Abram Tertz and the Poetics of Crime

Russian Literature and Thought
GARY SAUL MORSON, SERIES EDITOR

Abram Tertz

and the

Poetics of Crime

· ·

Catharine Theimer Nepomnyashchy

Yale University Press

New Haven and London

Published with assistance from the Mary Cady Tew Memorial Fund.
Studies of the Harriman Institute, Columbia University.
Grateful acknowledgment is made for permission to quote from *I and Thou* by
Martin Buber, translated and with a prologue and notes by Walter Kaufmann
(New York, Charles Scribner's Sons, 1970), translation copyright © 1970 Charles
Scribner's Sons, introduction copyright © 1970 Walter Kaufmann, and from
A Rhetoric of Irony by Wayne C. Booth (Chicago: University of Chicago Press,
1974), © 1974 by The University of Chicago.

Designed by James J. Johnson and set in New Aster type by Tseng Information
Systems, Inc.

Printed in the United States of America by BookCrafters, Inc., Chelsea, Michigan.

Library of Congress Cataloging-in-Publication Data

Nepomnyashchy, Catharine Theimer.
    Abram Tertz and the poetics of crime / Catharine Theimer Nepomnyashchy.
        p.   cm. — (Studies of the Harriman Institute) (Russian literature and
    thought)
    Includes bibliographical references and index.
    ISBN 0-300-06210-9 (alk. paper)

    1. Terts, Abram, 1925– / —Criticism and interpretation.   I. Title.   II. Series.
III. Series: Russian literature and thought.
PG3476.S539Z84   1995
891.73'44—dc20   94-40946
                                                                              CIP

A catalogue record for this book is available from the British Library.

To Rufus W. Mathewson, Jr.

Contents

Acknowledgments

I would first like to thank the National Endowment for the Humanities, the Social Science Research Council, and Barnard College for grants they awarded me, giving me the invaluable gift of time to research and write this book. I would also like to express my appreciation to the University Seminars of Columbia University for assistance in the preparation of the manuscript for publication. Material drawn from this work was presented to the University Seminar on Slavic History and Culture.

Aside from the generous institutional support I have received, I have also found myself rich in friends and colleagues who have contributed munificently of their time, expertise, and encouragement to the completion of this book. My heartfelt gratitude goes to Rufus W. Mathewson, Jr., who first introduced me to the writings of Tertz and to whom this book is dedicated. I have much regretted since his death the loss of those lively intellectual exchanges and incisive comments from which this book would certainly have benefited. I would also like to express my special thanks to Andrei Sinyavsky and Mariya Rozanova, who have given generously of their time, hospitality, and acquaintance with Abram Tertz, as well as to Galina Belaya, Irina Uvarova, and Lev Anninsky, who shared their memories. Deborah Martinsen, Richard Borden, and Ruth Mathewson read early drafts of this work and provided not only invaluable suggestions, but also consistent sympathy that kept me going in the darkest moments. Others who read all or part of this manuscript and to whom I am equally grateful for their comments and constructive criticisms are Maria Carlson, Ellen Chances, Caryl Emerson, Michael Naydan, Kathleen Parthé, Sylvie Richards, Bernice Rosenthal, and Greta Slobin. I have been fortunate as well in my colleagues in the Barnard Slavic Department—Richard Gustafson,

Marina Ledkovsky, and Mara Kashper—all of whom have made significant intellectual and technical contributions to this book and have provided me with much-needed support. I also wish to express my sincere thanks to Olga Meerson, who helped me greatly in polishing the English translations for this volume and supplied me with keen insights on the texts; to D. Barton Johnson and Tatyana Bomdast-Korainkina who generously gave me access to their bibliographical materials on Sinyavsky/Tertz; and to Nadezhda Azhgikhina, Michael Robinson, and Emily Johnson, who provided me with much-appreciated research assistance. Christopher Harwood challenged me to think through *Goodnight* more deeply. Carol Ueland, Jamey Gambrell, and Milla Trigos were always at the other end of the phone, and they know how much that meant. I would also like to express my deep gratitude to Jonathan Brent for his encouragement and ongoing support of this project and to my editor, Cynthia Wells, whose calm and professionalism helped push the book through to completion.

This book would not exist without the lifelong support of my father, Ernst Theodore Theimer, who passed away shortly before its writing was completed but left me his love of words, and of my mother, Jo-Anne Wright Theimer, who has always been there for me, as she was at the end of this project. Finally, to my husband, Viacheslav Nepomnyashchy, who has lived and, more often than not, suffered through this book from start to finish, I express my love and appreciation that he has been and still is willing to put up with me.

The defects in this book are, of course, all my own. My fondest hope is that readers will respond to the lapses and gaps they find in my approach to Abram Tertz by writing their own interpretations of his works, so that this book may contribute, in some small measure, to increasing the attention paid to this far-too-long underappreciated writer.

Note on Transliteration and Translations

In bibliographical references and Russian words cited in the text this book follows a modified version of the Library of Congress system of transliteration ("ya" instead of "ia," for example). Soft signs are omitted from Russian names and titles appearing in the text, and names are given in their standard English form when one exists. Unless otherwise specified, all translations from the Russian are my own.

Chapter One

. . . .

The Trials of Abram Tertz

When writers are tried and imprisoned in the Soviet Union for their books, and Western writers come to their defense and ask the powers that be in the Soviet Union how they can put writers on trial, the authorities have only one excuse to offer: "What kind of writers are they! They aren't writers, they're criminals!" When I heard this for the first time, I must confess that I experienced not humiliation, but a feeling of profound inner satisfaction. I should think so! Art is equated with crime. And not even with political crime, but rather with common crime. Art is equated with theft and murder. That means it's worth something! It's reality! And perhaps in fact—art, all art is crime? A crime against society. Against life itself. . . . So what is it—art? And what is the good and evil in it?

—ABRAM TERTZ, "Art and Reality"

For more than three decades Andrei Sinyavsky has published writings under the pseudonym Abram Tertz. Borrowed from Abrashka Tertz, a legendary Jewish outlaw whose exploits were celebrated in a thieves' song popular in Odessa in the 1920s, the Tertz pseudonym was from the beginning of Sinyavsky's career emblematic of the writer's approach to literature both as text and as process. In the years since Sinyavsky's true identity was discovered, the alias no longer a necessary cover, the writer has continued to sign all of his fiction and certain of his critical works with the name Tertz. In simple terms, the distinction between Sinyavsky and Tertz is stylistic and generic. Sinyavsky attributes those writings that conform to accepted conventions of critical discourse and structure to himself, while affixing the Tertz pseudonym to works of what he variously terms "fantastic realism," "fantastic literary scholarship" (*fantasticheskoe literaturovedenie*), and "exaggerated prose" (*utrirovannaya proza*)—writings that challenge linguistic orthodoxies and straddle boundaries between traditionally discrete genres.[1] In a deeper sense, in the course of Sinyavsky's career the Tertz pseudonym has come to entail a series of linguistic strategies and metaphors for the writer and writing which, taken together, define Sinyavsky's vision of literature. It is to an exploration of this vision, embodied in the figure of Abram Tertz and the writings attributed to him, that this book is devoted.

Over the years Sinyavsky's Tertz works have periodically precipitated explosive literary "scandals" that have polarized the Russian intellectual community and made Sinyavsky the target of attacks the virulence of which would seem to be out of all proportion with the immediate cause. While at first glance these outraged reactions might seem to have had only the most tenuous connection to the texts themselves, a closer examination of the "trials" of Abram Tertz[2] in relation to the works bearing that name shows that the aggravated reader response not only to the works themselves but to the circumstances of their publication is in fact immanent in the structure—linguistic and narrative—of the Tertz writings. If the writer is an outlaw, then the act of writing literature becomes a crime and the text a site of transgression. To begin to understand this link between text and context we must first review the basic facts of Sinyavsky's biography and the nature of the attacks directed at his Tertz publications over the years.

Andrei Donatovich Sinyavsky was born on October 8, 1925, and he came of age during World War II and the final years of Stalin's rule. Shortly after the beginning of the war he was evacuated with his mother to the town of Syzran. He was drafted into the army at the age of seventeen in 1943 and underwent a year and a half of training at the Moscow Aviation School, which also had been relocated to Syzran. Sinyavsky returned to Moscow when the school was moved back to the capital, and he served as a radio technician at an airfield outside of Moscow during the last year of the war. After his demobilization he studied literature at Moscow University. His undergraduate years thus corresponded with the heyday of Socialist Realism in Soviet literature and the cultural crackdown launched by Andrei Zhdanov in 1946. Following his graduation in 1949 Sinyavsky went on to graduate study at the same institution and completed the work for his candidate degree (roughly equivalent to an American doctorate) in 1952, the year before Stalin's death and a year after his father had been arrested. (Details of that arrest appear in Tertz, *Goodnight.*) He received an appointment in the Soviet literature section of the Gorky Institute of World Literature of the Academy of Sciences of the USSR and taught literature as an adjunct professor first, briefly, at Moscow University and then at the theater studio of the Moscow Art Theater. Having begun to publish as early as 1950, Sinyavsky participated in a number of prestigious projects, including the three-volume *History of Soviet Literature* put out by the Academy of Sciences. Not until the early 1960s, however, was he able to give greater scope in his publications to his unorthodox tastes in literature and art. Co-author during that time of books on Picasso and on Russian poetry of the postrevolutionary period, he also wrote a substantive introduction to a new edition of Pasternak, and published a series of articles in the Soviet Union's premier literary journal, *Novyi mir*.[3] By promoting writers who had earlier been repressed and urging a depoliticization of literary evaluation, Sinyavsky earned a growing reputation as an important liberal voice in the vanguard of the cultural "thaw" that, by fits and starts, accompanied the policy of de-Stalinization launched by Khrushchev in 1956. In 1965, in the fortieth anniversary issue of *Novyi mir*, the journal's editor, Aleksandr Tvardovsky, singled Sinyavsky out as one of the most talented literary critics of the younger generation.[4]

However, even as Sinyavsky was, as it were, winning a name for himself within the Soviet Union, he was also, beginning as early as the late Stalin years, writing works that could not be published in his homeland. Unlike Sinyavsky's "official" writings, which paid lip service to accepted critical as much as political orthodoxies, the writer's "unofficial" works, while neither politically sensational nor essentially at odds with the views expressed in his criticism published in the Soviet Union, were thick with linguistic ambiguities and fantastic flights of imagination designed to subvert the traditional literary commonplaces codified in Socialist Realism. In 1959 these works began to appear in Western publications under the pseudonym Abram Tertz. Over the course of the next six years an essay on Socialist Realism, three short novels, six "fantastic tales," and a brief collection of aphorisms made their way abroad, where Sinyavsky was rapidly making another—different—name for himself.

It is a testimony to the distinctness of Sinyavsky's and Tertz's voices that it took the Soviet authorities some six years to ferret out the true identity of the writer behind Abram Tertz.[5] Sinyavsky was arrested on September 8, 1965, and, after almost five months of detention in the Lubyanka and Lefortovo prisons, was brought to trial in February 1966—along with his friend and co-defendant Yuly Daniel, who had with Sinyavsky's help also published in the West, under the pseudonym Nikolai Arzhak.[6]

The trial of Sinyavsky and Daniel remains a landmark in the history of Soviet cultural politics, symbolically marking the end of the relative freedom of the Khrushchev years and serving as a catalyst to the burgeoning dissident movement.[7] The two writers were charged under article 70 of the criminal code of the Russian Republic (RSFSR) with having disseminated anti-Soviet propaganda. The case was tried before the Supreme Court of the Russian Republic, and L. N. Smirnov, one of the Soviet Union's leading jurists, presided, indicating the importance imputed to the affair by the powers that be. While the Soviet authorities made a pretence of adhering to the formalities of legal procedure, the trial was clearly staged and the verdict a foregone conclusion. In the weeks before the trial and during the trial itself, the Soviet press carried articles on Sinyavsky and Daniel, their works, and on the judicial proceedings all of which blatantly distorted and suppressed facts and assumed the defendants' guilt. As the prosecution had requested at the outset, at the end of the four-day trial (February 10–14), Sinyavsky was sentenced to the maximum sentence of seven years at hard labor and five years of internal exile, and Daniel received five and three years respectively.

Yet, the end result notwithstanding, the authorities' attempts to orchestrate the trial in the spirit of the notorious show trials of the Stalin years ran into serious resistance, most notably from Sinyavsky and Daniel themselves, who, despite months of pre-trial incarceration and pressure to repudiate their acts, broke the Stalinist tradition of public recantation and maintained their innocence throughout. The spectacle of writers being tried for the contents of their works understandably became an international cause célèbre, and a stellar array of foreign literary luminaries, including communist sympathizers, deluged representatives and institutions of the Soviet government, both before and after the trial, with protests and pleas for moderation and mercy. Within the Soviet Union, the Sinyavsky and Daniel trial became a focus for the emerging struggle between the Brezhnev regime and the cultural elite. Emboldened by the experience of the relative relaxation of governmental control under Khrushchev and unwilling to cede to the new crackdown without a fight, a certain segment of the intelligentsia openly expressed their dissatisfaction at the government's actions, both during the months when the accused were imprisoned before the trial and in its aftermath. On December 5, 1965, the first of the demonstrations on Pushkin Square in Moscow—demonstrations that were to become something of a dissident tradition—was held to protest the imprisonment of the two writers, and in the wake of the trial a number of prominent writers and cultural figures signed letters criticizing the verdict and pleading for leniency.[8]

The vast majority of the Soviet public was, however, privy to only half of this verbal confrontation. Not only were Sinyavsky's and Daniel's works completely inaccessible to the average Soviet reader, but pleas in defense of the two writers were suppressed, and when the works at issue were mentioned in the press or in official statements, it was only to condemn them as manifestations of a hostile ideological agenda. The press campaign against Sinyavsky and Daniel thus became an affirmation of the governmental control over language that the two writers had circumvented by publishing their works abroad, beyond the bailiwick of the Soviet censorship. The issues involved, however, went beyond the fact of institutional restraints on language to the cultural mythology behind them. Thus, in reviewing the attacks on Sinyavsky, one is most forcefully struck by the incommensurability of the criticisms with the works themselves. Sinyavsky's early Tertz works, although often clothed in a layer of satire directed against Soviet politics and everyday life, are primarily metaliterary and, on any level, are devoid of the political explosiveness of such works as Solzhenitsyn's *One Day in the Life of Ivan Denisovich*, which had been published in the author's homeland at the same time Tertz was surreptitiously appearing abroad. While, on the one hand, this apparent discrepancy serves to confirm that the issue involved in the trial was the government's power to decide what got published and what did not, on the other, it suggests that Solzhenitsyn's mode of writing, whatever the "contents," was more palatable to the Soviet authorities than was Sinyavsky's, that the central concern was not political dissent, but a certain understanding of the proper functioning of literature and language within the society.[9] The Soviet press coverage of the "Sinyavsky and Daniel affair" in the weeks preceding and during the trial gives an indication of what was at stake.

The first article in the press campaign appeared in *Izvestiya* on January 13, 1966, some four months after the writers' arrest and three weeks before the beginning of the trial.[10] The piece—written by Dmitry Eremin, a secretary of the Moscow section of the Writers'

Union, a laureate of the Stalin Prize, and most certainly a party hack—was a diatribe pointedly entitled "Turncoats." The Russian title of the article, "Perevertyshi," not only refers to an act of political betrayal, but, more important, carries deeper folkloric connotations, which are even more pronounced in another epithet applied to Sinyavsky and Daniel in this article and repeatedly in later Soviet press accounts: *oborotni.* In mythology and fairy tales the word *oboroten'* denotes a person who is transformed or has the ability to transform him- or herself into a completely different form, whether animal or object, through the use of magic.[11] Underlying Eremin's argument, then, is the implication of frighteningly uncontrollable supernatural forces at work capable of undermining the integrity of identity— forces, as we shall see, putatively inherent in the very workings of language itself.

Throughout his article, Eremin berates the two writers for their double-dealing (*dvurushnichestvo*), for having masqueraded as loyal Soviet men of letters while their overt activities were only "a false facade." Behind it he claims, "was hidden something different: hatred of our system, vile mockery of what is most precious for the Motherland [*Rodina*] and the people [*narod*]" (89). He links this duality of identity with a breakdown in ethical values: "The first thing that you experience when you read their works is disgust. It is repugnant to cite the vulgarities that embellish the pages of their books. Both with unhealthy voluptuousness rummage in sexual and psychopathological 'problems.' Both exhibit extreme moral degra- dation. Both spit out onto paper all that is most vile and dirty" (89).[12] The existence of a darker personality concealed under a mask of re- spectability is thus implicitly associated with the transgression of a language boundary, with the committing to words of that which should be suppressed and repressed.

Furthermore, Eremin maintains, as they reveal what should be denied, they denigrate what should be venerated: "They care for nothing in our country, they revere none of the things that are held sacred in its multinational culture, they are prepared to curse and run down everything that is dear to the Soviet person—in the present and the past" (90). The remarkably "unmarxist," religious tenor of the critic's language reaches a particularly high pitch when he comes to Sinyavsky's treatment of Lenin:[13] "For Soviet people, for the peoples of the world, for all of progressive humanity there is no more sacred name than the name of the leader of our revolu- tion Vladimir Ilych Lenin" (90). Eremin cannot even bring himself to repeat the offending lines, assigning them to a realm outside the

pale of acceptable language: "What a bottomless swamp of abomination must a so-called writer have sunken into to cast slurs with
his hooligan pen on a name that is sacred to us! It is impossible to
reproduce here the pertinent citations: this scribble is so malicious,
it is so revolting and dirty. These *blasphemous* lines are sufficient
to make a diagnosis: their authors place themselves outside Soviet
society" (90–91, *my emphasis*). Thus, underlying Eremin's argument
is the assumption that in violating linguistic taboos, the writers have
breached the social compact on which Soviet society rests. Sinyavsky and Daniel have placed themselves "outside our literature, outside the community of Soviet people" (93). They are "emigrants of
a particular sort: internal. They locked themselves up in their rotten little world. There their malicious passions seethed. There they
dipped their quills into inkwells with poison. There they lived, imagining it was life" (93). Membership in Soviet society is therefore
defined, at least in part, by adherence to linguistic rituals, which
regulate the limits of acceptable discourse. By their "blasphemy"
then, the two writers have excluded themselves from their society, a
society that has in effect been hallowed by a baptism of blood: "Our
people [*narod*] paid too dearly for the achievements of October, for
the victory over fascism, for the blood and sweat shed for the sake
of the Motherland to regard these two scum with indifference" (94).

The powerful appeal of Eremin's invocation of this religio-mythic
vision of Soviet society—as a community sacralized by shared suffering and victory over common enemies and preserved by adherence to language taboos—is reflected in the outraged letters published in *Izvestiya* in response to the critic's article. The letter writers
most certainly had no first hand knowledge of Sinyavsky's or Daniel's
works. Yet the tenor of their rhetoric indicates the depths of the
emotions unleashed by the specter of the abuse of public discourse.
One letter, signed by a woman agronomist from the Latvian Republic, is worth quoting almost in its entirety as a gauge of the extent
to which allegiance to the nation could be personalized. The letter
opens: "What could be more precious than the Motherland? It is
as necessary to a human being as the sun, as air, as a clear spring,
which fills the breast with life-giving strength as soon as it touches
the lips" (103).[14] The writer then invokes World War II as a time of
consecration, when, in face of threatened loss, love for the homeland
was confirmed:

There was a time when I could have lost it—my Motherland. Many years have already passed since that time, but

now from time to time I go back in memory to those terrible
days, when Latvia groaned under the yoke of the fascist occu-
piers. How many tears I saw at that time, how many horrors
I endured! I remember how once, on the road leading to Bau-
ska, Hitler's soldiers were driving along a crowd of people
with knapsacks over their shoulders, with small bundles in
their arms. Frightened children held on to the hems of their
mothers' dresses.

In fear I rushed into the forest. There were already others
like me there, local inhabitants—women, children, old people
who had hidden themselves in the fear that they would be
driven into slavery, separated from their paternal home. We
were ready to accept any hardships, if only the bitter cup
would pass from us, if only we could manage to stay here,
on Latvian land, which was covered with wounds and dese-
crated, but dear to our hearts. It was in those terrible days
that I understood particularly profoundly: the most precious
thing a person has is his Motherland! (103)

This effusion leads to the exclamation, "So how could anyone raise
their hand against the holy of holies—against their Motherland!
Against the Native Land that gave you everything: the possibility of
getting an education, growing, working creatively, of looking into
the future without fear for yourself or your children?" (103). Where,
she goes on to ask, did these "turncoats" (*perevertyshi*)—who "lived
on the same land as we do, breathed the same air as we do, enjoyed
the same blessings as we do," and yet wrote "rotten libels against
our country"—come from, a question that is left hanging, again suggesting inexplicable forces at work. She concludes her attack with
a categorical statement: "To betray one's mother, to betray one's
Motherland—it is after all one and the same thing" (103).[15] Most
striking here is the palpable force of metaphor. The motherland becomes a nurturing mother, and words uttered against her become
an act of treachery. Love for this "mother" is, moreover, defined in
terms of a threat from a hostile other, which, frighteningly, originates within the national community but is equated by implication
with a foreign enemy.

The reflex to construct the world according to a bipolar model, to
divide it into a community bound by blood and a threatening outside
force, repeatedly manifested itself in the press attacks. Only in those
terms does the strategy deployed in the second and last article published in the Soviet Union before the trial appear comprehensible.

The piece, entitled "Nasledniki Smerdyakova" (Heirs of Smerdya-kov), was written by Zoya Kedrina, a colleague of Sinyavsky's at the Institute of World Literature and later a witness for the prosecution at the trial. Seemingly incongruously, given the fact that the only exposure the average Soviet reader was allowed to Western reviews of Tertz's writings were those snippets cited by Kedrina herself, the critic sets it as her task to refute positive foreign responses to the writer's works and specifically to answer those foreign reviewers who placed those works in the tradition of one or another famous Russian writer. She sets up her argument against what she refers to in scare quotes as "literary amusements" by first citing brief phrases from foreign reviewers in praise of Tertz's works, followed by quo-tations, again from the Western press, that affirmed that the works were "anti-Soviet." The latter citations, tautologically demonstrating that the Tertz texts are anti-Soviet because they were called anti-Soviet by those who are unquestionably anti-Soviet, serve to place Sinyavsky in the enemy camp. Kedrina then devotes the rest of her article to a lengthy argument designed to demolish the positive judg-ments of Sinyavsky's writing made by his "foreign protectors." [16] She clearly aims to discredit the dissenting voice of the West on both political and literary grounds. Her ironic use of the phrase *literary amusements* at the beginning of her article underscores the profound unease that runs throughout the tortured course of her argument. This unease originates in the implicit assumption that there exists an alternative mode of evaluation that, invoking artistic complexity or quality, art as a form of linguistic play, would place literary works outside the simple bipolarity of mutually hostile ideologies.

Thus, at the core of Kedrina's argument lies her accusation that Sinyavsky employs literary devices as a "mask": [17]

> Having made your way through the seemingly impassable desert of rhetoric, through thickets of all possible symbols, allegories, and intersecting and mutually reincarnated char-acters, you discover a very open and clear rationalistic con-struction, so to speak, the ideological skeleton of all the works of these people. The extreme confusion of form in the works of A. Tertz serves only as a variegated camouflage for his "fun-damental ideas," and when you tear it away and throw it aside, at first the naked diagram even stuns you: that's all it is and nothing more?! Two or three of the most hackneyed theses of anti-Soviet propaganda, familiar from time immemorial. (108)

Formal complexity thus becomes nothing more than a subterfuge, a means of simultaneously conveying "propaganda" and cloaking it in a respectable guise. Apparently concerned, however, that this argument in and of itself is insufficiently compelling, Kedrina proceeds to impugn the authenticity and genealogy of the Tertz writings. In a bizarre realization of the writer's own metaphor, Sinyavsky becomes a literary "thief," who ruthlessly plunders the texts of others:

> The author of the stories of Abram Tertz, candidate of philology A. Sinyavsky, whom the reactionary foreign press with sensational fanfare has proclaimed "heir to the Russian tradition," is an efficient fellow and he knows what he's about, dipping his hand into others' books without a twinge of conscience. The moral nakedness of Abram Tertz, those anti-Soviet "ideas," which he has assimilated and is so eager to propagate, appears in the garb of the most varied literary reminiscences and parallels. Ripped with a bit of cloth out of the most various works of others, which are turned inside out and offhandedly tacked together into a patchwork of anti-Sovietisms, they define the "creative persona" of Abram Tertz as a man who brazenly lives parasitically off the literary heritage. (110)

Still not content to let her argument rest, however, she suggests that

> if Dostoevsky had not created Smerdyakov, putting into his image the whole force of his hatred for corruptors of human souls, but Smerdyakov himself had written novels, generalizing the phenomena of life from his Smerdyakovian position, we could easily establish Tertz's direct kinship with such a "tradition." For there is no abyss of moral decay and corruption that would intimidate the worthy heirs of Smerdyakov in their striving to defile and persecute everything human in the Soviet person: friendship, love, motherhood, the family. (111–12)

Tertz is thus an illegitimate son, representing all the hostile forces who will stop at nothing to undermine all that is good (that good being defined in terms of bonding and family) in the "Soviet person." All that is left when the purloined tropes disguising Tertz's true intent are ripped away, Kedrina finds, is "pornography next to which the most daring pasquinades of Artsybashev look like literature for pre-schoolers" (115). In effect, then, the anti-Soviet ideas suppos-

edly lurking beneath the camouflage of literary form are implicitly
equated with sexual perversion and moral decay. Sinyavsky and the
foreign other who defends him by proclaiming his literary merit—
specifically by assigning him a genealogy, defining a tie of kinship
with the national cultural heritage—are exposed as embodying a
profound threat to the bonds that hold the community together. Just
as Eremin claimed that Sinyavsky had forfeited membership in that
community, Kedrina denies him a lineage—or rather allows him
only a stolen or illegitimate one—in the literary heritage.[18]

Buried among Kedrina's extravagant accusations is a phrase
that suggests the true nature of Sinyavsky's "crime."[19] Toward the
end of the article, Kedrina refers to "the many-layered irony summoned to the aid of the author to establish at any moment his 'non-
participation' in what he himself wrote" (115).[20] Echoing her earlier
charge that literary tropes are merely a cover for anti-Soviet ideas,
this comment also reveals Kedrina's underlying concern that certain
uses of language resist control—in part at least, because they allow
the author to deny responsibility for what he himself has written,
but, in a deeper sense, because they allow for alternative readings of
the literary text.

The trial was the one place where the two sides, Sinyavsky and his
accusers, came into direct and public verbal confrontation.[21] From
the beginning, as in Kedrina's article, the potential ambiguity of the
legal status of the literary text, the possibility of claiming an exemp-
tion for literature from political polarities, proved to be a central
issue of the trial. The judge attempted to defuse this issue in his opening remarks by placing artistic evaluation outside the competence
of the court: "[T]he trial is investigating the issue not of the literary merits or defects of the works of these writers, but of criminally
punishable acts. Therefore artistic merits lie beyond the bounds of
the given trial" (170). Sinyavsky countered that approach later in the
trial by maintaining, "I am not a political writer," and went on to
generalize this statement, understandably provoking what the unofficial transcript of the trial described as "an indignant buzz in the
hall": "No writer's works convey his political views. Artistic works
do not express political views. It is impossible to ask either Pushkin
or Gogol about his political views" (224). It would be wrong to take
this statement as either a disingenuous dodge or a naive attempt to
negate any and all links between politics and text. Rather, it reflects
an understanding of how literary language works that places it outside reductive political taxonomies and even, ultimately, beyond the

jurisdiction of the law. The dynamics of the incompatibility and confusion of modes of discourse that characterized the trial throughout come into particular focus in the prosecution's questioning of Sinyavsky and in the writer's closing speech to the court, in which he attempts to deconstruct the linguistic malfunction underlying the proceedings.

In this context, Sinyavsky's interrogation at the trial may be roughly divided into two parts. During the first half of the exchange, the prosecutor asked the writer a series of questions regarding the factual background of the case—about how, for instance, Sinyavsky had sent his works abroad and with whom, who had read his works, and whether he had helped other writers smuggle their writings to the West. Understandably, under the circumstances, Sinyavsky was not completely open in his answers to some of these questions; he was very careful not to implicate anyone who was not already involved in the trial nor to exacerbate the charges against Daniel or himself. His responses were generally short and to the point, and on occasion he fastidiously held the court to strict legal definitions of words, as evidenced by the following:

> *Prosecutor:* You sent your manuscripts illegally?
> *Sinyavsky:* I sent them unofficially, and not illegally.
> *Prosecutor:* And what do you call the path you chose?
> *Sinyavsky:* Unofficial. I do not consider it illegal, and I do not know what that word means in the juridical sense.[22] (204)

If, however, in the part of his interrogation dealing with the extraliterary facts of his surreptitious publishing activities Sinyavsky made some attempt to invoke the letter of the law, his strategy changed when the questioning came to the literary texts themselves. This modulation was marked by a noticeable alteration in the rhythm of the exchange itself. Sinyavsky's responses to the prosecutor's questions, which were clearly meant to elicit brief and unambiguous answers, became lengthy, detailed, and—from the point of view of the prosecutor and the judge—circuitous and evasive. As one journalist reporting on the trial remarked in exasperation, "The accused—Sinyavsky and Daniel—answer almost stereotypically: 'Before answering this question I would like to express my views apropos . . .' Apropos various subjects. On the genre of the fantastic. On the theory of hyperbole. On their views on artistic creation. About everything. About anything. Except an answer to a direct question."[23] The motive, however, lay not in any simple or underhanded attempt to evade legal responsibility but in a conception of literature that placed it beyond the purview of the language of law and rendered it intractable to simple definition.

The point of shift in the interrogation came when the prosecutor asked Sinyavsky whether in the works on the basis of which he had been charged "your political views and convictions are expounded" (221). Sinyavsky responded, "My position as a writer is laid out in them," and in the essay "Chto takoe sotsialistichestskii realizm" (What Is Socialist Realism) "my artistic position is laid out in a free manner" (221). Clearly trying to circumvent this appeal to art, the judge then pressed the writer on the first section of the essay, asking whether it could be regarded as an "artistic work" (221). Rather than immediately answering yes or no, Sinyavsky pointed out the complexity of the issues touched upon in the essay and invoked the possibility of differing opinions: "In that article, which is devoted to complicated and unclear questions, of which there are many interpretations, I wanted to express my understanding of Socialist Realism. Different opinions exist on this topic. In the West it is often said that Socialist Realism is a fiction, an invention" (221). At this point, just as Sinyavsky raised the suggestion of competing voices, the judge broke in with "And the first part of the essay?" to which Sinyavsky responded, first, by saying that he wanted to answer in "greater detail," that he had no intention of trying to wriggle out of answering the question, and then by explaining at some length the approach "I find difficult to define [*opredelit'*]" (221)—that he had adopted in his interpretation of Socialist Realism. In the end, he did not give a simple answer to the judge's question, but rather established the essay as an alternative mode of discourse that eludes straightforward categorization and is open to multiple interpretations.

The sparring between Sinyavsky, on the one hand, and, on the other, the prosecutor and the judge—who, irritated by what he apparently believed was Sinyavsky's refusal to give direct answers, aggressively joined in the questioning—continued in this vein. The prosecutor and the judge repeatedly cited what they considered offensive passages from the writer's works, attempting to force the defendant to admit that his Tertz works expressed anti-Soviet views. Sinyavsky responded with detailed explanations of the use of imagery in his texts, again and again remonstrating his questioners for citing passages out of context, equating the words of fictional characters with those of the author, misapprehending irony, and, generally, for trying to find simple political meanings in texts that did not yield to unambiguous interpretation. In short, he implicitly accused them of being poor readers. At the end of his cross examination by his defense attorney, the writer laid out the basic premises about literature under which all of his arguments during his questioning can be subsumed and laid the groundwork for the more detailed remarks he would make in his closing speech to the court:

> [T]he artistic image is always polysemic [*mnogoznachen*]. Even I, the author, have difficulty saying what it means. I consider juridical trials of the literary text impossible. Because it is impossible to define juridically unambiguously [*odnoznachno*] the meaning of an artistic work. And all the same it is easier for me, as the author, to understand the logical meaning of my own works. The works of Tertz are very complex and multilayered, and it would be difficult even for me to analyze them. In my concluding speech I would like to touch upon the specifically literary aspect of the question, leaving to my lawyer the juridical aspect of the case. The court is interested in the political aspect. But I want to explain the literary aspect, defending precisely the literary text. (251)

Here Sinyavsky set up, as he said, the argument he would make in his final words to the court the next day.[24] These prefatory remarks also make clear one of the key difficulties of the writer's situation: he was essentially battling on two fronts at the same time. On the one hand, he postulated the inherent incommensurability of literary and juridical discourse, thus placing the literary text beyond the jurisdiction of the law. On the other hand, by pointing out that there were not two, but three—literary, juridical, and *political*—approaches to the text represented in the court, he not only subtly challenged the prosecution's manipulation of the law for political ends, but also prepared his assault on the abuse of language in Soviet society.

Thus, in his closing speech, Sinyavsky in essence deconstructed the dynamics of the trial and, in so doing, laid out the basic principles of his early Tertz works and of his vision of the literary process as it would be further elaborated in his later fiction and theory. He began by pointing to the linguistic impasse created by the prosecution's case: "The arguments of the indictment—they created the sensation of an impenetrable wall, through which it is impossible to break through to anything, to any truth" (301). The prosecution's strategy was to pull quotations out of context and repeat them over and over: "All the same terrible quotations from the indictment are repeated dozens of times and grow into a monstrous atmosphere that no longer corresponds to any reality" (301). He identified this linguistic strategy as a literary device, but a literary device removed from the context of the literary text and taken literally, endowed with an independent reality:

> The literary device—the repetition of one and the same formulations—is a potent device. A sort of shroud is created, a particularly electrified atmosphere, when reality ends, and the monstrous begins—almost as in the works of Arzhak and Tertz. This is the atmosphere of the dark anti-Soviet underground, hidden behind the bright faces of Candidate of Sciences Sinyavsky and the poet-translator Daniel, who are hatching conspiracies, negotiations, terrorist acts, pogroms, murders. . . . Here, truly, very horribly and unexpectedly, the literary device loses its stylized nature [uslovnost'], is taken literally, so that the court proceedings are plugged into the text as its natural continuation. (301)

The boundaries between discrete discourses have been violated. The artistic device has been usurped into life, taken out of the conventional context of the text, literalized, and given a life of its own. Reality, represented by the court, becomes a grotesque continuation of the literary text. As Harriet Murav observes, "Siniavskii sees his own trial . . . as the realization, or the making literal, of metaphor."[25] The trial becomes a fantastic tale brought to life, and with language running amok, the accusations against the defendants become progressively more absurd: "[T]his political underground turned into an underground of degenerates, cannibals, living by the darkest instincts: hatred toward mothers, hatred toward their own people, fascism, anti-Semitism. . . . Sinyavsky tramples on everything that is most holy, even motherhood" (301).

In an atmosphere where the boundaries between literary trope, political slogan, and juridical terminology have collapsed, there is no possibility of dialogue: "Therefore, it is extremely difficult to dissipate this atmosphere. Neither extensive arguments, nor conceptions of creation"—Sinyavsky's strategies in responding to the charges against him—"will help here" (301). The writer nonetheless reiterated the basic premises of his defense, which were, as he pointed out, rudimentary principles of reading a literary text: "I want merely to recall several arguments, elementary in relation to literature. This is where the study of literature begins: *the word is not an act, but a word: the artistic image is stylized, the author is not identical to his hero"* (302, ed. emphasis). However, the prosecution, Sinyavsky maintained, interpreted these "ABC's" of literary scholarship as merely a "means of taking cover" (302). Just as the respectable personae of Sinyavsky and Daniel were cast as covers for the moral monstrosities Tertz and Arzhak, just as "behind the bright appearance is revealed the dark interior—mine and Daniel's" (303), so the literary device became nothing more than a mask for political treachery: "In sum, everything is camouflage [*maskirovka*], everything is subterfuge, a screen, like the candidate degree as well. The feeble literary form is only a screen for counterrevolutionary ideas. Idealism, hyperbole, the fantastic—all of these, of course, are the subterfuges of a violently anti-Soviet person, who masked himself in every possible manner. . . . Then art itself becomes a subterfuge, a screen for anti-Soviet ideas" (304).

Following this logic, the literary text is nothing more than a political slogan. Sinyavsky pointed out that the very publishers' imprints that appeared on his works in the West served as proof that they were anti-Soviet: "[The prosecution] adduces as proof the imprints on the book (something like 'struggle with the CPSU' and something else, I don't remember). An imprint on a book turns out to be equal to the book itself. . . . An equals sign is drawn between a propaganda cliché and the literary work" (305). Sinyavsky's argument comes full circle. While he and Daniel have been transformed into their own literary images by the misappropriation of literary tropes into real life, the literary text has been reduced to the status of a political slogan: "The question arises: What is agitation and propaganda, and what is literature? This is the position of the prosecution: *Literature is a form of agitation and propaganda; agitation can only be Soviet or anti-Soviet, if it is not Soviet, then it must be anti-Soviet"* (305, ed. emphasis). The literary text—and the world—are reduced to the simple bipolarity dictated by the political cliché: "Here the law of 'either-or' begins to function, sometimes it functions correctly, sometimes— horribly. Whoever is not with us is against us. In some periods— revolution, war, civil war—this logic can even be correct, but it is dangerous when applied in peacetime, when applied to literature. I am asked: where is the positive hero? Oh, no? A-ah, not socialist? Not realist? A-ah, not marxist? A-ah, a fantast? A-ah, an idealist? And moreover abroad! Of course, a counterrevolutionary!" (306). Such language demands emotional reaction and action—unambiguous and univalent—rather than fostering analysis or dialogue. It creates an "impenetrable wall."

Sinyavsky concluded his remarks by maintaining that he was not an "enemy," but simply "different" (*drugoi*) and implicitly located his otherness in a profession of faith in the multivalence of the literary text:

> In the depths of my soul I think that it is impossible to approach literature with juridical formulations. After all, the truth of the artistic image is complex; often even the author himself cannot explain it. I think that if Shakespeare himself (I am not comparing myself with Shakespeare, that could never even enter anyone's head), if Shakespeare were asked: what does Hamlet mean? What does Macbeth mean? Is there not subversion here?—I think that Shakespeare himself could not answer that precisely. You, jurists, deal with terms, which the narrower they are, the more precise. In contrast to the term, the meaning of the artistic image is more precise the broader it is. (306)

The central issue Sinyavsky raises in his closing speech is thus the nature of meaning in the literary text, arguably the major concern of his Tertz texts both before and after the trial. He in essence draws strict lines of demarcation between the three modes of discourse—literary, juridical and political—represented at the trial.[27] Literature, he maintains, is not simply an expression of the writer's political ideas. Therefore it can be neither relegated to one half of a political bipolarity nor placed on trial. Meaning in the literary text is inherently uncontrollable, for the author, being at most a privileged reader of his own writings, cannot dictate how his texts will be read. While juridical language strives to define reality and order it by aspiring to absolute referentiality, the relation between sign and referent in the literary text is complex and problematical. Literature generates fictions out of language itself, fictions that have no binding relationship to the reality outside the text. Hence the danger of political discourse, backed by the power to act, that usurps the literary sign's prerogative to independence from reality and transforms word into deed.[28] Neither politics nor law can reduce the literary text to its own terms of reference, and, by the same token, the literary text that becomes nothing more than political slogan or judicial tract is no longer literature.

Attacks on Sinyavsky in the Soviet Union following the trial were, if anything, more virulent than earlier and therefore demonstrate even more clearly the mythic vision of the word operative in Soviet culture, which is both Tertz's context and the text his own texts seek to subvert. A brief analysis of two of the more abusive of these diatribes reveals both the workings of the linguistic mechanism Sinyavsky identifies as realization of metaphor and the extent of the official investment in maintaining control over the word.

A verse lampoon published in the journal *Agitator* by the pseudonymous feuilletonist Nikodim Troekurov some months after the trial answers Sinyavsky's assertion that the position of either-or —"he who is not with us is against us"—may be applicable in wartime, but not in peacetime. Troekurov's travesty, tellingly entitled "O 'samovyrazhenie' i mezhdunarodnom polozhenii" (On "self-expression" and the international situation), portrays the current period as indeed a time of war. His verses are cast as a talk in a workers' club on "self-expression" and "peace and war" (370).[29] The speaker begins by metaphorically linking writing to political bipolarization, identifying his two-color pencil as a model for the division of the world into ideological camps:

> Take up the pencil . . . Colored thus:
> There it's black, and here it's red.
> Thus, my friends, is all the world
> Also colored in our time.
> [*Vzyat' karandash . . . On tak okrashen:*
> *On chernyi tam i krasnyi zdes'.*
> *Vot tak, druz'ya, vo vremya nashe*
> *I shar zemnoi okrashen ves'.*] (370)

This politically bifurcated world is, moreover, at war:

> And even there, where all is quiet,
> An invisible war is being waged
> For human souls.
> [*I dazhe tam, gde tishina,*
> *Za chelovecheskie dushi*
> *Idet nezrimaya voina.*] (370)

"Mister Capital" wages this "invisible war" by seeming to promise— in words—humanitarian ideals, while in fact sending bombs:

> He goes into other countries,
> Proclaiming humanitarian ideals,

But hereafter it is with bombs
Himself he "self-expresses."
[*V chuzhie strany priezzhaet,
O chelovechnosti trubya,
Da tol'ko 'samovyrazhaet'
Otnyne bombami sebya.*] (371)

Words become merely a cover for bombs and—through the transposition of the verb *self-expresses*—are even equated with bombs. In this war in which what is at stake are human souls, words are weapons of destruction. Language unrestrained—masked as "self-expression"—threatens annihilation.

Mikhail Sholokhov's speech to the Twenty-third Party Congress, which was arguably the most notorious post-trial assault on Sinyavsky and Daniel, echoes the basic paradigm of the Troekurov doggerel and demonstrates more starkly than any other source the mythology of the potency of the word that underlay censorship.[30] The initial premise of Sholokhov's remarks is that the international situation is such that "an honest writer or artist" cannot "remain in the position of an observer from the sidelines" (387). Invoking "American aggression" in Vietnam and the arms race ("destructive methods of monstrous force [*sily*] are being tested"), the newly minted Nobel laureate ended his catalogue of global horrors: "Reactionary bourgeois art in every way kindles the basest passions in people, acts like the evil forces [*zlye sily*] from ancient fairy tales and legends of peoples of all countries, trying to transform the human being into his opposite, to deprive him of his human image and human soul" (387). Art, then, represents a threat as dangerous as the atomic bomb.[31] Art is perhaps even more dangerous, because rather than physical force, it wields a magic power capable of releasing the darker side of human nature. Thus, Sholokhov, like Troekurov, suggested that the world is in a state of war, that art is a weapon, and that the artist must choose sides: "And today Maksim Gorky's question sounds with its former urgency for the artists of the whole world: 'Who are you with, masters of culture?'" (388).

Having defined his context, Sholokhov compared his own appearances abroad—his Nobel speech in particular—and his current remarks at home, maintaining that in both places he spoke with the same voice. He proclaimed: "Wherever, in whatever language communists might speak, we speak as communists. . . . Wherever a Soviet person might speak, he must speak as a Soviet patriot" (388).

A writer like Sinyavsky or Daniel,[32] on the other hand, "writes about one thing in our country, and publishes something completely different abroad. He employs one and the same Russian language, but in order in one instance to mask himself, and in another to defile that language with rabid malice, hatred for everything Soviet, for everything we hold dear, for everything we hold sacred" (388). Language is simultaneously a gauge of the integrity of identity and a potentially dangerous instrument of deception and subversion. The nation becomes a family: "I belong to those writers who, like all Soviet people, are proud that they are a small fraction of a great and noble people [*narod*]. [*Prolonged and stormy applause*]. They are proud that they are the sons of a mighty and beautiful Motherland. She created us, gave us everything that she could, gave us immeasurably much. We owe her everything. We call our Soviet Motherland mother. We are all members of an enormous family" (388–89). Here Sholokhov takes the metaphor implicit in the feminine gender and in the root of the word *rodina* (*rod*, signifying close, familial relationship) and realizes it: the motherland becomes the mother who feeds and nurtures and to whom her "sons" are obligated for all they have. Sinyavsky and Daniel are the "miscreants" (*urody*) in the family, who have committed the most horrible of crimes: "There is nothing more blasphemous and loathsome than to slander one's own mother, to insult her vilely, to raise a hand to her!" (389). Again words become equivalent to physical violence.

Sholokhov concluded with a not very veiled suggestion that Sinyavsky's and Daniel's sentences may have been too lenient. He appealed to the delegates from the "kindred [*rodnoi*] Soviet Army" in the audience, asking them what they would do if traitors appeared in their ranks. Invoking with something bordering on nostalgia the revolutionary tribunals of the civil war period, he stopped just short of suggesting that the two writers should have been shot: "If these fine fellows with black consciences had turned up in the memorable twenties, when trials were conducted not on the basis of rigorously circumscribed articles of the Criminal Code, but 'guided by revolutionary justice' [*Applause*], oh, these *oborotni* would have received a very different measure of punishment" (389). Sholokhov's use of the word *oboroten'* here throws a bridge between his vision of the power of art to "turn the human being into his opposite, to deprive him of his human image and human soul" and his portrayal of Sinyavsky and Daniel as miscreants in the nation-family. The word contains the threat of the transformation of what is near and dear into its converse, of the transformation of "us" into "them," of the potential to unleash the darker forces of the human psyche. In the face of this threat—both from within and from without—the nation-family must band together to protect its "mother" from "blasphemy" by rigorously adhering to ritual language ("wherever a Soviet person might speak, he must speak as a Soviet patriot") and by mercilessly expelling from its midst those who transgress language taboos. These taboos originate in the reflex to deny difference within, to repudiate everything distasteful by externalizing it and attributing it to a hostile other.

Shortly after the trial Sinyavsky and Daniel were transported to different hard labor camps at Potma in Mordovia. Daniel served out his sentence and was allowed to return to Moscow in 1970. Sinyavsky was released approximately one year later, some fifteen months before the end of his sentence, and was also eventually permitted to resume residence in the capital.[33] Despite the rigors of camp life, Sinyavsky had not stopped writing. While at Potma, he wrote a brief monograph on Pushkin, which he smuggled out in letters to his wife, Mariya Rozanova, and the first chapter of what was to become a lengthy study of Gogol. After his release he also compiled out of passages from letters to his wife what might loosely be termed a camp memoir.

As one of the early beneficiaries of the Brezhnev policy applied throughout the 1970s of allowing, encouraging, and even forcing troublesome writers to leave the USSR, Sinyavsky was given permission to emigrate to France with his wife and son in 1973. The family took up residence in a town outside of Paris, and Sinyavsky received an appointment in Russian literature at the Sorbonne, where he taught until his retirement in 1994. Since his emigration, Sinyavsky has published under the Tertz pseudonym his three "camp" works— *Golos iz khora* (A voice from the chorus) in 1973 and *Progulki s Pushkinym* (Strolls with Pushkin) and *V teni Gogolya* (In the shadow of Gogol) in 1975—as well as a novella entitled *Kroshka Tsores* (Little Tsores) in 1980, the novel *Spokoinoi nochi* (Goodnight) in 1984, and a number of articles on the function of art and the nature of the creative process. Under his own name he has published a book-length study of Vasily Rozanov entitled *"Opavshie list'ya" V. V. Rozanova* (V. V. Rozanov's "Fallen Leaves," 1982), two books on Russian and Soviet culture—*Soviet Civilization* (1988) and *Ivan-durak: Ocherk russkoi narodnoi very* (Ivan the fool: An essay in Russian popular belief, 1991)—and articles devoted to "academic" literary scholarship and political issues.[34]

While Sinyavsky has evolved and remained productive under both of his names, he has also continued to be the subject of controversy both in the emigre community and, since the advent of glasnost, in Soviet and post-Soviet Russia. Originally welcomed by the mainstream of the emigre intelligentsia, he was recruited to participate in the journal *Kontinent*, published in Germany, and contributed articles to several early issues, including the inaugural one published in 1974. However, by 1976 he had broken with *Kontinent* and with the journal's editor, Vladimir Maksimov, who ultimately was to become one of his most persistent detractors.[35] Disgusted by the politics of emigre journalism, Rozanova, working out of the family home, founded the journal *Sintaksis*, the first issue of which appeared in 1978. Originally conceived as an outlet exclusively for Sinyavsky's writing, the journal from the outset attracted like-minded contributors both from the emigration and the Soviet Union, with Sinyavsky or Tertz publishing one and sometimes two articles in many issues. The journal—which, particularly in Sinyavsky's articles, adopted an aggressive stance against the anti-Semitic Russian chauvinism of many emigre intellectuals—and the publishing house of the same name, established by Rozanova soon after, exacerbated the couple's reputation as renegades from the emigre establishment.

It was not, however, Sinyavsky's polemical articles signed with his own name that raised the greatest furor, but rather his whimsical and idiosyncratic little book on Pushkin, written in Dubrovlag. In that work the writer lightheartedly "strolls" through Pushkin's life and works, mustering a virtuoso display of metaphor and wordplay in defense of art's independence from political and social mandates. Given its playfulness and linguistic complexity *Strolls with Pushkin* would seem to be an unlikely work to call forth strong passions on the part of a general readership. Yet twice *Strolls with Pushkin* has catapulted Sinyavsky to the center of cultural controversy—first, in 1975, in the wake of its publication in the West and, second, in 1989, following the appearance of an excerpt from the work in a Soviet journal.[36] The two uproars essentially replayed the attacks on Sinyavsky at the time of his trial. This continuity in the reflexes of response through different generations—with apparently discrete cultural backgrounds—of Russian readers takes us to the heart of the issues of reader, reading, text, and context enacted in the writings of Abram Tertz.

One of the earliest and most notorious attacks on *Strolls with Pushkin* was a review entitled "Progulki khama s Pushkinym" (A boor's strolls with Pushkin) published in the emigre periodical *Novyi zhurnal* in 1976 and written by the journal's editor, a first-wave emigre named Roman Gul. Gul draws the first epigraph to his article from Genesis 9:22–23: "And Ham, the father of Canaan, saw the nakedness of his father, and told his two brethren without. And Shem and Japheth took a garment, laid it upon both their shoulders, and went backward, and covered the nakedness of their father; and their faces were backward, and they saw not their father's nakedness." Gul maintains, somewhat disingenuously, that he is not using the Russian word *kham* in the sense of "boor," but rather in reference to the Old Testament name: "I am not using the term *kham* in an abusive sense. That would be unworthy. I am using it in the biblical sense—as the cynicism of man and mockery of that which in human society should not be mocked if society does not want to turn into a herd of orangutans."[37] Underlying Gul's argument then is a vision of language taboos as an essential means of concealment, a cover for the indiscretions of the body—like the clothing Ham's brothers place over their father's nakedness—shrouding figures of authority from a dangerously intimate and therefore inappropriate gaze that can threaten the very basis of human community.

Gul posits Abram Tertz and his *Strolls with Pushkin* as an example of the general "boorification" (*okhamlenie*) of Soviet society that he sees reflected in the use of language: "In our country everyone uses four-letter words: the prime minister and the pillar of literature Mikhail Sholokhov and prima ballerinas and members of the Writers' Union and academicians and Moscow drivers and thieves and factory workers and housewives. And these four-letter words are not at all a kind of 'exoticism,' it is the *language of Soviet life,* the language of everyday life, which speaks of the degree of universal boorification" (120, Gul's emphasis).[38] The vulgarization of language in the Soviet Union posited by Gul thus appears as a primary symptom of this "absolutely awful phenomenon: spiritually, culturally, politically, socially, in every way" (121).

Gul openly acknowledges that his quarrel with Abram Tertz and *Strolls with Pushkin* is first and foremost linguistic: "In this, in my opinion, precisely *khamskoi* (in the biblical sense, of course!) book what is remarkable is not *what* Abram Tertz wrote about Pushkin, but *how* he writes about Pushkin" (122). The central issue thus becomes what Gul considers to be the inappropriateness of Tertz's language to his subject, and the critic devotes the bulk of his article to examples of Tertz's supposed violations of linguistic decorum, fulminating (in an echo of Kedrina) against Tertz's "Smerdyakovish style" (126) and exclaiming, "What a style! Directly out of the thieves' barracks of Dubrovlag!" (128). Gul is particularly exercised by Tertz's treatment of Pushkin's "tragic death": "Here, before the poet's corpse, one would think Tertz would probably have doffed his cap. A vain expectation. Tertz plays the hooligan and the boor here as well" (128). As an example, he cites the purported vulgarity of the language Tertz employs in speculating about the question of Pushkin's wife's fidelity: "In Pushkin's family drama Tertz is particularly interested in one thing: 'Well, all the same, hand on your heart, did she put out, or didn't she?' Of course, Tertz could have written, "Was she, or was she not, unfaithful?' But Tertz deliberately chooses a *khamshoe*, prostitutish word" (129).

Gul's championship of linguistic decorum—and his consequent animadversion to Tertz's "dirty, hooliganishly-*khamsoi* and, in essence, insignificant book" (129)—is rooted in his vision of literature in general and of Pushkin in particular.[39] He cites Tsvetaeva's statement, "Art is *holy*," and concurs with her—"I agree with Tsvetaeva— true art is *holy*"—adding, "The name . . . of Pushkin . . . for me is *holy*" (123). Although he does not use the word, Gul, like Sinyavsky's Soviet critics, is in essence accusing the writer of blasphemy. Once again the point of contention lies in the violation of linguistic taboos and therefore in the link between appropriate use of language and the role of the writer in society. Gul maintains that "Tertz writes impudently [*naglo*], without any responsibility before the reader" (127).[40] The writer's "responsibility before the reader" consists in using language to conceal, to maintain social decorum. Adherence to conventionalized language becomes fundamental to the preservation of the social group, and the writer takes on the role of keeper of linguistic propriety, a role that he violates only at society's peril.

Aleksandr Solzhenitsyn's article on *Strolls with Pushkin*, entitled ". . . Koleblet tvoi trenozhnik" ('. . . Shakes your sacrificial altar') and published in 1984, echoes Gul's basic premises, while offering a more complex reading of the Tertz work.[41] Solzhenitsyn draws his title from Pushkin's 1830 lyric "To the Poet," in which Pushkin advises the poet to pay no heed to either the fickle love or the jeers of the crowd, but rather to be himself the "highest judge" of his own poetry:

> Are you satisfied? Then what matter if the crowd abuses it
> And spits on the altar where your fire burns,
> And in childish playfulness shakes your sacrificial altar.

Playing on Pushkin's imagery, Solzhenitsyn casts *Strolls with Pushkin* as a manifestation of the crowd's "childish playfulness,"[42] which is by implication sacrilegious in relation to the sacred person of Pushkin. Solzhenitsyn thus seconds Gul in hanging his article on the opposition between the sacred and the profane and in concomitantly criticizing Sinyavsky's use of slang and particularly thieves' slang (*blatnogo musora*, 144) as being equivalent to relieving oneself in a church. Solzhenitsyn's understanding of the implications of the linguistic daring of Sinyavsky's text and his attempts to defuse them—by turning metaphors from *Strolls with Pushkin* back on their author—are, however, far more penetrating than those of Gul and others who have criticized *Strolls with Pushkin*. Solzhenitsyn openly disagrees with the vision of literature the work enacts and with Sinyavsky's use of Pushkin to validate that vision. In this context, Solzhenitsyn's article on *Strolls with Pushkin* forms part of an ongoing polemic between Solzhenitsyn and Sinyavsky on the function of literature in society and the role of the writer.[43]

Solzhenitsyn builds his argument around a series of mixed, but interrelated, metaphors—linked by repetitions of the words *pustoi* ("empty" or "pointless") and *pustota* ("emptiness")—to describe the structure and method of *Strolls with Pushkin*. He describes Tertz's technique as a "dance around Pushkin," an "empty jig" (136) with an "artificial structure": "And how is one step linked to another? By associations, often artificial, though artful, vaults from subject to subject" (136). The dance then becomes a "labyrinth" (137) of "burrows" "gnawed" through Pushkin: "It is not a construction, but as if burrows had been gnawed through Pushkin and mostly on a lower level, and the system of burrows is so confused that toward the end we together with the essayist barely remember the beginning and the whole path" (136). Solzhenitsyn is disturbed that this "worm gnawing" (137) has no logical foundation: "The critic offers us there neither an inductive nor a deductive method, but takes us through deliberately confused twists and turns" (137). The first group of metaphors that Solzhenitsyn adduces to describe the structure of *Strolls with Pushkin* thus focus on the work's apparent lack of structure, direction, and purpose. This discussion is punctuated by phrases and paraphrases from *Strolls with Pushkin* in which Solzhenitsyn focuses on Tertz's description of Pushkin by absence or lack, which he rhetorically emphasizes by citing his use not only of words denoting emptiness, but also of words beginning with the prefix *bez* ("without"), for example *besputnyi* ("directionless") and *"Bezotvetstennost', beztrudolyubie, bezzabotnost' Pushkina"* (Pushkin's irresponsibility, lack of diligence, carelessness) (137). Solzhenitsyn clearly views "emptiness" or "pointlessness" as a potentially dangerous declaration of the independence of the literary text from controls imposed on the free play of language.[44]

Solzhenitsyn's analysis of *Strolls with Pushkin* thus differs from those of Gul and others precisely because he does not merely cite examples of "mockery" of Pushkin and inveigh against them. Rather, he is disturbed, above all, by the text's *ambiguity:* "Sinyavsky is in fact enthralled by Pushkin, laying this out with talent, enthusiasm, in some places vividly; however, the epithets are sustained in such a way that the form of the praise itself soils the poet. These are the conditions of the game proposed to us: ambiguity through and through [*skvoznaya dvusmyslennost'*], to seek what is spoiled everywhere or even to create it artificially" (139). Solzhenitsyn seems to locate the roots of this ambiguity in an inconsistency, a duality, in the text. Acknowledging that in some passages Tertz has done justice to his subject, he is unable to reconcile these instances with the sections he finds offensive. This leads him to his last metaphor for Tertz's method. He accuses him of having performed a "vivisection" on Pushkin by fragmenting the "genius" into poet and man.

> All of this is nothing new, has little significance, is empty exercises. As in all people everything is one [*edino*], organic in a genius as well: his conduct in life, his bright and dark sides, the colors and shadows of his personality, his thoughts and views, his artistic achievements and failures—and moreover at every minute [a genius] remains naturally true to himself. Genius is not a separate fluid poured [into a person]. If one judges by dissected parts, one condemns oneself to not understanding the essence. (145)

Solzhenitsyn thus takes Sinyavsky's metaphorical division of Pushkin into poet and man and "embodies" it. He invokes the tangible oneness of the body as proof of the integrity—the unity—of the personality, which is jeopardized by Sinyavsky's irresponsible use of language. Deploying the metaphor of the body, on the one hand, to validate the unity of the author—which in turn legitimates the author's control over his own text—Solzhenitsyn also employs the body as a demand for the simple referentiality of the text, invoking a sort of literary habeas corpus in response to Tertz's remark that in *Boris Godunov* "the dead body moves to the center of the work." "But, if you please," Solzhenitsyn counters, "he [the dead tsarevich in *Boris Godunov*] emerges again and again as a plot of conscience and not at all in a natural unburied aspect."[45] In effect, then, Solzhenitsyn insists on reading Tertz's metaphor literally, demanding that if he is going to talk about corpses in Pushkin, he must in fact produce the corpses. Language must be held accountable to the body.[46] The literary text must be held in check by the "physical reality" outside the text, or the uncontrolled figurative use of language threatens to undermine the integrity of the self.

The crux of Solzhenitsyn's argument thus resides in his understanding of Tertz's assertion in *Strolls with Pushkin* that "emptiness is Pushkin's content." While Tertz celebrates Pushkin's emptiness, Solzhenitsyn deplores it, as a gnawing away of substance, an evisceration. Solzhenitsyn devotes the rest of his article to salvaging "the volume not eaten away by the moves of the critics" (146). The Pushkin that, according to Solzhenitsyn, "remains" after the poet has been "dug out" by Tertz and his ilk hardly surprisingly reflects Solzhenitsyn's own ideas about the role of the writer. Solzhenitsyn's Pushkin was a political thinker who recognized the power of the printed word and believed that the government should respect and listen to writers, without allowing that "the writer should employ this divine weapon to achieve base or criminal aims" (147). He was equally suspicious of revolution, democracy, and the "passion for novelty" (147), concepts that are implicitly equated. Solzhenitsyn's Pushkin, moreover, serves as a touchstone of religious orthodoxy: "Russian literature as a whole was Christian to the extent that it remained . . . faithful to Pushkin" (150). Pushkin emerges as a paradigm for the Russian writer as the political and moral conscience of society, a defender of Russia and its traditional values. Solzhenitsyn thus meets the "emptiness" of Tertz's Pushkin with an affirmation of Pushkin's substance. Pushkin may neither be read nor written about freely; there is only one correct, harmonious, and unitary Pushkin, who serves as a gauge of the Russian writer's legitimacy.[47]

The interconnection between language and authority on which

Solzhenitsyn's argument implicitly rests becomes clear in the concluding paragraphs of his article. Writing of the trend in Russian emigre literature of which he perceives *Strolls with Pushkin* to be representative, he asks: "Could we have naturally expected that the new criticism, barely freed from the unbearable repression of Soviet censorship, that the first thing for which it would employ its freedom would be a strike against Pushkin? With our current belated experience we shall answer: yes, that is precisely what we should have expected" (151). It should have been expected, Solzhenitsyn maintains, because this recent tendency is a continuation of the "aesthetic nihilism" of the Russian radical critics of the 1860s, characterized by a "revolutionary disrespect for the classics" (151). He thus hints darkly that Sinyavsky and those like him share the same indiscriminate urge to challenge all authority that drove early political radicals and ultimately led to the revolution. The trend that, for Solzhenitsyn, *Strolls with Pushkin* represents threatens to undermine the very basis of Russian culture by tearing down "precisely that which in Russian literature was lofty and pure" (152). Solzhenitsyn links this assault with the "childish playfulness," the irreverent irresponsibility toward language, with which his argument began. Deploring the "all-embracing irony, play and liberty with the self-sufficient New Word" (152), in which he views Sinyavsky and his like as indulging, Solzhenitsyn associates the uninhibited and unrestricted use of language in literature with political pluralism and suggests that both represent dangerous threats to authority. Ultimately, then, the possibility of rival interpretations—inextricably linked with the irresponsible, empty use of language that violates "the boundaries of decency" (152)—endangers the very basis of society.[48]

Solzhenitsyn's analysis of *Strolls with Pushkin* reveals a series of associations—which arguably underlie all of the attacks on Sinyavsky—between literature's claims to referentiality, the author's pretensions to the status of a defining center who can control how the text is read, and language's ability to define identity. Solzhenitsyn's vision of literature rests on the assumption that the literary text has a responsibility to the reality outside the text, a responsibility to reflect and shape that reality. As he wrote in his novel *The First Circle*, "The writer is a second government." If, as the writer's aspiration to political power suggests, literature can transform word into act, can change reality, then unrestrained language, language that is ambiguous and therefore out of the writer's control, is potentially dangerous to society. In this light, Tertz's "emptying" of Pushkin appears not as a harmless metaphor, but as a threat of anarchy. On the other hand, postulating, as Tertz does, that literature is merely literature and not a political weapon devalues the writer's claims to authority. If literature is merely play, the writer becomes nothing more than an entertainer.

These same issues concerning the interrelationships among language, power, and identity resurfaced in the third "scandal" surrounding Sinyavsky, which erupted in the wake of the publication of an excerpt from *Strolls with Pushkin* in the writer's homeland in the spring of 1989. While the emigre uproar over Sinyavsky's work—and specifically the Gul and Solzhenitsyn articles—served as a subtext for the furor with which the publication was greeted in the USSR, the continuity between the first- and third-wave emigre reactions and the later Soviet response to *Strolls with Pushkin* testifies less to immediate influence than to the deep-rootedness of the cultural patterns it triggered. In the aggravated situation created by glasnost and perestroika, the issues of raw power and virulent Russian chauvinism largely implicit in the earlier attacks on *Strolls with Pushkin* came to the fore.

Early in 1989 the ban against publishing living emigre writers gave way, marking the beginning of the final stage of the collapse of Soviet censorship. At the beginning of January, Sinyavsky himself returned to the Soviet Union for the first time since his emigration in 1973, to pay his final respects to Yuly Daniel, who had died several days earlier.[49] In the wake of this visit, interviews with Sinyavsky and his wife were published in the Soviet press, and works first by "Sinyavsky" and soon after by "Tertz" started to appear in Soviet periodicals. In the superabundance of previously banned works filling the pages of Soviet journals, the "return" of Sinyavsky's works initially passed almost unnoticed, including the publication of a four-page excerpt from *Strolls with Pushkin* in the journal *Oktyabr* in April. This neglect, however, was not to last, and the later ferocity of the attacks more than compensated for their slow start.

The first real indication of things to come was the republication of Gul's "A Boor's Strolls", omitting the passages condemning Soviet culture, in the newspaper *Literaturnaya Rossiya* in June. The attack did not begin in earnest, however, until *Literaturnaya Rossiya* published on August 4 a letter addressed to the Secretariat of the Writers' Union of the RSFSR, castigating *Oktyabr*, an organ of the union, for having published such "Russophobic" works as *Strolls with Pushkin*.[50] The most notable of the letter's three signatories was

Igor Shafarevich, a noted mathematician and co-contributor with Solzhenitsyn to the dissident anthology *From Under the Rubble* compiled in the early 1970s. In June Shafarevich had published a lengthy essay entitled "Russophobia" in the self-styled Russophile journal *Nash sovremennik*.[51] In the article he defined the "Russophobia" that he claimed permeated the writings of Western Sovietologists and emigre publicists as "the view according to which the Russians are a nation of slaves, who have always worshipped authority, who hate everything foreign and hate culture, and Russia is an eternal breeding-ground for despotism and totalitarianism, dangerous for the rest of the world" (173). The essence of Russophobia, Shafarevich argues, is hatred, "and hatred toward one nation is most often linked with an acute sense of one's belonging to another nation" (187). Following this reasoning, Shafarevich locates the driving force behind this allegedly rampant Russophobia in "Jewish national sentiment" (188) and claims that Russian culture is in jeopardy precisely because all members of the liberal intelligentsia—and particularly emigres—are Russophobes, and all Russophobes either are Jews or are under the control of Jews.

In an article entitled "Fenomen emigratsii" ("The emigration phenomenon"), published in *Literaturnaya Rossiya* in September 1989, Shafarevich, while muting the blatant anti-Semitism of his earlier tract, directs his argument specifically against the third wave of emigration from Russia, which he portrays as a "stratum of people who have broken spiritually with the whole way of life of the country they have left to the most radical extent possible" (47).[52] He likens the return of the third wave—or of their writings—to "toxins" that threaten with further upheaval a nation that has been left vulnerable by seven decades of communist rule: "Readers—and primarily young ones—exhausted by the burden of nauseating propaganda and mendacious literature, are stunned and carried away by this extreme license and aggressive daring in overturning despised idols. . . . And is this the first time that the stagnation of life has made any overthrow sweet, no matter what precisely was being overthrown?" (53). Shafarevich selects *Strolls with Pushkin* as his primary example of these dangerous toxins, suggesting darkly that it represents a sort of loyalty test for Russians, an attempt at subversion of traditional values, for which he, rather extravagantly, finds an analogue in Salman Rushdie's *Satanic Verses:*

> An analogous situation recently resounded all over the world. Salman Rushdie's famous *Satanic Verses* is apparently

something like an Islamic variation on *Strolls with Pushkin*. And it must be said that the Islamic world, by its reaction to this "sounding out," once again proved its great vitality and thereby probably significantly weakened the pressure that it could have been subjected to in the near future. I am talking, of course, not about the calls by the late Ayatollah to kill the author; these in fact turned out to be a very convenient excuse to whitewash, under the pretext of protecting Rushdie (who will no doubt make more than one million on this uproar), the blasphemous insult that was leveled at a whole civilization, at many hundreds of millions of people. The real response was the vast demonstrations, the fact that hundreds of people gave their lives in clashes with the police, as a result of which the book was banned in many countries.

But our response is still to come. (5)

Spearheaded by Shafarevich, the outcry against *Strolls with Pushkin* escalated in the autumn of 1989, with attacks on the work—in the form of articles or letters from outraged readers—appearing in virtually every issue of the weekly *Literaturnaya Rossiya*. The uproar reached its peak at the sixth plenum of the Administration of the Writers' Union of the RSFSR held in Moscow on November 13 and 14. Speaker after speaker at the meeting accused Sinyavsky of being a Russophobe who had defiled Russia's "sacred object" (*svyatynya*), Pushkin. The tactics employed in the Soviet assaults on *Strolls with Pushkin*—especially the deprecatory formulas reproduced over and over in irate letters and newspaper articles and pronounced from official podiums, often by people who clearly had never read the work itself—unmistakably recalled the campaign that had accompanied the Sinyavsky and Daniel trial a quarter of a century earlier. However, if the attacks on Sinyavsky in the mid-1960s had been ordered "from above," the scandal over *Strolls with Pushkin* emanated from within writers' circles themselves.

On the surface of it, the furor over *Strolls with Pushkin* was merely a blind for a power play within the Writers' Union, a pretext to unseat Anatoly Ananev, the reform-minded editor of *Oktyabr*, and to replace him with someone closer in views to the conservative nationalist camp, while at the same time consolidating bureaucratic control over the union.[53] The fury unleashed by the Soviet publication of an excerpt from the Tertz book was clearly fed by the immediate situation of incipient institutional chaos: writers and literary officials who previously had monopolized the privileges of union mem-

bership and enjoyed healthy honoraria from their officially spon-
sored and subsidized publications saw their access to publication
and their hegemony over literary politics threatened by the influx of
formerly proscribed writings and writers, emigres foremost among
them. However, even within the writers' community, the issues involved went far deeper than immediate political or economic expe-
diency. What *Strolls with Pushkin* placed at issue, as Solzhenitsyn
had earlier recognized, was the role and status of the Russian writer.
Thus, one of Sinyavsky's defenders wrote: "I want to say immediately
that in *Strolls with Pushkin* Tertz truly does make a mockery. Not of
Pushkin however, but of the tradition, which has long reigned in our
country, of seeing in art above all a service, auxiliary category. For
almost two centuries the writer has been required to *serve:* society,
the state, the tsar, the fatherland, the liberation movement, patriotic
duty, the Russian idea—whomever was required."[54] By arguing in
Strolls with Pushkin that Pushkin's art is "purposeless," that it resists
subordination to goals outside itself, Tertz challenges the traditional
role of the Russian writer as, depending on the relevant political orientation, an "engineer of human souls" or a "second government"
canonized in the official image of Pushkin. Given the extent to which
this vision of the writer as society's conscience had historically been
the source of the Russian writer's social, political, and institutional
status and power, it is hardly surprising that *Strolls with Pushkin*
struck a deep nerve in the literary community.

However, the rhetoric of outrage—in the popular press as well
as among literati—that greeted the publication of *Strolls with Pushkin* makes clear that the threat represented by Tertz's work touched
the mainstays of national identity. Viewed within the context of the
cultural upheaval engendered by glasnost, the motive forces behind
the scandal and the bipolar mythic construct—pitting Jews and Jewish sympathizers against Russians—within which it was played out
appear obvious. First, the deluge of sensational revelations about
the horrors of the Soviet period unleashed by the collapse of censorship and the discreditation of the long-prevailing ideology led
many, especially of the older generation, to look for an alternative
source of self-validation in their "Russianness" and, concomitantly,
to seek vindication for their national identity by blaming Russia's
ills on "foreigners." Hence the alarming rise of anti-Semitism and
the persistent attempts by Shafarevich and his ilk to prove that both
the revolution and the collapse of authoritarian power structures
were engineered by Jews and their sympathizers. As a non-Jewish
Russian who had taken a Jewish pseudonym, Sinyavsky was a tailor-

made emblem for this culture myth. The same pressures led many to clutch ever more tightly to symbols—Pushkin foremost among them—of the worth of Russian culture. As one critic of *Strolls with Pushkin* maintained, "Pushkin is one of the last saints to remain to our people in this spiritually tragic time."[55] Before an American audience Ernst Safonov, editor of *Literaturnaya Rossiya*, elaborated on the sacralization of the figure of Pushkin in Russian society:

> Not long ago I was in my native village, and I was standing by a church that had been destroyed. An old woman came up to me and I asked her when the church had been destroyed. She told me in 1932. She had still been a little girl and now she was an old woman and obviously the offense had festered in her soul for such a long time that she told me, a stray passerby, who happened to have gotten out of a car and gone up to the church. . . . She told me, "I was a little girl and when they were destroying everything, I grabbed an icon and ran away with it, but when I was almost home, a man with a bag and with a revolver in his belt, tore the icon away from me and trampled it before my eyes." . . . When all of these holy things are trampled, when there are no more icons or very few, Pushkin is one of those icons. He is an icon equal to the icons of the church.[56]

The Russian sense of national identity and self-worth in part rests on such allegiance to fetishized figures, who must be protected against subversive language.

However, the fact remains that *Strolls with Pushkin* is *not* an attack on Pushkin. We are left with the question of why it was perceived as such. Part of the answer lies precisely in Pushkin's sacralization and the language taboos that it entails. Only ritualized, rigorously formulaic language is appropriate in writing about a sacred figure, a stricture that Tertz flouts in *Strolls with Pushkin* by writing about the poet in indecorous language.

Yet the issue goes far beyond the inappropriate use of language to the way language functions in Tertz's text. Rozanova, in an article analyzing the controversy over *Strolls with Pushkin* comes to the conclusion that, "the saddest revelation in this story was that the Russian people have unlearned how to read somewhat" (96).[57] She illustrates her point by citing examples of readers' responses to one of the most "notorious" lines in Sinyavsky's work: "Pushkin ran into high poetry on thin erotic legs and created a commotion":

It began, of course, with the thin erotic legs. "Marya Vasi-
levna," a respected old doctor, stopped me one day in a Russian bookstore in Paris: "Where did Andrei Donatovich get
the idea that Pushkin had thin erotic legs? After all even in
the notorious book *Pushkin's Don Juan List* there are no instructions to the effect that his legs were erotic." And I explained at length that since he was not running into a drawing
room, but into poetry, these were not literal legs, but what is
called a metaphor, and I consoled myself with the rationaliza-
tions: well, he's old; well, he forgot. . . . But then not long ago
the remarkable Russian writer Georgy Nikolaevich Vladimov
asked, "Andrei Donatovich," he said, "Where did you get the
idea that Pushkin had thin legs? After all, it is well known that
he was a very athletic person." It is some kind of sorcery: the
man wrote a whole novel-metaphor and stumbled over those
legs. . . . I have the feeling that after seventy years of realism—
socialist or not socialist—many people have begun to read by
syllables and only literally. (96–97)

As Stephanie Sandler has observed, "This has been a controversy
about figurative language, as much as anything else."[58] The allegiance in Russian culture to a belief in the referentiality of the literary text, its claims to authenticity—to meaning—are rooted in its
ability and obligation to reflect reality. The tangible reality of the
body—Pushkin's legs—defines the limits of semiosis. Tertz's text, in
undermining the illusion of referentiality, either forces the reader
tutored on "realism" to relearn how to read or elicits perverse misreadings.

All three of the "scandals" over Tertz's works, then, have arisen
out of what Sinyavsky himself has termed "stylistic differences."[59]
These differences emanate from conceptions of how language works
which entail an entire structure of relationships between writer,
reader, text, genre, society, and, in the final analysis, identity. The attacks on Sinyavsky beginning in 1966 and continuing to the present
reveal the workings of a mythical equation of word and deed deeply
rooted in Russian culture and born of a fear of language "unre-
pressed" (in both the political and the psychological senses). To restrain the dangerous "magic" power of the word—the power of language to produce action—controls on language emerged, of which
censorship was merely the most obvious manifestation. Seen in this
light, we can read cultural reflexes going back to the nineteenth-
century Russian critic Vissarion Belinsky's definition of literature

as "thinking in images" and his championship of "realism" through Solzhenitsyn's attack on *Strolls with Pushkin* as a lapse into the intentional fallacy, a belief that the writer can control what his text "says" and therefore dictate to the reader how to read. This led in the Soviet period to the reduction of the text to slogan, to the sacralization of cultural icons maintained by a protective veil of ritualized language. In his 1975 review "Lyudi i zveri" (People and beasts) Tertz asserts—in terms that, in the wake of glasnost and the consequent collapse of the Soviet empire, seem little short of prophetic—that the entire system rests on language control:

> We can't understand why the "masters," the "bosses" endlessly repeat phrases that everyone, including the "bosses" themselves, are fed up with, of the sort: "Socialist Realism," "cult of personality," the "anti-party group of Malenkov, Molotov, Kaganovich and Shepilov, who attached himself to them." Is it really impossible, we ask out of naivete, to move at least this Shepilov—about whom we have only heard that he was "attached"—just a bit to the right or the left, well, at least, to put him, the scoundrel, into the full complement of the "anti-party group" without this sickening epithet "attached," which means nothing? Indeed then we would have understood, felt, loved something: at last the bosses have given at least themselves some freedom of the word! Perhaps with this "Shepilov," shifted a bit, a new era would begin, enthusiasm would rise! Communism!
>
> No, it's impossible, and you don't understand that if you modify "Shepilov" just a little bit—everything will collapse. Because the whole ideological-political education of dogs and men is based on rote training. And it's impossible to say "lie down!" instead of "sit!": a revolution will take place in consciousness and everything will fly off the tracks, and so it is better to let "Shepilov, who attached himself to them" stay "attached"—it's more peaceful. (375–76)

In this model of the reading process, all utterances are designed to elicit acts, all words become deeds, all metaphors—to use Sinyavsky's terminology—are realized.

To this totalitarian paradigm for the relationship between reader and text, Sinyavsky counterposes an alternative vision, in which shifting Shepilov becomes a paradigm for the workings of the literary language, which in turn corresponds to the essential "uncontrollability" of the literary text. If at his trial he defined the writer as at best a privileged reader of his own works, in his "Tertz" article "Iskusstvo i deistvitel'nost" (Art and reality) he openly challenges the *author*'s *author*ity by insisting on the unpredictability of reader response:

> Of course, we all know that literature at times influences how people act. But we are not in a position either to gauge or to regulate that influence. And thank God. . . . In the camp an old criminal told me that he became a thief and a bandit after reading Maksim Gorky's wonderful story "Chelkash" at seventeen. We know that because of Goethe's *Werther* some young people even shot themselves. But that same *Werther* saved other young people from committing suicide. Reading, profoundly reading Lermontov's poem *The Demon*, one might possibly become a mystic. And one might just as possibly become an atheist. For example, my father, who came from a noble family, became a revolutionary after reading Dostoevsky. But I know boys who, having read too much Mayakovsky, went from the Komsomol over to the dissidents. But you could shoot dissidents under the influence of that same Mayakovsky. (117)

The text thus becomes a sort of neutral zone—beyond the bipolarity *for* or *against*—by opening up the possibility of multiple readings allowed, even encouraged, but not dictated by the text. While Tertz here begs the issue of misreading, and his comment cited above in fact places the concept itself in doubt, we may nonetheless suggest, on the basis of the scandals over his works, that misreading the writings of Tertz constitutes precisely the reflex to reduce the text to one half of a simple bipolarity or to simple referentiality, thereby negating its essential ambiguity.

In effect, the dichotomy between Sinyavsky and Tertz itself represents a paradigm for literature's essential otherness in relation to reality that informs Sinyavsky's understanding of how literature works. Here we may return to the apparent incongruity between juridical innocence and textual crime thrown into relief by Sinyavsky's trial. On the one hand, Andrei Sinyavsky pleaded innocent to the charges against him. On the other hand, in the persona of Abram Tertz, the writer brands himself a criminal. However, this self-identification entails a subtle subversion. Abram Tertz is not a "respectable" political offender, but a common thief, a discrepancy that is symptomatic of Sinyavsky's redefinition of the nature of the crime that is literature. Andrei Sinyavsky can be placed on trial, but

Abram Tertz cannot, because he has no juridical standing—he is a metaphor. If we return to Sinyavsky's closing words at the trial— "You, jurists, deal with terms, which the narrower they are, the more precise. In contrast to the term, the meaning of the artistic image is more precise the broader it is"—the nature of his understanding of literature as crime becomes clear. The essence of the language of the law court is to strive for transparent referentiality; the nature of literary language is to strive to unsettle semantic boundaries. Literature is criminal, but untriable, because it challenges the illusion of the unambiguous relationship between signifier and signified on which legality depends.

The duality of the writer—his difference from himself—crystallized in the bifurcation of Sinyavsky and Tertz is a figure of both the failure and the richness of literary meaning. By locating the threatening other—thief and Jew—within himself, Sinyavsky emblematizes literature's mandate to express what society might wish to repress. Yet in a deeper sense, the Sinyavsky/Tertz dichotomy challenges the very ability of language to name the body, to define the boundaries of the self, and therefore to refer unambiguously. Sinyavsky is both Tertz and not-Tertz, is both same and different. By the same token, in the writings of Abram Tertz, bipolarities are constantly frustrated: between writer and critic, reader and writer, self and other. The ability of language to name unities reliably is placed in doubt and with it all conventional taxonomies, including the integrity of identity itself.[60] The writer transformed into text becomes not an *author*ity, but an *empty* locus for verbal play.

The Tertz pseudonym serves, moreover, to locate the writer within his own cultural context. By adopting the name of a Jewish outlaw he identifies his literary persona with that which is considered other in his society. While creating an association between the writer's works and the semi-forbidden culture of the lower strata of society, Abram Tertz also evokes another famous Jewish outlaw in "high" Russian literature: Isaac Babel's Benya Krik.[61] By the same token, Sinyavsky's identification of his literary alter ego with a Jewish criminal echoes both Marina Tsvetaeva's provocative poetic statement

> In this most Christian of worlds
> Poets are Jews[62]

and Osip Mandelshtam's assertion in his "Fourth Prose": "I divide all works of world literature into those that are permitted and those that are written without permission. The former are rubbish, the latter—stolen [*vorovannyi*] air."[63] In his selection of his pseudonym Sinyavsky thus traces his literary heritage to the ornamental prose of the 1920s and, more generally, to the Russian modernist tradition cut short by the intervention of state-sponsored Socialist Realism.

In a broader sense the distinction between Sinyavsky and Tertz functions as a metaphor for the "death of the Author," an assertion of the noncorrespondence of the body of the author with the body of his text, of the flesh-and-blood writer with his representation, an abdication of the writer's claim to be the center of reference defining how his texts will be read.[64] Abram Tertz is thus a figure for transgression analogous to Derrida's violation of orthographic rules in writing the word *difference* with an *a:* it is a flouting of convention that opens up the play of difference. As Barthes writes, "the birth of the reader must be at the cost of the death of the Author." The text's denial of its origin, of an Author, the affirmation of the difference between Sinyavsky and Tertz, opens the text up to limitless possibilities of interpretation. In the words of Barthes, "Once the Author is removed, the claim to decipher a text becomes quite futile. To give a text an Author is to impose a limit on that text, to furnish it with a final signified, to close the writing. . . . [Writing], by refusing to assign a 'secret,' an ultimate meaning, to the text (and to the world as text), liberates what may be called an anti-theological activity, an activity that is truly revolutionary since to refuse to fix meaning is, in the end, to refuse God and his hypostases—reason, science, law."[65]

It is essential to note, however, that although the vision of the interrelationship between writer, text, and reader elaborated in the Tertz writings at points dovetails with several basic premises of deconstructionist philosophy and criticism, Sinyavsky and Tertz are the products of a fundamentally different intellectual, religious, and literary tradition, and Sinyavsky therefore parts company with Western theorists both with regard to the parameters of his project and the cosmology in which he places it. As Barthes's generalization of the death of the Author beyond the bounds of the literary text to all discourse, his assertion of the "world as text," makes clear, deconstructionism presents itself as a global theory of meaning, postulating an unbridgeable rift between all discourse and its origin, between word and body. Sinyavsky, as he made clear in his remarks at his trial, posits an essential distinction between the function of language in the literary text and the discourse of law, politics, and everyday life. At the core of his critique of totalitarian society lies a horrific vision of the world transformed into text, the word divorced

from its consequences to the body, the discourse of politics transformed into literary trope. Moreover, while Barthes identifies the exposure of the death of the Author as "an anti-theological activity"—
just as Derrida presents what he terms "decentering" as a corollary
of the death of God[66]—for Sinyavsky/Tertz the instability of meaning that results from the absence of a defining center is a symptom
of humanity's postlapsarian state. God is not dead, but inaccessible.
Writer, reader, and text are alienated from the transcendent by their
confinement in the substance of the fallen world.

As an assertion of the otherness of the text from the writer, the
Tertz pseudonym is thus a figure of the type of writing Sinyavsky attributes to Abram Tertz. These are texts that challenge the reader to
fill the gap left by the Author's open abdication of *author*ity, texts that
are, to use Barthes's terminology, "writerly," that "make the reader
no longer a consumer but a producer of the text."[67] Viewed within
their particular cultural context then, the Tertz writings represent a
challenge to the "readerly" texts of Socialist Realism, writings that
allow the reader only "the poor freedom either to accept or reject
the text" (4), and, in a larger sense, to reading as an institutionalized
process in Soviet society, which dictated that all readers interpret a
text in a single, prescribed way. Tertz as text thus seeks to subvert
the state's claims to be the defining point of reference and thereby to
return to the reader his or her right to find him- or herself in the text,
to affirm the infinitude of meaning. Yet, especially after the demise
of the Soviet state, it is essential to recognize that the significance
of Tertz's writings is not limited to a particular political context.
As Tertz maintains, all writers are dissidents. I shall therefore attempt to demonstrate in the readings that follow, that Sinyavsky's
understanding of the death of the Author and the birth of the reader
has profound ethical and theological ramifications. The crime of the
text, its acknowledgement of *differance,* holds forth the possibility of
liberation and redemption.

Chapter Two

. . . .

Subversion from Within:
What Is Socialist Realism
and *The Trial Begins*

For both its devotees and for those who fear it, irony is usually seen as something that undermines clarities, opens up vistas of chaos, and either liberates
by destroying all dogma or destroys by revealing the inescapable canker of
negation at the heart of every affirmation.

—WAYNE C. BOOTH, *A Rhetoric of Irony*

"So, that means, in your opinion, there also exists an *unofficial* definition of
Socialist Realism? . . ."

—ABRAM TERTZ, *Goodnight*

The essay *What Is Socialist Realism* (*Chto takoe sotsialisticheskii realizm*) and the novella *The Trial Begins* (*Sud idet*) were the earliest
of Sinyavsky's Tertz works to be written and to be sent abroad for
publication. Both first appeared in Western publications in 1959,
launching Sinyavsky's career as a tamizdat writer.[1] They also mark
the beginning of Sinyavsky's unofficial writing activities in that they
constitute an exorcism of sorts, a confrontation with and attempt
to overcome the then-prevailing hegemony of Socialist Realism over
Soviet literature through an exposure of its formal incoherence. The
two works thus may be viewed conjointly as the writer's declaration
of independence, his escape from the Soviet canon.[2] In each of them
Tertz begins by ostensibly positioning his narrator within the conventions of Socialist Realism in order, ultimately, to subvert those
conventions from within by calling into question the existence of a
single defining center and thus the authority of authorial voice.

The title of *What Is Socialist Realism,* which is echoed in the first
sentence of the essay, makes it clear from the start that the essay is

about a problem of definition.³ It also evokes the tradition of such nineteenth-century tracts as Dobrolyubov's *What Is Oblomovism?* (*Chto takoe oblomovshchina?*) and Tolstoy's *What Is Art?* (*Chto takoe iskusstvo?*), in which literature as a formal structure is subordinated to political, social, and moral aims.⁴ Tertz concludes his essay, however, by answering in no uncertain terms the question posed by another canonic text from the tradition of literature as social criticism, Chernyshevsky's tendentious novel, *What Is to be Done?* (*Chto delat'?*) "There is nothing to be done" (*delat' nechego*),⁵ Tertz maintains in his final paragraph, thus repudiating the basic premise that literature should serve social activism with which he began by denying literature's ability, and vocation, to define reality much less to change or transform it.

Tertz's subversion begins with the juxtaposition of competing voices, of rival points of view, in the first two paragraphs of the essay. The initial question—What is Socialist Realism?—posed by the title⁶ and opening sentence is immediately countered by a series of questions that call into doubt the coherence of the term *Socialist Realism*, exposing the internal difference, the incompatibility, of the two concepts out of which it is agglomerated:

> What is Socialist Realism? What does this strange combination of words which grates the ear mean? Can there really be socialist, capitalist, Christian, or Mohammedan realism? Can such an irrational concept even exist in nature? Maybe it doesn't exist? Maybe it's only the dream of a frightened intellectual in the dark, enchanted night of Stalin's dictatorship? The rude demagoguery of Zhdanov or a whim of Gorky in old age? A fiction, a myth, propaganda? (401)

This seems to preface a straightforward attack on Socialist Realism. In the second paragraph, however, the voice of the narrator intercedes: "Such questions, as we've heard, arise frequently in the West, are heatedly discussed in Poland, and have currency even among us, agitating ardent minds which have fallen into the heresy of doubt and fault-finding" (401). The narrator thus poses as an orthodox defender of Socialist Realism, locating himself—through his use of the second-person pronoun—within that system and imputing the linguistic quibble expressed in the first paragraph to a foreign or disaffected other. In support of his position he calls to witness the physical reality of the institution of Socialist Realism, which must be measured in "millions of printed pages, kilometers of canvas and film, centuries of hours" (401). Tertz thereby sets up the tension between word and reality on which the essay rests.

Having established himself as a champion of Socialist Realism, the narrator goes on to invoke what he calls "the most precise definition" (*naibolee tochnoe opredelenie*) of the term, which appears in the charter of the Soviet Writers' Union. The section on which he hinges his argument reads: "Socialist Realism, being the basic method of Soviet literature and literary criticism, demands from the artist a truthful, historically concrete artistic representation of reality in its revolutionary development" (402). This definition, he maintains, "contains both the link between Socialist Realism and the realism of the past and its difference, the new quality" (402). This "new quality" is the demand that Socialist Realism give a faithful depiction of reality "in its revolutionary development." To clarify what this qualification means, the narrator elaborates a theory of history that deploys analogy in order to destabilize the boundaries between words and thereby undercut the Marxist "teleology" that ideologically validates Socialist Realism.

History, as the narrator presents it, constitutes a cycle of periods each of which is defined in relation to the striving for a higher goal. Each in this series of goals embodies a human attempt to represent God, "the final goal of everything that is and that is not and the endless (and, probably, goalless) end [*tsel'*] in itself" (404): "There are periods in history when the presence of the Goal becomes obvious, when petty passions are consumed by the striving toward God. And He begins to call mankind openly to Himself. Thus arose Christian culture, which grasped the Goal, perhaps, in its most inaccessible sense. Then the epoch of individualism proclaimed the Free Personality and began to worship it as the Goal, with the help of the Renaissance, humanism, the superman, democracy, Robespierre, service, and many other prayers. Now we have entered the era of a new universal system—that of socialist purposefulness [*tselesoobraznosti*]" (404). While the narrator views history as a succession of goals, all of which are responses to the same impetus and therefore analogous, he maintains that history as conceived from within any given goal, by adherents of that goal, appears as a linear progression in which all events are reinterpreted in terms of the appropriate teleology. While "a consistent Christian, if he wants to be consistent, must consider the life of the whole world before the birth of Christ the prehistory of Jesus Christ" (407), for a Marxist, history is "transformed into the history of humanity's coming to communism"

(406): "Everything immediately fell into place. Iron necessity, strict hierarchical order forged together the flow of the centuries. The ape, having stood up on his hind legs, began his triumphal march to communism. The original commune structure was necessary so that the slave-owning structure could emerge from it; the slave-owning structure was necessary so that feudalism could appear; we needed feudalism so that capitalism could begin; capitalism was necessary so that communism would arise. That's all! The beautiful Goal is attained, the pyramid is crowned, history has ended" (406). Thus, each goal subordinates all of history, all of society to itself, and, because it conceives itself as the single, unique, and final goal of all history, is absolutely intolerant of all other goals, of everything that does not accept its authority: "Even the most liberal of gods grants only one freedom of choice: to believe or not to believe, to be with him or with Satan, to go to heaven or to hell" (413). Therefore, the narrator postulates, the elevation of any particular historical goal to the status of absolute defining center inevitably reduces the world to a binary opposition, which can only be escaped by dethroning the center, recognizing that it is not unique but only one of many attempts, all inevitably failed, to name the transcendent goal in itself— God.

In essence, then, the entire argument laid out in the first of the three sections of Sinyavsky's essay, hinging as it does on the juxtaposition of cyclical versus linear conceptions of history, revolves around the ability to define boundaries between similarity and difference. Each goal falls victim to a false specificity of naming that renders it blind to analogy, unable to recognize its fundamental similarity with other goals. This blindness in turn entails a further error in definition. In relation to the goal, the world is reduced to a simple bipolarity of "them" versus "us," those who are for the goal versus those who are against it. It is to this bipolarity that the narrator turns his discussion next.

Just as the first section is structured around, and its argument rooted in, the opposition between two competing visions of history, the second section counterposes two stock literary terms, the *positive hero* and the *superfluous man*, as embodiments of mutually incompatible approaches to definition—or the inability to define. The positive hero embodies Socialist Realism's goal-directedness, its portrayal of reality refracted through the prism of "revolutionary development." The most distinctive trait of the "positive hero" is his or her "definiteness" (*opredelennost'*): "The most important of them [the merits of the positive hero], I guess, is the clarity and direct-ness with which he sees the goal and strives toward it. Hence the amazing definiteness in all his acts, tastes, thoughts, feelings, and evaluations. He knows firmly what is good and what is bad, says only "yes" or "no," does not confuse black with white, for him there exist no inner doubts or waverings, no unresolved questions or unsolved mysteries, and he easily finds a way out of the most complicated business—by the shortest route to the goal, by a straight line" (418). The positive hero experiences no internal difference, no conflicts or blurred borders within him- or herself, and effortlessly names exter-nal boundaries in terms of polarities. To illustrate the positive hero's intolerance of linguistic ambiguity, the narrator recounts an episode from Leonid Leonov's novel, *The Russian Forest:*

> The courageous girl Polya is making her way to the enemy's rear on a dangerous assignment—it takes place during the Patriotic War. For purposes of disguise she is ordered to pre-tend to be a German sympathizer. In conversation with a Hit-lerite officer, Polya for awhile plays this role, but with great difficulty: it is morally difficult for her to speak like the enemy and not like a Soviet [*govorit' po-vrazheski, a ne po-sovetski*]. Finally, she can no longer hold out and exposes her true face, her superiority over the German officer: "I am a girl of my epoch . . . perhaps the most ordinary of them, but I am the world's tomorrow . . . and you would stand up, stand up when you talk to me, if you had the least bit of self-respect! But you sit in front of me, because you're nobody, just a performing horse under the main executioner. . . . Well, there's no reason to sit now, go to work . . . take me, show me, where do you shoot Soviet girls here?" (421–22)

As the narrator points out, Polya's inability to "speak like the enemy," to adopt the language of the other, undermines her mission. Practi-cal results are not the point, however. Rather her words serve to illus-trate "the immutability, definiteness [*opredelennost'*], and straight-forwardness raised to the second power of the positive hero" (422). The positive hero is incapable of using language as a mask: "It is impossible to hide them, to mask them [the positive hero's posi-tive qualities]: they are written on his brow and sound in his every word" (422).

    The primary characteristic of the superfluous man, on the other hand, is his "goallessness" (*bestsel'nosti*, 425) and "indefiniteness" (*neopredelennost'yu*, 430). He seeks an equally "indefinite" (427) goal incarnated in the woman he loves and inevitably loses. The superfluous man, moreover, shares with his creators a cacophony of inner voices, as exemplified by Dostoevsky: "The nineteenth century was completely taken up with seekings, castings, and wanderings with fervor and without, with the inability or the lack of desire to find oneself a permanent place under the sun, with uncertainty, bifurcation [v razdvoennosti]. Dostoevsky, who regretted that Russians were too broad[7]—they should be narrowed!—himself was broad enough to combine Russian Orthodoxy with nihilism and could find in his soul all the Karamazovs at once—Alesha, Mitya, Ivan, Fedor (some say Smerdyakov as well), and it is still not clear which one predominated" (423–424). This multivoicedness is the root of Dostoevsky's "blasphemy," which is "insulting to the one God" (424). Fragmented into conflicting voices within, the superfluous man has difficulty drawing boundaries without. For him the line between bipolarities—so clear to the positive hero—is blurred. He is confused "his whole life long between 'yes' and 'no'" (429).

To the positive hero, the superfluous man is completely incomprehensible:

> But the superfluous man is some sort of a good-for-nothing, a being of different psychological dimensions that do not yield to calculation and regulation. He is neither for the Goal nor against the Goal; he is outside the Goal, and this cannot be, it is a fiction, blasphemy [koshchunstvo]. While the whole world, having defined [opredeliv] itself in relation to the Goal, had clearly divided itself up into two hostile forces, he feigned incomprehension and continued to blend colors into an ambiguously indefinite [dvusmyslenno-neopredelennuyu] range, declaring that there were neither reds nor whites, but simply people—poor, unfortunate, superfluous people. (428)

The superfluous man's ambiguous indefiniteness—the inability to define and to be defined—is blasphemous in relation to the definiteness, definedness, of the goal. In the bipolar universe of the "new culture" boundary-straddling is intolerable. The superfluous man is transformed from simply being other to being against. Moreover, the ability to draw clearly the line of demarcation between "them" and "us" entails a corresponding dismissal of the diversity within each term of the bipolarity:

> It goes without saying that we differ from one another in age, gender, national, and even mental particularities. But to any-

one who adheres to the Party line it must be clear that all
of this is diversity within the bounds of uniformity, discord
[*raznoglasie*] within the limits of accord [*edinoglasie*], conflicts
in conflictlessness. (419)

To these superfluous people, who had already irritated
him by their indefiniteness, Gorky shouted 'No!' and called
them "petty bourgeois." Eventually he expanded the concept
"petty bourgeois" to its limit, lumping together under it everyone who did not belong to the new religion: small and large
property owners, liberals, conservatives, hooligans, human-
ists, decadents, Christians, Dostoevsky, Tolstoy. . . . Gorky
knew that everything that is not God is the Devil. (430)

The ability to define therefore rests on a paradox: defining difference, the difference between "them" and "us," means denying difference, the heterogeneity within each term of the bipolarity. And it is
precisely by exposing this inherent contradiction that the narrator
in the concluding section of the essay will subvert the term *Socialist
Realism* itself.

In the third part of *What Is Socialist Realism*, then, the narrator
focuses on the issue of naming—redefining and ultimately challenging the boundaries of similarity and difference. While the second
section of the essay establishes a distinction—the mutual incompatibility between the positive hero and the superfluous man—the
final section opens by positing an analogy: "In its hero, content,
spirit, Socialist Realism is much closer to the Russian eighteenth
century than to the nineteenth century. . . . Like the socialist system,
the eighteenth century imagined itself to be the center of the universe" (431). The similarity between eighteenth-century classicism
and twentieth-century Socialist Realism is, moreover, largely rooted
in their common difference from the nineteenth-century tradition,
in their intolerance of "destructive laughter" (433).

The narrator cites Aleksandr Blok's 1908 essay "Irony," in which
the poet identifies irony as the "disease" infecting the age—a disease
that begins in laughter and ends in blasphemy. The narrator then
concludes, again invoking Blok's words:

Irony in that sense is the superfluous man's laughter at
himself and at everything sacred in the world. "I know people
who are capable of choking with laughter as they are reporting that their mother is dying, that they are dying of hun-

ger, that their fiancée betrayed them. . . . Before the face of
cursed irony everything is the same to them: good and evil, the
clear sky and a stinking hole, Dante's Beatrice and Sologub's
Nedotykomka. Everything is mixed together, as in a tavern or
a fog."

Irony is the unfailing companion of unbelief and doubt; it
disappears as soon as faith, which does not permit blasphemy,
appears. (433)

The nature of irony is to collapse boundaries, and in this destruction
of borders lies its blasphemy. By subverting clear linguistic boundaries, it threatens to undermine the ability to define unambiguously
embodied in the positive hero.

The rejection of ambiguity by both Socialist Realism and classicism emanates from their common impulse: "to give an ideal interpretation to the real, to write what should be as what is" (434).
Romanticism, the narrator maintains, also depicts life as being "better than it is" (435). However, it openly acknowledges the shortfall
between language and reality, between the ideal and the actual. This
admission of nonreferentiality is completely unacceptable: "It is impossible to admit openly that we need a beautiful lie. No, no, God
forbid, we are against deception, against embellishment, we write
only the truth" (435). Romanticism, he goes on, belongs to the early
period following the revolution, "before the fiery rush to the happy
future and worldwide scope were completely regulated by a rigid
state order" (435). It is too "anarchic and emotional" (437), it is
"powerless to express our clarity, our definiteness [*opredelennost'*]"
(438). Romanticism is inadequate because it is incapable of incar-
nating authority in language: "Romanticism does not have enough
compulsoriness in its assertion of the ideal. It passes off what is
desired for the real. That's not bad, but it is redolent of willful-
ness, of subjectivism. The desired is real because it is what must
be" (438). Romanticism, in speaking from the point of view of the
"I," implicitly acknowledges the possibility of competing ideals. In
contrast, Socialist Realism and classicism regiment language, reducing it to clichés that pass "from author to author without essential changes" (441). The authorless discourse of the set phrase finds
its validation in the unanimous "we." Socialist Realism should have
been called classicism, the narrator maintains, but the term would
have "called to memory undesirable analogies" (439). Again, the possibility of drawing analogy, of recognizing classicism as a "pseudo-

nym" for Socialist Realism, exposes the co-existence of rival centers of meaning, discrediting the equivalence between ideal and real, word and referent, putatively legitimized by the monologic "we."

The fatal flaw in both the conception and practice of Socialist Realism, the narrator concludes, is inscribed in the term itself. Instead of writing "large-scale, poster-like, Homerically," authors strive to write "like Chekhov":

> They, despite the classicist nature of our art, still consider it realism, orienting themselves on the literary models of the nineteenth century, the farthest from us and the most inimical to us. Instead of going the way of stylized forms, pure invention, fantasy, which great religious cultures have always taken, they strive for compromise. They lie, dodge, trying to combine the uncombinable: the positive hero, who naturally gravitates toward schema, toward allegory—and the psychological development of character; elevated style, declamation—and prosaic portrayal of everyday life; an elevated ideal—and truthfulness to life. This leads to the ugliest mishmash. (443)

He maintains, moreover, that this "mishmash" is terminologically incoherent: "It is semi-classicist half-art of a not-too-socialist-completely-not-realism" (444). The disintegration of the term inheres in the term itself: "Evidently the very name 'Socialist Realism' contains an insurmountable contradiction" (444). The essay thus comes full circle back to its opening paragraph. The narrator, however, has reversed roles. He now speaks with the voice of the other.

The narrator admits toward the end of the essay that he has "more than once caught [himself] using in some places the unworthy device of irony" (437). In fact, irony colors the essay throughout, an index of the noncorrespondence of the narrator's voice with itself, of the inherent duality of his project, which demands that he speak from outside Socialist Realism in order to define it, while he proposes to speak from within. The root of the narrator's irony lies in its embodiment of competing centers of meaning in his language. His discussion of the language of Stalin's *Short Course* provides an example:

> Here each word is permeated with a spirit of purposefulness. Even ideas that do not further the movement toward the goal have their purpose—to hinder the movement toward

the goal (Satan probably once had the same purpose). "Idea," "Superstructure," "Base," "regularity," "economics," "forces of production"—all these abstract, faceless categories suddenly came alive, acquired flesh and blood, were likened to gods and heroes, to angels and demons. They conceived goals, and from the pages of philosophical treatises and scholarly analyses sounded the voice of a great religious Mystery: "The superstructure is created by the base precisely so that it would serve it." (409)

By exposing the religious models embedded in Marxist rhetoric, the narrator draws an implicit analogy—thereby collapsing the boundary between the two "goals." This subversion of the discourse's claims to authority based on its uniqueness, its ability to draw borders between "us" and "them," places the narrator outside the bipolarity embodied in this confrontation of pronouns. The passage in which the narrator confesses his use of irony is, moreover, one of two places in the essay in which he speaks in the first person, thus asserting his difference from both "us" and "them."

Irony is "blasphemous" because it rests on disrupting the illusion of a simple relationship between word and referent: irony is a product of the noncorrespondence between the literal meaning of an utterance and the sense it conveys, a noncorrespondence that undermines the referential use of language. Seen in this light, Sinyavsky's project in *What Is Socialist Realism* goes beyond the definition and consequent subversion of Socialist Realism to a questioning of the straightforward referentiality of language, at least the language of literature and literary criticism. He plays throughout with the boundaries between words in order to subvert the very concept of definition.

Thus, in his analysis of Socialist Realism, classicism, and romanticism, the narrator describes each in terms of a disparity between language and reality. While he resists a frontal assault on realism, he undermines the concept in subtle ways, placing the word in scare quotes toward the end of the essay and identifying the nineteenth-century tradition with irony. *What Is Socialist Realism* is punctuated, moreover, with references to the inadequacy of language to express that which transcends boundaries, a transcendence the narrator himself can convey only by resorting to the indirections of analogy and irony. The narrator twice uses the phrase "words are insufficient" (*ne khvataet slov*, 405, 421) in relation to attempts to describe the "goal." By the same token, late in the essay the narrator maintains that Mayakovsky—who is paradoxically "the most Socialist Realist of them all" (446)—eludes terminological definition: "either because he caught the voices not only of Russian, but of world contemporaneity, and, being a romantic, he wrote like an expressionist, while in classicism he approached constructivism or, finally, because he was a genius" (441). True art resists reduction to simple terminology, just as it defies definition.

The essay itself ends in a failure to name. The last two paragraphs of *What Is Socialist Realism* are generally considered Abram Tertz's literary manifesto:[8]

> In the given case, I place my hopes on a phantasmagoric art with hypotheses instead of a purpose and grotesque in place of realistic descriptions of everyday life. It would correspond more fully to the spirit of our day. Let the exaggerated images of Hoffmann, Dostoevsky, Goya, Chagall, and the most Socialist Realist of them all—Mayakovsky—and of many other realists and non-realists teach us how to be truthful with the help of absurd fantasy.
>
> In losing our faith, we did not lose our ecstasy at the metamorphoses of God which take place before our eyes, at the monstrous peristalsis of his intestines—the convolutions of the brain. We don't know where to go, not having understood that there is nothing to be done; we begin to think, to construct conjectures, to suggest. Perhaps we will think up something amazing. But it will no longer be Socialist Realism. (446)

The narrator thus leaves this new approach to literature without a name, specifying only what it will *not* be called. The absence of purpose dictates the impossibility of naming. We may infer here that this namelessness is temporary, a state that will last only until the emergence of the new "goal." Yet the relativity of naming, deployed in this essay specifically to undermine the pretensions of Socialist Realism, becomes in Tertz's writings a fundamental principle of his understanding of literature. All literary terms are provisional, just as all attempts to name and thereby define the "goal" are inadequate, because we live in a world fragmented into competing subjectivities, and the vantage point of the ideal observer, the harmony of the unanimous "we," is denied us.

Tertz elaborates these implications in *The Trial Begins*,[9] exploring in fictional form the premises outlined in *What Is Socialist Realism*. Like the essay, the novella turns on a subversive reversal. The "positive hero," who begins by prosecuting what he considers to be the murder of a child, ends by himself becoming a child-murderer.[10] It is, however, the writer-narrator, at the start a loyal practitioner of Socialist Realism, who finds himself in a labor camp at the end. Again, the interplay of multiple voices reveals the ambiguity of naming in the text and thereby undermines the course of the narrative.

The linguistic instability, the failure of univocality, that ultimately subverts the writer's project is immanent in the opening scene. The writer is alone in his apartment when he is visited by "two men in civilian clothes," who are "as similar to one another as twins."[11] After a search of the apartment, during which letters of the alphabet are gathered off a manuscript page and confiscated and the writer is declared loyal, the wall of his apartment grows transparent, and he sees an enormous fist hanging in the sky. He falls on his knees and hears the voice of the Master (*khozyain*): "Arise, mortal. Do not turn your eyes from the right hand of God. No matter where you hide, no matter where you conceal yourself, it will find you anywhere, merciful and punishing. Behold!" (252). *Khozyain* was one of the common epithets used to refer to Stalin, and later in the text the term is applied to the figure of Stalin—who is never called by name. The ecclesiastical tenor of the language he employs, however, also identifies the Master with God. He goes on to point out the man who is to serve as the writer's "hero," "my beloved son and faithful servant Vladimir" (252) and issues his order:

"Follow in his footsteps, do not deviate by a step. In moments of danger, shield him with your body. And glorify him!

"Be my prophet! Lo the light will shine, and enemies will quaver at the words uttered by you!" (252)

The language of the opening scene thus simultaneously evokes images of Stalin issuing a social command and God summoning a prophet.[12] As in *What Is Socialist Realism* then, the text draws an analogy that discredits attempts to appropriate the prerogatives of the divine.

The double-voicedness of the presentation of the Master in the prologue prefigures the competing voices that structure the text as a whole. In allowing this polyphony the narrator apparently—but, as it turns out, only apparently—violates the letter of the Master's instructions: "Follow in his footsteps, do not deviate by a step." The writer does first turn to his "hero," the municipal prosecutor Vladimir Petrovich Globov. In the wee hours of the morning when the writer's task begins, Globov is looking over the case file of an illegal abortionist named Rabinovich. The defendant's Jewishness, indicated by his surname, immediately marks him for Globov as an enemy, a hostile other: "He had had occasion to prosecute one Rabinovich and maybe two or three. How could you remember them? That by their petty bourgeois nature they were hostile to socialism— every schoolchild knew that now" (252–53). Globov's transvaluation of Rabinovich's proper name into a generic designation of alterity determines the role the invocation of that name will play in the narrative.[13] The dissociation of the name from its specific referent is underscored by the repeated invocation of Rabinovich's name in the absence of the character himself, who makes his appearance as an autonomous character only in the epilogue, outside the boundaries of the text proper. It is, moreover, not with Globov's name, but with Rabinovich's, that this text so concerned with naming begins: "Citizen Rabinovich S. Ya., gynecologist, performed an illegal abortion" (252). Rabinovich and his crime therefore in a sense give birth to Globov's and the writer's narrative,[14] raising the issues of otherness, criminality, self, and text on which the novella rests.

The tension between rival perspectives that destabilizes meaning in the text is enacted in the structure of the narrative. Despite the order to dog Globov's footsteps, the narrator abandons him almost immediately, shifting his focus to a meeting between the defense attorney, Yury Karlinsky, and Globov's wife, Marina. This apparent digression from the prescribed path establishes the pattern followed by the narrative throughout.[15] The plot is fragmented into a series of discontinuous scenes, constantly moving back and forth from Globov to Karlinsky, Marina, and Globov's son, Serezha. Each of the characters' trajectories in the narrative is determined by that character's pursuit of his or her goal and his or her projection of the world into means for the attainment of that goal. Globov, as befits his role as positive hero, defines the world in relation to the striving toward communism and is willing to resort to any means to reach that goal. Karlinsky, an embodiment of self-absorbed individualism, seeks to distract himself from fears of the annihilation of the self in death by seducing Marina, thereby attempting to turn her beauty into a means to his end. Marina, for her part, considers her beauty an end in itself, an end that does, however, demand means—Karlinsky's purported adoration. Serezha, who in the metaphorical trial

being played out in the novella wants to be a judge, foments world
revolution to sweep away the corruption of the old order and establish and maintain the ideal state through violence. The counterpoint
of conflicting points of view, by underscoring the relativity of each
one of them, calls into question the locus of semantic authority in
the text, a situation dramatized by the image of the planetarium in
the third chapter and a conversation that takes place there between
Karlinsky and Marina: "Above them—over the whole cupola—they
kindled the universe. It hung in billions of stars and quietly rotated,
creaking at the turns, like the real sky. It opened up its shaggy en-
trails, and, having thrown out the contents, proved that God does not
exist" (272). In this Godless universe, under the "cupola" of the dark-
ened planetarium, Karlinsky makes his play for Marina: "Marina
Pavlovna, be my Sun. Indeed your face is the center of the orbit along
which I rotate" (273). As he cynically utters these words, however,
Karlinsky thinks to himself that he is the true center, "priceless and
first" (273). In the absence of an absolute defining center, ends and
means become relative and the distinction between them collapses,
as will happen in the course of the text.

Serezha raises the question posed by the episode in the planetarium and by the structure of the narrative in a conversation with
his father toward the beginning of the novella. He is disturbed by
the distinction between just and unjust wars drawn by his history
teacher:

> "But Valeryan Valeryanovich says that Ermak acted justly
> in subduing Siberia. And Shamil's rebellion was also correctly
> suppressed."
> "Yes," mused Vladimir Petrovich, "We couldn't do without
> Siberia. Or without the Caucasus. Oil. Manganese. What is it
> the people sing? 'Ermak, engulfed in thought, sat on the quiet
> bank of the Irtysh.' Have you heard it?
> "The English in India also . . ."
> "Leave off these comparisons." Vladimir Petrovich became
> upset. "The English are no authority for us. Where do we live?
> In England, or what?" (255–56)

Serezha, however, counters with an argument he has learned from
Karlinsky: "It all depends, he says, on your point of view. For some it
is just, for others—the opposite. Where then is true justice?" (256)[16]
Globov in turn responds with a story illustrating the premise that
whatever furthers the goal of building communism is just. Serezha's

question, however, hangs over the text. If all language is relative, how can one judge?

The issues concerning the workings of language—the relationship between word and deed, between subjectivity and referentiality —around which the text revolves are raised most squarely in the middle of the novella. At the end of the third of the seven chapters, we hear the voice of the writer speaking to us directly, in the first person, for the first and only time in the text of the novella proper. At this point in the text he is literally trailing in his hero's footsteps and follows Globov in crossing over a geographical boundary into forbidden space. Globov, looking through the empty courthouse afterhours, enters the ladies' restroom to make sure there is no one there. This penetration violates a taboo. It represents a border-crossing into the private territory of the other, suggesting both a transgression of propriety and a parody of the sex act. It appears as a parody because the other is absent—the room is empty. The only sign of presence is the graffiti that women have written on the walls, which Globov decides to order to be washed away the next day.

Globov seeks to efface the traces of alterity, but the writer remembers and records them in his text, crossing a further boundary into an enclosed stall: "In the common lavatory, having locked yourself up in a small, quiet stall, you, at last, remain one on one with yourself. Here you can do what you want. No one will see, no one will interfere. Usually in such circumstances men write only obscenities. Women are better than us, they write words of love and indignation" (277). These women's words, which will never be seen by the men to whom they are addressed, become a paradigm for writing as an end in itself:

> The person to whom these words are addressed will never learn of them. And they are not written for a reader at all. But simply tossed into space, onto the wind, to the farthest distances. Only God or the random eccentric amateur can pick up these prayers and incantations.
>
> I would like to believe in the word as these women believe. And sitting in my room, which resembles a toilet stall, late at night, when everyone is sleeping, write words, short and direct, without afterthoughts or address. (278)

The narrator compares this inherently naive writing, about which he can express only the nostalgia of the impossibility of return, with prelapsarian language—a language before dialogue, the language of God's creation of the world. Uttering the word, God brought the object itself into being: the connection between word and referent was direct and unmediated, because there was no other to whom it was addressed. Word equalled deed: "In the beginning was the word. If this is true, then the first word was just as beautiful as the inscriptions in the women's restroom in the municipal courthouse. When it was pronounced, the world began to live like a bill of fare. Name plates hung everywhere—'fir tree,' 'mountain,' 'infusorian.' Planets and stars hatched out of wordless emptiness. And everything was called forth by its word, and the word was deed [*slovo bylo delom*]" (278).[17]

The voice of the Master interrupts the writer's musings, "'Legal action [*Sudebnym delom*],' the Master corrected me. 'Do you hear, author! All words are indictments [*obvinitel'noe slovo*]. Word and deed!'" (278). The equivalence of signifier and signified, word and deed, in God's creation of the world is debased in the Master's equation of language with legal prosecution. The author, however, imagines himself called before a higher tribunal:

> I hear.
> Court is in session [*Sud idet*]; court is in session throughout the whole world. And it is no longer Rabinovich, exposed by the city prosecutor, but all of us, as many as there are taken all together, who daily, nightly, are taken to trial and questioning. And this is called history.
> The bell rings. "Your surname? Given name? Date of birth?"
> That's when you begin to write. (278)

This passage echoes not only the title of Tertz's novella, but also the text that may have suggested that title. In *The Death of Ivan Ilych* Tolstoy's title character is confronted by the inadequacy of legalism in the face of death: "What is it you want now? To live? Live how? To live as you live in court when the usher proclaims: 'Court is in session [*Sud idet*]!' Court is in session, the judge is coming [*Sud idet, idet sud*]!, he repeated to himself. Here he is, the judge. But I'm not guilty!"[18] Ivan Ilych grasps in the end that the law courts and conventional morality by which he has ordered his life falsify, and distract from, what is most important: our common mortality, the judgment to which all human beings are finally called. By the same token, the narrator of *The Trial Begins* implicitly locates the genesis of writing in the recognition of the gulf that separates human from transcendent judgment. The nameless narrator is summoned to personal responsibility—to name himself, not before Stalin, but before God—and the mandate to write originates in the realization of the discrepancy between the two, which is simultaneously a recognition that human attempts to lay claim to the divine language of the creation, to transform word into deed, must inevitably end in disaster, just as the bloodletting of the Stalin purges becomes a grotesque parody of the Final Judgment.

Karlinsky's explication of original sin to Marina in the following chapter serves as a gloss on the writer's postlapsarian situation:

> "All cognition consists, I would say, of two elements: linking and distinction [*svyaz' i razlichenie*]. Is it not true that in cognizing a thing we, first of all, link [*svyazyvaem*] it with other things and, second, distinguish [*otlichaem*] it from other things, as something original? In the sex act . . . are contained the protoelements of cognition. Adam and Eve merged in amorous embraces and immediately understood the difference: which one was the man and which one the woman. Having come together, they were distinguished, and, having been distinguished, they came together [*Svyazavshis', oni razlichilis', a razlichivshis', svyazalis'*]. And thus, having known themselves [*poznav sebya*], they began to get to know [*poznavat'*] everything else." (280–81)

This passage postulates a break between the language of the creation—in which word is deed, and word and referent are united in an unambiguous relationship of absolute equivalence—and language after the fall, which is born out of the recognition of alterity. Original sin thus becomes a metaphor for the difference of language from itself that arises from intercourse—sexual and verbal—and its inability to return to the ideal state of univocal isolation. The continual failures to engage in or complete the sex act—Marina's unsuccessful seduction of Globov, Karlinsky's abortive intimate encounter with Marina, Serezha and Katya's innocence—mark failures of knowledge that are all linked, in one way or another, with the characters' claims to be able to define the center of meaning.

The fourth chapter, the midpoint of the novella, in which Karlinsky's commentary appears, presents a paradigm for the fragmentation of the postlapsarian self. The scene here shifts back and forth from Serezha and his co-conspirator, the schoolgirl Katya, at the zoo to Karlinsky and Marina at the Pushkin Museum, and to Globov asleep at home. The zoo and the museum provide architectural models of the problem of boundary delineation and collapse. The zoo with its caged exhibits represents a model of taxonomy, based on the distinction between animal and human and ordered by divisions into genus and species. These borders, on which the zoo as an institution rests, are, however, challenged in the narrative by metaphor and misnaming. When Katya argues that zoos should be abolished along with prisons when the ideal state comes into being, Serezha counters with a vision of the zoo of the future: "Serezha reasonably objected: science demands sacrifices. In the name of world progress. But in the future society, menageries would be completely reorganized. Instead of these kennels there would be bright and spacious cages. Barbed wire would be disguised as the boughs of trees, so that it would not be so noticeable. The beasts would feel almost as if they were free" (282). The figure here is transparent. The zoo of the future is an image of human society in the future; the metaphor thus erases the line between animal and human. By the same token, Vitya—one of the "two men in civilian clothes" who have followed Serezha and Katya to the zoo—addresses one of the animals: "What can you do, zebra, in comparison with a human being?" (282). The line of demarcation drawn in the question is immediately undermined by a simultaneous act of misdesignation: Vitya is in fact addressing a leopard. And while Vitya imagines the skin of the leopard, "all covered with birthmarks" (282), hanging over his bed, the leopard sees the man as "living food, wrapped up in an overcoat and slacks, just like a piece of candy in paper" (282). Each defines and names the other in relation to a subjective goal, which transforms that other into something to be used or, literally, consumed. As underscored by Vitya's misnaming of the leopard, all individual perspectives are limited and, therefore, fallible.

Like the zoo, the museum also institutionalizes taxonomy, labeling exhibits and partitioning them according to temporal periods and geography. The museum, however, confounds boundaries of chronology and place by combining in one space that which in its original context is temporally and spatially discrete. The collapse of boundaries inherent in the structure of the museum is, moreover, metaphorically actualized by the conversation between Karlinsky and Marina that takes place within the precincts of the museum and metonymically underscored by the juxtaposition with the scene at the zoo. Thus, Karlinsky's explication of original sin is in fact an attempt to distinguish humans from animals—and gods: "Gods and

animals do not experience shame. When Adam and Eve were transformed from apes into humans, they were ashamed. Original sin—
knowledge—shame. They cannot be torn asunder!" (283). Karlinsky,
however, immediately infringes on his own categorical boundary.
When Marina objects that she prefers sphinxes to "your ashamed
apes," Karlinsky retorts, "You yourself are an Egyptian sphinx! . . .
They should put you into the museum, as an exhibit!" (283). Karlinsky thus blurs the boundaries not only between human and animal,
but also between animate and inanimate, life and art. Marina, "killed
into art," becomes a metaphor for the noncorrespondence of the self
with its representation, a recasting of the riddle of the sphinx into a
problematic of the objectification of the self in the artistic image.[19]
While the sphinx conceived as a museum exhibit represents a reification, a denial of the selfhood of the other equivalent to Karlinsky's
reduction of Marina to a means toward his end—and to Vitya's misnaming of the leopard, and the leopard's of Vitya—the additional
reference here to the confrontation between Oedipus and the Sphinx
is inescapable. This allusion itself, moreover, contains an inherent
ambiguity. Oedipus's solution to the Sphinx's riddle—his recognition of that which walks on four legs in the morning, two in the
afternoon, and three in the evening as a human being—represents
a realization of the plurality of the self, its mutability over time. Yet
he does not recognize the multiplicity of his own self, because he
fails to decipher the duality inscribed in his name.[20] Like Oedipus,
all of the characters in *The Trial Begins,* blinded by their goals, disregard the ambiguity of naming inherent in the heterogeneity of the
self. The writer, attempting to fulfill his task, is entrapped by the
multiplicity the characters deny, and his text is transformed into
a crime.

Thus we learn at the midpoint of the text that the writer has
not in fact violated his original instructions—to follow in his hero's
footsteps without deviating by a step—but has, if anything, followed
them too well. The section of the fourth chapter that precedes the
conversation between Karlinsky and Marina analyzed above ends
with a vision of a tiger sleeping in the zoo. The next section opens
on Globov sleeping, thereby blurring the boundary between Globov
and the cat. Marina and Karlinsky talking of sphinxes in the Pushkin
Museum suddenly become characters in Globov's dream, and the
distinction between discrete characters, between dream and reality,
disappears. The text in effect moves inside Globov's head.

The implications of this transgression come through most clearly in the final pages of the chapter, when Rabinovich also appears in Globov's dream, serving out his term as a guide in the Push-kin Museum. He has been assigned to acquaint the prosecutor with "some secret material" and leads him to a brain kept preserved in alcohol in a glass jar. The brain, Rabinovich tells Globov, "just thinks and thinks, invents ideas" (284).[21] When Globov expresses his con-cern that it might produce some "reactionary nonsense," Rabinovich offers to let him see for himself and takes him on a tour of history that reiterates the vision of the historical process as a succession of goals laid out in *What Is Socialist Realism*. Globov watches the pre-sentation as it passes through bloody images of the Crucifixion and burning heretics to the rise of individualism. Before the next goal can appear, he says he does not want to watch any longer.

> But Rabinovich seemed not to hear.
> "In the name of this freedom one personality began to squeeze out the guts of another personality. See how they compete? Now it's not far to the next goal. In the name of communism . . ."
> "Shut up! Stop the machine!"
> But it was already too late.
>
> > "We'll destroy the whole world of violence
> > To its foundations, and then . . ."[22]
> > > > Fire! (286)

With these words the chapter—and Globov's dream—ends. The positive hero finds the other whom he has labeled criminal within himself, in the figure of Rabinovich and in the historical analogies Rabinovich forces him to see. The writer, following his hero even into his dreams, has been led to the multiplicity of the self that inherently undermines the authority of language to define fixed cate-gories, and because his text reveals and acts out this discovery it will be branded criminal.

In the second half of *The Trial Begins*, Globov's world collapses, as the strivings of each of the characters toward goals articulated in the first half are frustrated or discredited in a tangled drama of conflicting ends and tainted means. Serezha's revolutionary "con-spiracy" is uncovered when Katya, incited by Karlinsky, scatters her notes, which are retrieved as evidence, and Serezha is arrested. Abandoned by the rest of her admirers in the wake of Serezha's ar-rest and estranged from Globov after she admits that she herself has had an abortion, Marina finally yields to Karlinsky's importunities. In bed with her at last, however, Karlinsky finds that desire and even lust have deserted him. Their relationship remains unconsummated, and in the aftermath Marina begins to discern signs of age eroding her beauty.

Globov, for his part, attempts to act out the externalization and destruction of the other only to be himself exposed as being that which he wished to destroy. After Serezha's arrest and Marina's revelation that she has had an abortion, he drinks himself into a state of alcoholic hallucination and imagines that he is holding in his arms the baby daughter Marina has aborted. Marina, afraid of being alone, comes to his room and tries to seduce him. Having rebuffed her advances and shut her out, he turns to look for the imaginary child and "discovers" her to be missing. Conflating in his alcoholic delusion Marina with the abortionist Rabinovich and the "doctor-murderers" of the Doctors' Plot[23] into which Rabinovich's case has mushroomed, he goes on a rampage, hacking away with a sword at the inanimate objects in the room to destroy the "enemies, [who] having slipped away through deception, had hidden in nooks and crannies and were rummaging about in all the corners" (305). The chapter ends as Globov, having reduced the room to a shambles, "reports" to a bust of the Master that has miraculously remained intact: "Master! Our enemies are on the run! They killed my daughter, stole my son. My wife betrayed me, and my mother disavowed me. But I stand before you, wounded, abandoned by everyone, and say: 'The goal is attained! We are victorious!' Do you hear, Master? We are victorious. Do you hear me?" (305). The response to his question follows immediately. The seventh chapter opens with the words: "The Master died" (306).

The scene of Globov's wanton destruction is, in effect, recapitulated in the last chapter of the novella. Here, as in the reference to the Doctors' Plot, historical events are woven into the fabric of the fictional text. Globov finds himself in the midst of the lethal crush created by the blocked exit that trapped the crowds that flocked to view Stalin's body.[24] The historical event is recast into a grotesque image as Globov is lifted out of the crowd by an enormous hand—the same hand with which the Master threatened the writer in the prologue—which strikes out with him at the people caught in the bottleneck:

"Let me go! It hurts!" the prosecutor groaned. "Everyone here is one of us [*vse svoi*]. They are guilty of nothing. Here

there are many women, children, there are even invalids from
the war, who brought you glory."

But the hand did not release him from its tenacious,
lethally clenched fingers. Mourning and embittered, it used
him like a cudgel to beat and beat the crowd wailing with
pain. (308)

When the carnage is over a "little girl", who later turns out to be
Serezha's friend Katya, is dead. Globov, renouncing the alterity
within himself—emblematized by the dream-figure of Rabinovich
and by Globov's conflicting obligations as husband, father, and son
—becomes the true child-killer at the very moment when he seemingly achieves the positive hero's repudiation of the other within and
his complete subordination to the goal. The scene, and the text of the
novella proper, ends with a cry from the crowd calling for the criminal to be brought to justice. The prosecutor, however, is himself the
culprit, and there is no judge.

The final irony comes in the epilogue when Globov is promoted
and the writer-narrator arrested for his text. He has been caught
by the very dragnet imagined by Tolya in the course of the novella,
that is, he has in a sense been skewered on his own fantasy. Aside
from blurring the line between the "author" and his characters, the
narrator's appearance in the epilogue gives him a chance to report
the judgment on his work by the powers that be.[25] What primarily
defines the criminality of the text is its failure to draw clear lines
between positive and negative characters:

> Particular censure was excited by the fact that the posi-
> tive heroes (the prosecutor Globov, the lawyer Karlinsky, the
> housewife Marina, the two men in civilian clothes, et cetera)
> were not depicted here many-sidedly [*mnogogranno*] in their
> labor practice, but maliciously presented to the reader in their
> untypical aspects. The negative characters, on the other hand,
> (the childkiller Rabinovich, the saboteur Serezha and his ac-
> complice Katya, who realized her mistakes too late and there-
> fore was trampled under the feet of the indignant people),
> although they were punished according to their just deserts in
> my slanderous work, were not completely unmasked in their
> reactionary basis. (310)

The irony of the narrator's use of "many-sidedly" here is clear, for it
is precisely his purportedly unwitting revelation of the plurality of
the self—his failure to draw a sufficiently clear borderline between

positive and negative characters, "us" and "them"—that constitutes the criminality of the text.

The epilogue, however, goes on to pass final judgment on this condemnation of the text. The narrator is sent to a labor camp, where he finds himself with Serezha and Rabinovich. While the three are working, they unearth a rusty sword, its handle shaped like a crucifix. Rabinovich, playing the role of historical *raisonneur*, pronounces the "moral" of the work: "Look where they stuck God. On the handle of a death-dealing weapon! You say no? He was the end and became the means. So that it would be easier to grasp. And the sword went the other way: It was the means and became the end. They exchanged places. Ai-yai-yai! Where now is God, and where the sword? Both the sword and God are in age-old frozen ground" (312). God, embodied in the handle of the sword, a work of art which is also a tool of violence, ceases to be the end in itself and becomes a means to destruction. The sword thus figures the fatal paradox intrinsic to all representation, which is played out by the characters in the novella. In a world fragmented into competing subjectivities, rendering all definition relative, it is impossible to return to the Edenic ideal of monovocal language in which word equals deed, in which naming is in itself an act of creation and therefore transformation. The attempt to assert the authority of definition and to act it out is inevitably undermined by the inherent unreliability of linguistic boundaries. The borders between opposites collapse. Because there is no center of authority to pass judgment, to define unambiguously, ends become means and means become ends.

At the heart of both *What Is Socialist Realism* and *The Trial Begins* lies an implicit rephrasing of the question posed by Dostoevsky: If there is no God, can there be morality? In Tertz's rendition this becomes: If there is no God, can there be meaning? If there is no absolute validation for language's authority to define, the competition of each separate "point of view" to establish its priority leads to a failure of dialogue and, at least potentially, to violence.[26] Alternatively, if God exists, is it then the existential state of postlapsarian humanity to be trapped in language that is unable to name Him, because the recognition of difference has irreparably dislocated the Edenic relationship of absolute equivalence between signifier and signified, between word and deed, rendering all attempts to reclaim it inherently doomed? In either case, the writer's task becomes in essence a sublimation of failure, an attempt to employ language to transcend language. Striving to articulate "what is most important," he finds himself continually reiterating the failure to define. Thus, the crime committed by *What Is Socialist Realism* and *The Trial Begins*—and by all of Tertz's other works—consists in posing a challenge to claims to linguistic authority, to the right to define and therefore judge, including those staked by the literary text.

Chapter Three

The Writer as Criminal: "Pkhents" and "At the Circus"

At the end of the day there's still another theme concerning the Suprematist quadrilateral (more exactly, the square). It's worthwhile dwelling on the
question of who it is and what it contains. Nobody has given any thought to
this.

And I, too, am peering into its mysterious black space—one which is
becoming a kind of form of the new face of the Suprematist world, its external appearance and its spirit. Perhaps you consider my ideas excessively
audacious.

Oh, no. I see in it what people at one time used to see before the face of
God.

—KAZIMIR MALEVICH, *Letter to Pavel Ettinger, 1920*

In his closing speech at his trial, Sinyavsky, deploring the impulse
to categorize everyone different as an enemy, invoked his story
"Pkhents" as an example of alterity that eluded the binary opposition
of "for" and "against": "In my unpublished story 'Pkhents' there is a
sentence that I consider autobiographical: 'You think that if I simply
am different, you must immediately curse me . . .' So there it is: I
am different. But I do not regard myself as an enemy, and my works
are not hostile works."[1] His two earliest "fantastic stories,"[2] "At the
Circus" and "Pkhents," are constructed around metaphors that cast
the text as a "criminal" body in order to explore the origins of art's
alterity.

As Sinyavsky acknowledged at his trial, there are obvious autobiographical allusions in "Pkhents."[3] The first-person narrator of the
story claims to be a creature from another planet. Assuming the
story to have been written in 1957, the alien's arrival on earth thirty-
two years earlier corresponds with Sinyavsky's own birthdate.[4] His
adopted earth-name, Andrei Kazimirovich Sushinsky, clearly echoes

Andrei Donatovich Sinyavsky, just as his supposed half-Russian, half-Polish ancestry mimics Sinyavsky's own background.[5] Moreover, the extraterrestrial's dual identity, fear of exposure, and recording of his secret in writing parallel Sinyavsky's own status at the time of the story's conception as a pseudonymous underground writer. These references to Sinyavsky's own biography in "Pkhents" underscore the problem of the relationship between author and text, between the self and its representation, addressed by the story.

The status of these references to Sinyavsky's autobiography is rendered ambiguous by the complex interplay of names in the story.[6] First of all, the narrator in essence remains nameless throughout, since his "true name" is lost to the reader. This lacuna throws into doubt the very possibility of naming the author of the text. His "pseudonym," moreover, articulates a complex problematic of construction of the self. Sinyavsky, after all, endows his fictional character with his own proper name—*Andrei*—only, so to speak, provisionally, since it is *not* that character's real name, but only a marker for his "forged" identity. Similarly, the alien's adopted surname, *Sushinsky*, does not simply echo *Sinyavsky*. It also contains the Russian root *sush-*, which denotes dryness. This signals an essential disparity between the name and the named, since the extraterrestrial, who resembles a cactus, lives on water. The name contains the possibility of the destruction or negation of what it names, since dehydration is the greatest threat to the creature's survival. *Sushinsky* also suggests a conflation of *Sinyavsky* and *Pushkin*. This assertion of parentage contains an acknowledgment of the cultural burden borne by the self that intrinsically calls into doubt the integrity both of the proper name and of the boundaries of the self. This play with Pushkin's name also extends to the narrator's "double," the hunchback Leopold Sergeevich, who not only bears Pushkin's patronymic, but is described by his neighbors by analogy with Pushkin—an analogy that originates in an expression of his difference:

> "See, Leopold Sergeevich's brother . . ." "No, you're mistaken. Next to him our hunchback is the spitting image of Pushkin." (240)

Pushkin's name thus becomes a marker for the interplay among shifting borders of similarity and difference out of which the text and the alien's assumed identity are composed. Coupled with the text's allusion by name to Tolstoy and its invocation of Gogol in the specter of a burned manuscript, the buried reference to Pushkin in the narrator's pseudonym marks the alien's plight as not simply an autobiographical representation of the dilemma of the underground writer Andrei Sinyavsky, but a metaphorical dramatization of the existential predicament of all writers—who are trapped in language, while the ability of language to mean, to express the self, is called into doubt.

Other names in "Pkhents" appear to allude directly to the problem of representation. The narrator's Polish patronymic, *Kazimirovich*, most obviously serves as a marker of foreignness, signaling the otherness of the being it purports to name, and of the difference within—connoted by his "legal" description as half-Russian and half-Polish—that renders the self resistant to simple, unambiguous labeling. The name would also seem to allude, however, to the painter Kazimir Malevich, constituting yet another claim to cultural parentage—a genealogy in which the writer figure at the center of "Pkhents" has been "fathered" by the early twentieth-century avant-garde. This name again is problematized by its simultaneous pseudonymity and illegality; its authenticity rests on the alien's faked documents. Moreover, the evocation of Malevich, taken together with the name of the narrator's neighbor and would-be mistress, Veronica, introduces the central problem of representation posed in the story. According to legend, St. Veronica, on the way to the Crucifixion, gave her veil to the suffering Christ to wipe his face, and his image was miraculously transferred to the veil. Veronica's veil thus came to signify the representation of the divine "not made by hands" (*nerukotvornyi*), untainted by human agency.[7] The allusion therefore both raises the question of the possibility of human representation of the divine and postulates the authenticity of art as a function of direct contact with the body. Malevich, who, for the first public display of his painting *Black Square*, had it hung "diagonally across one of the upper corners of the exhibition space" (the equivalent of the icon corner [*krasnyi ugol*] in a Russian peasant hut) and who claimed that in looking at the "Suprematist quadrilateral" he saw "what people at one time used to see before the face of God," aspired to attain the authenticity of the image "not made by hands," to represent the divinity of the self "made in the image of God" through nonmimetic, objectless painting.[8] As we shall see, Tertz broaches the same issue in "Pkhents."

The references to Malevich and to St. Veronica in the names of the characters thus provide a cultural context for the primary concern enacted in the narrative and epitomized in the story's title. Just as

critics have recognized the echo of Sinyavsky's name in his protagonist's terrestrial name, so have they also noted the acoustic similarity
between *Tertz* and *Pkhents*.[9] This reflection of the duality between
Tertz and Sinyavsky in the duality of Pkhents and Sushinsky re-
verses the "real-life" roles of the two hypostases, casting Sinyavsky/
Sushinsky as mask. Tertz/Pkhents thus becomes an embodiment of
the "true" self, as opposed to the "legal" identity. While it has been
suggested that the invented word is the name of the alien's home
planet,[10] we cannot in fact know from the information given in the
text what it denotes. All we are told is that it is *"indescribably* beautiful" (245, my emphasis) and that it is a "sacred name" (241) that
serves in the text, as we shall see below, as a sign of recognition of
true identity. The point lies precisely in the fact that *Pkhents* is a
signifier loosed from its signified; only the narrator remembers the
language in which it is a meaningful word, and it is untranslatable
into human language. The name thus becomes a metaphor for the
impossibility of the text itself, which struggles vainly to explain the
meaning of the word and fails because of the inadequacy of human
language to convey the concept.

The proper names in the text of "Pkhents" thus chart a map of
a text that calls into question the very possibility of "mapping," of
representing reality. The narrator, imagining himself trying to explain to earthlings who he is, writes:

> You can see for yourself—a creature from another world.
> Not from Africa, not from India, not even from Mars or your
> Venus, but even farther, even more unattainable. You don't
> even have such names, and I myself—if you were to lay out
> before me all the astronomical maps and plans there are avail-
> able—I would not be able to find, honestly, I would not be
> able to find that magnificent point where I was born.
>
> First of all, I am not a specialist in astronomy. I went where
> I was taken. Secondly, it's a completely different picture, and I
> couldn't recognize my native sky in your books and papers.
> Even now—I go out on the street at night, raise my head and
> see: again it's not right! And I also don't know in which direc-
> tion to grieve. Perhaps, from here it is impossible to see not
> only my earth, but even my sun. Perhaps it is registered on
> the other side of the galaxy. It's impossible to figure out! (243)

The narrator's dilemma challenges the possibility of all representation by positing the relativity of the defining center—the sun—and

of all perception to the extent that it is a function of visual perspective determined by bodily location. It therefore articulates the basic problematic of body, perception, and representation around which the story revolves.

The narrator's body serves as both the origin and the gauge of his otherness. Trying to situate himself in relation to a human system of reference, the narrator maintains: "I am neither human nor beast, and, if you please, I tend most nearly—out of that which you have—to the vegetable kingdom" (244). As he views human reality from the point of view of a plant, he radically dislocates basic coordinates of orientation. His "reading" of human cooking practices provides a most unsettling example of this estrangement:

> I have always been struck by the sadism of cookery. Future chicks are eaten in liquid form. The innards of pigs are stuffed with their own meat. An intestine that has swallowed itself and been covered by the foetuses of chickens—that is what an omelette with sausage is in fact.
>
> They treat wheat even more mercilessly: they cut it,[11] beat it, grind it into dust. Is that not why flour and torture [muká i múka] differ only in stress? (235)

He then imagines the same operations performed on a human being: "And what if a human being were prepared by the same procedure? If an engineer or writer were larded with his own brain and a violet stuck into his roasted nostril—and given to his coworkers for dinner? No, the torments of Christ, of Jan Hus, and Stenka Razin are a veritable trifle next to the torments of a fish pulled out of water on a hook. They at least knew—for what" (235). These two fantasies locate the origin of estrangement in the narrator's dual perspective, as a being caught in two worlds between which he must translate. Representation thus becomes the dislocation of taxonomy effected by the writer's looking on from a vantage point of alterity.

The narrator's discovery of his own difference is enacted in the narrative in his confrontations with Veronica and Leopold Sergeevich, confrontations that explore the interplay between body and sight, on the one hand, and language and representation, on the other. The episode with Veronica plays out the disruption of a binary opposition by difference within one term of that opposition. The narrator is disturbed that Veronica's amorous interest in him will undermine their union against their "common enemies" (234), the other tenants in the communal apartment. He most fears that Veronica will declare her love and thereby force a recognition of the difference between them: "Was it worth spoiling our military alliance against the evil neighbors?" (236). When Veronica does speak, she attempts to authenticate her words by exhibiting her naked body, which she exposes to the narrator's estranging vision. The narrator has previously studied the human body in an anatomy textbook and observed little boys swimming in the park. Now, however, he views the female of the species in the flesh for the first time. Long disturbed by the "problem of sex," he directs his gaze at the genital region:

> And now, overcoming my confusion, I decided to seize the opportunity and glanced there where—as was written in the textbook—the genital apparatus was located, which, like a catapult, shot out already-finished infants.
>
> I caught a glimpse there of something that looked like the face of a human being. Only it was, it seemed to me, not a woman's but a man's face, elderly, unshaven, with teeth bared.
>
> A hungry, ill-tempered [zloi] man dwelled between her legs. Probably he snored at night and used foul language out of boredom. It must be from there that the duality [dvulichie] of woman's nature comes, about which the poet Lermontov aptly wrote: "as beautiful as a heavenly angel, as perfidious and evil as a demon." (238)

The body, as perceived by the narrator, reveals its difference not only from the narrator, but from itself. On it is inscribed an essential duality—between feminine and masculine, good and evil, human and divine. The narrator is relegated to the status of a voyeur, viewing without allowing himself to be viewed, recognizing difference without revealing his own difference. The narrator's vegetable, and therefore transgendered, body precludes sexual intercourse and true dialogue. He rejects both Veronica's words and her body.

The destabilization of one bipolar categorization—his "alliance" with Veronica against their hostile neighbors—leads the narrator to seek to construct another bipolarity by finding his like: "At least one—the same [odinakovyi]" (239). The story in fact begins with the narrator observing another hunchback leaving his dirty linen at the laundry. As we later learn, the narrator believes the hunchback to be a creature from his world, like himself masquerading as a deformed human. After fleeing Veronica, the narrator seeks out the home of the hunchback, whose address he has discovered on a laundry receipt. When the two are alone, he immediately tries to elicit an admission of common origin, of kinship: "'I recognized you at first glance. You and I are from the same place. Relatives so to speak. PKHENTS! PKHENTS!' I recalled to him in a whisper the name that for both of us was sacred" (241). When Leopold Sergeevich claims not to understand, the narrator persists, finally taking him by the shoulders. It is this contact with the body, rather than Leopold Sergeevich's words, that convinces him of the hunchback's difference, that authenticates his words: "Suddenly through his wool jacket warmth—which came from an unknown source—reached me. His shoulders became hotter and hotter, just as hot as Veronica's hands, like thousands of other hot hands, which I preferred not to shake" (242). Leopold Sergeevich is not a fellow being from his home planet, but "a human being, the most normal human being, although humpbacked" (243).[12] As in the encounter with Veronica, the evidence of the body here frustrates the narrator's attempts to find an ally, someone like him. In this instance, the difference between bodies is even more directly linked with a failure of language: because his body is different, because he is not an extraterrestrial being like the narrator, Leopold Sergeevich cannot understand the word *Pkhents*.

Forced to acknowledge his difference from others, his uniqueness, the narrator considers revealing his alterity: "Why shouldn't I, after all, legalize my position? Why for thirty-two years, like a criminal, have I pretended to be someone else?" (243). His difference from others thus leads him to focus on his difference from himself, to a juxtaposition of his official identity as Andrei Kazimirovich Sushinsky with the story of how he came to earth, to a confrontation between legal language and fantastic narrative. He relates how, en route to a resort, the spaceship in which he was traveling was hit by a meteorite and fell to earth. The only survivor of the crash, he was soon forced by the inclement environment to take refuge with a tribe of nearby Yakuts (identifying his landing place as eastern Siberia). Initially fearing that they would eat him, he disguised himself in "some rags": "that was my first theft, excusable given the situation" (244). Because he required central heating to sustain the temperature necessary to his plant-like body, he made his way to Moscow, where he has remained, under his assumed identity, ever since.

Aware of the disparity between his legal identity, authenticated by official words, and his story, inscribed in his body, the narrator foresees three equally unpalatable outcomes, each defined by the relationship between language, body, and society. The first alternative is that his story, divorced from his body, will simply not be believed:

> Tell this sad story [*povest'*] to whomever you like, in the most popular form there is—they won't believe it, they won't believe it for anything. If I could at least cry as I told my story [*rasskaz*], but while I have more or less learned how to laugh, I don't know how to cry. They will consider me a madman, a fantast, and moreover they could place me on trial [*k sudebnoi otvetstvennosti mogut privlech'*]: a false passport, forgery of signatures and seals, and other illegal acts. (245)

The apparent paradox embodied in the narrator's vision of being both disbelieved and branded a criminal for forging a false identity dramatizes Tertz's vision of literature. The writer's crime resides precisely in the noncorrespondence between his "legal" identity and his story. The figure of the narrator's body here becomes a marker for the unabashed fictionality of the text: the body cannot be produced to validate the narrator's story because it has no material reality, it is a figment of the writer's imagination. This fantastic body, which ultimately will be equated with the text itself, stands outside the law, has no legal status but to undermine the narrator's claim to a lawful identity, to brand him a criminal.

It would, however, be "even worse," the narrator imagines, if he were to be believed:

> Academicians from all the academies would come together from all over—astronomers, agronomists, physicists, economists, geologists, philologists, psychologists, biologists, microbiologists, chemists, biochemists—to study me to the last little spot; they would forget nothing. And they would do nothing but ask questions, investigate, examine, elicit.
>
> Millions of copies of dissertations, movies, and poems about me would be sold out. Ladies would begin to paint their lips with green lipstick and order hats in the shape of cactuses, or at least ficuses. And all hunchbacks—for a few years—would enjoy colossal success with women.
>
> They would call by the name of my homeland models of automobiles, hundreds of newborn infants—not even to mention streets, and dogs. I would become as famous as Lev Tolstoy, as Gulliver and Hercules. And Galileo Galilei. (245)

Recognition turns the writer and his writing into parodies of themselves. Canonization transforms the writer from a representing subject into an object of representation; the line between reality, fiction, and myth—Tolstoy, Gulliver, and Hercules—is erased. People remake their physical appearance and trade on their likeness to the fetishized body. The word is detached from its referent and is used to name what has no relation to it. The writer may attempt, like Galileo, to redefine the center, but he cannot communicate its essence:

> But despite all this general attention to my humble person, no one would understand anything. How can they understand me when I myself in their language can in no way express my unhuman essence. I do nothing but dodge all over the place and make do with metaphors, but as soon as it comes to what is most important—I fall silent. And I only see the solid, low GOGRY, I hear the swift VZGLYAGU, and the indescribably beautiful PKHENTS overshadows my trunk. Ever fewer and fewer of these words remain in my fading memory. The sounds of human speech can only approximately convey their construction. And if linguists were to crowd around and ask what it means, I would say only GOGRY TUZHEROSKIP and make a helpless gesture. (245)

Metaphor thus becomes the writer's tool of final resort, the closest he can come to conveying his experience, his self. "What is most important," however, reduces him to silence.

The third alternative faced by the narrator is a logical extension of the second, of his reduction to silence. If revealing his "true" identity will lead either to being branded a criminal or to being reduced to a fetish, it is better, he decides, to "drag out his solitary incognito" (245). This course, however, will inevitably end in his death and the discovery of his body, which, wordless, will be made into a display in a zoological museum, put "into an acid bath, into a glass crypt, into history; for the edification of future generations—for all eternity—they will submerge me—a monster, the most important monster of the Earth" (248). Envisaging the visitors viewing his preserved body, the narrator foresees that his corpse will be perceived as threatening, as ugly precisely because it is a "hybrid": "And filing past, they will begin to tremble from fear and, in order to buck themselves up, will start to laugh insolently, to stick out their squeamish lips: 'Oh, what an abnormal, what an ugly mongrel [*ublyudok*]'" (245).[13]

The body, transformed from a speaking subject into a mute ob-

ject, comes to represent the opposite of what the narrator himself
sees in it. The corpse thus suggests an image of the writer, divorced
from his self, transformed into the body of the text. His viewers, or
"readers," kill the body by seeking in it some "educational" value. Attempting to find some use in it, they "misread," seeing in the corpse
only an exemplification of impure and ugly heterogeneity. Art, reduced to didactic aims, becomes dead art.[14] The narrator, on the
other hand, finds in his body the epitome of harmonious beauty.
This discovery is prompted by his stay on earth, by his juxtaposition with the other: "Perhaps if I had not lived in foreign parts for
thirty-two years, it would never have entered my head to admire my
own exterior. But here I am the only exemplar of that lost harmonious beauty that is called my native land. What is there for me to
do on earth but delight in myself?" (247). This disparity in vision
articulates two incompatible views of art: the ideal of beauty as an
end in itself, versus the practice of subordinating artistic creation
to a didactic end. This discrepancy is rooted in the impossibility of
viewing the other as subject rather than object. The alien's disguise
impairs his ability to see the human beings around him: his multiple
eyes are concealed and damaged by the human clothing with which
he must cover them.[15] Alone, his limbs freed from their disguise, he
is able to look at himself through all the eyes in his "arms and legs,
on the top and back of the head" (246):

> But I turned my head, not limiting myself to a semicircle—
> the pitiful one-hundred-and-eighty-degree norm allotted to
> the human neck—I began to blink all of my eyes that re-
> mained intact, dispelling fatigue and darkness, and I suc-
> ceeded in seeing myself from all sides—simultaneously in
> several perspectives. How captivating is this spectacle, unfor-
> tunately accessible to me now only in rare hours of the night.
> All you have to do is lift up your hand and you see yourself
> from the ceiling, so to speak, rising and hanging over yourself.
> And at the very same time—with your remaining eyes—not
> losing sight of the bottom, the rear, and the front—all your
> branching and forking body. (247)

In viewing his own body, the narrator is vouchsafed a transcendent
vision. He is able to see himself from outside, from multiple perspectives. He therefore sees beauty and harmony where others, looking
on from a single angle of vision, can discern only a monstrous cross-
breed.

Rejecting the three fates that would seem to await him upon discovery, the narrator decides on a fourth path: to abandon human society, to find the hole left when his spaceship crashed, and, freeing himself of human disguise and human language, to live out a final summer before immolating himself when the weather turns cold in the autumn. This retreat into a "private" language, however, is problematized by its negation of the very nature of language as a social institution, reiterating the question of meaning posed by the story's title. The narrator's recognition of signs of assimilation in himself, moreover, calls into doubt the possibility that he can abandon human language: "Strange desires at times visit me. Sometimes I long to go to the movies. Sometimes I feel like playing checkers with Veronica Grigorevna's husband" (249). The narrator, as he becomes more "human," is thus drawn to forms of representation and play, a development that he views as threatening to his very nature and that he seeks to flee. The possibility of flight, however, is finally challenged by the ending of the narrative itself, which degenerates into a mishmash of foreign expressions, animal sounds, and nonsense words:

"O motherland! PKHENTS! GOGRY TUZHEROSKIP! I am coming to you! GOGRY! GOGRY! TUZHEROSKIP! TU-ZHEROSKIP! BONJOUR! GUTENABEND! TUZHEROSKIP! BU-BU-BU!

MIAOW-MIAOW!

PKHENTS!" (250)

Even with no one to speak to, the narrator cannot return to a perfect language. Instead, as he tries to express himself in words, language itself fragments him into competing stances. The attempt to translate the beautiful harmony of the self into language is defeated by the medium itself.[16]

While enacting in his text language's inability to represent, however, Tertz does not negate the possibility of literature, but rather affirms it in terms of paradox: the impossibility of representation becomes the ontological condition of the text. Key here are the biblical references that underlie the narrative of "Pkhents." The images of water and water deprivation are clearly allusions to baptism and to Christ's suffering from dehydration on the Cross, just as the narrator's decision to burn himself in his thirty-third year echoes the Crucifixion.[17] The narrator's situation thus can be read as a metaphor for the dual nature of Christ, simultaneously human and divine, caught between heaven and earth. At the same time it has been recognized that the "fall" of the narrator's spacecraft—"we fell [*padaem*], deprived of support, not knowing where, we fell for seven and a half months" (244)—echoes the fall of humanity, thus casting the narrator as an image of the soul trapped in a fallen world.[18] Like the narrator's equation of his true self with the sacred Pkhents, this implied equivalence between the soul and the divinity of Christ has some correspondence with the Russian Orthodox belief in the purity of the true self created "in the image of God." The problem of the representation of the true self, the soul, thus becomes the same as the problem of embodying the divine: the impossibility of representing the transcendent in the "fallen" substance of human words.

The narrator's "irregular diary," in which he records his attempts to define himself in relation to and preserve himself against the alien world into which he has "fallen," is his attempt to convey in human language what he himself has recognized the impossibility of translating: the totality of meaning and therefore absolute meaninglessness betokened by the name *Pkhents*. The problem is figured in the distortion of the legend of Veronica's veil out of which his text, in a sense, arises.[19] The narrator borrows ink from Veronica to write his diary. As a metonymy for the words he will write with it, the ink simultaneously recalls the episode of the veil and diverges from it. While the representation of Christ's image on the veil draws its authenticity from direct contact with the divine body, the narrator's writing is marked as a failure of contact and its authenticity therefore called into question.

The central issue addressed in the text thus hinges on the correlation between the narrator's body, as an emblem of his otherness and "the only exemplar of that lost harmonious beauty that is called my native land," and his diary, in which he attempts to "embody" it. Both will be burned in the end. The text we are reading, moreover, is clearly the very same text that the narrator says he will burn. We are therefore reading a text that ostensibly has been destroyed. Thus, the narrator's fantastic body—which asserts its own fictionality, its status as a sign with no referent, no body with which to authenticate its story, which exists only in the text—and the text that exists despite the impossibility of its existence merge. Mimicking metaphorically the identity of body and representation postulated as the source of legitimacy in the legend of Veronica's veil, the text places in question the issue of authenticity. Like the alien being, the text has no "legal" status. Its criminality inheres in its simultaneous denial that language can contain the self and its assertion of the priority of the imaginary over the real.

In "At the Circus" the body becomes the medium of art: the stunts of circus acrobats serve as a prototype for the artistic creation that exhausts itself in its own performance, in spectacle that points to no referent outside of itself. While the narrator of "Pkhents" is a voyeur who conceals what he considers sacred under a guise of legality, the central character of "At the Circus" is an exhibitionist and a thief who imagines he can become "like God" in creating a spectacle out of his own person. The first is an incarnation of otherness who is tormented by his difference; the second seeks to escape his ordinariness and assert his uniqueness. Yet both begin their careers with a theft that is construed as a usurpation of an alternate identity. Following from this point of contact, I would suggest that the two stories approach the same problem from different points of view. While "Pkhents" explores the drama of the artist as representing self, "At the Circus" focuses on the writer transformed into the body of the text. The latter story thus in effect enacts the metaphor personated in the Tertz pseudonym, casting the artist as a thief and art as a transgression against legality.

The title and opening scene of "At the Circus" place the story from the beginning in the realm of art, a place set apart where the laws governing reality are suspended. The circus's star performer, a magician called the Manipulator, after pulling a white mouse from behind a female spectator's ear and then giving her to drink a sparkling liquid drawn from her male companion's nose, begins returning to members of the audience various and sundry personal belongings he has "stolen" from them. The Manipulator thus both violates the boundaries of body and identity and commits "theft" with impunity.

The magician's act strongly affects a young electrician named Kostya, who, as he is leaving the circus, laments his own inability to perform acrobatic feats: "Without preliminary practice he probably could not even toss up his cap so that it would do a somersault [sal'to] and land by itself on his skull."[20] Under the influence of this sense of his own inadequacy, Kostya decides to take action, to imitate the Manipulator's performance by picking a man's pocket. Immediately there appears a promising victim, who observes in a snatch of conversation: "A true woman acrobat should be seen undressed. And not in a circus, but in an apartment, on a tablecloth, amidst pineapples" (115). This comment, which transfers the performing body out of the world of performance, foreshadows the fatal path that Kostya himself is about to pursue.

Kostya's theft, mimicking the Manipulator's act, constitutes both a dislocated bid for an audience and a collapse of boundaries between identities. The man he will rob is specifically described as ignoring, not looking at, Kostya: "His eyes, directed into the distance, deep blue, with green sparks, did not pay the slightest attention to Kostya" (115). The crime itself is cast both as a confusion of the boundaries between criminal and victim and as a magic trick: "They kept bumping into one another and as a result became so entangled that it would have been difficult to distinguish where Kostya's client was and where Kostya was. And the fur coat even more energetically threw open its fluffy interior, and the big-bosomed, double-breasted coat opened of itself, and all of this happened like a magic trick [fokus], without human intervention" (115). Taking the identity confusion a step further, the narrative at this point changes from third person—in which all but the following two paragraphs of the story are related—to first person:

> My breathing stops, and my pulse moves into my fingers. They quietly tick in time with the surrounded heart, running in someone else's [chuzhoi] breast, near the inner pocket, and it methodically jumps up into my palm, without suspecting the substitution, without suspecting my disturbing, otherworldly [potustoronnem] presence. And with one stroke of the hand I work a miracle: a thick bundle of money flies, like a bird, through the air and settles itself under my shirt. "Your money is my money," as the song goes, and in this fairytale-like transformation lies the whole trick [fokus]. (116)

Not only are the boundaries erased here between magic and theft, between criminal and victim, between author and character, between artist and audience, but the language of the text merges with the act it describes, through a play of pronouns performing a "fairytale-like transformation" that turns Kostya's heart into the victim's heart into the stolen money, so that in the end the "substitution" becomes an exchange of hearts, of identities.

The first-person narrator then anticipates taking the victim's place, going to a restaurant and eating his food, drinking his cognac, and kissing his women

> at your personal expense, but to my full satisfaction. I won't be stingy, and if we meet in the restaurant, I will fill you with liquor until you're drunk and feed you to satiety—with that same food you did not manage to eat in time on your

own. And you moreover will be grateful to me for this, I dare
to assure you. You'll think that I'm some writer, an actor,
an honored master of sports. But I am none other than a
magician-manipulator. Let's get acquainted. Hello! (116)

This passage, first of all, reveals Kostya's action specifically as an
attempt to usurp the identity of the Manipulator. Moreover, these
imaginings, which are attributed to Kostya but spoken by the first-
person narrator, link the figure of the writer with that of an actor
(who plays roles, assumes alternate identities), an athlete (an artist of the body), and finally a magician. This intrusion of the "I"
into the text and the confusion of identities between Kostya and the
voice telling the story disorients, because it simultaneously posits
a link and a distinction between the author and his fiction. On the
one hand, this blurring of voices establishes thief, actor, athlete, and
magician as metaphors for the writer. On the other, by disrupting
the narrative, the writer calls attention to the artificiality of his text,
thereby discriminating between Kostya, who in becoming a thief
takes the art of the circus into the real world, and the writer, whose
crime and magic are confined to his text. Symptomatic of this same
disjunction is that while the Manipulator's performance is greeted
by applause from his audience, Kostya's act remains secret, and he
garners the attention he craves only by masquerading as someone
else.

Beginning with this first theft, Kostya—now Konstantin Petrovich—starts a "new life" (116), frequenting the restaurant envisaged
in the earlier fantasy. The restaurant, where waiters rush to serve
him, makes him feel like a circus acrobat: "As if he were walking
a wire at a height of four hundred meters, and, although the walls
sway, threatening to cave in, he walks with a springy and light bal-
anced step, in an absolutely straight line. And the public is all eyes,
holding its breath, and relies on you as if you were God" (117). The
audience's "faith" is a demand for spectacle: "And you must, you
must without fail show them something; some *salto mortale* or an
amazing trick [*fokus*], or simply find and express some word—the
only one in your life—after which the whole world will turn upside
down and be transformed in the blink of an eye into a supernatural
state" (117). Here the artist becomes like God, magic trick becomes
like miracle, and, in the course of the narrative, the boundaries are
blurred between circus and church. The impecunious Jew Solomon
Moiseevich, whom Kostya treats to drinks in the restaurant in ex-

change for conversation, asserts the false etymology: "church comes from circus" (120). Kostya, for his part, goes to the circus "every Sunday" (123), and his "estranged" vision of the church recasts religious images in terms of theater, spectacle, and stunt: "He had had occasion to glance into a church. He liked the various miracles painted on the ceiling and walls in acrobatic poses. He particularly liked when one magician [*fokusnik*] disguised himself as a dead man and then leapt out of the grave and amazed everyone. And another man—of the same nation as Solomon Moiseevich by the way—treacherously denounced him, but they didn't catch the magician, but caught that same Judas traitor[21] and nailed him alive to the church cross" (119–20). Kostya's blasphemous "misreading" of the Crucifixion and his conflation of circus and church figure the same shortfall between human expression and interpretation, on the one hand, and, on the other, divine act, incarnated here in the performing body and enacted through the central metaphor of "Pkhents." In the world of "At the Circus," where "there are no gods and no devils, although it would be very merry if there were" (119), Kostya, in his longing to escape the everyday, to fill the vacuum left by the absence of religion, usurps the place of God. In the process he plays out his distorted vision of Judas changing places, swapping identities, with Christ.

Kostya, against his better judgment—"I deal with living beings" (121)—is talked by the bath attendant Leshka into robbing an apartment that they expect to find empty. They take Solomon Moiseevich along as lookout. In what they thought would be a deserted apartment, Kostya finds the Manipulator sleeping, his clothing and toupee, the accoutrements of his artistic persona, removed and lying nearby, marking his removal from the space of art, where the laws of reality are suspended. The magician awakes and, ignoring Kostya and the gun he is pointing at him—"paying no attention to the muzzle of the foreign Browning" (123)—runs to the balcony and begins calling for help. To stop his shouting, Kostya, "almost crying" (124), pulls the trigger, and the Manipulator falls dead:

> At first it seemed as if, having wriggled for effect, he would sit on the floor and clear his throat, and announce for all to hear that he had deceived them to frighten them. But, evidently, this artist was giving a road show to go, and, inspired by Kostya's shot, was playing his best part, transforming himself in miraculous fashion into a dead man, who recognized his superiority over those who remained among the living. His

face moved away with the smoothness of a sailboat, acquiring
the innate pride of stone and hardened water. He died im-
perceptibly, not even winking in farewell, and leaving Kostya
in confusion before the completed trick [*fokusom*], which belonged equally to both of them. (124)

This miraculous transfiguration, performed by the Manipulator, "inspired" by Kostya, is not a simple aestheticization of death, but
rather dramatizes the confrontation between life and art. The body,
which "in reality" is dead, is simultaneously "resurrected" through
the force of the artistic metamorphosis. Kostya, here cast in the role
of Judas to the Manipulator's Christ, will now go on to play out the
rest of the garbled biblical figura, replacing the mentor he has betrayed in a final transformation of his own body into art, echoing
the Manipulator's death.

The concluding section of "At the Circus" plays out the metaphors around which the story is constructed specifically in terms
of the opposition law/reality versus crime/art. The trial of the thief-
turned-murderer, at which his legal fate is decided, is for Kostya an
opportunity to play before an audience, to occupy the center of attention: "He had a good parade with a large gathering of the public,
at the trial. . . . All the gazes of the men and women were riveted
on Konstantin Petrovich, and, standing at the center of the arena,
he experienced many wonderful moments, which tickled his jealous artistic self-esteem" (125). The trial thus serves to establish the
dichotomy between law and spectacle, between legal process and
"parade," the full implications of which are realized at story's end.

The concluding scene opens on a convoy of shackled prisoners.
Suddenly the "frightened voice" of an old guard rings out: "Stop!
Stop! I'll shoot!" (125). Kostya has made a dash for freedom that
ends, with the story, in his death:

Kostya could see a space flooded with electric light, with
kilometers of wires stretched out beneath the cupola of the
universal circus. And the farther he flew from the initial point
of his running start, the more joyful and anxious became his
soul. He was overcome by a sense akin to inspiration, when
every nerve plays and romps, and, romping, awaits a flood of
that otherworldly and magnanimous supernatural force that
throws you into the air in a powerful jump, the highest and
lightest of your slight life.

Ever nearer, nearer . . . Now he will turn . . . Now he will show them . . .

Kostya leaped, turned over, and, having performed the long-awaited somersault [*sal'to*], shot through the head, fell face first to the earth. (125–26)

Thus Kostya's death merges with the salto mortale to which he has aspired since the beginning of his career in crime, his feat played out "beneath the cupola of the universal circus" echoing both the Manipulator's death and the acrobats in the opening scene of the story. Kostya's somersault becomes the quintessential artistic act, performed for itself, not in order to represent something beyond itself—the body literally becoming the medium of execution, transformed into art at the very moment of its physical destruction. The metaphor thus "embodies" the complex and ultimately paradoxical relationship between art and reality that runs throughout the Tertz writings. The frightened guard becomes an incarnation in word and deed of the law, of that which defines the legal boundaries of "reality," as well as an unwilling accomplice in Kostya's art. Kostya's performance is both a violation and a transcendence, not only of the borders defined by the guard, but of the limitations of the body's physical reality.

Michel Aucouturier has postulated that running through Sinyavsky's works is an image of "the ideal of the text as an object." He points to the "acrobatic performance" and the "sleight of hand trick" as figures that "assimilate the written text to a physical, palpable, material reality." The Tertzian text thus aspires simultaneously to the sui generis status of the artistic object as an end in itself and to the absolute authenticity, the identity with the represented body, of the image "not made by hands." As Aucouturier observes, however, "what is involved is an inaccessible ideal. A text is made up of words, which are never purely material, and by men, who can never completely remove the mark left by their hands."[22] But, though they express art's aspiration to transcend the limitations of representation, the early Tertz writings also continually play out the inevitable frustration of that aspiration. Just as the narrator of "Pkhents" can never find anyone who can understand the word *Pkhents*, someone who is exactly like himself and who will therefore be able to see the same "harmonious beauty" in his embodied self as he does, so Kostya's transformation of his own body into a work of art ends in annihilation. The guard, Kostya's only audience, sees in the thief's salto mortale only a transgression of boundaries, an illegal attempt to escape the confines imposed on the body. We are left at the end with only a corpse. Most important, in both stories the protagonist's "crime" is the theft of an identity that is not legally his. Looking forward to Tertz's later writings, art here begins with imposture. The texts thus underscore their own inauthenticity. The work of art can never attain the ideal of the image not made by hands because it always remains at the mercy of the perception of the audience. As we shall see in following the evolution of Tertz's images, it is only by acknowledging its inherent deception, by openly admitting that the only link between circus and church lies in metaphor, that art holds open the promise of transcendence.

Chapter Four

Confrontations with God:
"You and I" and "Graphomaniacs"

The world is twofold for man in accordance with his twofold attitude.

The attitude of man is twofold in accordance with the two basic words he can speak.

The basic words are not single words but word pairs.

One basic word is the word pair I-You.

The other basic word is the word-pair I-It; but this basic word is not changed when He or She takes the place of it.

Thus the I of man is also twofold.

For the I of the basic word I-You is different from that in the basic word I-It.

—MARTIN BUBER, *I and Thou*

Tertz's fantastic tales "You and I" ("Ty i ya") and "Graphomaniacs" ("Grafomany") stand in roughly the same relation to one another as do "Pkhents" and "At the Circus." Both take as their focus self-absorbed characters—one who flees attention and another who craves it. These stories, however, in essence originate out of their characters' misreadings of the texts in which they figure, misreadings that in each case entail misconceptions of crime. Both characters fall prey to solipsism, pitting themselves against the rest of the world and imagining themselves the targets of conspiracies hatched by ill-intentioned antagonists. The limitations of their perspectives, which cause them to misread, are exposed by biblical figurae enacted in the texts, placing each man in confrontation with God. The two encounters, however, end differently, one in the character's destruction and the other in the character's regeneration.

"You and I" is the most profoundly disturbing of Sinyavsky's early stories and has, for the most part, left critics baffled and dissatisfied.[1] The story has arguably frustrated interpretation because it so radically disrupts traditional conventions of literary discourse. On the one hand, Tertz here deploys stock images and characters from the nineteenth-century fantastic tale, which prompts the reader to interpret the story, as critics have tended to do, as a study in mental unbalance.[2] On the other hand, convincing textual and intertextual evidence identifies the narrator of "You and I" as God.[3] Reading the story in this light, we find that "You and I," like "Pkhents," posits a figure of the divine as that which transcends the limits of human representation precisely by trapping it in body and human language.

The story that unfolds in "You and I" arises out of misunderstandings created by the limitations of the characters' visions and the competing claims of different defining centers. The first of its six sections establishes the basic misreading on which the narrative rests. The main character's sense of being under constant surveillance and his fear of falling prey to a plot to compromise him politically encourage us to read his story—as, in a sense, he does himself—as an allegory of life in the totalitarian state. Yet to confine ourselves to a purely political—or, for that matter, psychological—interpretation of the story is to replicate the central character's failure of vision, which leads in the end to his destruction. "You and I" rests on the tension between alternative readings and on the exposure of the limitations of the "human" readings of the text, which trap the characters and, in the end, even the narrator himself.

In the first section of the story events are related from the point of view of a character addressed only as "you" (*ty*). The as-yet-unnamed man reluctantly accepts an invitation to a party celebrating the twenty-fifth wedding anniversary of his co-worker Henrikh Ivanovich Graube. The character is convinced from the outset that the anniversary celebration is not at all what it purports to be, but rather serves as a cover for an elaborate provocation engineered to compromise him politically, to draw him into "illegal participation in the diversion taking place."[4] He assumes that Graube's wife and the other women at the party are men in disguise and imputes sinister interpretations to apparently innocent actions, as when he says that one of the guests "grasped in both hands a large portion of duck and took a big bite out of its side, hinting that in an allegorical sense an analogous end would overtake you as well" (128).[5] He has a strong sense of playing a role in someone else's plot, which he desperately tries to read in order to avoid this "analogous end," and ultimately he goes to his destruction precisely because he misreads as a result of the limitations of the perspective he brings to his interpretation of events. His consciousness of being in someone else's "story," in which he casts himself as the center of attention, is underscored by his reading of the clatter of cutlery as an esoteric text echoing the "threatening phrase—'It's time to begin'" (127) spoken at the start of the party by Graube: "The guests ate swiftly, making noises with their knives and forks, and with the help of these sounds maintained a secret communication in a ciphered code like the Morse alphabet. 'It's time to begin! It's time to begin!'" (127–28).

The focal character's apprehension springs from his awareness of being watched. He feels Graube's eyes on him as his would-be host insists that he come to the anniversary celebration:

> "If you don't come, I'll be mortally offended!" he said with emphasis and directed at you eyes similar to convex lenses.
> There the icy little sparks of the pupils [*zrachkov*] quivered hypnotically. (126)

At the party he has the same consciousness of Graube's eyes upon him, but heightened by an apprehension that he may be the focus of some other, far more powerful viewer: "Henrikh Ivanovich's gaze, sniper-like, microscopic [*mikroskopiinii*], scoured your face. In addition to everything you suddenly imagined that someone unseen and all-seeing [*nevidimyi i vsevidyashchii*] was at that moment looking (through the window perhaps, from the wall or through the wall?)— at you and at all those sitting straight-backed before their plates, as if they were about to be photographed for a group portrait" (128). The opening section closes with a reference to this same unseen observer, hinting that Graube and the other guests are his minions: "And that all-seeing eye [*vsevidyashchii glaz*], which was keeping watch over everyone, ironically screwed itself up over its hapless intelligence officers and ran like a yellow stain [*rasteksya zheltym pyatnom*] blending into the color of the yellow wallpaper, as if it didn't exist [*budto ego i ne bylo*]" (129). The characters' misconceptions result precisely from "reading" as if "it didn't exist."

The misinterpretation of events presented in the first section of the story is exposed in the second section, when the narrator— now speaking in the first person—opens up a completely new perspective. While a direct tie with the story's opening situation is not immediately established, word echoes in the first paragraph of this second division of the narrative foreshadow the connection, linking the narrator's vision to the yellow stain invoked earlier. As the narrator looks at the city through falling snow, "Suddenly my field of vision crawled away like a blind slush, and a yellow tear half-and-half with sparkling snow, ran out of my eye" (129).

The first half of the second section of "You and I" reveals the scope of the narrator's vision. As he looks on at the twilit scene, he sees a "panorama" (130) of human actions:

> Snow was falling. A fat woman was cleaning her teeth. Another woman, also fat, was cleaning a fish. A third woman was eating meat. Two engineers were playing Chopin four-handed on the piano. In maternity homes four hundred women were simultaneously giving birth to children.
>
> An old woman was dying.
>
> A ten-kopeck coin rolled under a bed. A father, laughing, was saying: "Oh, Kolya, Kolya." Nikolai Vasilevich was running at a jog-trot through the frost. A brunette was rinsing herself in a basin before a rendezvous. A brown-haired woman was putting on slacks. Five kilometers from there— her lover, also for some reason Nikolai Vasilevich, was slinking with a suitcase in his hand through an apartment covered with blood.
>
> An old woman was dying—not that one, another. (130)

Underscoring the ostensible lack of connection between these events, their apparent meaninglessness, the narrative becomes a mosaic of phrases thrown together in seemingly random fashion from the preceding paragraphs:

> Ay-yai-yai, what were they doing, what were they engaged in! They were boiling semolina. Shot out of a gun, missed. Was unscrewing a screw and crying. Zhenka was warming his cheeks, having clutched his ice skates under his arm. A shop window into smithereens. A brown-haired woman was putting on slacks. A yard-keeper spit with loathing and said: "Here we have it! They've arrived!"
>
> In a basin before a meeting he was running at a jog-trot with a suitcase. He was unscrewing cheeks out of a gun, laughing gave birth to an old woman: "Here we have it! They've arrived!" A brunette was dying. Nikolai Vasilevich was dying. Zhenka was dying and being born. A brown-haired woman was playing Chopin. But another brown-haired woman—the seventeenth by count—all the same was putting on slacks. (130)[6]

As the narrator points out in the following paragraph, the significance of these events is concealed from those who perform them: "The whole meaning consisted in the synchronicity of these acts, each of which had no meaning. They did not know their accomplices. What is more, they did not know that they were serving as details in the picture that I was creating, looking at them. It never occurred to them that each of their steps was being registered and was liable at any moment to thorough study" (130). The narrator thus makes claims to being an artist creating a "picture"—which echoes the reference to the party guests posed as for a photograph in the preceding section—the meaning of which is clear only to himself because only he has the scope of vision that can take in all the fragmented parts. The perspective and therefore comprehension of the human figures in his "picture" are circumscribed by their lack of awareness of their roles in this process of creation: "True, some of them experienced pangs of remorse. But to feel incessantly that I was watching them—directly, without taking my eyes off them, penetratingly and vigilantly—this they were unable to do. In their delusion they acted, perhaps, very naturally, but in the highest degree shortsightedly" (130).

At this point the narrator's gaze is drawn to a man "whom it was impossible not to notice" (130–31), who keeps "glancing back" and acts "as if he were a criminal who was just about to be caught and exposed" (131). The narrator concludes:

> Nothing threatened him, and I reasoned sensibly that a presentiment of my presence manifested itself in him. Probably he caught my sharp gaze on himself and squirmed under it, without understanding what the hitch was, ascribing to the people around him a power they did not have. It seemed to him that someone was personally spying on him, and it was I, but he thought it was they, and that made me laugh. I focused on him, I zoomed in on him through the light spot of my pupil [*pyatno zrachka*]. He was like a bacillus under a microscope, and I examined him in all the pitiful details. (131)

Here the narrator reveals the misapprehension, the disparity in perspective on which the story hinges, underscoring the discrepancy through the repetition of words from the first section of the story. Thus, for instance, Graube's "microscopic gaze" becomes the figurative microscope through which the narrator observes his subject. The main character's fatal error lies in "ascribing to people around him a power they did not have," in confusing Graube's gaze with the narrator's scrutiny. We thus learn in the concluding paragraphs of the section that the man who has drawn the narrator's attention is the "you" of the opening of the story and that that character's reading of the anniversary celebration as a political provocation is a figment of his paranoia. Sensing that he is embroiled in someone else's plot, the "you" misattributes authorship of the creation in which he figures. The alternation between first- and second-person narration throughout the story serves to throw the discrepancy between perspectives into relief.

At the end of the second section of "You and I," another character—who will quite literally become a figure of the grammatical third person later in the narrative—makes her appearance in the story. Back at the party the central character turns to the only guest he is sure is truly a woman, the librarian Lida. As the section closes, he announces to her, "Lida, I love you!" (131), words that set the story on the course to its fatal denouement.

In the third part the narrator reverts to second-person narration and to the perspective of the "you." Seeking to stave off Graube's next "attack," the "you" casts about for a way to divert suspicion. Through a strange twist of reasoning that exemplifies his ethical shortsightedness, he imagines a paradigm for proving innocence by indulging in crime and indecency: "After all it sometimes happens that an elderly, serious man, even, for example, an academician, comes to visit and drinks a couple of shots and—just look—he's already packing the host's silver into his pocket or declaiming out loud verses of an intimate content" (132). Such behavior inspires confidence, "Because it's immediately obvious that he's one of us [svoi paren'], he didn't study in any gymnasium and in the moral sense is as pure as Jesus Christ. A man like that won't divulge military secrets and won't betray the motherland at a decisive moment" (132). The note of political satire here is obvious: in this corrupt system theft and obscenity become demonstrations of patriotism, proofs against implication in the only crime the society condemns, which is political disloyalty. Once again, however, the issue goes deeper. The "you"'s misguided actions and distorted sense of values are driven by a misplaced sense of guilt, a limitation of perspective that confuses political surveillance with the eye of God.

In order to prove that he is "as pure as Jesus Christ" the "you" turns to Lida as "the only woman capable of saving [spasti] your reputation" (132). He thus both lays claim to divinity and defines the path to salvation. It is not he, however, who will take that path, but the narrator, who will consummate the relationship in his place. The connection between the "you"'s fear of physical intimacy and his failure to find redemption is likewise suggested by his attempts to prove his sexual prowess by accosting Graube's wife: "To confirm these words you, reeling like a drunk, went right up to him and, fighting down your innate timidity, cautiously fingered with one brown-and-orange-flecked hand the bulging camouflage attached to his chest. You knew it: it was only a rubber pillow, inflated with empty air" (133). To understand the implications of this image we must remember that Graube's wife's name is Vera or "faith." Inverting "doubting" Thomas's demand to touch Christ's body before he will believe in the resurrection, the "you" here disclaims the evidence of the body, taking it as proof of his own delusion that Vera Ivanovna is merely a "fiction" (133), a man in disguise. Rejection of the body thus becomes, in effect, renunciation of faith, just as the "you"'s refusal of Lida's body will lead to his perdition.

Before fleeing the party under the pretense of physical desire for Lida, the "you" takes a parting shot at Graube, which suggests that his self-obsession is in some sense an attempt to usurp the narrator's place. Having taken as a political provocation Vera Ivanovna's earlier remark that she bought the duck for dinner at the market because the produce there was better than in the state stores, the "you" claims to see through the plot against him and protests his loyalty:

> "Lidiya, I am abducting you. Let's get out of here. Let these people carry on their petty conversations without me. They'll be more comfortable running down state ducks without me. What am I? I'm okay [*ya—nichego*], completely loyal. But you, Henrikh Ivanovich, I see right through you [*vas ya vizhu naskvoz'*]."
>
> And you looked him right in the eyes with his own piercing gaze, as if it were not you, but he who was under scrutiny by you.
>
> "Yes! Yes! Yes! I see right through you!" (134)

Thus, while, on the one hand, the "you" misattributes the gaze he feels upon him to Graube, on the other, in a telling spurt of bravado, he appropriates the penetration of that vision to himself. In fact, precisely by imagining himself the center of universal attention, he challenges God's status as defining center, a challenge that precipitates an exchange of roles in the next two sections of the story.

At the beginning of the fourth section the "I" and "you" come into direct confrontation in the narrative for the first time, as the narrator, continuing to speak in the first person, addresses his antagonist in the second person. This narrative stance mirrors the duel of vision between narrator and character. The section opens:

> He has been in my field of vision for four days. I seem to him a python whose cold-blooded gaze causes a rabbit to lose consciousness. His notions about me are complete nonsense. But even taking these absurd fantasies as a basis, I don't know who holds whom on a leash: I him or he me? We have both fallen into captivity, do not have the strength to tear our glazed eyes away from one another. And although he does not see me, from under his bleached eyelashes beats in my direction such a shaft of fear and hatred that I want to shout: "Stop! If not I'll swallow you! All I have to do is slam shut my eyelids— and you will vanish like a fly!" This contest begins to tire me.
>
> Fool! Understand—you live and breathe only while I am looking at you. Indeed you are only you because I am addressing you. Only being seen by God have you become a human being . . . Oh, you! . . . (135)

Here the narrator announces himself, and the significance of the epigraph to "You and I" becomes clear: "And Jacob was left alone; and there wrestled a man with him until the breaking of the day" (Genesis 32:24). The passage is drawn from the account of Jacob's struggle with an antagonist he identifies as God. The biblical text continues:

> And when he saw that he prevailed not against him, he touched the hollow of his thigh; and the hollow of Jacob's thigh was out of joint, as he wrestled with him. And he said, Let me go, for the day breaketh. And he said, I will not let thee go, except thou bless me. And he said unto him, What is thy name? And he said, Jacob. And he said, Thy name shall be called no more Jacob, but Israel: for as a prince has thou power with God and with men, and hast prevailed. And Jacob asked him and said, Tell me, I pray thee, thy name. And he said, Wherefore is it that thou dost ask after my name? And he blessed him there. And Jacob called the name of the place Pēn-ī-ēl: for I have seen God face to face, and my life is preserved. (Genesis 32:25–30)

The "contest" between the "I" and the "you" thus replays the struggle between Jacob and God—with significant differences, however. While God's attention is drawn to the "you" by that character's awareness of being watched, that awareness springs not from humility, but from an inflated sense of importance which amounts to a usurpation of God's place at the center of the universe: "Oh, if it were only the persecution mania which sometimes afflicts people highly gifted with a consciousness of their guilt and insignificance! No, he was sooner possessed by a different ailment, called in medicine 'mania grandiosa.' The universe had only one worry: to vex him personally. And running out in the mornings for bread, for sausage, he brazenly put down to his own account everything that came before his eyes" (136).

The biblical story, moreover, is about naming and recognition.[7] While Jacob's antagonist refuses to name himself, Jacob recognizes him as God. The "you" in Tertz's tale, however, blinded by his self-obsession, misidentifies and therefore misunderstands the source of the gaze fixed on him. In this, moreover, he is not alone. When in the latter half of the story's fourth section the "you" ventures from his apartment, he encounters Graube. Terrified that his co-worker will compromise him politically, either because of his wife's comment about state stores or because of an imagined rivalry over Lida, Graube offers to grovel before him: "but I, dear boy, would like a tête-à-tête [*s glazu by na glaz*]. Oh, you prankster! My wife still remembers with pleasure. What a good time we had! What laughter, laughter! And you believed the old fool? She wanted to roast a duck, she wanted to give the guests a treat, that's all. . . . You were joking— I understood immediately. 'Right through [*naskvoz'*],' he says, 'I see right through [*naskvoz' vizhu*]!' Ha-ha-ha! Oh, oh! Oh, you, prankster! Do you want me to get down on my knees?" (137). The duel of eyes between Graube and his opponent thus becomes a parody of the struggle between the "you" and the "I." Misreading the "you"'s words, Graube does indeed go down on his knees before him in a travesty of prayer. In a world where God is not recognized, human relations are perverted by the misattribution of divine power. Trust is impossible. Thus, fearing that even Graube's act of supplication is a strategy to get the better of him, the "you" strikes Graube in the eye and flees.

The story reaches its climax in the fifth section. There the alternation between first- and second-person narration breaks down completely as the narrator turns to Lida, who is keeping vigil outside the apartment of his antagonist, and tries to distract her gaze: "I counted on enticing Lida away from her post and thereby easing the situation. I thought to lessen the number of eyes that by the force of imagination he was concentrating on himself. But there was another point as well: I wanted to distract myself. I needed a third person [*ya nuzhdalsya v tret'em litse*] to forget and to defend myself against my persecutor" (140).[8] Lida, however, encourages the blurring of identities between the "you" and the "I," the exchange of roles implied in the narrator's reference to the target of his gaze as "my persecutor." As she sits with the narrator in a cafe, she harps on his physical resemblance to the man from whom he is so intent on being distracted, finally suggesting that he shave his beard, presumably to enhance the likeness. At this point the minds of the "you" and the "I" have so merged that when Lida mentions shaving, the idea of a razor enters the other's head as well, and, at the very moment when the narrator, in a final attempt to distract himself, copulates with Lida, his antagonist slits his own throat.

While the epigraph to "You and I" suggests Jacob's struggle with God as a paradigm for the confrontation between the two opponents, the story's denouement clearly invokes, albeit in grotesquely distorted form, the incarnation of Christ, his taking on of a human body to save humanity. The narrator, echoing the "you" earlier, turns to Lida as a means of salvation: "Before it was too late, I wanted to leap out of the game, which could end badly, but there was no other means of salvation [*sredstv spaseniya*] besides Lida at hand" (142). In having intercourse with Lida, then, the narrator plays out the path to human redemption: "Of course, it would have been better if you had been in my place. Openness was precisely what you lacked in life. No matter what, in the embraces of a woman every man, even the most secretive, arrogant, is forced to behave unconstrainedly whether he wants to or not. Perhaps, had you not turned Lida down, this might have helped even you, and—how can one know?—if you had been a bit more trusting, perhaps, you would have managed to understand me better as well" (142). Sexual intimacy, relationship and contact with the body of the other, thus becomes a means to trust and even to understanding of God.

The play of pronouns in "You and I," which might better be translated "Thou and I," suggests a fantastical extrapolation of the terms of relation and alienation—among human beings and between human beings and God—elaborated by Martin Buber in his philosophical dialogue *I and Thou*.[9] Buber posits the inherent duality of human existence defined by the two postures toward the other between which the human "I" alternates:

> The I of the basic word I-You is different from that of the basic word I-It.
>
> The I of the basic word I-It appears as an ego and becomes conscious of itself as a subject (of experience and use).
>
> The I of the basic word I-You appears as a person and becomes conscious of itself as subjectivity (without any dependent genitive).
>
> Egos appear by setting themselves apart from other egos.
>
> Persons appear by entering into relation to other persons.[10]

I-You represents relation, direct and unmediated, while I-It signifies turning the not-I into that which the I experiences and uses. While "no purpose intervenes between I and You" (62–63), the realm of I-It is the "sphere of goal-directed verbs . . . of activities that have something for their object" (54). "Man becomes an I through a You" (80), and a human escapes the realm of I-It by confronting "its detached self for a moment like a You" (80). Dialogue and sexual intercourse between human beings become a "metaphor for the relation to God":

> Here language is perfected as a sequence and becomes speech and reply. Only here does the word, formed in language, encounter its reply. Only here does the basic word go back and forth in the same shape; that of the address and that of the reply are alive in the same tongue; I and You do not only stand in a relationship but also in firm honesty. The moments of relation are joined here, and only here, through the element of language in which they are immersed. Here that which confronts us has developed the full actuality of the You. Here alone beholding and being beheld, recognizing and being recognized, loving and being loved exists as an actuality that cannot be lost.
>
> This is the main portal into whose inclusive opening the two side portals lead.
>
> "When a man is intimate with his wife, the longing of the eternal hills wafts about them."
>
> The relation to a human being is the proper metaphor for the relation to God. (151)

God is "the eternal You" that "cannot become an It" (160), "the center in which the extended lines of relationship intersect" (148). "Through every single You the basic word addresses the eternal You" (123).

Viewed in this light, the narrative structure of the story represents a failure of relation. From the beginning the narrator takes both parts in what fails to become a dialogue because the "you" is unwilling or unable to participate. The "you" personifies ego, perceiving others as impersonators or "plants" (*podstavnymi figurami*, 136), refusing to enter into an I-You relation either with another human being or with God. He exists completely, to use Buber's terminology in the realm of I-It, unable to see himself as a you and casting everything that is not I as it. His argument dovetailing with Tertz's vision elaborated in *What Is Socialist Realism* and *The Trial Begins*, Buber writes of the alienated individual: "His world is devoid of sacrifice and grace, encounter and present, but shot through with ends and means" (110). "When he says You, he means: You, my ability to use" (109). In like fashion, when the central character in "You and I" says "I love you" to Lida, what should be an intimate expression of relation—a recognition of the fullness of the other as a "you"—becomes merely a tactic to transform her into a means to his own end, just as he suspects others of trying to make him into an instrument of their own machinations.

At this point we are faced with the problem that the narrator of "You and I" also resorts to the third person, also turns Lida into a means to an end. Here I would suggest that Tertz is positing the ontological paradox implicit in the representation of the divine: How can the transcendent be "embodied," whether in human form or in the substance of the artistic sign? The mystery of the dual nature of Christ becomes a testing ground for the limits of art.

As in "Pkhents," names in "You and I" are suggestive.[11] Neither the narrator nor his failed interlocutor names the other in the text, but both are assigned names for the first time in the fifth section of the story. The narrator "misnames" himself to Lida, taking on a "human" name as he apparently has a human body: "I called myself by the first name that came to mind, Ippolit, I think" (140). This purportedly random name in fact most obviously suggests an association with Ippolit Terentev from Dostoevsky's *The Idiot*. In its most general sense, this reference to *The Idiot* signals the fact that by casting God as the narrator of his text Tertz is posing himself a narratological challenge roughly analogous to that addressed by Dostoevsky in the figure of Myshkin, "PRINCE CHRIST."[12] More specifically, the allusion to Ippolit, who fails to commit suicide in the presence of a character for whom the narrative makes claims to divinity, speaks to the narrator's immediate situation at the moment he names himself to Lida: he is hoping to avert the "you" from taking his own life. The reference to the Dostoevsky character here, moreover, evokes a particular passage from Ippolit's tormented public confession, "My Necessary Explanation." In the course of his lengthy explication of the events and considerations that have led him to the decision to shoot himself, Ippolit describes his response to Holbein's profoundly disturbing painting of Christ, a copy of which he saw hanging in Rogozhin's home:

> This picture depicts Christ just after he has been taken down from the cross. It seems to me that painters usually follow the custom of depicting Christ, both on the cross and taken down from the cross, still with a trace of extraordinary beauty in his face; they seek to preserve this beauty in him even in the face of the most horrible torments. But in Rogozhin's picture there is not a word about beauty [*o krasote i slova net*]; it is absolutely the corpse of a man who endured interminable suffering even before the cross, wounds, torture, beating by the guards, beating by the people, when he was carrying the cross on himself and fell beneath the cross, and, finally, the torments on the cross, which went on for six hours (at least by my calculation). True, it is the face of a man *just* taken down from the cross, that is, it retains a great deal that is living and warm; nothing has yet had time to grow stiff, so that suffering is still perceptible in the face of the dead man, as if he could still feel it even now (that was caught very well by the artist); but to make up for it the face has not been spared at all; there there is only nature, and in truth such should be the corpse of any man, no matter who he is, after such torments. I know that the Christian church established even in its first centuries that Christ suffered not figuratively [*obrazno*], but actually, and that his body therefore on the cross was fully and absolutely subjected to the law of nature.[13]

Ippolit finds the vividness, the raw physicality, of this representation of the marks of suffering on Christ's body so horrible that he asks how faith can withstand this proof of the power of the law of nature, imagining that even Christ himself could have been turned from his path by this depiction: "And if that teacher himself could have seen

his image [*obraz*] on the eve of his execution, would he himself have
mounted the cross and would he have died the same way now? This
question also involuntarily occurs to you when you look at the picture" (339). Here Ippolit addresses the paradox of the transcendent
incarnated in a human body and the danger of its representation.
Commenting on his own musings, he queries, "Is it possible for that
which has no image [*obraza*] to appear in an image [*v obraze*]?" (340).

"You and I" arguably plays out the implications of the issue raised
by Dostoevsky: divinity—in the person of the narrator of "You and
I"—falls victim to its own representation. Confined within human
body and human language, the transcendent becomes indistinguish-
able from the human. Buber's "eternal You" has recourse to the third
person, and the path to redemption leads instead to damnation, to
suicide, the final rejection of relation.

The only name assigned to the central character, the "you," adds
a further dimension to the story's meditation on the limits and
dangers of representation. In conversation with the narrator, Lida
refers to the "you" as Nikolai Vasilevich. This attribution of Gogol's
name and patronymic to the narrator's antagonist raises questions
of authorship and authority which complement the issue of the embodiment of the transcendent in the artistic text and look ahead to
Tertz's portrayal of Gogol in *In the Shadow of Gogol*. In seeking to
control the plot in which he finds himself, Nikolai Vasilevich stakes
a rival claim to authorship of the text that is in fact being composed
by the narrator. Blind to the fact that he is only one of many Nikolai
Vasileviches, whose actions make sense only from the vantage of the
all-seeing narrator, he imagines himself the center of the universe,
in effect attempting to usurp the place of God. Misreading, which
is here implicitly tantamount to miswriting, thus appears as a function of a failure to enter into relation, to view oneself as a "you" in
relation to God. This failure, moreover, entails an inability to see
another human being as a full-fledged "you," to share intimacy based
on trust. Only by committing suicide can Nikolai Vasilevich attempt
to gain control of his own plot. At the conclusion of the story, however, he remains in the narrator's memory, a sad testimony to the
nonconsummation of the dialogue inscribed in the story's title.

While the encounter with God in "You and I" leads Nikolai Vasilevich to destroy his own body, the first-person narrator and central character of "Graphomaniacs," Pavel Ivanovich Straustin, confronted by the "Author" of earthly life, undergoes a conversion and
renounces his egocentric ambitions, which are rooted in his confu-

sion of the writer's body with his texts. As in "You and I," Straustin's initial misconception culminates in a misapprehension of crime. In the course of events, however, he realizes the inadequacy of his interpretation. The story itself is presented as a chronicle of his regeneration and therefore owes its very existence to its author's transformation.

Like "You and I," "Graphomaniacs" opens with the central character accepting an invitation from another character he would rather avoid: "On the way to the publisher I met the poet Galkin. We reservedly exchanged greetings. And I intended to pass on when suddenly he, having caught up with me, proposed that we eat ice cream and drink a bottle of cranberry juice on him." [14] As in the other story, the initial confrontation between Straustin and Galkin [15] sets up a tension that continues throughout the narrative. While in "You and I," however, the contention between the "you" and Graube serves primarily as a parodic counterpoint to the struggle between narrator and character, in "Graphomaniacs" the rivalry between the two writers is the focus of the narrative. Straustin and Galkin propound mutually incompatible conceptions of the role of the writer and the process of creation, one of which will be discredited and the other vindicated in the course of the narrative. Their disagreement, moreover, hinges on differing connotations they attribute to the term *graphomaniac.*

The story's second paragraph both poses the central problem of the nature of authorship and defines Straustin's artistic stance:

> It was hot and stuffy. Pushkin Boulevard was drying up.[16]
> The breath of an approaching storm could be felt in the air. I liked that. I would have to remember and use it: "The breath of an approaching storm could be felt in the air." I would conclude my novel *In Search of Joy* with it.[17] I would insert it without fail, even directly into the proofs. The approaching storm enlivens the landscape and sounds in unison with events: a subtle allusion to the revolution, to the love of my Vadim for Tatyana Krechet. (154)

Not only the title of his novel but also his appropriation of nature description to the ideology of his text identifies Straustin from the outset as a conventional, Socialist Realist writer.[18] The location of the scene on *Pushkin* Boulevard suggests that the roots of Straustin's understanding—or rather misunderstanding—of the literary process lie in the institutionalized cult of the writer (which, as in

"Pkhents," is linked with the fetishization of the writer's body) and the vision of literature it is called on to validate. Yet his conception of the sentence, "The breath of an approaching storm could be felt in the air," leaves itself open to alternative readings: Does the phrase "mirror" reality or have the words simply popped into the writer's head from some unknown source outside himself? The implications of this distinction become clear in the course of the story.

While Straustin is a prose writer whose genre appears to be the monumental historical epic, Galkin, judging by Straustin's less-than-sympathetic description of his work, is an avant-garde poet, who has a fondness for declaiming his verses to anyone who will listen: "While I refreshed myself with an ice cream and drank the sour water, he managed to bring down on me over a dozen verses. There were 'hairy legs,' 'pilasters,' and 'chrysanthemums' in them. I don't remember anything else: run-of-the-mill balderdash" (154). What truly sets the two writers apart, however, is their differing understandings of the word *graphomaniac*, a disparity that illustrates the relativity of meaning. When Galkin refers to his own writing as "graphomania," Straustin expresses his disbelief that the poet is truly willing to acknowledge himself a graphomaniac, prompting Galkin to elaborate:

> "Graphomania! A disease, psychiatrists say. An incurable, wicked inclination to produce verses, plays, novels—in defiance of the whole world. What talent, what genius, tell me please, what genius didn't suffer from this noble ailment? And any graphomaniac—take note!—the most wretched, the littlest graphomaniac in the depths of his weak heart believes in his genius. And who knows, who can say in advance? After all the Shakespeares and Pushkins were also graphomaniacs—brilliant graphomaniacs. . . . They were just lucky. And if they hadn't been lucky, if they hadn't been published, then what?" (155–56)

Galkin then challenges the common negative interpretation of the term: "Do you understand—I'm sick of it. Everywhere all you hear is: *graphomania, graphomania.* Another word for untalented. But I say to them—not out loud, of course, but to myself, in my innermost soul—I say: 'Go to the devil, all of you! There are after all, for example, drunkards, there are libertines, sadists, morphine addicts. . . . But I, I am a graphomaniac! . . . Like Pushkin, like Lev Tolstoy! . . .

So leave me in peace! . . .'" (156). While Galkin repudiates and attempts to redefine the meaning of the term *graphomania*, Straustin
credits the generally held negative connotations of the word. Their
conversation coldly ends on his refusal to allow the term to be applied to himself: "'Please don't call me a graphomaniac,' I responded
sharply. 'You can consider yourself whatever you like, but leave me
out of it! . . .'" (157). Thus, as in "Pkhents," the meaning of the story's
title becomes the main issue addressed by the narrative.

Straustin's next two encounters undercut his pretensions and
reveal the envy and inflated ego that feed his literary aspirations.
At the publishing house he learns that his novel has been rejected
and the manuscript returned to him. Angered by the offhanded manner the receptionist adopts toward him, he indulges in a revealing
fantasy:

> A girl available to any proofreader, and in the daytime
> hours to the editor, who had the habit of slapping her on the
> back, dares to lecture me! Slapping on the back. . . . As a man
> who had given himself up completely to the lofty business
> of art, I was absolutely free of these base interests. But if I
> had the good fortune to publish *In Search of Joy*, I'd be able
> to slap her on the back as much as I liked, and she wouldn't
> object and would moreover be flattered. But I wouldn't act
> like that, I'd think up something else: I'd invite her first to the
> art theater, then—in a beautiful light-gray suit, to the curtsies
> of lackeys—I would weaken her to the point of losing con-
> sciousness with dry Georgian wine. Then I would take her,
> weakened, by the arm to a hotel, where there is a "deluxe"
> room at any day or hour for a major writer, and there, under a
> canopy, I would perform on her every imaginable degrading
> procedure. Not because I need it so much, but just for the sake
> of justice. Then she'll understand whom she's dealing with.
> Then she won't insult a person who is gigantically above her,
> but for the time being has no way of proving his superiority.
> (158–59)

Authorship represents for Straustin a means to power, an affirmation of his manhood.

Straustin's obsession is thus rooted in a desire for control, here
likened to sexual domination. While Galkin extends the term *graphomaniac* to all writers, beginning with himself, Straustin seems to

apply it to everyone but himself. He views himself as the only true writer and dismisses all others as mediocrities, or resents what he sees as their unfair advantages:

> The nineteenth-century classics had it good. They lived on quiet estates, had a steady income, and, lounging on glass verandas, between balls and duels, wrote their novels, which were immediately published in all corners of the globe. They knew foreign languages from birth, were taught diverse literary devices and styles in lyceums, traveled abroad, where they replenished their brains with fresh material. And their children—they turned their children over to the care of governesses and sent their wives off to dances or to the dressmaker or shut them up in the country.
>
> But here just try—awaken inspiration when your organism is famished and your head stopped up with the thought of how to hit the necessary mark, how to force your way through the obstacles erected in your path by upstart graphomaniacs, who entered literature by shady means and bricked up all the entrances and exits after themselves. Where to get nourishment three times a day? And besides—for gas, for electricity, and your soles have worn through, and to settle accounts with the typist for two hundred pages of typed text at a ruble a page. (160–61)

Straustin presents his willingness to sacrifice everything else to his devouring desire for publication as proof of his superior claim to authenticity as a writer: "Go and compare me after this with Lev Tolstoy, with Ivan Turgenev! I don't know which of them, of the classics, would agree to accept my proposition: just let them publish me, and then let me get sick and immediately die, without even properly experiencing all my posthumous fame. Publish only one book (best of all if it were the novel *In Search of Joy*), and then kill me or do with me what you will—I'll accept any ultimatum, and which of you would accept this, which of you would agree to those conditions?" (161). Straustin's self-proclaimed devotion to literature is thus driven to the exclusion of all else by a desire for immortality, which he assumes will follow inevitably upon publication. He seems to view the making public of the text as a guarantee of the continuation of himself. The body of the text is literally to replace the body of the author.

Straustin's obsession with the fruits of writing rather than with the process, his overweening desire for his fame to live on in place of his body is exposed by his reaction to his young son's first attempt at writing fiction. When he returns home from the publishing house, Straustin discovers that the child—also named Pavel—has written a "story" (*rasskaz*, 162) about dwarfs. He forbids the boy to write any more "fairy tales" (*skazok*, 163) and suggests that when his book is published and they become rich, they will buy a typewriter and little Pavel will become his personal typist. Straustin's resentment of the obstacles to writing posed by his physical needs and his willingness to renounce his body for renown are paralleled by his fears that his son, the physical continuation of his own body in a separate and therefore independent body, will challenge the immortality of his name: "But I knew very well that writers do not give birth to writers and that geniuses do not have descendants. Lev Tolstoy's children did not have the right to write. The Dumas don't count: neither of them is any good at all, especially Dumas *fils*. And Zinaida [Straustin's wife] was stupid enough to name our son Pavel. She never loved me. Pavel Straustin—on spines, on covers, on everybody's lips. In two or three hundred years just try to figure out—which one is I and which one he—a graphomaniac?" (163).

When his wife comes home, Straustin precipitates an argument with her over the fact that she concealed his returned manuscript from him. For Straustin, Zinaida has become an emblem of the gap between art, which is timeless, and life, which changes over time. He is appalled that this "aging, unattractive woman" (164) once served as the model for the heroine of his novel: "After all it is her image filled with enthusiasm and passion, with flying hair the color of ripe rye, that I immortalized [*zapechatlel*] from memory in the image of Tatyana Krechet, altering only the name, so that readers would not suspect, and placing her in different historical surroundings" (164). Zinaida, for her part—validating Galkin's tirade about the abasement of graphomania earlier—denounces her husband's obsession with writing as being worse than abuse of the body: "It would be better if you were an alcoholic. Morphine addicts are better. At least they have lucid periods" (164). "You," she accuses him, "have only one thing on your mind—going down in history. You don't have the courage to be a simple mortal" (165). Straustin's approach to literature as the copying of physical reality (the body) and his literary drive, to overcome the mortality of the body, are thus simultaneously discredited.

In the wake of this quarrel, Straustin flees his home and takes refuge at Galkin's apartment. His visit ends in a paranoid fantasy that all literature is a crime against himself, a fantasy triggered by his misunderstanding of Galkin's views on literature. Just as his initial conversation with the poet ended in a failure of communication caused by the disagreement of the two writers over the term *graphomaniac,* so Straustin here consistently misapprehends Galkin's statements on literature, interpreting them to fit his own delusion. The roots of his misinterpretation of Galkin's words lies in Straustin's insistence on considering literature a means to self-affirmation. Galkin, on the other hand, views writing as a sort of self-effacement:

> "You know, old man," Galkin said, smiling stupidly and broadly, "the more I work, the better I understand: all the best that I've written doesn't belong to me and was written, the devil take it, seemingly not by me. It just came into my head from somewhere else, flew in from the air. . . . They say 'immortalize yourself' [*zapechatlet' sebya*], 'express your personality.' But I think that every writer is engaged in one thing: self–e-lim-i-na-tion [*sa-mo-us-tra-ne-ni-em*]! That's why we labor in the sweat of our brow, cover trainloads of paper with writing—in the hope of eliminating ourselves, overcoming ourselves, giving access to thoughts from the air. They arise of themselves, apart from us. We only work, only work, only go, go our way and from time to time, overcoming ourselves, give way to them. And suddenly!—indeed it always happens immediately and suddenly!—it becomes clear: this is what you wrote yourself and therefore it isn't any good, but that isn't yours, and you no longer dare, don't have the right to do anything with it—neither to change nor try to improve it. It's not your property! And you recoil in bewilderment. You're dumbfounded. Not because of any beauty that has been accomplished. But simply out of the fear that you had no part in what's occurred." (168)[19]

Galkin's attempt to elucidate his vision of the creative process, however, only serves to sow seeds of suspicion in the uncomprehending Straustin: "I listened attentively to Galkin's frank admissions. They seemed very interesting to me. So that's how it is! He doesn't consider it his property? That must be taken into consideration. . . . Who then is the author? . . . Who does he borrow this all from? . . . Events confirmed my worst apprehensions" (168–69). Straustin draws false inferences from Galkin's words because he confuses authorship with ownership, viewing his writing as an extension of his self.

Straustin's misconstrual of Galkin's words comes to a head at a gathering of writers, all of them apparently unpublished, at the poet's apartment. Galkin regales the odd assortment of would-be writers with his ideas on the "analogy between the graphomaniac and the genius" (170), elaborating it into an evangelical vision of the world transformed into a text: "He called graphomania the foundation of foundations and the beginning of beginnings and called it the swampy soil out of which the purest springs of poetry take their sources. This soil, said Galkin, is oversaturated with moisture. It has no exit, said Galkin. The time would come, said Galkin, when it would spout from the bowels of the earth and inundate the world. He who was nothing, said Galkin, will become all [an allusion to the *Internationale*], and if there's not enough paper for all, we'll cover the walls of buildings and the naked pavements of the streets with texts in verse and in prose, said Galkin" (170). The company listens for a time to Galkin's exhortation, but eventually they become impatient and drift into corners to read aloud their own works. Straustin finds himself engulfed in a babble of muddled texts. Suddenly in the midst of the cacophony he distinguishes his own sentence:

> "The breath of an approaching storm could be felt in the air."
>
> It flashed like lightning and drowned in the darkness of words swirling around me, and, turning swiftly, I could not understand which of these muttering mouths had just uttered a quotation from my novel *In Search of Joy*. But I couldn't be mistaken either, because I'd inserted the sentence about the approaching storm into the text only yesterday—precisely in that variant in which it had been repeated here.
>
> And then again, in confirmation of my horrible conjecture, another voice at the other end of the room said softly, but distinctly:
>
> "Brea . . . oaching . . . orm . . . fel . . . air . . ."
>
> There could be no doubt: they'd robbed me, they'd stolen my pearl. (171–72)

Straustin now believes that he understands the true significance of Galkin's ideas "from the air." Galkin, he thinks, must have looked at his manuscript and given his "pearl" to his "graphomaniac friends" (172): "And now it [the sentence] was passing from hand to hand like small change among cheats and swindlers" (172).

When Straustin confronts Galkin with his imagined crime, the two writers again talk at cross purposes. Straustin approaches Galkin and asks him if he does not want to take notes on the proceedings so that he can use it later, and the poet responds enthusiastically: "'I would like to,' he said without even blushing. 'I would like to! But after all I'm not a dramatist or, unfortunately, a prose writer. I wouldn't be able to do it. . . . If I were you, Straustin, I would write something of the sort. . . . A story, or even better—a novella, a novel, an epic! I'd call it "Graphomaniacs"! An epic about unsuccessful writers. The material, what material is going to waste! . . .'" (172). When Straustin persists with his accusations, asking Galkin what he thinks of the sentence about the approaching storm, Galkin dismisses it as a cliché: "'A bad sentence,' he said coldbloodedly, 'Hackneyed, old, like a twenty-kopeck coin'" (172). Straustin is thus exposed as claiming ownership of that which is intrinsically "authorless."

Still unwilling to part with his delusions, Straustin spends the night rummaging through Galkin's books, all of them by politically acceptable Soviet and foreign writers, and imagines that in all of them he finds passages stolen from the manuscripts he submitted for publication: "And while I suffered in expectation, the agile hands of various Galkins, Fedins deftly reworked them and launched them under other [*chuzhimi*], under false names" (174). Since he views his writing above all as a means to the immortalization of his name, Straustin considers the true injustice of this "plagiarism" (174) to lie in the theft of "the fruits of fame, which by rights belonged to me alone" (174).

The next day, Straustin so irritates Galkin—by tapping on the glass of the bookcase with the now-materialized twenty-kopeck piece and by calling him a graphomaniac—that the poet drives him from his apartment. Wandering the streets in the dead of night, with only the twenty-kopeck piece in his pocket, he—like the "you" of "You and I," who imagines the windows of all buildings to be eyes glaring at him—projects his own self-obsession onto the urban landscape, fancying that the city is swarming with scribbling graphomaniacs. Bitterly ruminating that he is the only "true writer," that the others "do not write themselves, but copy me," he postulates himself as the unacknowledged source of all creation: "I did not enter as a victor in a laurel wreath through the front door, but I penetrated into their bodies and souls through their food and through the air, as poison penetrates the blood, and now they will never get rid of me" (176). Straustin thus inverts Galkin's vision, identifying himself as the source of all words. All other writers therefore become thieves masquerading under false names.

His final burst of *ressentiment* is triggered by the streets named after famous writers along which he finds himself wandering:

> The classics—that's who I hate worse than anyone! Even before my birth they grabbed all the vacancies, and I was faced with competing with them, without having at my disposal even a fraction of their puffed-up authority. "Read Chekhov, read Chekhov," they've repeated to me my whole life, tactlessly hinting that Chekhov wrote better than I do. . . . But how can I struggle with them, when at Yasnaya Polyana even Lev Tolstoy's fingernails, clipped a thousand years ago and collected by the far-sighted count in a special bag are kept as a sacred relic [*svyatynya*]?! And in Yalta, they say, Chekhov's dried-out spittle is preserved in special little packets, yes, yes! The original spittle of Anton Pavlovich Chekhov. (176–77)

The root of Straustin's obsession is thus located in the sacralization of writers, manifested grotesquely by the preservation of the remains of their physical bodies, in the investment in the "classics" of the authority to define all writing. Straustin's tirade serves both to discredit authorial claims to sacred authority, by casting them as a perverted bid for physical immortality, and to reveal that his own delusion stems from a lust for the same misplaced authority and immortality. Thus, he asks rhetorically, "But who will write memoirs about me? Who, I ask you, will remember and perpetuate me?" (177).

Straustin receives an immediate answer to his question:

> From fatigue and vexation I traced out a monogram with my feet, stumbled, staggered. My painful way along the roadway was whimsical and zigzagging. Suddenly it seemed to me that I was not myself walking down the street, but that someone's fingers were guiding me, as a pencil is guided along paper. I walked in cramped, uneven handwriting [*pocherkom*], I hurried as fast as I could after the movement of the hand that was composing and jotting down [*sochinyala i zapisyvala*] on the asphalt these solitary streets, and these

houses with unextinguished windows here and there, and me myself, all my long, long unsuccessful life.

Then I tore myself away, abruptly slowed down, stopping at full speed, and almost fell down, and looked sullenly into the dark sky, hanging low over my forehead. I said not loudly, but substantially enough, addressing myself directly there:

"Hey, you, graphomaniac! Quit working! Everything you write is no good. Everything you've composed is devoid of talent. It's impossible to read you." (177)[20]

Thus, Straustin suddenly realizes that he is in fact a character in someone else's text, that his body, like all of the earthly reality around him, is merely a writing instrument in the hand of God. God Himself becomes a graphomaniac.

That Straustin's encounter with God is in fact a conversion experience becomes clear only in the concluding pages of the story, when Straustin returns home chastened and promises his wife that he will now finally give up writing. As soon as she leaves for work, however, he sets out to compose his "swan song about myself. No, no, not for print. Let my son at least read it. And on this I'll give it up" (179). Now he is writing for the sake of writing, rather than for fame, and not epics about the revolution, but stories about himself. Echoing Galkin, moreover, he encourages his son to write as well: "Write, Pavel! Write! Don't be afraid. Let them laugh at you, call you a graphomaniac. They're graphomaniacs themselves. All around there are graphomaniacs. There are a lot of us, a lot, more than are needed. And we live in vain and uselessly die. But one of us will make it. Either you, or I, or someone else. Will make it, will carry it through. Write, Pavel, compose your fairy tales about your funny dwarfs. And I will about mine. . . . You and I will think up so many fairy tales. . . . It won't be possible to count. Only take care—don't say anything to Mama" (179). Thus, his perspective radically altered by his realization that he is merely a character in the divine text, Straustin sits down to write the story the reader has just finished reading, the tale that Galkin suggested that he write, setting down the title "Graphomaniacs" and adding in parentheses the subtitle that does in fact appear at the head of the story: "(from stories about my life)" (179). His recognition of God thus becomes a realization of self as well, marked by his turning from revolutionary epic to autobiography. Writing has now ceased to be a means for him and has become an end in itself. Having, moreover, renounced his delusion that he is the victim of the crime of plagiarism, Straustin embarks on a writing career that is criminal in the exemplary sense invoked again and again in Tertz's writings. As his words to his son and the subtitle to the story ("stories from my life") make clear, Straustin's "swan song" will not be his final work. He will continue writing in secret, under prohibition, against the rules, in defiance of the injunction to "write like Chekhov."

The biblical figura that Straustin plays out in the text is revealed in the title of one of Galkin's collections of poetry: *In the Belly of the Whale* (167). The reference is, of course, to Jonah, who, fleeing God's summons to act as His prophet, boarded a ship for Tarshish. When the ship was already en route, however, God raised a storm, and those on board cast lots to see who had brought the evil upon them. When the lot fell on Jonah, he was cast overboard and swallowed up by a "great fish" sent by God. Just as Straustin spends three days at Galkin's apartment, so Jonah spent three days "in the belly of the whale." During that time, Jonah prayed to God in the form of a poem repenting his disobedience and vowing submission. God, in response, caused Jonah to be vomited out of the fish and then came to Jonah a second time to call him to serve as His prophet. This time Jonah agreed.[21] Straustin is thus a modern Jonah who out of arrogance misconceives his vocation and initially rejects the divine call, only in the end to express his capitulation in a work of art, which is the story "Graphomaniacs" itself. Art becomes, as Galkin preaches, not an assertion of the autonomy and authority of the self, but rather a form of "self-elimination," of openness to words "from the air."

"You and I" and "Graphomaniacs" suggest two paradigms for the writer that will recur and be amplified in Tertz's later writings. Nikolai Vasilevich, through his onomastic identification with Gogol, looks ahead to the writer who strives to control his text by speaking with the voice of God, an attempt that ultimately leads to the writer's destruction. Galkin's credo, apparently adopted by the "converted" Straustin, on the other hand, introduces the vision of writing as a form of self-elimination—paradoxically, as Straustin acts it out, through autobiography—as a receptivity to words "from the air," reiterated throughout Tertz's later texts. Both stories, moreover, one through failure and the other through success, posit writing as a function of the ability to enter into relation and, implicitly into dialogue, to be open to the other, exemplified in Straustin's acceptance of the designation *graphomaniac* and the change in his relations with his son. Both, finally, by associating "miswriting" (or the failure to write in "You and I") with misreading serve as an appropriate introduction to the texts we will examine in the next chapter, texts that explore the problematic of writing and reading as collaborative activities.

Chapter Five

The Fantastic as Metaphor: "Tenants," "Icy Weather," and *Lyubimov*

If we realize metaphors, it will be the end of the world. We say, "It's raining cats and dogs," "Falling stars" . . .

—ANDREI SINYAVSKY, testimony at trial

But even though something gradually dies out "in the end," it doesn't mean it must be liquidated before the gradual process is over, does it? The mammoth is extinct, but it did exist and we can still admire its form, although we never set eyes on it. But it did exist; that's what is so marvellous. Yet had some terrible, all-powerful creator decided, "The mammoths will die out eventually anyway, so let's do away with them now," there would have been no mammoths, no mastodons, nothing at all from the past—and all destroyed in the name of the Future, in the name of the Final Objective. What a terrible temptation, to put everything ahead of you, with nothing at all behind you.

—[N. BOKOV], "Andrei Sinyavsky, on Dissidence"

The figurative use of language, metaphor in a broad sense, stands at the core of Tertz's conception of literature as crime. His remaining early fictional works—the stories "Tenants" (*Kvartiranty*, 1959) and "Icy Weather" (*Gololeditsa*, 1961) and the novel *Lyubimov* (1962–63)[1]—all explore the generative and potentially destructive force of metaphor. In each of the three works the ability of language to create figures is identified with the fantastic—with the self-proclaimed fictionality of the text, originating in language's ability to give birth to itself in narrative—and, in each text, metaphor ultimately eludes restraint and runs amok. The issue of control over language thus becomes key, and each work pits its narrator against figures with claims to legal authority who seek to repress or harness the power of the storyteller. Perhaps most important, metaphor is realized to disastrous result in each work precisely because of a failure of dialogue, highlighted by the existence of, or the implication of the desirability of, a multiple narrative persona. These failures take on particular significance because in each case the narrator is a reader-turned storyteller.

The narrative of "Tenants" is cast as a series of four conversations between two characters, corresponding to the four sections into which the story is divided. The text, however, consists of the words of only one of the two participants in the purported dialogue. The other's presence and ultimate reduction to complete unresponsiveness and silence are indicated only by the verbal reactions they elicit from the single speaker. The silent partner in the narrative is identified as a writer, and the narrator characterizes himself as a reader, making frequent references and often humorously inappropriate allusions to the books he has read. The narrator repeatedly accuses the writer of being unobservant, while he himself claims to be a house spirit (*domovoi*) with the power to see behind his back, through doors, and beneath the surface of external appearance. As critics have pointed out, the genesis of the plot is open to alternative readings: either the supernatural narrator of "Tenants" may be taken at face value, or he and all the story's events may be interpreted as figments of the alcohol-besotted writer's imagination.[2] The possibility of the coexistence of multiple readings, inherent in the disorienting and suggestive images of all of Tertz's texts, here stands as a paradigm for the uncontrollability of the reading process. The narrative plays with the idea of a failed collaboration between multiple narrators, between reader and writer, and ends with the narrator's words producing a result opposite to that which he desired. Either reading postulates the text as self-generating, growing out of figures invoked in the course of the narrative itself and ultimately brought to a close, "suppressed," by the very images its language has unleashed. The text as a whole thus realizes the metaphorical expression "to drink to the point of seeing devils" (*napit'sya do chertikov*), which the narrator invokes at the end of the story as the writer lapses into a drunken stupor: "And devils [*chertiki*] are already capering in his eyes."[3] In the story's concluding lines these very "devils," materialized in the characters of the tenants, have risen up and threaten to exile the narrator "under the floor. Into the dampness, the cold, to the microorganisms" (150–51) and to do away with the writer, the "last human being" (150), by transforming him into a rat, a "wordless creature" (152).[4]

The story opens with a markedly ambiguous comparison, a simultaneous invocation and negation of not only likeness but the bounds of simile: "Oh, Sergei Sergeevich, Sergei Sergeevich! Can you really be compared with Nikolai Nikolaevich? It's even funny" (144). The narrator thus begins by rejecting the possibility of comparing the writer, Sergei Sergeevich, with the previous tenant, Nikolai Nikolaevich. The equivocal status of the comparison is reflected in the interplay of the story's parallel plotlines. The narrator, Nikodim Petrovich, in the course of his narrative relates the story of Nikolai Nikolaevich and his wife, Ninochka, and as he reveals the events of the past, the story of Sergei Sergeevich unfolds in the narrative present, his plot essentially repeating the plot of Nikolai Nikolaevich in reverse. While Nikolai Nikolaevich began as a devoted husband and ended up separated from his wife and carted away to a madhouse, Sergei Sergeevich, the story's conclusion suggests, will finish as Ninochka's "spouse" (154), transformed into a "wordless beast" and confined in the communal apartment, assumedly to the end of his days. Sergei Sergeevich as the story concludes is about to take the place of the very character with whom he supposedly could not be compared at the story's beginning. The opening sentence therefore sets in motion the problematic of identity and comparison—the basis of metaphor—that the narrative enacts.

Though, viewed retrospectively, the beginning of "Tenants" determines its ending, the narrator's opening patter seems to give little hint of what is to come. The first section of the story appears to be nothing more than the report of half of a quite ordinary conversation between two quite ordinary tenants of a communal apartment. Only at the end of the first part does the narrator make the quite extraordinary claim, which he apparently proceeds to carry out as the section closes, that he can make himself disappear: "If you want—on the spot, I'll disappear. I'll up and vanish. One, two, three! Now you see me! Now you dooonn't!" (146). As the second section opens, moreover, apparently in mid-conversation, the narrator unfolds a startling series of images of supernatural figures caught in modern technology, immortal beings trapped in history:

> Thus soon only mermaids were left. And even they . . . You yourself know: the industrialization of natural resources. Give way to technology! Streams, rivers, lakes stunk with chemical substances. Methylhydrate, toluol. The fish simply died and floated belly up. But they would come to the surface, snort

with difficulty, while from their eyes—you won't believe it!—
tears of sorrow and disappointment. I saw it myself. All over
their sumptuous busts—ringworm, eczema, and even, excuse
my immodesty, venereal relapses.

Where can you go to hide?

Without thinking long—the same place, following the
wood demons, the witches—to the city, to the capital. By the
Moscow-Volga Canal, through those same sluice-gates—into
the water-supply system, where it's cleaner and more nour-
ishing. Farewell, native land, primordial surroundings!

How many of them perished here! Multitudes. Of course,
not for good. Immortal creatures after all. You can't do anything about it. But some of the meatier ones—got stuck in the
water pipes. You've probably heard them yourself. You turn on
the tap in the kitchen—suddenly from there float sobs, various plops, swearing. You think—whose tricks are these?—
Their voices—the mermaids'. They get stuck in the sink and
start to act capricious, to sneeze. (146–47).

The narrator maintains that all of the other tenants in the apartment are in fact supernatural beings—including a mermaid, a wood
demon, a witch, and himself, a house spirit.

Just as the invocation of comparison at the beginning of the
story ultimately determines the course of the narrative, so the fantastic materializes out of metaphors adduced by the narrator. Thus
the transformation of the tenants into supernatural creatures is set
in motion by a seemingly innocent comment the narrator makes
toward the beginning of the story. Claiming that one of the tenants,
Krovatkina, has been listening in on their conversation, the narrator
calls her a "real witch" (*sushchaya ved'ma*, 146). It later transpires
that the metaphorical "real witch" Krovatkina is in fact a *real* witch,
just as Ninochka—called "Witch [*Ved'ma*]! Whore [*Potaskukha*]!"
(149) at the height of a kitchen argument—becomes both: "She became a complete witch [*Sovsem ved'moi sdelalas'*]. Made peace with
Krovatkina. Even began to learn how to fly on a toilet seat at night.
Like a rocket engine. By means of intestinal gas" (152). When Nikolai Nikolaevich has had enough of his wife's goings-on, all he has to
do is say the words expressing his desire for Ninochka to leave him
for the purported wood demon Antchutker, and his wish becomes a
material reality:

Kolya put up with it for a long time, but one day he said, "Go to the wood demon, Ninochka [*Nu tebya, Ninochka, k leshemu*]. I'm sick of these scandals."

And as soon as he uttered these fatal words, Anchutker came into their room. Ostensibly on business, for a cigarette. And he looked fixedly at Ninochka, and Ninochka looked at Anchutker, and at that moment they found one another very much to their liking. (152)

Putting something into words makes it happen. Metaphor is realized. Words become acts. As soon as Nikolai Nikolaevich employs the expletive *tebya k leshemu*, which is synonymous with the expression "Go to the devil!" the wood demon appears and Ninochka goes away with him to become his "whore."

Andrew Durkin has pointed out:

In the course of the story, characters are apparently transformed into the things, mostly animals and supernatural beings, to which they are first compared by the narrator (whether the changes are actual or imagined by the narrator is insoluble for the reader, given the mode of narration). Inhabitants of the communal apartment are first metaphorically referred to as a witch, or a *rusalka* [a sort of mermaid], or a forest demon (*lešij*), often with metonymic evidence for the metaphor (the *rusalka* spends a great deal of time in the bath and flounces about in a suggestive robe; the *lešij* works in the forest ministry and reads books with titles like *Les šumit* and *Russkij les;* his name Ančutker is connected by the narrator with *ančutka*, a dialect term for the devil). These metaphors gradually become realized, turning people into their metaphorical folkloric counterparts; this metamorphosis reveals natures previously obscured or hidden.[5]

The narrator's "crime"—the crime of metaphor—lies in the revelation of "natures previously obscured or hidden," in the exposure of what is concealed behind external appearance. Metaphor is, after all, the postulation of a similarity between two entities that appear different, with the simultaneous possibility of disclosing each entity's difference from itself. Thus, the narrator warns the writer against one of the other tenants, Sofya Frantsevna Vinter, who "takes water procedures from morning to evening" (147) and sings, in German,

Heine's verses on Lorelei. She is, the narrator claims, a mermaid: "Be careful, Sergei Sergeevich. God save you from running after her. She'll tickle you to death. And as regards what is more essential—I'll say: she has fish blood and everything else is piscine. She only has the external appearance of a lady, to tempt" (147). The invocation of metaphor unleashes the other within, with dire consequences for the narrator and the writer.

In the third section of the story the narrator disguises himself— "Now I'll mask myself a bit" (150)—as a drinking glass in order to hide his latest visit to Sergei Sergeevich from the other tenants, who, he holds, want to suppress his storytelling:

> I know—they want to put me on trial [*menya sudit' khotyat*]. For divulging their secrets.[6] Tomorrow at twelve midnight the Soviet will meet in the kitchen. It would be nothing, except Shestopalov is unhappy with me. He gave the order: "We trusted him," he said, "while he has periodic acquaintances with alien elements [*s chuzhdymi elementami*]. We forgave him," he said, "the incident with the newlyweds, so now he has again struck up a friendship with an unauthorized person. And his new friend, a writer, is jotting down all his words on paper. This could cause trouble. Punish the tattler to keep others from doing it." (150).

As the story ends, the "Great Kitchen Soviet" (151) has apparently resulted in a decision to take action against the troublemakers. The tenants are coming to suppress the narrator and the writer, who has drunken himself into a state of unconsciousness. The narrative is thus literally brought to an end by the forces of censorship, seeking to stem the flow of metaphor which threatens to expose the ambiguity of the self.

The story, in portraying the tenants as wrangling petty demons, clearly pokes fun at the institution of the communal apartment, just as it suggests a bleak picture of the Soviet literary process reducing unruly writers to silence or exiling them to the underground ("under the floor"). Yet, as with all of Tertz's works, the political satire in "Tenants" is a collateral issue to deeper questions about writing, reading, language, and act. Thus, paradoxically, the narrator is quelled by the very metaphors he has himself unleashed. The story enacts the author's inability to control his own text, the impossibility of using narrative to realize authorial intent.

Nikodim Petrovich makes it clear that he wants his words to elicit certain acts on the part of his "audience." He first of all wants Sergei Sergeevich to help him escape the communal apartment, since his "physiology" (151) will not allow him to leave the premises on his own. His idea that he will take up residence together with the writer in more congenial surroundings is suggestively allied with an offer of literary collaboration:

> Besides—I'm not going to pretend to be modest—you too will be lost without me. But with me—God willing—you'll gain worldwide recognition. Charles Dickens. Mayne Reid. After all I know—I know everything, you're such a slyboots. I'll man the door, you'll take up the pen. Even when you're not completely yourself and have a poor command of language. . . .
>
> What are they, our conversations! A miserable fraction. I have a whole decameron of these fables. And all from personal experience. They could be published in five volumes. With illustrations. You and I, Sergei Sergeevich, will leave the Brothers Grimm in our dust. (151–52)

This vision, which the narrator attempts to bring into being through his words, comes to naught because the audience of one at whom his tirade is directed does not respond, allowing the narrator to be "repressed" by his own metaphors. The author cannot dictate how his text will be read. His words may give birth to acts, but not necessarily—perhaps not even probably—those he either desires or expects.

Just as the narrative structure of "You and I" enacts a failure of dialogue (the narrator incorporating both the "I" and the "you" into his own unanswered monologue), so also does that of "Tenants." The suppression of the second speaker's voice in "Tenants," which apparently reflects his growing unresponsiveness, marks a failure of collaboration between two narrators, and between reader and writer. Metaphor, the story suggests, requires both a multiple narrative persona and a creative interaction between storyteller and listener, reader and text. In the absence of these conditions, metaphor malfunctions, is transformed from harmless trope into destructive act. The narrator, seemingly by taking his own metaphors too literally, is destroyed by the very text he constructs to save himself.

"Icy Weather" dramatizes the problematic of the workings and misworkings of metaphor in similar terms. Like the narrator of "Tenants," the nameless narrator of "Icy Weather" is vouchsafed a perspective that transcends the temporal bounds of the human. His expanded vision is specifically linked with the plurality of the narrative self that encompasses a multiplicity of points of view, out of whose coexistence metaphor is conceived. Yet, again as in "Tenants," the narrator's failure to communicate, to enter successfully into dialogue, results in a series of fatally realized metaphors. The text of "Icy Weather" in fact presents itself as an attempt to rectify the failure that gave it birth. Significantly, in the course of the narrative, the addressee and concomitantly the message to be conveyed by the text are subtly redefined.

The preface, "From the Author," with which "Icy Weather" begins identifies the narrative as an effort on the part of the narrator to establish contact with a certain Vasily, who, we later learn, is a future incarnation of the nameless narrator himself. Like the narrator of "Tenants," the narrator of "Icy Weather" is a reader turned writer—"I've read a lot of stories and novels and conceive how it's done"[7]—who wants to use his narrative to elicit action on the part of his target audience, to reunite his future self with a future incarnation of his lost love, Natasha. From the beginning he labors under no illusions about the possible success of his project:

> I am writing this story [*povest'*] as one who has suffered a shipwreck sends word of his misfortune. Sitting on a solitary fragment of debris, or on a lifeless island, he throws into the stormy sea a bottle with a letter in it—in the hope that the waves and wind will carry it to people and they will read it and recognize the sad truth, when the poor author has departed life long before.
>
> Will the bottle reach its destination?—that's the question. Will the tenacious hand of a sailor pull it out by the neck, and will the sailor on deck shed tears of sympathy and pity? Or will the sea salt gradually soak through the sealing wax and eat away the paper and will the undiscovered bottle, filled up with astringent moisture or smashed on the reefs, remain lying motionless at the bottom of the sea?
>
> My task is even more complicated. Possessing neither scientific nor literary experience, I want my labor to be published and to receive recognition. Only by such a roundabout route can I count on reaching you, Vasily. O Vasily! Believe me, I don't need money or homage, I need only your sympathy.[8] I am seeking no other readers except you, although my story

will float through many hands, perhaps, before it reaches your eyes by chance. (179–80)

The narrator's tenuous hope that his words will reach their destined reader and prompt him to act speaks to the work's central concern: the volatile relationship between word and deed. By the end of the text, the narrator's own understanding of this relationship seems to have altered as evidenced by the change in the addressee of his "letter to the future."

The longest of Tertz's "fantastic stories," "Icy Weather" also has the most complicated plot, composed of three separate series of relationships between characters intricately intertwined in a counterpoint of metaphor and misreading. The premise underlying the interconnections between the various strands of events is set in motion on the opening pages of the narrative proper. The narrator, by some inexplicable fluke of memory, apparently gains the ability to see into the past and future lives of both himself and others. As in the case of the narrator of "Tenants," the question of the first-person narrator's reliability, of whether he is truly endowed with the supernatural powers he claims, cannot be conclusively resolved.[9] A thread of uncertainty, spun by frequent references to his dubitable sobriety and questionable motives, runs throughout, feeding the dialectic between word and deed, prediction and realization, on which the story hinges. As the narrator's recognition of the scope of his powers grows, he comes to believe that Natasha's life is in danger from an icicle that he predicts will fall on her head and kill her as she is walking along Gnezdnikovsky Lane on Sunday, 19 January, at ten in the morning. He consequently takes steps, ultimately futile, to save her from the threat he quite literally sees hanging over her. Simultaneously, Natasha is carrying on a surreptitious affair with her estranged husband, Boris, and has become pregnant by him. When the narrator attempts to flee Moscow with Natasha to remove her from harm's way, he is arrested on the train by security officers who have been tipped off by Boris and who seek to make use of the narrator's clairvoyance for their own ends. As the narrator is being held in prison under the supervision of one Colonel Tarasov, Natasha meets the fate he has foreseen, and at the moment of her death, his powers disappear. The narrator's relations with Natasha and Tarasov, and Natasha's relations with Boris, are linked less by the peripeteia of the plot than by the question of whether words predict or create events, whether the narrator truly foresees

a foreordained future, or whether his own utterances bring it into
being.

As the story begins, the narrator is sitting with Natasha on
Tsvetnoi Boulevard shortly before the new year. Because of the
"icy weather" (*byla gololeditsa,* 181), the two find themselves alone.
Suggestively, given the fact that the freeze will ultimately cause
Natasha's death, the couple does not fear the slippery conditions:
"Natasha and I were an exception, because we loved one another
and on that evening were not afraid of falling down and getting
hurt" (181). The icy weather of the title becomes a metaphor for the
fragility and apparent unpredictability of human existence against
which love appears to be a shield. The narrator's love will not, however, save Natasha, either because the immunity of the lovers is
merely an illusion or because his love for her is essentially flawed in
that it is based on a denial of the fullness of the other's self.

In the course of a conversation about the unseasonable absence
of snow, Natasha claims to remember a snowfall that took place in
May when she was only two years old. Incredulous that she can remember back so far—"the scope of our memory has limits" (182)—
and irritated that she can remember farther back in her life than
he can, the narrator stretches the boundaries of his own memory,
which precipitates the radical expansion of perspective his narrative
purports to document. His first intimation of his new powers comes
as an immediate change of scene, as if he were suddenly transported
into the Ice Age:

> I found myself in a long gorge, ringed by rows of bare
> mountains and smooth hills. Its bottom was covered by a
> crust of ice. Along the edge of the ice, in front of the sheer
> cliffs, grew trees which were also bare. They were sparse, but
> the proximity of large tracts of forest made itself known in
> a dull, windy noise. There was a smell of carrion. Pieces of
> rotting wood shone in great number. They were not rotting
> wood, however, but most likely scraps of the moon, torn apart
> by wolves and awaiting the time when its bones, cartilage,
> joints would again be covered with white, luminous meat and
> it would ascend into the sky to the envious howling of the
> wolves. . .
>
> But I didn't have time to comprehend and think through
> all of this: a beast with gaping jaws was running me down.
> It quickly, quickly pawed the ground with invisible legs, and

I could guess that it had not four or five legs, but at least as many as I had fingers and toes taken together. That's how many. It was shorter than a mammoth, but to make up for it plumper and stronger than the largest bear, and when it had come right up close, I noticed that it had a belly as transparent as the bright swimming-bladder of a fish, and little human beings swallowed alive were horribly plopping around there. Probably it was so voracious that it swallowed them without chewing, and the victims that had ended up in its stomach were still fidgeting and jumping up. (182–83) [10]

The narrator snaps out of this horrific vision only when he thinks of the sparks cast by the frightening beast as "electrical": "And probably because these sparks were all the same recalled in my blacked-out brain as 'electrical,' I realized immediately that it was a harmless trolley that was driving past me" (183).

As it turns out, he has never moved from his spot beside Natasha, but has experienced a drastic shift in point of view, briefly seeing the world through the eyes of another self, of a wordless, prehistoric ancestor. Thus he comments on the paragraphs cited above: "Of course I am conveying these sensations approximately, in my own words. Then there weren't even any words in my head, but there were, so to speak, only conditioned reflexes and various, as they are now called, vestiges of religion, and I, tormented by fear, muttered incantations, the character of which I cannot now bring myself to reproduce on paper" (183). Presaging the complex interconnection between word and act elaborated in the course of the story, the narrator notes that at the time, before he realized that the monster bearing down on him was merely a "harmless trolley," it seemed that "these meaningless incantations had some effect" (183), apparently diverting the beast away from him. Thus here, as in the narrative as a whole, the relationship between word and deed remains ambiguous. The narrator's words seem to accomplish their end, to save him from danger, but their effectiveness is revealed as the by-product of the limitation of his perspective. On the other hand, his ability temporarily to see quite literally through new eyes, through the eyes of what we will later learn is his first self (*pervenets*, 211)—embodied in his attempt to translate his wordless experiences into words, to describe the Moscow cityscape as seen by prehistoric man—becomes a paradigm for narrative estrangement.

The wellspring of the writer's vision is cast as the ability to step into an alternate self and, simultaneously, out of the confines of his own historical era. The very narrowness or inadequacy of the alter ego's scope of vision opens up an arresting new perspective precisely through its juxtaposition to that of another, also necessarily limited, self. Most important, this estrangement, this coexistence of alternate selves, is revealed as the origin of metaphor. The twentieth-century trolley becomes *like* a rampaging prehistoric beast, the cityscape becomes *like* a prehistoric wasteland precisely because the narrator, remaining in his own time and space, sees through the eyes of a self from another age. To function properly both terms of a metaphor—both the original entity and that to which it is compared—must remain in play. If the second term of the metaphor becomes detached from the first and takes on a life of its own, disaster ensues. Thus the narrator here—unlike the narrator of "Tenants," who is done in by his own realized metaphors—is saved from the "monster" bearing down on him only by realizing that it is a "metaphor" that originates in the plurality of his self. His inability later to extend this awareness to encompass the woman he loves will, however, lead to the same malfunction of metaphor that transforms word into destructive act in "Tenants."

In the wake of this first experience of his newfound awareness of other selves, the narrator soon learns that he now can see into the past and future lives of others as well. At a New Year's party he attends with Natasha, he tests his recently acquired faculties in a sort of supernatural parlor game in which he reveals details from the lives of the other guests and predicts the future. Suddenly, before the narrator's eyes alone, the bodies of the other guests begin to undergo a series of grotesque transformations: men sprout female bosoms, women grow beards, hair color changes; wrinkles appear on some, while others appear to turn into children. In short, the boundaries between identities collapse: "Just a little while ago I knew very well which one of them was a thief and which one a bigamist and which one the secret daughter of a fugitive white guard, but now everything was mixed up and in the process of development, and I could not figure out where one person ended and the next began" (191). As it turns out, what the narrator is seeing are apparently past and future incarnations of the guests.

Looking at one of them, an engineer named Belchikov, the narrator discerns prostitutes and priests alternating back into the past at least as far as 237 B.C. and as far into the future as the twenty-fourth century. This vision of Belchikov changing back and forth from male to female, sacred to profane, over the course of some three millennia leads the narrator to conclude that "the human, so to speak, individual, character, personality, and even—if you will—soul—also play no role in life, but there is only the misprint of our vision [*opechatka nashego zreniya*], like the spots in our eyes that arise when we poke them with our fingers or look for a long time at the bright sun without blinking" (193). What we take to be identity is merely an empty hole in the air inhabited at different times by different states, by diverse angles of vision:

> We are accustomed to the idea that people move in the air, which seems to us empty and transparent, while the figures of people, fanned by the wind, have a semblance of solidity and great density. We erroneously transfer this uniform substantiality and completeness of the silhouette, which stands out particularly well against the light and airy background, onto a person's inner world, and call it "character" or "soul." In fact there is no soul, there is only an aperture in the air, and through this opening sweeps past a nervous vortex of disconnected psychic states, which change from occasion to occasion, from epoch to epoch. (193)[11]

This conception of the fragmentation of identity leads the narrator to affirm the multiple personas he carries inside himself, vestiges of past or future states. This realization precludes the possibility of drawing clear boundaries between self and other:

> Everyone of us, if we pay attention to ourselves, will easily discover the most unexpected relapses of past and future states, like, for example, the desire to steal, to kill, or to sell oneself for good money. I can honestly say of myself that at times I have violently experienced in my, if you will pardon the expression, soul far worse urges, and you also will find all of this in yourself in great quantity, if you don't start to dodge and evade shamelessly. The most important thing is not to play the hypocrite, and you will realize that you have no right to say, "He is a thief, while I am an engineer," because at bottom no "I" or "he" exists, and all of us are thieves and prostitutes and perhaps even worse. If you think that you are not, it means that you are temporarily lucky, but in the past, even if it was a thousand years ago, we were all like that or in the future will certainly reach that level, as our sweetest

memories and bitter forebodings ceaselessly reiterate. (193–94)

In the days following the New Year's party the narrator must come to terms with the consequences of his expanded self-awareness. He makes the acquaintance of a motley assortment of previous and future selves, including an Italian man who rapes a corpse, a little boy named Mitya Dyatlov, a woman with a husband and children, the future Vasily, to whom the narrative is addressed, and, perhaps, the future famous writer Boldyrev, who may or may not be the narrator in his present incarnation. Assailed by "fragmentary and unsystematic visions" (197) of his other lives, the narrator runs the risk of losing his present self: "At times in the torrent of memories rushing over me I lost my clarity of thought, who I was [*kto ya takoi*] and where I was located. I began to think that I didn't exist [*chto menya net*], but there was only an endless series of disparate episodes, which had taken place with other people—before me and after me" (198). To get hold of himself—as he puts it, "to restore and certify my authenticity" (198)—he turns to his reflection in the mirror. While apparently seeking affirmation of his self in the image of his physical body, the narrator compares the experience of looking into the mirror to viewing one's own corpse: "It is a feeling of discordancy with that which takes you somewhere outside, while you are located here, inside. Someone, I suppose, sits in us and heatedly protests every time when they try to persuade him that he is the very same person [*lichnost'*] he sees before him. . . . 'No, no, it's not me, not me [*eto ne ya, ne ya*]!'" (198–99).

Standing before the mirror, the narrator finds himself literally playing out the otherness of his reflection when his own image is replaced in the glass by the faces of his other selves. On one occasion, while looking into the mirror, the narrator realizes that one of these others—"a brown man, small, elderly, angular, resembling a bat with folded wings" (200)—is looking back at him. As in the episode with the trolley, he now finds himself seeing through the eyes of an earlier incarnation, and this time looking at himself:

> Desert. Quartz. Sun. A crystal in my fingers. What will happen to me after seventy-five renewals? Will I ask? . . . It's forbidden to ask! I will ask! No one will find out. . . . I see myself. A wise, handsome, leathern head . . . . Who is that? Who is that? White, slippery, bathed in sweat. Resembling a

snail. How disgusting! Some sort of meat in rags. A rope on its neck. Strangled. A monster. He's noticed me. He's looking! He's looking from there!! Is it possible that he sees? He sees, he sees . . . the lips are shaking. And it is I, I [*eto ya, ya*]! That's what I'll be like?!

And almost simultaneously with him, against his dark brown background, I saw myself in the mirror—as he saw me then in his crystal—and the memory of my impression at that time of my current state for a moment pictured him for me: in an unthinkable little jacket, in a tie knotted around his white, mongrel head . . . I, the leathery one, choked with hatred toward the other one, jacketed and jelly-like. And I rushed away from the crystal (from the mirror?)—through the desert (through the room?) and, falling on the bed (on the sand?), covered my face with my hands. It seemed to me that he did the same with his—I no longer know which, leathery or jelly-like?—face . . .

So they met and parted—
—the one who remembered the one
WHO saw
him remember
and the one who saw the one
WHO remembered
that he had seen.

Between them lay a span of five thousand years. There were two of them. But I wasn't among them [*A menya sredi nikh ne bylo*]. (200–201)

The self dissolves in recognizing its plurality.

Just as the narrator turned to Natasha when his powers got out of hand earlier—when he was becoming lost in the changing shapes of the guests at the New Year's party—here his self is saved from complete disintegration by her appearance. She finds him prostrated by his "ordeal by mirror" (199) and asks him how he is: "This tender 'you' [*nezhnyi 'ty'*], uttered by Natasha, referred to me personally, because there was no one but her and me in the room" (201). His love for her becomes the touchstone of his identity: "Next to her I felt myself stronger and more confident in life, which did not seem so inconstant when Natasha, about whom I knew firmly that I loved and love her, was here" (201).

From the beginning of the strange chain of events related by the narrator, however, there are things that remain—fatally, as it would seem—unsaid between the two lovers. While he turns to Natasha to protect the integrity of his self from his new powers of vision, the narrator does not tell her about those powers, about the multiple selves he has found within himself and others, and this silence apparently leads Natasha to misread his intentions at a fateful juncture. There also is something that the narrator initially does not know about Natasha: she is sleeping with Boris. Natasha's affair with Boris, which seems at first glance to be something of a subsidiary narrative embellishment, is in fact a primary motivation of the plot. Natasha is, after all, killed by the icicle when she is on her way to meet Boris. What is more, if we look again at the events that lead to the narrator's expanded vision, we find that he is initially prompted to prod his memory by the revelation that there is something about Natasha—ostensibly her memory of the snowstorm—that he does not already know: "I was a bit hurt, because I thought I knew her through and through. . . . And suddenly it turned out that Natasha's life was more full of events than I had supposed" (182). In light of Natasha's continued relations with Boris and of the changes subsequently undergone by the narrator, this statement comes to appear markedly ambiguous. It is, on the one hand, the realization that Natasha's life is "more full of events" than he thought that triggers his recognition of the multiplicity of his own self. On the other hand, he does not disclose this plurality to Natasha, just as he consistently denies the heterogeneity of her self, emblematized by her secret dalliance with Boris.

The inherent ambiguity of the situation, the semantic interplay of the other lives that the narrator and Natasha hide from one another, comes to the fore in the fourth and penultimate section of the story, as the two lovers flee Moscow by train. The narrator, now apparently at peace with the other selves he has discovered within, continues his ruminations on the implications of this discovery. The trees covered with frost and snow that he sees from the window of the train prompt him to meditate on tropical vegetation that he maintains grew in prehistoric Russia. He finds in the contemporary landscape an "imprint" (*otpechatok*, 207) of the long-extinct past and concludes, "Nothing perishes in nature, but instead everything takes root one in the other, leaves an impression [*otpechatyvaetsya*], hardens" (207). He then extends his hypothesis to himself and to human beings in general:

They say that the human embryo undergoes stages. First—
a fish, then, it seems, an amphibian, then it gradually grows
into the likeness of an ape . . . so that's how it is! Fish and
even frogs are in my body given some opportunity to jump
and run a bit, to show themselves off, to have a look at
people. . . . These are not abstract stages that my organism
passed through when it was a stupid embryo, developing part
by part in the maternal womb. But an absolutely concrete,
live, unique carp was my twin and, so to speak, held my place
in those golden hours—probably the same carp that swam in
the Amazon River 18 million years ago. The remaining fish—
each taken separately—were stowed in others of my contemporaries. (208–09)

This vision of the fish *cum* embryo inside him casts the multiplicity
of the narrator's self as a sort of alternative pregnancy, which becomes an affirmation of immortality as he envisages himself and his
past incarnations in the future: "We will stow ourselves inside some
spacious future citizen. And, I think, this citizen will not remain indifferent to us. He will be a sensitive, polite, advanced person, and
science in those progressive times will tell him in detail about everything. And so, sitting by the window on a quiet summer evening, he
will suddenly feel a restless swarming in his soul. Sudden moods
will spill from his heart, and fantastic ideas will dawn upon his
tired head" (209). The consciousness of alternate selves, of the other
within, thus explicitly appears as the source of "fantastic ideas," a
pregnancy giving birth to metaphor.

While the narrator is now reconciled to, even delights in, the
multiple identities he feels within him, he admits that he is unwilling to recognize the same heterogeneity in Natasha: "She was riding
next to me, remaining immutably the same person she had always
been for me—my beautiful Natasha, and no one else. And although
I could conceive purely speculatively that she also had someone else
inside her, for some reason I did not want to know anything about
it and I thought such a possibility inconceivable. My unfettered fantasy preserved her as the untouched, eternal, unique, and indivisible
Natasha" (210). The significant ambiguity here lies in the narrator's
simultaneous denial of Natasha's multiple selves and of her pregnancy, that is, of the fact that she is carrying another being, fathered
by Boris, inside herself. This confusion of "pregnancies," of the literal

and metaphorical, of what she does not know about him and what he does not want to know about her, results—after an absurdly comical conversation in which the two lovers talk at cross-purposes—in their final separation. The narrator's initial comments, hinting to Natasha without directly explaining to her his sense of "inner fullness" (211), sound like an admission of pregnancy. He asks Natasha if she notices anything different about him, if he looks "fatter" (211). Then, when he goes on to ask her to live with him and have his children, he claims: "I personally, for example, am quite ripe for fatherhood. The same thing has awakened in me that, probably, happens in pregnant women" (211). The narrator's confession prompts Natasha to make a confession of her own, a confession of what the narrator claims to know already, but does not want to hear. The mere mention of Boris's name sets a fatal train of events in motion: "As soon as Boris's name was uttered, I had the thought that he, of course, did not leave us without consequences, and pursuit must be expected at any moment" (212). This thought, moreover, gives rise to the conviction that agents of "some state institution" are already searching the train for the narrator. Still not explaining his motives to her, the narrator flees with Natasha, urging her to jump from the train. She, apparently thinking he is trying to kill her out of jealousy, hesitates long enough for the authorities to catch up with them. As they take him away, he tells her, again without explaining why, not to go to Gnezdnikovsky Lane at ten in the morning on the following Sunday. He immediately realizes, however, that this last warning was a mistake: "And as soon as I expressed this thought, which had been eating away at me all this time, I realized I shouldn't have said it. If I hadn't told Natasha, perhaps it might never have entered her head to go there, and now I was the one who had prepared and marked everything out, and it was no longer possible to call off or redo anything" (215). As he looks at Natasha for the last time, her head cut off from his view by a railway bridge, he professes not to understand why the "little stain" inside her does not respond to his powers of vision: "Why does the rotten little stain, with which she had been infected by Boris, not grow and develop according to the laws of nature? After all, I'm willing to adopt the future child, I'm willing to do anything . . . Why won't it show itself at least in the image of a little fish and wave its future little hand at me in farewell?" (215). This vision confirms that the narrator's words have indeed sealed Natasha's fate, that she will be killed, along with her future child, by the icicle, which will itself be conjured up by the narrator's own words.

The narrator himself admits that perhaps his predictions are self-fulfilling, that his words make the future he claims to foresee: "Indeed all it takes is to start to speak or to think about something, and everything immediately begins. I noticed that a long time ago. Perhaps my predictions come true only because when everything is known—there's no way out, and if we didn't know in advance what was supposed to happen to us, nothing would happen" (211). In fact, the narrator's predictions, viewed closely, appear as a series of similes or metaphors that are ultimately realized. The narrator becomes a modern-day Oedipus, hopelessly fleeing not the prophecies of the Delphic Oracle, but the potency of his own words.

Looking back to the beginning, we find that the narrator's first exhibition of supernatural powers originates out of a simile. Having barely recovered from his regression into the Ice Age, he sees an old woman making her way along the icy boulevard, "swaying like a ballerina" (184). The woman, who falls on the ice as the narrator predicts, turns out in fact to be a retired ballerina, thus in effect becoming what the narrator named her. By the same token, Natasha's fate is set in motion by a metaphor that occurs to the narrator in the wake of the ballerina's accident: "I didn't lead my Natasha, but almost carried her suspended, as one carries a package of eggs from the store. I tried not to remember how eggs break" (185).

The metaphor that kills Natasha is precipitated by his encounter, in the final chapter, with the state security forces. After his arrest, he is taken to prison and put into the charge of Tarasov, a secret police officer who presses the narrator into the service of state security. Although he maintains that he has "accomplished something for the good of the people and of all peace-loving humanity" (217) in his labors with Tarasov, the narrator balks at the colonel's urgings that he use his gifts to uncover "some large conspiracy" (217):

> These plans held little enticement for me—not because I sympathized with conspirators, but simply from the force of the intelligentsia's habit of considering it not completely proper for oneself to catch people and to institute inquiries with the aid of telepathy and clairvoyance. It has always seemed to me that there should be an element of romance and, I would put it, sporting competition in the capture of a criminal. Otherwise espionage and investigation would be turned into a mass production business and would lose all of their luster and attractiveness for our youth. Besides, I still remem-

bered how they had caught me myself not long before, and I was in no hurry to encourage my chief in his far-reaching projects. (217)

Having begged off participating in what, given the setting of the story in the latter years of Stalin's rule, could only have meant the launching of a purge, the narrator finds himself being urged into far more grandiose interventions in the course of history. After working-hours, indulging with the narrator in cognac, Tarasov brings out a map and tries to chart the future course of Soviet conquests. The narrator demurs that divining from maps is not in his "competence" (218) and challenges the colonel's reckless seizure of territory: "Really, I should know better what will happen" (218). When the narrator insists that Australia will fall to "them" only "at a higher stage of historical development," Tarasov begs him to intercede, to speed up historical development and "give Australia a hand" (219). The narrator, however—in a remark that is both disingenuous and cautionary—claims: "He, it seems, was confusing me with the Lord God. But if I was in some small measure omniscient, that in no way entitled me to omnipotence. And what can I do? I know everything and can do nothing. And the more I know, the worse, the less legitimate are the grounds I have for doing anything or relying on anyone" (219). The distinction between word and act drawn here by the narrator focuses the central problem raised by this narrative in which words do make things happen, generally to disastrous result.

The problematic of word and deed played out in "Icy Weather" culminates in the final metaphor conceived by the narrator before he loses his powers. When he looks into Tarasov's incarnations, he finds a very different pattern from the one he discerned in Engineer Belchikov:

> Their [Tarasov's past incarnations'] shapes stretched back into the shadows of the most ancient cultures and hatched out of the darkness in such strict succession that at first they all looked alike to me. But then I noticed the difference: each later one was one rank more prominent than his predecessor. As if they had been born specially to rise one more step in the course of their lives. The most recent colleague came to a halt as a lieutenant-colonel in the reign of Alexander the Emancipator. No one stood closer than him in rank. Colonel Tarasov was the acme of this whole evolution. (220)

Tarasov and his other selves, which in their alikeness represent a denial of the multiplicity of the self, embody the force of will capable of overcoming the natural variety of human nature (represented by Belchikov), the power to remake the world in the image of the word: "In the final analysis—I felt—no Australia, no New Zealand, not to speak of more trivial tasks, could withstand this invincible need for self-perfection, this merging of all actions in one unanimous progress" (220). The narrator's subsequent vision of Tarasov's incarnations to come presents an even more daunting perspective. His vision opens out to the distant future of a planet covered with what appears to be ice: "However, I am using the concept of 'ice' with reservations and sooner figuratively, for we don't know yet what these stalactites and stalagmites, which jutted out everywhere like giant icicles, consisted of" (226). These "giant icicles," the narrator maintains, are living beings, with a descendant of Colonel Tarasov at their head. In the midst of this vision, which apparently coincides with Natasha's death, the narrator's powers disappear. Tarasov, compared by the narrator to an icicle, becomes the icicle that kills Natasha.

The pattern of prediction and fulfillment, of metaphor and realization, out of which the narrative of "Icy Weather" is constructed challenges Marxist pretensions to forecast the future course of historical development. As the narrator remarks when he learns that Boris has died from a disease with which he threatened him in the heat of argument, "even these lies out of my mouth came true" (231). Words, invested with the authority of prediction, become self-realizing. Tarasov, who imprisons the narrator in order to exploit his potentially criminal faculties, embodies the dangerous force that tries to remake the world in the image of a text, destroying Natasha and transforming the world into a future ice age inhabited by artificial creatures made out of "petrified gas or spirit, compressed under high pressure" (226). Tarasov—past, present, and future—is the peril of language control incarnate, the absolute suppression of otherness.[12]

The text of "Icy Weather" itself, a message thrown into the sea which may or may not reach a reader after it is too late to take action to save its author, becomes an emblem of the fragile and unpredictable relationship between text and reader, between language and act. While the narrator initially addresses his "letter to the future" to Vasily, it is Natasha he sees—in what may be either a glimpse into the future or a dream—reading what may be his book. The final words of the epilogue are to her: "The story is not yet finished. I want to say something to you. The last thing I still have the strength for . . . Natasha, I love you. I love you, Natasha. I love you so very, very much" (233). In the narrator's vision, however, Natasha is reading the book only after Vasily is dead, and he fears that she will "again and again slip from my outstretched arms" (223). The narrative becomes not a call to action, not an attempt to turn word into deed, but an expression of love. This redesignation of the text's ideal reader from an alter ego of the narrator to his beloved marks an evolution in Tertz's views which, as we shall see, comes to fruition in his later writings. Here we should note that while in "Tenants" the projected collaboration between narrators—between writer and reader—is suppressed by the unresponsiveness and hostility of the "audience," in "Icy Weather" the text as a written document survives, although it remains in doubt whether it will reach its destined reader.

An implied expression of love is also inscribed in the title of *Lyubimov*, which means "beloved city."[13] *Lyubimov* is both the last of the early Tertz fictional writings and, in a sense, their culmination. The novel develops patterns played out in "Tenants" and "Icy Weather." It harks back to *What Is Socialist Realism* and explicitly traces its genesis to *The Trial Begins*.[14] The novel generally was read by the Soviet authorities as well as by some Western critics as a satire of the Soviet system, yet the political implications of the work are, again, subsidiary to deeper issues of language, control, fantasy, and the self. Like "Tenants" and "Icy Weather," *Lyubimov* enacts the uncontrollability of metaphor in the absence of mutuality and locates the origin of metaphor in the multiplicity of the self. The narrative starts, like *The Trial Begins,* as an official chronicle and ends as a banned text, its original project subverted by the alterity that in Tertz's writings inevitably undermines the pursuit of utopian ideals. Echoing the writer's call at the end of *What Is Socialist Realism* for a "phantasmagoric art with hypotheses instead of a purpose," *Lyubimov* openly proclaims its own "purposelessness": it is the record of an historical experiment that leads nowhere and finally ends up by leaving no trace in history but the narrative itself.[15]

The events related in *Lyubimov* are triggered by disastrous misreadings. The local bicycle mechanic, Lenya Tikhomirov, becomes infatuated with a teacher of foreign languages who came to Lyubimov from Leningrad, Serafima Petrovna Kozlova. Both her background and profession mark her as an outsider. When Lenya divulges his feelings to her, she demands that he lay the town of Lyubimov at her feet, that he make himself into a hero from her reading: "When you come to me on a shield, like Spartacus, crowned with grape leaves, then we'll talk in more detail" (30). The town librarian, Savely Kuzmich Proferansov, who has been secretly listening in on the conversation, warns Lenya against Serafima, pointing out that she is older than he, may even already have children, and is, moreover, a Jewess: "It's better for a Russian man not to get mixed up with Jewesses" (31). Lenya dismisses the librarian's words as "slander and ignorance. For me all nations are equal, and then no Jewish mannerisms have been observed in Serafima Petrovna, and she has the most ordinary, Russian surname—Kozlova, from the simple Russian word 'goat'" (31).[16] Lenya refuses to recognize the alterity concealed behind Serafima's "Russian" name, just as in his utopian experiment he will attempt to deny the unruly "otherness" of the citizens of Lyubimov and even of himself. This blindness will in the end defeat his pursuit both of love and of the ideal state, when what he tries to suppress rises up to defeat him.

After his initial rebuff by Serafima, Lenya, prompted by the librarian, instead of becoming a criminal ("There is only one road for me now—to become an outlaw or a bandit," 31), takes up reading. He begins with books "on the subject of great people: Copernicus, Napoleon, Chapaev, Don Quixote . . . He reread the novel from Roman life *Spartacus* four times." He then turns to works on "nervous psychology and magnetic physics" (32). The role models he finds in his reading define his efforts to become a "hero": Napoleon invokes not only the historical figure himself as conqueror, but also the rich tradition of Napoleonic pretenders in literature from Julien Sorel to Raskolnikov; Chapaev and Spartacus mark him as a populist leader and positive hero. Lenya's attempt to make the provincial backwater Lyubimov into the "center of the world order" parodies Copernicus's redefinition of the sun as the center around which the earth revolves. Most telling, perhaps, is the allusion to Don Quixote, with its suggestion that Lenya, like his fictional predecessor, misreads in attempting to translate his reading into the transformation of life. The book that sets events in motion, however, is presented as a sort of "revealed text," which, as Lenya tells Savely, fell on his head "from the ceiling," where "all sorts of antiquities were dumped in several layers" (33). The tome, entitled *The Psychic Magnet*, purportedly discloses "how to have influence in life by using the cerebral force called 'magnetism'" (34). The book, as Savely guesses, was brought from India by the prerevolutionary *intelligent* Samson Samsonovich Proferansov, whom Savely claims as a common ancestor to both himself and Lenya. Samson Samsonovich, as it turns out, tries to orchestrate both the events of the plot and the narrative of those events from beyond the grave. The meddling spirit later harangues Lenya for abusing the book he has entrusted to him and, at the end, takes it back. Lenya's project appears throughout as an emblem of the uncontrollability of the reading process and of the peril inherent in the transformation of reading into life, word into deed.

Armed with the knowledge garnered from his reading—the "scientific" nature of which he defends by citing such authorities as "Darwin, Jules Verne, and Count Caliostro" (35)—Lenya sets out like a latter-day Don Quixote to build communism in Lyubimov through mind control, which he claims is the key to changing human nature. His rise to power, launched at the town's May Day celebration, tellingly begins with a struggle over language. When Comrade Tishchenko, Lyubimov's leading official, gets up to speak, he finds that he cannot control his own words: "His cracked voice struck like an axe along the square. He would say a word and fall silent, say another and again fall silent, and then would say two more words. As if he were being pulled by the tongue this second to make an extraordinary announcement to the people, but he didn't even have time to collect his thoughts and himself did not understand where the devil was taking him" (21). He even risks strangling himself to cut off the flow of words, but to no avail:

> There he faltered, jumped up and seized himself by the throat—tightly—with both hands, as if he wanted to hold back the speech streaming from there. His eyes goggled strangely. It seemed that any moment he would collapse, suffocated, onto the platform, which clanked and heaved under the kicks of his taut, big body. But, apparently, a power higher than him opened his frozen fingers and withdrew his crooked hands, freeing his flabby, bruised throat from the death grip. He began to resemble a crab with claws pulled apart to the sides and in this impotent pose concluded his address:
> ". . . to elect as supreme ruler, judge, commander," he whispered, his bronchial tubes whistling, "Comrade Tikhomirov, Leonid Ivanovich, hurrah!" (21–22) [17]

The struggle over speech enacted here casts Lenya's social experiment as a form of language control. He suppresses other voices by making all the citizens of Lyubimov speak with the same voice—his own. His challenge to the center becomes an attempt to redesignate the defining center as Lyubimov, whose inhabitants are forced to speak—and act out—his words.

Lenya's rule is officially inaugurated by the public celebration of his marriage to Serafima Petrovna. The biblical allusions embedded in the account of the event intimate the inherent flaw in his project. About to drink the traditional wedding toast, Lenya sniffs his wineglass, sets it back down with distaste, and demands an explanation: "Why do I not see around me the fruits of abundance? Vodka and pickles!" (48). Informed that there is nothing left in the inventory of the town store but mineral water, imported canned red peppers, toothpaste, and vitamin C, Lenya demands that what there is be brought, and, as the narrative proclaims, "A miracle occurred: the water was transformed into alcohol" (49). The motley offerings from the store and from the townspeople become a lavish wedding feast, which culminates in the local river flowing with champagne. As critics have pointed out, these events clearly echo Christ's first miracle, the transformation of water into wine at the wedding at Cana.[18] In the words of Savely, who has now become official historiographer to the new regime and who speaks—according to Lenya—"by inspiration from on high," Lenya has created paradise in Lyubimov: "The age-old dream of the people has come true, has been fulfilled. There they are—rivers of milk and banks of honey! There it is— the Heavenly Kingdom, which it would be more scientifically correct to call a leap into the radiant future [svetlee budushchee]" (53). The irony of this conflation of biblical imagery and Soviet Marxist rhetoric, of this attempt to perform miracles on a scientific basis, is underscored by the fact that, in the Lyubimov the characters survey as Savely utters these words, nothing has in fact changed. Just as Savely's description of the reality of Lyubimov viewed through the prism of the ideal parodies Socialist Realism, so the mineral water, red peppers, toothpaste, and other products only appear, through the power of suggestion Lenya exercises over his subjects, to have changed. The local dogs, who turn up their noses at the "roast meat" that is really hot peppers, attest that the changes wrought by the new leader represent an alteration not of essence, but of perception, a radical dislocation of the relationship between sign and referent. Thus, when an old woman asks for vobla (a type of dried fish) at the wedding feast, Lenya hands her a tube of toothpaste:

> "But where's its head, its air-bladder," the old woman asked in wonderment.

"It's paste, you fool! In simple language, *vobla* dough. With-out bones, without an air-bladder, just the soft part. See, it's written: 'toothpaste.' For people without teeth. For people like you!" (51)

Lenya's usurpation of the sole authority to define stands at the heart of his attempt to create a utopia in Lyubimov—and of the reasons for its failure. He seeks to define the good of humanity simultaneously in terms of the body and in defiance of the physical evidence of the body and ultimately finds language, in concert with the body, rebelling against his control.

His troubles begin at the wedding celebration. The network of children that has been established to patrol the town informs him that a drunk "outsider" (*chuzhoi muzhik*, 50) is making untoward advances to a townswoman. Lenya directs his gaze at the malefactor, who immediately releases his prey:

> The outsider, who in a state of drunkenness had attacked the defenseless Dasha, released her weak body from his clutches and, retreating a step, said:
>
>   "Forgive my unseemly behavior, madam. It will never hap-pen again, I swear it to you on my honor! . .
>
>   And the young woman, torn from the jaws of the lion, instead of raising a ruckus, answered with modesty:
>
>   "It's nothing, it's nothing, please . . . I didn't even have time to notice . . . Here, if you like, is my address and photograph."
>
>   And what might have been a scandal ended in nothing. (50)

Lenya controls the bodies of others by putting his own words in their mouths. The contrast here between attempted rape and linguistic decorum is reminiscent of the clash between real life and the conventions of chivalric romance precipitated by the efforts of Lenya's literary forebear, Don Quixote, to make life conform to the books that have driven him off his head. The texts that Lenya makes others speak generally sound as if they had been lifted from his reading, from a bad Socialist Realist novel or a tract on Marxism–Leninism.

If Lenya manages successfully to use conventional word to sup-press criminal deed in meeting the first potential disruption of the new order, he is hard-pressed to deal with the second, which comes hard on the heels of the first and again involves an "alien." After Lenya's wedding feast, as his new bride is about to embrace him, the child spies again come running, to tell him "an outsider [*chu-*

zhoi chelovek] has died" (54). When they go to examine the corpse, the town physician, Dr. Linde, pronounces the man dead of alcohol consumption. Lenya, although he knows that all the man has had to drink is Kharkov mineral water, does not dispute the diagnosis, assumedly because his admission would reveal the shortfall between seeming and reality on which his putative utopia is based. Yet he is also loath to verify the physical evidence: "But for some reason Lenya did not dare to interfere, or to check whether or not the deceased, as Dr. Linde had declared, truly smelled of alcohol" (54). He is unwilling to face the implications of this fatality, the possibility that he cannot control the effects of his powers, that the words he puts in people's heads can destroy their bodies, can produce results opposite to those which he intended. Lenya's redesignation of mineral water as alcohol acts as a sort of parody of metaphor—which consists, like all metaphors, in calling one thing by the name of another. However, whereas Tertz locates the source of metaphor in the discovery of different voices within, Lenya tries to impose his own voice on others, to pass metaphor off as reality.

The dead man, the single casualty of Lenya's bloodless coup, becomes an emblem of the fatal flaw in his utopian experiment, as Tertz again deploys a biblical allusion to undercut Lenya's pretensions to place himself at the center of meaning. The position of the man's body makes him look like a victim of crucifixion: "The man lay on the ground, his palms spread apart, as if he were Jesus Christ" (54). Despite the invocation of Christ's name, which undercuts Lenya's own claims to be Lyubimov's savior, the reference here might more appropriately be traced to the image of the unrepentant thief crucified with Christ.[19] As the assembled officials of Lyubimov try to identify the body, Savely remembers that he is "not one of ours, not from the town" (55), but "yesterday's thief from the prison" (54). Prompted by the librarian, Lenya himself recalls his encounter with the criminal when he had amnestied him from prison the day before:

> "So is that who you are [*Tak vot ty kto*]?" burst involuntarily from Lenya, and the prisoner in the pale-blue shirt came alive [*ozhil*] in his memory.
> At first he listlessly spat and drawled: "Give me a cigarette, boss . . . Order them to give out grub for the holiday, boss . . . It's due, boss." And then loudly and distinctly, as if he were reading an article in the newspaper, he told how in Melitopol he'd had the luck to filch a gold watch with a bracelet from a

woman working in the snackbar, which he regretted and was
ready to mend his ill-considered act and deep-rooted character. (55)

As he recalls the words he put into the criminal's mouth, words
belied by the latter's subsequent alcoholic debauch, Lenya also remembers his own speech to the freed prisoners: "Be human beings!
Do not steal, do not kill, do not forge documents, and do not commit other crimes that impair your human dignity." . . . "Remember:
Man—that sounds proud [*chelovek—eto zvuchit gordo*]!" (55). Most
striking here is Lenya's implicit equation of illegal language use with
the crimes of murder and theft. The citation from Gorky—Satin's
speech from the *Lower Depths*—with which he ends his harangue
underscores the hackneyed and derivative nature of the words Lenya
dictates to others. It also locates Lenya's utopian aspirations in the
tradition of Gorky's God-building, which denied the existence of
God and put human beings in His vacated place at the center of a
rationalistic, utilitarian cosmology. Continuing in his mind his conversation with the dead thief, Lenya asks the corpse what more he
wanted, why, when he had been "made a human being, did [he] drink
like a pig instead" (55). While his imagined interlocutor has now
been silenced for good, Lenya in a sense simultaneously suppresses
and internalizes the other's voice, and a hint of dissent sounds in
his own words: "No, wait, don't object . . . You wanted freedom?
What more freedom, when you were granted more than enough of
it? Freedom from your own life, from your mind, and from your
fatal human flesh, which, when you drink, becomes light and airy so
that it seems as if you were leaping out of yourself and were soaring
around your body, like some kind of spirit. Well—did you leap out?
Are you free now?" (55).

"There's something I didn't take into account" (55), Lenya concludes out loud. What he has not taken into account is precisely the
urge to be free of the limitations of the body—to assert oneself as
other than the physical self—and the inevitability of death, which
his psychic meddling can bring about but not reverse or annul. Thus,
when Serafima asks him to "resurrect" the dead thief ("Please, resurrect him," 55), he can only exclaim, "Have you all gone out of your
minds! I'm not a miracleworker!" (56). Death marks the insurmountable limit of human aspirations to divinity. Having freed the thief's
body from prison, Lenya does not have the power to free him from
his body. The silent corpse forces Lenya to confront the noncorre-

spondence of the body with the self, forces him to enter into dialogue with the other inside himself, the other that he will become at the end of the narrative.

In *Lyubimov* Tertz poses the same problem raised by Dostoevsky's underground man and reprised in Zamyatin's dystopian novel *We*. Just as the underground man sticks out his tongue at the Crystal Palace, and as Zamyatin's One State is challenged by the square root of minus-one, so Lenya's "scientifically based" utopia is undermined by human irrationality. The episodes discussed above demonstrate that Tertz casts the confrontation between rational self-interest and freedom as above all a problem of language control, which is inevitably undermined by the discrepancy between body and self. The erosion of Lenya's power thus is charted by dissenting voices, coming from both outside and inside himself.

In the fourth and middlemost of the novel's seven chapters, Lenya is compelled to face head-on the problem of competing voices. Upholding the "ancient Russian custom of dragging oneself to the tsar himself for every bit of rubbish" (64), Lenya meets with the petitioners who line up outside his office every morning: "Though there could be no question of needs, because Lenya knew better than the visitors themselves what they needed for complete happiness" (64). A woman who comes to ask for thatch for her cowshed goes away ready to give up her heifer and pig and become a tractor driver. Whether merely by the power of suggestion or by the force of magnetism, Lenya redefines her aspiration, again, putting his words in her mouth. When an American "tourist," who introduces himself as a journalist and claims his nickname is "Old Gangster," turns up among the petitioners and begs Lenya to sell his "discovery," Lenya makes short work of this ideological adversary, forcing the American to spout his own "theses" on "historical development"— an absurd muddle of Soviet political jargon and Russian nationalist platitudes—back to him: "Silently, as if this were not coming from him, Leonid Ivanovich looked at the transformed American, who, like a parrot, repeated everything that was secretly [*neglasno*] dictated to him" (68).

When his own mother shows up in his office, however, Lenya finds that it is not so easy to make her regurgitate his own words. She objects to his plans to tear down the ruins of the local monastery. He responds by trying to implant in her mind the idea that God does not exist and, again, by making her repeat his words back to him: "You are free from the dark fears that have entwined you since childhood, poor mommy. Don't be afraid, don't be afraid of anything: there is no God! And you yourself, yourself with your own senile lips will now utter these beneficial, liberating tidings: there is no God!" (71). On this occasion, however, Lenya's ventriloquism meets with serious resistance. His mother declaims a verbal pastiche in which her words mingle with those inculcated by her son: " 'There is no God,' she said, staring and accompanying her speech with distinct swallowing pauses, like hiccups. 'There is no God. The Prophet Elijah has been shot down. Electricity. Thunder is from electricity. Lenyushka, eat some curds with sour cream. You're thin as a rail, transparent . . . There is no God. And there are no heavenly angels either. No cherubim. Eat, little son, restore your strength. You've grown thin, Lenya, turned black . . . There is no God. Curds, curds with sour cream . . .'" (71–72). The voice of his mother's concern for him, which he is unable to drown out, calls forth a discordant voice within Lenya himself:

> There was in her appeal to eat such importunity, such pity for his famished thinness that it suddenly seemed to him that if he were to kill his mamma by slow and agonizing torture, even then she would not forget to say before her death: "Curds, curds, Lenyushka, eat . . ." And when the last faith in God on earth is extinguished and the whole crowd of us falls into the power of Satan, only this unnatural, maternal incantation will remain to us in memory of our bitter loss. "Stop!" he suddenly caught himself, "Where's the loss? Where did loss come from? What absurd thoughts are getting into my head! What is this 'whole crowd,' what 'Satan,' what curds with sour cream? (72).

In the wake of his mother's visit and this discovery of the dissonant voice within himself, Lenya finds himself confronting the disembodied voice of the elder Proferansov, who berates him for abusing the book that he, Samson Samsonovich, has temporarily put at Lenya's disposal. The elder Proferansov thus proclaims Lenya a poor reader while simultaneously representing the voice, divorced from body, that Lenya cannot control.

As his powers, overextended, start to wane, Lenya begins to seek out the voices of others. He goes incognito into the town pubs, among the townsmen taking their daily ration of mineral water *cum* vodka. When he asks one bar patron—"a legless war invalid who had already drained his legal glass and was clinging to a second, evidently acquired illegally with a stolen coupon" (91)—what he thinks of the political situation, the man complains that the alcohol to be had in the town is "counterfeit, gotten from normal water by means of hypnosis" (91). He knows it is fake, he tells Lenya, because "you drink and drink this fascist brew, and all the same your head doesn't ache from a hangover. Is that really booze?" (91). The man's comical logic challenges the whole basis of Lenya's experiment, from the dictator's usurpation of the right to define the relationship between sign and referent to his assumption that corporeal needs dictate humanity's highest good. Alcohol without the requisite after-effects is not alcohol, no matter what it is called, just as pleasure without pain remains unsatisfying.

Echoing Savely's words earlier, the invalid furthermore asserts that "the tsaritsa is a Jewess" (92). While before Lenya was unwilling to listen to the librarian, he now, for the first time, asks Serafima about her background. Not only does she tell him that she is, in fact, half Jewish, but this first revelation lets loose a string of other admissions: a previous marriage, a daughter in Leningrad, and a long list of past love affairs. Having unleashed this flood of confession, Lenya becomes obsessed with it. He neglects affairs of state and spends days on end forcing Serafima to recite to him every detail of her past life and then ordering her to be silent and forget everything, repeating over and over this cycle of eliciting and then suppressing her words. He pursues "with the persistence of a geologist" his "scientific work," his research "into the deep mines of the female soul overflowing with love" (94), eventually going beyond merely listening to her obediently dredge up for him all the details of her various loves to "remov[ing] the psychic blockade and observ[ing] the development of the woman in natural conditions" (94). He finds himself caught between two Serafimas—the one he can control and does not want and the one he wants and cannot have: "How he loved her in those fatal minutes! How he craved the reciprocal love, sympathy, and approval of the arrogant beauty, of *this* one [*etoi*], and not of the one [*toi*] who in another state wearied him to death with her submissive gaze, dog-like in its devotion. But in order to work her up and put her beside herself [*vyvesti iz sebya*] and all the same attain a merger of *this one* and *that one* [*toi i etoi*], Lenya reminded her what kind of tsaritsa she was if all he had to do was move his eyebrows a bit and she would crawl on the parquet floor like the lowest scum" (95). The bifurcation of Serafima emblematizes the unruliness of the self, which eludes control. No amount of psychic tinkering can produce unity from plurality, the ideal from the real. Lenya's goal slips from his grasp just as he seems to have attained it, paralleling the failure of the utopian experiment into which Serafima initially lured him.

Her words finally degenerate into a muddle of nonsense combining her own voices with the dissident voices of the citizens of Lyubimov and heralding her own flight from the town and the suppression of Lenya's insurrection by forces from the center: "Ai-yai squinting devil caress me squinting devil have mercy puny creature burns sweetly to give birth to puppies with fangs of Feuchtwanger I cannot distribute pants tanks are coming I will extract the cyst tanks are coming I want to bite off crested we run to Leningrad!" (95). Thus, as exemplified in Serafima, Lenya's attempt to remake human nature finally results in a disintegration of personality mirrored in a complete failure of language.

In the end, just before the tanks come from outside, Lyubimov is destroyed from inside, as Lenya, having lost control of everyone else, finally loses control of himself, and his powers run wild. As he walks through the town, he overhears the woman who once wanted to be a tractor driver using his popular nickname, "the Squint-eyed one" (103) and mentally calls her a "witch" (104). His metaphor is immediately realized. When he turns back to look at her again, she is astride a broom, and the moment he wonders, "Will she really take off?" (104), she indeed soars into the air. Lenya's powers, as it turns out, have returned one last time in full force, and his every thought, even those "whose presence he didn't suspect" (104) is played out before his eyes:

> Only his own thoughts could not be kept in check, and the tiniest little thought, an imperceptible cerebral flourish, any foolishness that popped into his head, was immediately acted out by the people around him.
>
> Does a human being really have control over his soul? Can he take into account all the caprices of fantasy that seethe in his mind? He ordered the population, "Comrades, don't panic!" and himself at the same time realized, looking at a huge fellow: "What a bull!" And the lanky man immediately began pawing the ground with the heels of his heavy shoes and, frowning, bellowed like a bull and butted passersby, who calmly endured his blows (after all they had been told, "don't panic"), which confused and complicated the situation even more. (104).

As chaos breaks out among the townspeople, and even domestic animals fulfill his mental commands, Lenya exclaims to the man acting like a bull, "Drop dead, cursed man!" (105), and the man immediately falls dead. Attempting to bring order, Lenya tries to give the command "Sleep!" (*usni*), but "against his will" it comes out "Die" (*umri*, 105), and others perish, brought down—like the thief before them— by the power of Lenya's words made deeds. Every time he almost manages to bring the situation under control, a "voice whispers" inside him some new mental vagary, and confusion erupts anew. As he stands on the sidelines, afraid that "if he were to say one superfluous word, make one unpremeditated gesture . . . it seemed, the town of Lyubimov would be torn from its place and would set off squatting through the forests and swamps" (105), the "witch" on her broom appears soaring above, repeating word for word the linguistic nonsense to which Serafima was reduced earlier. The townspeople are released once and for all from Lenya's power as tanks plow into the town. Thus, the uncontrollable voice of the other within Lenya himself gives rise to metaphor, which is realized and ruinously turned into action. Its power is suppressed only by the imminent arrival of another defining authority. By the end of the novel, Lenya has become the very other that he has tried to root out in his attempt to remake human nature. He is a murderer and an attempted thief (he tries to pry off one of the hundred-ruble notes with which he papered his office when he abolished money in Lyubimov), he wants a drink, and he plans to restart his life elsewhere under "someone else's [*chuzhoi*] passport" (110).

As much as the novel *Lyubimov* is about the town after which it is named, it is also, like virtually all of Tertz's narratives, about the text itself, about its own eponymous production.[20] Lenya Tikhomirov begins as a positive hero trying to remake the world in his own image and winds up as precisely that which he strove to suppress. In like fashion, the novel *Lyubimov* begins as an authorized chronicle and ends up as a banned text. Lenya's experiment is subverted by competing voices, and the initial course of the narrative itself is undermined by the collaboration and rivalry of two narrators, whose sometime contention and ultimate cooperation stand as a paradigm for the multiplicity of the narrative self.[21]

The first narrator we meet is Savely Proferansov, who, although he admits to having read banned books himself, presides over a reading-room that lends readers only works that have not been proscribed by instructions "from the center" (15). Savely, like the narrators of "Tenants" and "Icy Weather," is a reader turned writer. In 1926, when Savely was a youth, a "professor" who came to the town to excavate the remains of the local monastery had encouraged him to record Lyubimov's history. Decades later Lenya's takeover provides him with a "story."[22] Having become in the interim an avid reader, Savely describes his preferences in literature at the outset:

> Only one thing is sad—when a writer suddenly sets out into fantasy. There you sit, suffering, and perhaps with shivers running down your spine, while he, it turns out, has thought this all up out of his head. No, if you've undertaken to write, then write about what you yourself have seen or at least heard from reliable sources. So that the reader's soul, traveling through the pages, does not spoil its precious sight in vain, but receives reliable and useful information for inner development. It wants to live, that soul does, to live and grow rich, its eyes sucking out of a book someone else's [*chuzhuyu*] warm blood, and not empty air. (17)

Savely here postulates authenticity and utility, which he views as equivalent, as the values that define the worth of a work of literature. His claims for his own text, however—that it is both a scholarly historical chronicle and an eyewitness account of actual events—are undercut by the blatant "fiction" in his "science." *Lyubimov* the novel, like the fictive town of Lyubimov itself, turns out in the end to be no more than "empty air."

Savely's project is subverted immediately by an intrusion from outside. Echoing Galkin's creed in "Graphomaniacs," Savely expresses his wonderment that, as he is writing, the words seem to originate from somewhere outside himself:

> You write and you don't understand what's happening to you and where all these words are coming from, which you have never even heard of and didn't think of writing, but they of themselves suddenly popped up from under your pen and struck out swimming, swimming in single file [*gus'kom*] along the paper, like some sort of ducks, like some sort of geese [*gusi*], like some sort of black-winged Australian swans . . .
>
> At times what you write is such that you are seized by fear and the fountain pen[23] slips from your fingers. I didn't do that [*Ne ya eto*]! Word of honor, I didn't! But you read it over and you see: everything is correct, everything did happen like that . . . Lord! What is this? I have no direct part in this business! Perhaps, like this whole dear bewitched town as well, I am only set in motion by someone's invisible hand? . . .
>
> If stern judges call me to account, shackle my arms and

legs in irons, I warn in advance: I will renounce all of this; without a second thought, I'll renounce it. I'll say, Oh, citizen judges, I was swindled, confused. Shoot me if you want, but I'm not guilty! (18)

Savely here describes writing as a form of "self-elimination." The writer loses himself in writing and therefore cannot be held legally accountable.

Savely soon finds himself engaged in an all-out struggle for control of his own text. As he writes, he is interrupted by a dissenting voice that pops into the narrative against his will and challenges his command of his pen. After some bickering between the two would-be narrators, the interloper introduces himself as the professor who originally encouraged Savely to write years before and reveals that he is in fact the disembodied spirit of Samson Proferansov, from whom Lenya received the fateful book that set the story in motion. Just as Lenya later, when conversing with the voice of Samson, seems to be talking to himself, so Savely speculates: "Perhaps from all these experiences, bifurcation has begun in my head, and I'm conversing here, not with you, not with the professor, but with myself" (38). The confusion is underscored by the identity of their surnames:

> "My name is Proferansov."
> "No, now if you please! . . . My name is Proferansov! Indeed I said, I said it was not with you, but with myself that I was conversing." (39)

Samson Samsonovich personifies the bodiless voice of the other, the same voice that undermines the narrative's legal status and Lenya's utopia. It is, moreover, a voice that transcends the boundaries of chronology, since not only is Samson Proferansov a ghost from another century, but his biography, as later told by Savely to Lenya, fantastically violates any credible chronology.

The wrangling over the text by Savely and Samson tellingly begins as a conflict between text and footnotes.[24] When Savely initially introduces the footnotes that appear throughout the text of *Lyubimov*, he justifies them as a means of structuring the text— "In order not to get scattered, in historical books and chronicles, as is customary, special notes are set up, situated below, under the page" (18–19)—and as a means of distinguishing the "main content" from the "little secondary notes" (19). The disjunction between the scholarly convention of the footnote, heightened by the apparently arbitrary selection of material that Savely periodically relegates to the notes, and the fantastic events of the narrative runs as a comic leitmotif throughout. The footnotes, however, far from being merely a curious structural eccentricity, serve to orchestrate graphically the interplay of voices in the text. Thus, when Savely refuses simply to allow the voice from outside to dictate words to him, Samson offers to work with him, suggesting the footnotes as an analogy for their collaboration:

> "Ach, Savely Kuzmich, really how insufferable you are. . . Well, all right, all right, we'll write jointly, in layers.
> "In layers!"
> "Yes, in layers. The tricks [*fokusy*] of Russian history demand flexibility, multi-layered writing. Do you remember— at the excavations, in the monastery, one historical stratum is exposed after another: soles from the 18th century, broken pots from the 16th? It's the same thing here. One cannot dig up everything on one level . . . You yourself continually resort to footnotes, to digressions, dig burrows, cellars for the preservation of facts." (37–38)

The footnotes, like the excavation of Lyubimov's monastery and like Lenya's excavation of Serafima's soul, expose the variegated strata of voices which Lyubimov, town and narrative, comprises. Like the narrative itself—which alternates between first-person narration, sometimes by Savely and sometimes by Samson, and third-person narration, which apparently results from a merging of their two voices—the footnotes come to represent, in relation to the text proper, the possibility of alternative centers of meaning, differing points of view, dissenting voices.

The distinction between the page and the region "under the page" becomes, moreover, a means of mimicking the spatial disposition of the actors in the plot, of creating a graphic and metaphorical division between "above" and "below." The final footnotes in the novel clearly identify the space "under the page" as a sort of subversive underground. The last note, foreshadowing the fate of the manuscript of *Lyubimov* itself, tells of the secretion of banned books "under the cupboard in the public library" (95). The counterpoint between the penultimate series of footnotes and the text proper is not only the most daring use of the footnotes to mirror graphically the space of the plot, but also the most explicit representation of metaphor as a response to repression, as a means of challenging authority in Tertz's early works. As forces from the center bomb Lyubimov, Lenya's role shifts from that of dictator to that of dissident, and he is moved off the page into the footnotes as the planes in the air—in the text—bear down on him and the town:

> Imagine first—high, high in the sky—a dive bomber . . . [1]
> The bomber, imagine, dives with horrifying speed . . . [2]
> . . . from the murderer.
> He, still diving, notices with amazement . . . [3]
>   . . . into the snout of the beast, ready to drive its claws . . . [4]
> . . . and stuck the spears of their pointed summits into the sky. As if . . . [5]
>   . . . the roaring airplane . . . [6]
>   . . . above:
> "Go away, you whore, go away, bitch, if not you'll be in for it! . . .

---

[1] . . . and here, below—a man thrown down, lying on his back.

[2] . . . downwards, directly into the face, which does not lower its intense gaze . . .

[3] . . . that beneath him are disposed not the structures of the town with the face distorted from fear, but remote forests, here and there sweating out swamps and ravines. It was Lenya, who despairing in the face of death, strained his pupils and flung them . . .

[4] . . . into his eyes, which, like the trunks of giant larches, rose . . .

[5] . . . the earth itself, planted with spikes, rocked and shook, in wild fanaticism, broke through, went to meet . . .

[6] . . . shouting at it from below . . . (87–88)

This confrontation between airplane and man, between text and footnotes, becomes a clash between the forces of authority and metaphor. The disappearance of the town of Lyubimov before the eyes of the bomber pilot, the transformation of Lenya's frightened face into a desolate landscape of forests and swamps, realizes the earlier comparison of face to topography that the narrative ironically locates in the pilot's mind:

His [Lenya's] face, stretched along the cobbles, the whole width of the market square, served as an excellent target, and the pilot knew that it is just as simple to finish off a man lying on his back as to blow up a forest wasteland with a bomb. That's it precisely, he knew, and saw that Leonid Ivanovich's sunken cheeks would burn as easily as the slopes of ravines overgrown with dry spurge. That his lips, dotted with knobs of swampy eruptions, had no power to avert a blow inflicted on them. That his eyes . . . Wait! What comparison should we urgently think up for human eyes, which have no other weapon but this despair directed upwards, at the enormous steel thing, falling with each instant, no, with each thousandth of an instant? (87)

The narrative asks, "Is it worth trying to shield our toppled hero with a clumsy, old-fashioned metaphor?"—and immediately answers: "But where is the justice?! They have airplanes, newspapers, magazines, radio, madhouses, the telephone, while we have—nothing, well, you understand, nothing at hand. Naked imagination. So how could we, pressed against the ground and awaiting the hour of death, not fling ourselves to meet it and not poke the first monstrous bleeding hyperbole that comes into our head into the roaring snout?!" (87). Thus the metaphor realized in the "underground" of the footnotes becomes an emblem of language as a means of subversion, whose strength lies not in physical force but in the possibility of transforming the way we see the body.

Lyubimov is, in a sense, itself a realized metaphor. A curious, seemingly gratuitous detail slips into the opening description of the environs of the town: "And although Doctor Linde continues to try to prove to everyone that one day at twilight he ran across a prehistoric pterodactyl rather than a black grouse, it's all invention [*vymysel*], humbug, and there's nothing like that in our parts" (14). The pterodactyl pops into the narrative again some pages later as Savely laments that the words he puts down on paper are not his own, that they come from someplace outside him: "There it is again! Where did that alien word [*chuzhdoe nam slovo*] fly in from? I don't even know how to pronounce it, this pterodactyl, and, after all, as I said—nothing of the sort is found in our parts. Scat! Scat! Fly away, vile creature!" (18). This fantastic pterodactyl appears in the flesh, so to speak, hovering over Colonel Almazov, the official sent from outside to put down the rebellion in Lyubimov, as he lies dying from a "deliverance powder" (60) he has apparently taken in the wake of the failure of his mission. As Sinyavsky observes in the interview cited in the second epigraph to this chapter: "The mammoth is extinct, but it did exist and we can still admire its form, although we never set eyes on it. But it did exist; that's what is so marvellous. Yet had some terrible, all-powerful creator decided, 'The mammoths will die out eventually anyway, so let's do away with them now,' there would have been no mammoths, no mastodons, nothing at all from the past—and all destroyed in the name of the Future, in the name of the Final Objective."[25] The pterodactyl that intrudes into the text of *Lyubimov* is just such a fantastic, extinct creature, an image of art flying in the face of teleology, simultaneously preservation and pure invention.[26] Savely's manuscript—hidden under the floorboards from the repression that has come in the wake of the tanks ploughing through Lyubimov, "trampling down and hewing out passages for the future" (107)—his fantastic chronicle of a town that never was and a utopian experiment that led nowhere, is just such a "purposeless" beast, what Savely himself dismissed as "empty air." Yet, paradoxically, as an incarnation of the "alien word," it is dangerous, persecuted, perceived as a threat by the powers that be—criminal.

Each of the texts examined in this chapter exposes the noncorrespondence of the self with itself, the plurality of points of view encompassed by the consciousness of the single individual which belies the oneness of the body. As we see particularly clearly in *Lyubimov*, the heterogeneity of the self undermines attempts to construe human good exclusively in terms of the body as well as all claims to an absolute authority to define the relationship between word and referent. Metaphor, which arises from the juxtaposition of multiple angles of vision, is therefore inherently subversive, criminal, in relation to totalizing systems of meaning. On the other hand, in the absence of an active collaboration between reader and text, metaphor malfunctions. The second term of the comparison, that to which the original entity is likened, parts company with the first and takes on a destructive life of its own: the narrative of "Tenants" is cut off by creatures spawned by its own metaphors; Natasha is killed by the metaphorical icicle conceived by the narrator of "Icy Weather" himself; and the town of Lyubimov is thrown into chaos by Lenya's realized metaphors. Here Tertz elaborates in fictional form Sinyavsky's analysis of the workings of language in Stalinist society, to which he made reference at his trial and on which he expands in the chapter entitled "Stalin: The State-Church" in *Soviet Civilization*. In that work he writes:

> Lenin, of course, was speaking metaphorically when he used the term "agents of the bourgeoisie" to describe Mensheviks or Western Social Democrats; or when he accused them of "selling" the interests of the working class. But Stalin took everything literally: an "agent of the bourgeoisie" equalled

an actual spy. In this sense, the trials and executions of the thirties were nothing other than literal translations of Leninist metaphors. On Stalin's orders, the Soviet Chekists and investigators began torturing people arrested as agents of the bourgeoisie so that they would confess to spying for the Japanese, the Germans, or the English. The metaphor was taken to its real-life conclusion.[27]

As we shall see, in *Goodnight* Tertz himself becomes a realized metaphor spawned by the suppression of dialogue in Stalinist society.

The three texts examined here present alternative models of discourse that counterpose or condemn the failure of dialogue from which the literalization of metaphor stems. In "Icy Weather" the text is transmuted from a call to action into an expression of love. At the end of "Tenants," the house spirit tries unsuccessfully to convince the writer to pray. By the same token, in *Lyubimov*, Lenya's mother's prayer constitutes the only words that truly have their intended effect: Samson Samsonovich's spirit is released from his body. In Tertz's later works, prayer and the intimate letter to the beloved woman recur as paradigms for the aspirations of the literary text. Yet, just as Savely Kuzmich is left alone with his criminal manuscript by the translation of his coauthor's soul, so the text, despite its aspiration to attain an ideal form of communication, remains trapped in the fallen world. As the later works of Tertz suggest more explicitly only by acknowledging the free play of difference, by encouraging a creative mutuality between reader and text, can the literary work reestablish the boundaries between life and art and stem the destructive force of literalized metaphor.

Chapter Six

. . . .

"It Is Forbidden to Write Like That":
Thoughts Unawares and
A Voice from the Chorus

The wind rustles at midnight and carries away leaves . . . So life also in fleeting time plucks from our soul exclamations, sighs, half-thoughts, half-feelings . . . Which, being scraps of sound, have that significance that they "descended" directly from the soul, without being reworked, without a goal, without premeditation—without saying anything foreign . . . Simply—"the soul lives" . . . i.e. "lived," "died" . . . For some reason I have for a long time been fond of these "unexpected" exclamations. Strictly speaking, they flow uninterruptedly inside of us, but it is impossible to note them all down, and they die. Then for the life of you you cannot remember them. However, I have managed to note down a bit on paper. What was jotted down kept accumulating. So I decided to collect these fallen leaves.

—VASILY ROZANOV, *Solitaria*

The aphorisms, meditations, scraps of overheard conversations, and anecdotes collected under the title *Thoughts Unawares* (*Mysli vrasplokh*) and the compilation of excerpts from Sinyavsky's letters to his wife *A Voice from the Chorus* (*Golos iz khora*) belong to distinctly different periods of Tertz's evolution and are quite dissimilar in scope. Yet *Thoughts Unawares*, composed during the period of Sinyavsky's illicit tamizdat career, anticipates the more mature and ambitious *A Voice from the Chorus*, written during the years of Sinyavsky's incarceration at Dubrovlag. Both challenge conventional genre classifications, experimenting with what I would term structured formlessness in an attempt to confront the problems posed a priori by the representation of the self. Eschewing plot and character, the two texts formally mimic the instability of the self, which dissolves in its own plurality—its noncorrespondence with itself over time—and in the permeability of the boundaries between self and other. Both texts thus embody the conception of writing as "self-elimination" adumbrated by the poet Galkin in "Graphomaniacs." Challenging the illusory unity imposed on the self by ideologies, formal structures, and systems, both *Thoughts Unawares* and *A Voice from the Chorus* postulate the true self—the pure soul liberated from the body—as an emptiness. Yet while *Thoughts Unawares*, in the face of its recognition of the self as negation, concludes by asserting the impossibility of its own project, the impossibility of the representation of the self, *A Voice from the Chorus* affirms art's vocation to transform the "I" into the "not-I." It celebrates the text as imposture.

A number of critics have recognized the indebtedness, both formal and conceptual, of *Thoughts Unawares* and *A Voice from the Chorus* to the writings of the turn-of-the-century Russian religious thinker Vasily Rozanov. Sinyavsky's study of Rozanov, entitled *"Opavshie list'ya" V. V. Rozanova* (V. V. Rozanov's "Fallen Leaves"), his only book-length work on a single writer signed with his own name, represents a tacit admission of Rozanov's importance to his own literary and philosophical development. A brief survey of this work will help to pinpoint issues relevant to an understanding of the two Tertz writings.[1]

In the chapter appropriately titled "The Apotheosis of Formlessness," Sinyavsky suggests the significance of the form of the book *Fallen Leaves* as an approach to representing the self: "Aphorisms—as a genre, as a literary form—free the author from the necessity of laying out his thoughts consecutively and gradually, in the form of some system or doctrine, in the form of cohesive narrative. Aphorisms, as a genre, presuppose discontinuity. Aphorisms presuppose as it were that the author's 'I' is multi-faceted and many-faced. It is impossible to write aphorisms entirely on one theme. Aphorisms are always characterized by a diversity of thoughts, a diversity of subjects."[2] The form of the text thus imitates the construction of the self as a process unfolding in time, as a series of discontinuous moments that jostle and sometimes contradict one another, eluding reduction to any external ideology. Sinyavsky portrays the inconsonances in Rozanov's writing in terms of metaphors of organic growth: "It is such contradictoriness that for him comes closest to the natural state of the human being, who, like a tree, sends out roots in several directions at once, who grows like living thought and does not follow a course chosen once and for all" (66). *Fallen Leaves* then becomes a formal extrapolation of this metaphorical tree of the self:

Fallen Leaves is not simply the title of the book, but a definition of genre. And this, as in the case of the definition of any
genre, defines the way the book is written and the method of
its existence. A tree grew, a human being lived, and he lived
by the foliage of his thoughts, of his sometimes random emotional experiences. And these sprouts become detached from
him, like falling leaves. That is, speaking in literary terms, the
leaves fall as sheets of paper, scraps of paper, which the writer
covers with records of his thoughts. And he does this periodically, from day to day, and at the same time does it rather
randomly, unpremeditatedly, in passing, composing nothing
specially and not even imputing any particular significance to
these random records. (111–12)

The writer's embrace of "randomness" marks a relinquishment of
conscious control over his text, a repudiation of externally imposed
structure in the interests of arriving at the existential actuality of
the self. Yet, significantly, the very mode of the text's embodiment
exposes the unbridgeable gap between self and representation. The
leaves that fall from the tree of the self are, by definition, *dead* leaves.[3]
The reproduction of the self in the body of the text is thus a form of
death, an alienation from the living process of development.

Yet, while the metaphor invoked in the title of *Fallen Leaves* acknowledges the inherent impossibility of reincarnating the self in the
discarded body of the text, the text nonetheless challenges the conventional boundaries of representation. The undertaking to record
without prejudice or preconception, hiding nothing, inevitably takes
the writer over the border into territory traditionally closed to literature. Rozanov "overcame the literary tradition that expected an
author to appear in print tidied up" (123), Sinyavsky maintains; he
"does nothing but undress and bare himself before us" (220), taking
us not only into the "kitchen," but into the bedroom with frank
discussions of sexuality. It was precisely Rozanov's "nakedness," according to Sinyavsky, that called forth the rancor of his critics: "Indeed one does get the sense from *Fallen Leaves* that in it Rozanov
reached some final boundary and even crossed over it in his ability,
philosophizing about this and that, to be naked or, so to speak, to appear 'in negligee.' Rozanov's contemporaries, who protested against
the publication of such books as *Solitaria* and *Fallen Leaves*, experienced the same emotion even more keenly. As much as to say, it is
forbidden [*nel'zya*] to write about that, the writer has no right to

bare himself to that extent!" (217). The baring of the self thus goes
hand in hand with the conception of art as transgression, becoming
a means of simultaneously revitalizing literary form and redefining
the relationship between reader and text: "[Rozanov] places the book
in the position—'It is forbidden [nel'zya]': 'It is forbidden to write
such things.' He thereby produces, as it were, a renewal of genre and
creates the illusion that he is utterly frank with his readers" (223).

The word that should most readily draw our attention here is
"illusion." Sinyavsky, throughout his discussion of Rozanov, repeatedly makes the point that Rozanov the "hero" of *Fallen Leaves*, the
literary character, is not identical to the flesh-and-blood Rozanov:
"Rozanov's prose leaves us first and foremost with the image of
Rozanov himself—not the author, not the creator, but the character in *Fallen Leaves*. Before us appears the character or image of
the hero, which should not be confused with the author's 'I' of the
writer, although, of course, the origin of this image has its source in
the author's 'I'" (147). Paradoxically, then, Rozanov's presentation
of himself before the reader "naked" ("I am portraying myself as I
am in fact—naked!" (218)) is a "mask" that "becomes a form of self
revelation" (173).

Sinyavsky consequently explicates Rozanov's representation of
himself in *Fallen Leaves* as a polemical strategy with implications
that include but transcend the narrowly political. Rozanov, in Sinyavsky's reading, presents himself in his prose in deliberately "lowered" and "exaggerated" terms: "And for him the human being on
earth is small. With this tendency of his book and of his style Rozanov in the literature of the beginning of the century withstood the
high-flown thesis, famous at the time, the aphorism that belonged
to Maxim Gorky: 'Man—that sounds proud'" (237). As in *Lyubimov*,
Sinyavsky invokes Satin's words from *The Lower Depths* as a catch-
phrase that conjures up the entire rationalistic and utilitarian tradition in Russian thought, which placed the human being, rather
than God, at the center of the universe. Sinyavsky thus portrays
Rozanov's "smallness" in relation to God as a rebellion against the
reduction of human beings to political bodies and the concurrent
constriction of literature to social tract. Rozanov, he claims, rejects
"politics, which conceives humanity in terms of abstractions and
parties, in general categories (they sold themselves to the Bolsheviks
or they sold themselves to world capital). By appealing to the human
being as a private person he stands counter to this sort of politics
and hence the higher meaning, the statement that this private person

makes out of household articles" (233). Rozanov's representation of himself "naked" and "small" becomes a literary strategy designed to reclaim the self from abstract categories by transgressing into the realm of intimacy: "Intimacy is both the sphere of battle with public spirit and a principle of style" (107).

There is, in this context, a certain irony in Sinyavsky's allusion to Gorky's words—which Sinyavsky treats less as a quotation than a stock phrase—as an "aphorism." Although he refers to Rozanov's "leaves" as aphorisms "in order to underscore their disjunctiveness and fragmentariness" (190), he is careful to distinguish them from what he considers traditional aphorisms:

> An aphorism, in principle, is a ready-made formulation. But the distinctiveness of Rozanov's thought and prose consists precisely in his refusal to think or write in ready-made formulations. An aphorism is always something congealed. But Rozanov's notes grasp thought on the wing, in the process of its birth, of movement, in the process of speech and in the process of recording it. Hence the particular fluidity of Rozanov's prose. An aphorism is a crystal, usually a polished crystal. But Rozanov's prose is a river with many confluences, with many forks. Therefore Rozanov's aphorisms both exist and do not exist in isolation, but reside in the context of neighboring, adjacent, and distant entries. (191)

Rozanov's rejection of standardized language, moreover, corresponds to the destabilizing context in which the aphorisms are presented: "They clash, argue, and flow one into the other" (191).

Just as Rozanov seeks to transform the relationship between reader and text by drawing the reader into the intimate sphere of private life, so "he attempts to knock the reader out of the routine, usual rut through the very way he poses questions and through the form of his exposition" (247). Sinyavsky recognizes the idiosyncrasies of Rozanov's writing as a form of estrangement: "The device of estrangement is important as a means of freeing the reader's perception from its habitual automatism, from clichés of literature, everyday life and language, as a means of refreshing, of renewing the reader's vision" (250). He pits Rozanov against cliché taken in its broadest sense as that which must be overcome "if we want to get through to the soul of the human being, to the soul of the world. . . . Cliché excludes the individual face, abolishes the separate person with his soul and love, levels the world and style, imposing dead abstraction on everything. Cliché for Rozanov is in some sense equivalent to death. And death is his main enemy and main fear. And correspondingly, the accession of the bureaucratic phrase, the accession of cliché, threatens Rozanov with destruction. Therefore, even though he was a conservative and loved Russia fervently, Rozanov was deeply alien to bureaucratic patriotism, official cliché" (248). All systems, including conventional moral dictates, imposed on the self from without turn human beings themselves into clichés—"clichéd people" (*zashtampovannye*, 265). Sinyavsky thus opposes Rozanov's works to the socially tendentious strain in Russian literature by maintaining that Rozanov's writings seek neither to teach nor to harangue the reader, but rather to transform the nature of the reading process: "Rozanov does not require that people, in reading his books, change their views on life. He desires changes as it were in the very makeup, in the structure of the soul of readers, and he employs as synonyms the concepts 'crumbliness,' 'friability' of the soul, and its 'expansion' to the point of being able to 'breathe everything' and to 'absorb everything into itself'" (242). The reader is thus to be shaken out of clichéd systems of thought, out of clichéd constructions of the self, and opened up to the possibility of reclaiming the messy, at times counterrational, contradictory, and paradoxical diversity of the self inscribed in the very "formlessness" of Rozanov's writings.

Throughout *V. V. Rozanov's "Fallen Leaves,"* Sinyavsky views the work within the context of its time, as an embodiment of Rozanov's "repudiation of the heritage of the [18]60s and '70s" (187), that is, of the tradition of the radical critics and their intellectual progeny. By the same token, *Thoughts Unawares*, as something of an appropriation of Rozanov's strategies to a later historical context, challenges both formally and conceptually the hegemony of the public discourse of Marxism-Leninism and Socialist Realism in the Soviet Union at the time of its composition. Like *Fallen Leaves* it is an exercise in writing as "it is forbidden to write," transgressing into the forbidden realms of sexuality and religion and thereby drawing the reader into an intimate relationship with the text. Likewise, by renouncing traditional structures of character and plot and asserting the "smallness" of the human being in relation to God and eternity, *Thoughts Unawares* rejects the reduction of the individual to political formulas and attempts, through its affirmation of naked and unruly subjectivity, to jolt the reader out of conventional modes of thought and language.

In a manner roughly similar to Rozanov's *Fallen Leaves*, *Thoughts Unawares* is composed of a series of discontinuous prose texts that vary in length from a sentence to a page. The work opens: "You live like an utter fool, but sometimes superb thoughts come into your head." The title and this first fragment—echoing both Rozanov's insistence on the "randomness" of his "fallen leaves" and the idea of words that catch the writer off-guard, coming into his head from outside, as they do in "Graphomaniacs" and *Lyubimov*— locate the origin of the text beyond the author's conscious intent. The author's attempt at self-representation paradoxically becomes a form of "self-elimination." *Thoughts Unawares* concludes: "Thoughts end and come no more, as soon as you begin to collect them and think them over."[4] The project thus negates itself and so, like the burned manuscript of "Pkhents," testifies to the impossibility of capturing the self in words. Here the failure is presented as the inevitable result of accretion. Accumulation, as the antithesis of emptiness, appears throughout *Thoughts Unawares* as that which conceals and falsifies the true nature of the self.[5]

While *Thoughts Unawares*, like Rozanov's *Fallen Leaves*, suggests the messiness of random thought through the often jarring juxtaposition of discordant scraps of text, the collection as a whole has a discernible structure.[6] The "thoughts" tend to be arranged in topical "clumps." They also frequently echo one another, creating thematic threads that run throughout the composition. Moreover, just as the opening and closing sentences form a tidy frame enclosing the whole, so the collection divides rather neatly into two parts, the boundary between them marked by a text fragment—"Enough of repeating over and over about human beings. It's time to think about God" (324)—placed roughly halfway through. This statement signals a change in perspective. While the "thoughts" in the first half concentrate on the human condition in the face of death, on the existential situation of imprisonment in the body, those in the second half view the self in relation to eternity and the soul's ultimate liberation from the body. What binds the whole together formally and thematically is the attempt to arrive at the naked self, freed of accumulations that obscure its essence.

From the outset *Thoughts Unawares* establishes God and death as the basic measures of the human condition. The overarching presence of God cuts human pretensions down to size: "It is necessary to trust God the way a dog trusts its master. Whistle, and it comes running. And, wherever you go, it, asking no questions, without thinking, gaily runs after you even to the end of the earth" (315). The first relatively long text introduces both the recurring first-person persona and the fundamental coordinates of the self viewed in relation to God. The observing self is sitting in a restaurant: "It was in the afternoon, there were few people, and the people were all somewhat random [*sluchainyi*], having come in from the provinces or taken it into their heads to dine in luxurious circumstances once in life. It was interesting for me—here by chance [*sluchainomu zdes'*]—to examine these random [*sluchainykh*] people" (315). The repetition of the word *sluchainyi* underscores the importance of randomness as a means of access to the naked self. The chance encounter with a person unknown runs throughout *Thoughts Unawares* as a paradigm for the confrontation with the naked human being, disencumbered from official marks of identity. The other is reduced to an anonymous body, which is what the first-person persona "examines." His attention is drawn by a woman laughing loudly, and he is offended by her ugliness: "It seemed to me that she had no right not only to sit at the table, but to exist on earth at all, and how could this young woman not be ashamed to be so ugly, and how could she moreover laugh, given her ugliness?" (315). He suddenly thinks, however: "But, strictly speaking, what right do you have to condemn this woman if God himself endures her presence? If He has allowed all of us, who are so ugly and insignificant, to exist. Here we sit and scorn one another and are ready to wipe one another from the face of the earth, while He, seeing our ugliness perfectly well, permits us to live, although He could in a single stroke put an end to our lax, arrogant existence. What authority do you have not to tolerate this monstrosity if He, immeasurably beautiful, tolerates her?" (315). Echoing *The Trial Begins*, the first-person persona postulates God as the defining center that invalidates human authority to judge. The perspective of God, which is beyond human compass ("*immeasurably* beautiful"), transcends human differences (the male narrator "examines" a woman), rendering all human beings alike "ugly" and "insignificant." Adopting this frame of reference, *Thoughts Unawares* strips the human being first down to the naked body and then to the naked soul.

A number of the meditations in the first part of *Thoughts Unawares* are thus devoted to sexual intercourse, the coming together of naked bodies.[7] Among the several overheard voices and conversations incorporated into the text, foreshadowing the structure of *A Voice From the Chorus*, the first reduces sexual relations to numbers:

"'I was her 67th, she was my 44th'" (316). Here physical intimacy is trivialized, becoming merely statistical accumulation. The first-person persona, on the other hand, counters by portraying sexual intercourse as blasphemy and transgression, as an attempt to escape the grayness of the human condition. Physical desire originates out of prohibition, out of the very fact that "it is forbidden [nel'zya] to do this, and the more 'forbidden' it is, the more one wants to do it" (317). By its very nature desire demands new partners, not for the sake of sheer numerical cumulation, but to renew the sense of transgression: "Hence—inconstancy, betrayal. From the strictly physiological point of view the new object of love differs little from the old. But that's the whole point, that the new object appears 'sweeter' beforehand, because with her you are violating the law for the first time and, consequently, are acting more sacrilegiously" (317). With a new, "unknown" (neznakomaya) woman, "you experience anew the sense of falling, lost with the 'old object' by force of habit. Repetition there legalized the blasphemous act, and it no longer seemed so attractive" (317). Married couples must be more imaginative: "Acting from the same motives, having secured the moral right, a husband and wife indulge in depravity on lawful terrain more inventively than chance fornicators. For strangers there is enough shame in that they are strangers. But whom do loving spouses have to be ashamed of, with whom do they fornicate? They have no alternative but to violate the law within its own limits and to equip the family unit with such shamelessness that it might have at least the semblance of original sin" (317).

Death reduces the body itself to excrement, the last waste that human beings, who soil the earth their whole lives long, leave behind them: "The final trash is the dead body, which has to be removed as fast as possible. A left-over pile of manure" (318). The nearness of the sexual organs to the organs of excretion implicates sexuality in the impurity of the body:

The location of sex is in itself appalling—in immediate proximity to the organs of excretion. As if nature itself made provision for a squeamish, sarcastic grimace. That which is located next to urine and feces cannot be pure, inspired. The physically unpleasant, putrid surroundings reek of the mark of ignominy on our private parts. The shamelessness of copulation, apart from shame and fear, must overcome the nausea called forth by sewage. In general this pleasure resembles a

feast in a cesspool and disposes one to flee from the polluted
source. (319)

Yet, paradoxically, sexuality, associated by continguity with shame
and defecation, is also a means of flight: "A long, barren life, and
there is nothing at hand, except the private parts, which dangle, like
a child's rattle, and why should a miserable person who is bored not
play with it a bit? Or should a woman amuse herself a little with
an unknown man—it's the same as going to see a new movie" (319).
Trapped in the body, human beings have nothing but the body with
which to express the desire to escape the confines of the body. Sin
becomes a "safety-valve": "All this triviality of human life does not
so much remove or justify sin, but next to it sin, taken separately, as
such, in its primordial abomination is not as frightening and seems
to be a safety-valve. Sin is the end, crime, the hole, hell, death—that
is, all extreme, maximal concepts—while here, the everyday, life, is
dull vegetating, in relation to which even death is better" (319–20).
As we shall see, this vision of bodily transgression as an expression
of the aspiration to something higher, to something that lies beyond
the confines of the fallen state of the body becomes transmuted in
Tertz's later works into a conception of art as redemptive sin. Given
the fallen state of humanity, textual transgressions, like the sins of
the body, offer the only hope of release.

Sexual intercourse, the encounter of naked bodies, also provides
a metaphorical paradigm for human relations. As we have seen, the
text suggests two diametrically opposed possibilities: sex reduced
to numbers and physical intimacy, preferably with an "unknown"
woman, as a transgression of the boundaries of the everyday. By the
same token, the recurring image of the chance meeting with an unknown other is posed as an antithesis to the image of the self defined
by socially sanctioned gauges of identity. The figurative nakedness of
the individual stripped of social convention is juxtaposed to identity
conceived as accumulation:

A human being becomes truly near and dear when he loses
all his official attributes—profession, name, age. When he
stops even being called a human being and is simply the first
person one meets [*pervym vstrechnym*].

* * *

The accumulation [*nakoplenie*] of money. The accumulation of knowledge and experience. The accumulation of books

read. Collectors: kings of numismatics, the wealthy in candy wrappers. The accumulation of fame: one more poem, one more role. Lists of women. Stores of admirers. Notches on the butt of a sharpshooter. The accumulation of sufferings: I've gone through, endured, so much. Journeys. The pursuit of vivid impressions. Discoveries, achievements, the growth of the economy. He who has accumulated more is better, more distinguished, more cultured, smarter, more popular.

And amidst this general urge to accumulate:

"Blessed are the poor in spirit!" (320)

Scientific progress also is denounced as the destructive accumulation of thought: "If we are fated to perish from some sort of radiation, it will be completely logical. Thought develops to the limit where it kills itself" (321). Technological progress, the accumulation of knowledge, which seemingly has broadened the horizons of human life, in fact has narrowed them. In earlier times domestic life "was linked with universal—historical and cosmic—life" (322). The rituals of peasant life drew the individual "into a circle of concepts of universal meaning. Observing feasts and holidays, the human being lived by a worldwide-historical calendar that began with Adam and ended with the Last Judgment" (323). Modern life, by contrast, has only the appearance, created by futile accumulation, of universal scope:

Although we have newspapers, museums, radio, aerial communications, we only take note of this worldwide background and are not much involved with it, think about it little. In Czech shoes, with a Mexican cigarette in his teeth, he read a report about the appearance of a new state in Africa and went to consume broth made from French meat. All this external, seeming contact with the world has the character of random, incoherent information: "There's an elder grove in the garden, and an uncle in Kiev."[8] That there's an elder grove in the garden we learn many times a day and do not attach any particular significance to these facts. The quantity of our knowledge and information is enormous, we are overloaded with it, without changing qualitatively. It's possible to travel around our whole universe in several days—to get on an airplane and travel around it, without receiving any benefit for the soul and only increasing the dimensions of the information coming in. (322–23)

All of this "knowledge and information" is ultimately negated by death: "The peasant maintained a constant link with the enormous world order and died in the heart of the universe, next to Abraham. But we, having read the paper, die alone on our narrow, useless couch" (323). Progress has driven out God: We are indebted to urban comfort and technological progress for the decline of faith in God. Surrounded by the things we have made, we feel ourselves the creators of the universe. Can I see the Lord God in a world where I run across a human being at every step? The voice of God sounded in the wilderness, in the silence, and silence and the wilderness are precisely what we lack. We have drowned out and clogged up everything with ourselves, and after all that we are still amazed that the Lord does not show himself to us" (323–24). Accumulation thus crowds God out of the world.

Within this conceptual framework the Russians as a people appear exemplary. Accumulation is alien to the Russian nature: "All the same what is most important about a Russian is that he has *nothing to lose*. Hence both the unselfishness of the Russian intelligentsia (except where the bookshelf is concerned). And the directness of the people: in a state of drunkenness, for Russia, chest bared! Shoot, you vipers! Not hospitality—despair. The readiness to share one's last morsel, because it is the last and there's nothing more, at the limit, on the edge. And lightness in thoughts, in judgment. All hell breaks loose. They accumulated nothing, learned nothing. But who dares condemn them? When all are already condemned" (321). Like sex, drunkenness becomes, if not a virtue, an inspired response to the limitations of the body: "Drunkenness is our fundamental national vice and more—our idée fixe. The Russian people drink not out of poverty or grief, but out of an age-old need for the miraculous and the extraordinary, drink, if you will, mystically, striving to help the soul out of earthly equilibrium and to return it to its blissful incorporeal state. Vodka is the white magic of the Russian peasant" (321–22). Drunkenness, the seduction of the "white magic" of vodka, represents an aspiration to escape the body and, as in *Lyubimov*, goes hand in hand with thievery, which paradoxically appears as the opposite of accumulation: "In combination with an inclination to thievery (the absence of a firm faith in the interrelations between real objects) drunkenness imparts to us a vagabond unconstraint and places us among other peoples in the suspicious position of lumpen" (322). The Russians become that which the law condemns, the criminal other: "We are now all thieves (who of us has not sensed something roguish in his own soul and fate?)" (322). The Russian predisposition to drunkenness and theft places the people at odds with the country's legal structures: "From us, as from a thief, as from a drunk, anything can be expected. It's easy to order us about, to rule us by administrative measures (a drunk is inert, incapable of self-government, trails along wherever he is dragged). And at the same time—how difficult it is to manage this unsteady people, what a hard time our administrators have with us! . . ." (322).[9] The unruliness of the Russian people is matched by its openness to the "chance passerby": "How pleasant it is when a chance passerby says 'please' or 'thank you.' And says this 'thank you [*spasibo*]' with such frankness, as though he in fact desired your salvation [*spasenie*]. This sincerity is all that holds up the world, particularly the Russian world. A 'brother,' 'papa,' 'be so good as to.' Without any politeness, but with an intonation of kinship" (322). The depiction of Russianness in *Thoughts Unawares* crystallizes the antirationalistic strain that runs throughout the collection, as well as through Tertz's other works, casting suspicion on conventional morality, legal and political institutions, technological progress, and official status and rank as empty forms. Conversely, transgression, the attempt to escape the body and the deadening burden of accumulation, to emulate within the confines of the body the final release of the soul in death, is portrayed as the most appropriate response to the human condition.

The discontinuities and even contradictions between the passages that make up *Thoughts Unawares* underscore the temporality of the self, its changeability over time. In this context, the focus of the meditations in the second half of the collection shifts from the death of the body to eternity as a measure of humanity. The projection of necessarily time-bound human values into a supratemporal context reveals the unbridgeable gap between the human and the eternal:

Probably sinners, grouped in hell by various classes and parties, also envy one another and put on airs in front of one another. He who is being roasted on a spit laughs at those who are hanging upside down. Resentments fester, conflicts ripen: it seems to each that he is worse off than others. And the haughtiness of some sufferers (for example, pederasts), who comprise a special caste with a refined method of torture. And sudden fashions, when everyone dreams of getting into the gas chamber intended for child-murderers and ascribes to himself retroactively uncommitted crimes: all would be glad to kill a babe; there are none to be found in the hellish darkness. The eternal struggle for primacy in the netherworld and disputes about liberty, equality and fraternity. (325)

Extrapolating the pretensions of mortal life into eternity creates a radical shift in perspective, exposing the inherent absurdity, pointlessness, even horror, of human measurements of self: "Imagine a genius in the other world. He runs from corner to corner—in hell—and tries to prove to everyone: 'But I'm talented'" (325).

Thus eternity becomes the yardstick against which the insignificance, the "smallness" of the human body is exposed: "the natural world that surrounds us—forest, mountains, sky—is the form of eternity that is most accessible to us, visible, its material imitation, likeness, personification. The very extent of nature in time and space, its duration, its magnitude in comparison with our body, inspires thoughts of the eternal and induces in human beings distrust in their limited existence" (328). Nature as a material surrogate for eternity becomes, as the following text fragment suggests, an immovable point of reference: "When you sail on a steamship, and around you there is nothing but the sea, you begin to grasp that no matter where we walk, no matter where we ride, we always stand in the same place in relation to the sky" (329). The next passage contrasts the location-bound, and therefore inadequate, perspective of the human individual with the expanse and constancy of the sky (*nebo*), which is also heaven and eternity:

> For some reason it is supposed that what is started here should be disentangled and untied somewhere *there* (in the future or in eternity). That we should be compensated for our sufferings, efforts, sins, virtues. Meanwhile, perhaps it is not we who should be paid, but rather we are compensation or retribution to someone for something. Looking at the universe from our own angle, we take ourselves as the beginning and mentally try on a fitting end for ourselves. But in the world balance we are not the point of departure, but a curve drawn between quantities unknown to us, and it therefore is not meet to demand justice for *ourselves*. (329)

Eternity, the existence of a cosmological scope beyond human comprehension, discredits the limited human point of view. Again, the authority of human judgment is undermined by juxtaposition to a superior and ultimately defining frame of reference.

The prevailing imagery of the second part of *Thoughts Unawares* thus concerns the point of contact between the human being and eternity, the body as a cover for the soul: "What is the body? An external casing, a diving-suit. And I, perhaps, sitting in my diving-suit, keep wriggling" (327). Death is both the measure of the body— "What's good about death is that it puts us all in our place" (328)— and the liberation of the soul: "Death cleaves the soul from the body as a butcher cleaves meat from bones. It is just as agonizing. But only thus does liberation come" (327). Sleep recurs as a locus of inter-section between mortals and immortality, an interim state where the living in dreams can meet with the dead. Sleep, the penultimate meditation in the collection suggests, is a "rehearsal for death," a state in which we return to the disencumbered "I":

> In falling asleep we take the position of an embryo. We press our legs to our stomach, curl up, build a nest—a cozy and safe maternal womb. We become children and breathe heavily and smack our lips, setting aside later stratifications. In this universal, daily falling into childhood there is some return to oneself, to one's primal position, which was and will be the most important in life, and everything else is trifles. Falling asleep we break with the world, shed the mask of pro-fession, age, culture, nationality, return home and remain, finally, in our original guise, ridiculous and defenseless. This is our root, our ultimate "I," which is even difficult to call an "I," because we are all here as similar as infants. (337)

As he reaches the end of *Thoughts Unawares* the first-person per-sona thus concludes that virtually all marks of the uniqueness of the self, including memory and meditation, are merely forms of accu-mulation: "So, if all of these—sleep and childhood and death—are compared, it turns out that life lived as the 'development of con-scious personality' easily disappears and is good for nothing. No matter who we have become, what we have learned, we remain only with that store we had in childhood and we have before sleep. With it, only with it will we leave here, having forgotten forever all other acquisitions—the knowledge, money, fame, labor, books that bear the imprint of our personality, but have no value in the face of the child, sleep, and death" (338).

Beth Holmgren has pointed to the antithesis between "accumula-tion" and "negation" or "emptiness" that runs throughout *Thoughts Unawares:* "In positive contrast to these attributes and impulses of the flesh are Terc's entries which advocate a renunciation of earthly possessions and distinctions. In almost all of these entries, Terc expresses this desired state in terms of negation—be it an absence of waste, or an absence of distinguishing human features."[10] Freedom, as Holmgren goes on to point out, is defined by Tertz as an absence: "Freedom is always negative and presupposes an absence, an emptiness, which craves to be filled as swiftly as possible" (325). Freedom thus corresponds to self in its purest sense, which is, paradoxically, the absence of "personality" (*lichnost'*):

> Any personality is repellent if there is a lot of it. Personality is always capital, even if that capital is composed of virtues, intelligence, and talent. "Give away your possessions . . ." Christ loved those who were "no one" [*nikem*]. And wasn't he himself "No One"? As a personality He is rather inexpressive [*nevyrazytelen*] (and therefore unexpressible [*nevyrazym*]) and in any case not in the least original. The "personality" of Jesus Christ sounds blasphemous. It is personality in the inverse, minus, sense. You would not call Christ a "genius." Genius is full of itself; a genius is a capitalist. The vampirism of geniuses, the worship of geniuses, which began with the Renaissance, and the unselfishness of holiness, which always shines not with its own, but with Thy light, O Lord. (324)

Christ epitomizes self-abnegation. Clearly invoked here is Christ's kenosis, his "emptying" himself of divinity to accept corporeal suffering and death out of love for humanity. On the model of the kenotic ideal (*imitatio Christi*) all personality is condemned as accumulation, just as the text of *Thoughts Unawares* itself falls silent in the end, renouncing its own body, the passages of which it is constructed, as accretion. The true self, the soul released at death, remains in the realm of silence and absence.

Yet the text of *Thoughts Unawares* survives, reaches us as readers, as does the burned manuscript of "Pkhents." Its formlessness stands as a challenge to forms imposed from without on either the self or the text, endowing both the one and the other with a false veneer of legitimacy. Subverting conventional representations of the self, stripping the self naked, *Thoughts Unawares* simultaneously exposes the fallacy of identity as accumulation and draws the reader into a new, intimate relation with the text. In the same way that conventional understandings of the self merely obscure its true nature, its absence, so the text is revealed as merely that which fills the silence, attempting to embody that which lies beyond the body. *Thoughts Unawares,* in discrediting its own attempt to represent the self, tentatively looks ahead to the major concern of Tertz's later writings: the acknowledgement and even celebration of art as illusion.

Although there are obvious continuities between *Thoughts Unawares,* especially as viewed through Sinyavsky's interpretation of Rozanov, and *A Voice from the Chorus,* there are essential dissimilarities as well, dissimilarities that mark the dividing line between the early Tertz writings and his works dating from the years spent in labor camps and in emigration.[11] Rather than marking a radical shift in the writer's views, the distinctions that can be drawn between the earlier and the later works suggest a maturation of the writer's voice, coupled with a subtle reorientation of focus. Developing the central images elaborated in his pretrial oeuvre, Tertz returns again and again to the question of the relationship between art and reality—to the simultaneous interconnection and essential difference between them—repeatedly giving art pride of place in the comparison. In essentially declaring itself a failure, *Thoughts Unawares* reiterates the motif, which recurs throughout the early Tertz works, of the impossibility of capturing the self in art. *A Voice from the Chorus* approaches the problem from a different angle. The central issue becomes not the replication of the self in art, but rather art as transformation, the transformation of the "I" into the "not-I." The self becomes a site of experiment for the question "What is art?"

Sinyavsky wrote *A Voice from the Chorus*[12] during his imprisonment. Yet unlike *Strolls with Pushkin,* which was also written in Dubrovlag and sent out of the camp in letters to the writer's wife, *A Voice from the Chorus* was not originally conceived as an independent work. Sinyavsky has explained its genesis:

> I thought up *A Voice from the Chorus* after I got out of the camp, but I rewrote almost nothing in it, only compiled it out of passages from real letters. In my letters I set off some passages as literary prose. One such piece in each letter. I wrote about anything and everything—about nature (if something happened to strike me), or reminiscences about paintings. That kind of passage. It was like storing up material, but not a book. At the same time I listened to camp speech and tried to incorporate the voices I had heard. But I had nothing definite in mind. At first there was no book, but later, after I was released, I simply began to pull these passages out and made a book out of them. In the camp I had the feeling I was filled

to overflowing; sometimes I even thought that my head would split from all the impressions. So after I was released I decided to make a book out of them.[13]

As Sinyavsky's description suggests, *A Voice from the Chorus* is composed of a remarkable diversity of materials: text fragments in the "voice" of the authorial persona—which range from aphoristic observations to relatively lengthy disquisitions—are combined with scraps of overheard camp conversations, songs, snippets from other people's letters, and quotations from literary and scholarly writings and apocrypha. The book's structure produces an illusion of purely chronological arrangement. Dated passages, many concerned with changes in the seasons, are interspersed in temporal sequence throughout *A Voice from the Chorus*, creating the impression that the first six sections of the book correspond to the six years of Sinyavsky's incarceration in labor camps (the last cut short by the writer's early release), while the seventh and final section is devoted to his liberation and return to freedom.[14] Yet this apparently simple temporal order overlays a far more intricate contexture, which, taking our cue from the title, we might term "choral." The texts tend to be arranged, as in *Thoughts Unawares*, in thematic clusters in which the author's[15] voice alternates with the voices of others. Melding the sonic and the semantic, these clusters are frequently bound together by word repetitions, and, mimicking variations on melodic phrases in a choral work, key words and themes are periodically reprised, imparting a complex organic unity to the whole. In other words, *A Voice from the Chorus* is a carefully orchestrated work organized around discernible structural principles, the most important of which is the evolution of the counterpoint between the voice and the chorus— the voices of the author's fellow camp inmates. The chorus seemingly disappears in the penultimate chapter, but, as we shall see, this apparent suppression of other voices represents rather a merger, a true joining of voices in chorus.

   A Voice from the Chorus—like Rozanov's *Fallen Leaves* and, following in its footsteps, *Thoughts Unawares*—clearly eludes conventional genre classification. As an experiment in transcending form, however, it surpasses its predecessors in the complex interplay of its structure.[16] I would suggest that any attempt to define *A Voice from the Chorus* generically intrinsically falsifies the work's conception, at the root of which lies the attempt to overcome the limitations of form, the materiality of the word, through the body of the text. *A Voice from the Chorus* incorporates many genres—straddling divisions between oral and written, "high" and popular literature—in order to transcend genre. Just as the self in exploring its "nakedness" dissolves in the manifold voices of the chorus, so the text, because it incorporates elements of many genres, can be subsumed under no single one and thereby subverts the very concept of genre.

The text "embodies" the problem of defining art posed by the author early on:

> When people ask me what art is [*chto takoe iskusstvo*], I start to laugh quietly in wonder at its exorbitance and at my own inability to express what, after all, its endlessly changing content, which attracts like light, consists of. O Lord, I have spent my whole life just trying to get to the heart of its meaning and now as a result can do nothing and don't know how to express it. I say, "perhaps," "probably," "let's hope," "is it not one thing or another," and immediately get lost in the unsolvability of the problem. That's why the definitions of official aestheticians, who know exactly what art is (as if anyone had succeeded in that, as if it were possible to know!), are so lethal. Art is always more or less an improvised prayer. Just try to grab hold of that smoke. (442)

The author invokes prayer here not as a formal category, but rather as the aspiration of the text to rise beyond the confines of earthly existence. Characteristically, he opposes metaphor—art as "smoke" —to "lethal" definition. Art, like smoke, is a physical substance which yet eludes the grasp of those who would "kill" it by defining it. The text's renunciation of conventional form, its transmutation into different genres, corresponds to its continual destabilization of the relationship between word and referent. The claim to define is an assertion of the self as defining center. The genesis of metaphor, by contrast, lies in the ability to see through "other" eyes, to be open to other "selves." By the same token, the incorporation of diverse voices into the text undermines genre. Both the privileging of metaphor and the formlessness of the text thus represent expressions of the author's acknowledgement of his own emptiness, his "self-elimination." The text incarnates difference, the plurality of selves, and seeks to transcend it by offering itself up to God in prayer.

A Voice from the Chorus also clearly represents a challenge to the Russian tradition of writing about imprisonment and, more specifically, to the labor camp memoir's preoccupation with the sufferings of the body.[17] Yet, while asserting his right not to dwell on the physical conditions of his imprisonment, Tertz does not deny the body. The soul's confinement in the body, like the confinement of meaning in words, is an existential state that the living being, like the work of art, continually strives to transcend. The author directly addresses the problem in a question he poses himself:

> I ask myself: "To think about the bird-*sirin* while carting sawdust—is that really how it should be?"
> And I answer: "Yes—it is." [18]

The very form of such a text fragment, in which the authorial persona casts himself as two voices in a dialogue, encapsulates the inherent duality of the self—caught between body and soul, word and meaning, the self-affirmation of the "I" and the forgetfulness of death: "The 'I' is a point that, endlessly wailing, 'Give me! Give me!,' at the same time fumbles about in a whisper trying to figure out how to get rid of itself. The unstable equilibrium of the personality, pulsing between life and death" (490). In asserting his right to think about the *sirin* while his body is engaged in physical labor, the author does not simply repudiate the body, but rather affirms the aspiration, embodied in art, to transcend this state.

Furthermore, the *sirin* itself incarnates the inherent impossibility of this striving and thereby serves as a nexus for the images of birds, singing, and prayer that run throughout *A Voice from the Chorus*. Thus the text fragment that immediately follows the one cited above reads:

> . . . Play, guitar, play!
> And the song—a bird that has lost its
>   way—
> Was searching for paradise lost.
> The formula for art. Its most general and broadest formula.
> (551)

Here the author posits the bird-song art as a quest—doomed because the seeker is invariably lost—to return to a prelapsarian state. Both the aspiration to escape difference and the conditions that make it impossible of realization are inscribed in the very form of the utterance. The popular song—an "authorless" creation and an image of disembodied words, words sung and therefore not confined to the materiality of the text—represents art's impulse to overcome the conditions of its own creation. Yet, in citing the words of an other, even an anonymous or collective other, the author acknowledges the existence of the other, which is the source of difference, of the relativity of meaning. The text cannot escape its fallen state, but can only embrace it by incorporating a plurality of voices in which the single voice of the author, his authority as defining center, dissolves.

The *sirin* in medieval Russian folk mythology was, to cite one authoritative source, "a paradisiacal bird-maiden, the image of which goes back to the ancient Greek sirens. In Russian spiritual verses the *s[iren]*, descending from paradise to earth, bewitches people with its singing."[19] In the third and last of this series of texts on the *sirin*, bird, and song, the author speculates on the seductiveness of the *sirin*-siren's song, which lures with the promise of loss of self:

> I used to imagine (I checked with others and they also thought so) that the sirens Odysseus encountered resembled mermaids in appearance. Suddenly I saw that they are just like our *Sirins*—in the scene with Odysseus on an Attic vase from the fifth century B.C. That's how far back it goes—in the guise of birds. Does their singing not, by the way, herald the identification with heaven at the hour of death, as a result of which the "I" dissolves in beautiful sound and the soul, having forgotten everything, leaves the body? There are inscriptions on Russian caskets saying of the *Sirin* and *Alkonost* (in the spirit of the theory of music in Ancient India): "When it lets free its voice in song, it ceases to feel its own self." The same with a human being: "And his mind is so captivated thereby that a great change comes upon him." Self-consciousness has ended—the delights of paradise begin. (552)

This passage brings together several of the key images of *A Voice from the Chorus*. The author's speculations are sparked by his viewing of an Attic vase—an emblem of art as material substance, combining pictorial representation with clay vessel in an artifact of the past. The vase, art as body, represents the opposing pole from the pure sound of the sirens' song, art's striving to be free of the body. The writer becomes a modern Odysseus. He also will return home at the end. He thus paradoxically casts his confinement as a journey. Trapped in the body, confined in space, he is lured by the siren song of art. True oblivion, the release of the soul from the body, can be achieved only in death. But art, like the nearness of death, approximates—both for performer and audience, author and reader—the heavenly state of self-forgetfulness.

The writer, then, transmutes the very real circumstances in which

A Voice from the Chorus was written into a series of metaphors for the artistic process. The basic circumstances of the work's creation—the writer's imprisonment and the letters he sends out of the camp to his wife[20]—correspond to Tertz's understanding of the inherent nature of artistic creation. In his 1974 article "The Literary Process in Russia," Tertz argues that the repression of writers in the Soviet Union, their treatment as criminals, coincides with art's fundamental impulse to escape restraint: "The writer with his whole writer's innards does not crave freedom, he craves *liberation* (give me chains!). What is important is to open the valve, and in order to do this the valve must first be sufficiently blocked up. And, this means, the tighter the noose is drawn around the neck of the writer (within certain limits, of course), the more lightly and gaily he will sing as a result."[21] The writer therefore is in his element in the camp. Yet while his body remains imprisoned, his letters escape, becoming an emblem of art's craving for liberation.

Both the camp and the letters are, moreover, sites of encounter with others. As the author observes in *A Voice from the Chorus*, "Art is a place of meeting. Of the author with an object of love, of spirit with matter, of truth with fantasy, of the line of a pencil with the contour of the body, of one word with another, and so forth" (482). He proposes a sentence composed by two different people as a paradigm for language as a "place of meeting":

> It would be interesting to write a sentence that flowed over, that began from the perspective of one person and ended with another, in order that, through its structure and development, it would carry two faces, which would go along it to meet one another and would oscillate, as on a swing, coordinating and embracing space more broadly than generally possible. That is the charm of participial naivetes of the sort: 'Approaching the station, my hat flew off.' Besides, isn't it the task of language, to link diverse planes and things,' not necessarily along a straight line, but so that there is a branching out, growing, obeying its own caprice . . . If, let's assume, I walk toward you, then, having said 'I' at the beginning, why should you not stretch out your hands to me at the end? . . . (488)

Here we can see how, for Tertz, violations of rules of form—"participial naivetes"—constitute tacit acknowledgements of language as a collaboration between self and other. The camp, the locus where the voice and the chorus come together, and the letters, where the writer communes with his wife, become emblems of the text's confinement in difference, exemplified by the sentence with "two faces" and its striving to escape difference in intimate communication with the beloved other.

The dedication to *A Voice from the Chorus* reads: "I dedicate to my wife Mariya this book which is compiled almost completely out of my letters to her during my years of imprisonment, 1966–1971" (439). The text as a "place of meeting" thus has its ideal reader inscribed within it from the very outset. She is Penelope to the author's Odysseus: "While Odysseus sails, Penelope weaves" (550). The wife is physically absent in the text, that is, her answering letters are not included in *A Voice from the Chorus*. Yet this omission is not a suppression, but rather an eloquent silence, which represents simultaneously a collaboration and an ideal toward which the text itself strives.

"Everything interesting that happens inside and around me," the author writes, "has a secret footnote to narrate to you, and I am so accustomed to referring all of this to you that it is precisely this orientation of objects toward you that gives them meaning" (442). Meaning, like the text, thus arises out of the desire to relate specifically to the beloved other. Writing, paradoxically, becomes a form of listening:

> It's strange, but my idle chatter in letters is, to a considerable extent, not speech, but listening, tuning in to myself. Sometimes from one perspective, sometimes from another. And what will you say to this or that? It's important to me when I write to hear you. Language as a means of catching, listening. Language as a means of meditating silence. Absolutely empty. Snares, nets. A net of speech, thrown into the sea of silence in the hope of pulling out a golden fish. In a pause, in a moment of silence a little fish is pulled out, but words have nothing to do with it. They only help to arrange the pauses. Words only help us to distract ourselves, thereby opening up access to the most perfect silence. (643)

Words are only excuses for the pauses between them; language is only a poor substitute for the silence, the absolute emptiness, in which the only possibility of true communication, to which language aspires but which it cannot achieve, resides. Through their omission from *A Voice from the Chorus*, Rozanova's letters become pauses in the text, representing the unattainable ideal text, which is silence and emptiness.

The possibility of perfect communication, achieved through silence, rests on the intimacy between the writer and his spouse, between the text and its ideal reader. Speech becomes listening, words give way to the pauses between words, dialogue becomes equivalent to silence, because the boundaries between self and other vanish. Love, like death, is a surrender of self: "I am not. I am you. 'Oh, I am dying'!" (480). Love is a violation of order:

> Cato, according to Plutarch, said: "The soul of a lover lives in the body of another," and although this was probably said in condemnation, it is obvious from this that love always means a passage, a shaking off of one's own personality. Unfortunately, you can't get along without an "I." The nucleus. The law and form of existence, I am, the point of departure, the measure of things, the instinct for the continuation of the species, egoism, in conformity with which everything for the time being stands in place and remains itself. Love does not believe in this and violates the order of the world for the sake of its unity, mutuality. Love is formless, and it builds bridges, conceiving every object not in my, but in your, image. (482)

Thus, law, form, and order all rest on the "I," which is the source of difference, while love, the genesis of the ideal text, transgresses, is formless, and "bridges" difference. By the same token, the letters represent the possibility of bridging the space that separates the bodies of the lovers, of escaping the confinement of the body and the confinement of the text: the letters leave the camp, while the body cannot, and by communicating through silence, they surpass words.

At the same time, the letters take the place of the absent body: "I often begin a letter not because I intend to write you something serious. But simply to touch a sheet that you will hold" (466). A book may be precious, not for its contents, but as a point of contact with a person one cares for:

> An old man is reading a reference book on elementary mathematics. His son sent it to a neighbor. He doesn't understand any of it. Some sort of sines and cosines. All the same he reads it. From cover to cover. His son sent it!
>
> (This concerns the soul of objects. If you were to send

someone here a book of geometry problems, I probably would also not be able to restrain myself and would also take it—to have a look. Contact with the person is more important than the content of the book.) (441)

Following this line of reasoning, the letters between the spouses become analogous to the dolls that Eskimo women fashion of their absent or dead husbands. Characteristically, the author introduces this image into the text through the citation of another voice, this time an academic treatise, on which he comments:

"Eskimo women, in the event of a husband's prolonged absence, made a representation of him; fed, dressed and undressed the figure; put it to bed, and in every way took care of it as if it were a living being. Similar figures were made also in the event of a person's death . . . Also often those real dolls with which Eskimo girls played were representations of those who had died . . . The doll thus turned out to be a vessel for the soul and the 'representative' of the deceased among his kin. The soul contained in the doll, according to these concepts, passed into the body of the woman and was thereupon resurrected to a new life. It was thus considered the soul of the dead relative and the soul of the future child" (A. P. Okladnikov).

I have not read anything more significant about dolls, although all this is set forth with scholarly viscosity. Our dolls, perhaps, are the last-born children of those messengers who transferred news from the dead body into the living. And art? Did it not all issue from that doll? (556)

Like the Eskimo figures, the writer's letters to his wife become vessels containing the soul of the absent husband. Just as the love between the spouses promises to overcome difference, so the doll as the mode of transfer of the soul from one body to another depends on relations of kinship. Most important, the transmigration of the soul figures the possibility of perfect communication between bodies. The soul becomes a metaphor for meaning.

The text counterposes the dolls of the Eskimo women to "stone images" (*kamennye baby*) that serve as prisons for the souls of enemies: "Some scholars think that the stone images (of Turkic origin, in contrast to the Polovetskian Black Sea goddesses) represent not dear deceased people, buried somewhere nearby, but slaughtered enemies. This unproven theory is based on the fact that among some peoples (the Yakuts, Tungus, and others) the souls of the dead were considered dangerous and hostile to the living, and, in order to render a dead person harmless, they immortalized him. The Turks strove, naturally, to remove from play as many enemies as possible and transform them into stone" (559). The Turkic stone figures and the Eskimo dolls represent two antithetical models for art as well as the two poles—entrapment in the body and release of the soul— between which art exists. While relations of love and kinship allow the soul, through the medium of the art work, to pass into a new body, relations of enmity imprison the soul in the stone. By the same token, while Eskimo girls receive the souls of their dead ancestors by playing with the dolls, the souls of enemies are "taken out of play" through confinement in the image. Intimacy and play thus hold the possibility of meaning, of releasing the soul from the material vessel in which it is contained and allowing it to be reborn into a new body.

Just as in the image of the Eskimo dolls (figures of either dead or absent husbands) the line between death and absence is blurred, here the absent husband, translated into the body of the letters to his wife, suffers a kind of death. In the final section of *A Voice from the Chorus* the author depicts his return to freedom not as a rebirth, but as a posthumous existence: "Coming out of prison, you appear in this world seemingly posthumously. It's not quite a second birth, because you are old and weak. . . . All that remains is a naked point of view, that is, you experience your sojourn in the world as the presence of a specter" (664). The author suggests that he has exhausted himself in the creation of the text: "What form can a book have? That of a pulsing heart, let's assume, driving the text at once along many roads. Or that of a road leading away, along which the author travels farther away as the story flows, and he moves away hard on the heels of the text, until he disappears from view, physically taken up into the animated [*odushevlennoe*] movement into the distance of the book, which, having secured the author's soul and body for itself, comes to an abrupt end in large letters, carved almost beyond one's powers, childishly, having taken the pen in both hands, almost from the other world—in short, the author writes himself out in the material formation of the book, which carries him after it and is lost in silence" (643).

This death of the author, however, holds the promise of a new birth. Just as the Eskimo dolls serve as a vessel of intersection between death and birth, so the writer suffers a form of self-annihilation in creating the new body of the book into which his soul is transferred. While this new body has its genesis in the intimate discourse between spouses, in being published it is transformed into a public text and, like a child come of age, slips from the control of the author-parent and enters the realm of difference. Thus one explanation the author proffers for the ancient practice of transmitting wisdom exclusively orally, for taboos against "entrust[ing] the preservation of secrets to lifeless letters" is: "Perhaps the blame for this lies in a book's indifference to the reader, its readiness to associate with the first person it comes across, while profundity requires a profound receptor?" (642). The penultimate passage of *A Voice from the Chorus* expresses the author's realization of, and resignation to, the text's uncontrollability:

> You leave [the book], throw it away (almost send it flying) and say carelessly—I'm finished; you listen to the critics, some say to correct one sentence, chapter, page, others—another, but you no longer care. It lives. It was born and already lives apart from you, not asking permission, with all its deficiencies, abandoned—how will it feel when you are gone, dead, when, no one will help it, no one will even say a word, no one will correct the defective sentence, and it—gaping with its and your infirmity—will just stand, being gradually obliterated, as you left it, insignificant, amidst the decades, rejected, homeless, barely in three copies; and how can this be, that it alone, without you, will remain and will gradually begin to recoup, will profit not by your efforts, but more by blunders and omissions, spreading its wings in the grave, forgetting you, casting you away (why are you needed?), hundred-mouthed, and will begin to live by the fate and lot of a book. (668–69)

The text, born like a child out of the intimacy of man and wife, goes on to live its own independent existence. While the spouses read less the words than the pauses between words, the random reader reads the text's "omissions and blunders." Unlike the ideal reader, the wife who is a soul-mate of her husband, the random reader brings difference to the text.

Like the letters, the camp is transformed by the text from merely the physical condition of its creation into a complex metaphor for the representation of the self. It is, like the text, like all language, a "place of meeting" between self and other. The opening passages of *A Voice from the Chorus* establish the basic parameters of the author's project:

"I'll speak directly, because life is short."

In general it is interesting how a human being seeks a loop-hole in order to exist. And poses himself the question: and what if I try to live from the contrary? When it's impossible? When thought itself is extinguished by fatigue and indifference to everything? And right there, on that naked point, to stand up and begin! (440)

The text commences not with the author's voice, but with a line from the chorus, from one of the other inmates with whom the writer is thrown together by his confinement in the camp. The author then presents himself as beginning from a "naked point." *A Voice from the Chorus* therefore grows out of the same basic situation which functions as the central image of *Thoughts Unawares:* the meeting of the "naked self" with the "random passerby." Here it is the camp that not only serves as the impetus for and locus of encounter, but also reveals the emptiness of the self:

Creatures pulled out of life and put behind bars possess a capacity for pensiveness and for thinking things out to extreme degrees of profundity. There is something transcendent in the consciousness of one who has been pulled out. In him personality inevitably recedes into the background.

As a result: they are not people but expanses. Not characters but spaces, fields. The boundaries of the human being extend into contact with the infinite. The overcoming of the biographical method and genre. Beyond biography! Every person is beyond. The moment we rely on any rudiments of character, we fall through up to the waist. Personality is a pit, barely covered with a brushwood of psychology, temperament, life habits and practices. I fall into this pit when I stride to meet a stranger who is approaching me. (485)

In *Thoughts Unawares* the authorial persona strips himself down to the "naked self." In *A Voice from the Chorus*, on the other hand, the camp performs this function; the writer begins as a "naked point." Thus, while in the former work the realization that the self is a void leads the writer to capitulate before the impossibility of its representation, in *A Voice from the Chorus* the hole becomes filled up with the multitude of the voices of the chorus, in which the voice of the author dissolves—the all transmuted into the body of the text and offered up as prayer.

In the early pages of *A Voice from the Chorus*, the author suggests three literary models that define the intersection of his experience of the camp with the representation of the self. In one lengthy passage he juxtaposes Swift and Defoe, arguing that *Gulliver's Travels* and *Robinson Crusoe* approach the same issue from opposite directions. He opens his discussion with the observation:

> Let us note: Swift describes the contents of our pockets as an amazing phenomenon, or a peculiar case requiring proof. Gulliver's watch is not a watch, his comb is not a comb, his handkerchief is not a handkerchief but something unimaginable in the eyes of the Lilliputians, which does not yield to understanding and therefore is stretched out into pages of exciting plot. Swift's discovery, fundamental for art, was that there are no uninteresting objects on earth as long as there exists an artist who fixes his gaze on everything with the incomprehension of a dullard. "It's understood, it's been understood for a long time!"—voices are heard all around—"They are just scissors! What's all the fuss?" But the artist cannot and should not understand anything. He is unfamiliar with the word *scissors*. Stepping back a few paces and continuing to be amazed, he undertakes to describe them in the form of a riddle [*zagadka*]. "Two ends, two rings, and a tack in the middle." Instead of comprehension, instead of answers—he proposes representation. It is enigmatic [*zagadochno*]. (452)

In this passage, as elsewhere in his works, Tertz invokes the Formalists' conception of estrangement as the defamiliarization of the familiar through the adoption of an unconventional angle of vision. He, however, locates the origin of the estranging perspective specifically in contact with an alien other who views the world within a framework of radically different coordinates of measurement. He also explicitly connects the other's vision with an inability to name, which turns description into riddle. Gulliver—subjected to the same shifts in context as his watch, comb, and handkerchief—becomes a gauge of the precariousness of definitions of the self: "Next to the other characters Gulliver is characterless. He, better than others, fits under the rubric of man in general. What can you say about him except that this is Homo sapiens, only illuminated in different ways by the criteria of his surroundings? But those very changes in the proposed conditions of the experiment deprive Gulliver of reliability and constancy—he is small by comparison, he is big by comparison, he is pure by comparison and impure by comparison, he is a human being by comparison and a nonhuman by comparison. Among the Lilliputians he is a giant, among the giants he is a Lilliputian, among the Houyhnhnhms a beast, among people a horse" (452–53). Swift's "vivisection" (452) reveals that the possibility of naming Gulliver, his very status as a human being, rests exclusively on an inherently unstable conventional framework, which crumbles when confronted by other, equally relative centers of definition: "the human being is a fiction, the human being is an imaginary construct" (453).

While Swift strips Gulliver of his identity by sending him traveling among disorienting others, Defoe confines Robinson Crusoe on a desert island and chronicles his "accumulation" of identity: "a naked human being is left on the naked land. And what happens? After shedding a few tears, the prisoner Robinson Crusoe began to accumulate capital. The pristine desert was transformed into a profitable farm, the Bible into a handbook for the use of future Fords" (453). Robinson Crusoe, removed from civilization and reduced to a "naked human being," proceeds to accumulate, to acquire for himself a new furniture of identity which resembles the old and to which even the other—Friday—is to a greater or lesser extent assimilated. There is nonetheless a point at which Gulliver in his travels meets Robinson Crusoe in his confinement:

> Defoe's hero is saved from banality and his novel from boredom by the alternative of life or death, productivity or savagery, between which Robinson's fate vacillates. Starting from the other end from Swift, Defoe moved the scale of the interesting into the realm of ordinary objects and actions, which are entertaining only as a result of the point of view chosen by the author—the unusual technical difficulty of their execution, manufacture. He showed that cultivating a garden, sewing clothing, building a table are all in the highest degree amazing and responsible occupations, fraught with obstructions, snares, and crafty victories, which strain the lean body of the plot. When one's life is staked on a little kernel of grain, as if on a card, the sprouting of the hapless grain will attain the suspense of a detective story. (454)

Art is the transformation of the ordinary into the extraordinary, a transformation that entails the removal of the self and of language from automatized contexts, whether through encounters with conflicting scales of definition or through confrontation with the final measurement of death.

The camp is to Tertz what the travels are to Gulliver and the desert island to Robinson Crusoe. His imprisonment strips him bare, denuding him of external marks of rank and status. It serves as a gray backdrop against which the face stands out more vividly:

> If life is empty and poor, clothing gray, then against this dull background the face is granted the right to a heightened vividness. It is assigned the place of supplying the missing links and answering for the person. And so the face becomes overtly exaggerated [*utrirovannym*]. Why do the faces of city dwellers, of respectable people generally, appear indistinct? The contours are blurred, effaced by an indefinite fattiness— when there is character, proper clothing, and social position. But in old age or in prison, there where nothing is left, suffering cuts through faces, and they are thrust out at the viewer: the nose juts out like a spear, and the eyes cast pearls, and the mouth is bared, for lack of a standard smile, in an unconcealed greediness—to be. The face carries the honor of final representation [*predstavitel'stva*]. (441)

Anticipating his later, repeated use of the term "exaggerated prose" (*utrirovannaya proza*) to describe his own works, the author explains how the camp heightens his vision, throwing into relief that which is normally obscured by convention. The person is subjected to what he terms the "law of Robinson Crusoe": "Not from nostalgia or from snobbishness, but objects that are difficult to obtain or scarce here gather force and weight and demand respect toward themselves. Not to go and 'listen to music' would be the same as refusing breakfast, ignoring an invitation to drink coffee. The point lies not in the satiation of the flesh (or spirit), but in the demands of the object, which from the ordinary and insignificant has become precious—the law of Robinson Crusoe" (456). Stripping the individual of excess accumulation, the condition of confinement makes what remains worthy of attention. "It's possible," the author observes, "that grains of art, like salt, are spilled into life. It's left to the artist to discover them, distill them, and gather them in their pure form" (461). Imprisonment, by reducing people and life to essentials, allows the artist to discover these grains of art, revealing them in their "exaggerated" fullness.

The camp thus exposes the writer, as Gulliver's travels do Gulliver, to a radical change of perspective, which discredits conventional conceptions of character. The author's displacement from Moscow to the labor camp "at the edge of the earth" (508) represents, both geographically and conceptually, a movement from the center to the periphery, which the author proposes as the source of culture: "A question—where is the source? By the law of contrast (by the law of pain) it should be situated not in the capital, but off to the side, on the periphery—of the text, of the city, of society, of civilization. Just as a monastery, removed beyond the precincts of the city, into the desert, to the edge of the earth, in ancient times was nonetheless the spiritual center of culture—the center, which, for all this, always for some reason lies outside the circle of life and even somewhere beyond the field of attainability. Prophets come more frequently from the lower classes or from outside, in any case—not from the elite. Is that not because from below, from a distance, it's handier for them to rise above the common, and even above the highest, level and go beyond the limits of the culture?" (507–08). In relocating the writer, his imprisonment places him within an utterly different set of spatial and temporal frames of reference: "Rather there functions a general psycho-physical climate—an isolation from the commonly accessible, pan-human flow of life. Just as terrestrial marks of time are not applicable on Mars. A completely different system of coordinates" (455). The author finds himself looking from a different angle of vision: "All the same the shift in time and space introduces into existence an inexpressible nuance—a new dimension, perhaps, which makes it possible to look at everything from a height, as if you were looking with a somewhat otherworldly eye. It's not clear: is something long or short, small or big, good or bad—experiencing a cold feeling of distanced amazement" (450). Just as in *Thoughts Unawares* the author refutes conventional definitions of identity by measuring the "naked human being" against the gauges of death, eternity, and God; just as Swift exposes the relativity of definitions of the self by juxtaposing his Everyman Gulliver to a series of disproportionate others; so the camp—as not merely a place of confinement, but a different scale of calibration—places in doubt the integrity of the self as a coherent entity, concomitantly turning it into an object of wonder, of art.

The third of the literary models Tertz invokes on the early pages of *A Voice from the Chorus* provides a model for the imprisoned self. The author maintains that the person confined, deprived of free movement in space, has no recourse but to turn inwards:

Where do things come from? Probably it is all a matter of space. A human being, open to space, strives all the time into the distance. He is sociable and aggressive; he would have newer and newer delights, impressions, interests. But if you compress him, reduce him to standard—to the minimum—the soul, deprived of forests and fields, restores the landscape out of its own fathomless stores. Monks made use of this. Distribute your property—is that not a shedding of ballast?

Not rejected people, but immersed ones. Not imprisoned, but—immersed. Reservoirs. Not human beings—wells. Lakes of meaning.

The minimum cell—exactly tailored to the dimensions of the body—is given in sleep, and we leap out—where? We give up the ghost, moving away, not, however, outwards, but into ourselves. We melt away in sleep and, burdened with nothing, easily float across to the other bank of the river.

Nothing else remains to the soul driven into a cage but to go out into the expanses of the universe through the back entrance. But, for that to happen, it is necessary as a preliminary to bring it well to bay. (451)

The Life of Archpriest Avvakum by Himself—the first major autobiographical work, as well as the first major writing about confinement, in Russian literature—serves the author as the paradigmatic instance of this turning inward: "Why did so much fit into Avvakum's one pit? Is it not because it was a pit, a hole? And the smaller, the more cramped, the more would fit into it? Otherwise there is no way of explaining the appearance of a panorama hitherto unknown in the iconography of ancient Rus" (450).[22] Avvakum's "pit" or "hole" becomes a metaphor for the "fathomless" expanses of the soul: "If, while sleeping, we dream of a street along which people are walking, it means that it is spacious inside of us, as in a city, and our soul is large, and it is possible to walk through it and descend stairs to the sea, and sit down on the shore and look" (485). This inner space is also a repository of the past: "in our soul a house is built where long-past images are preserved, as in a museum, capable of coming alive at any moment and returning to their former place, continuing now outside time and space, so that it's even terrifying to lug this store around with you" (602). The self, freed of "ballast," is an empty hole, populated by memories and experiences of other people and other places. Avvakum, writing his "Life" while imprisoned, narrates his travels, encompassing his relatives, spiritual fellows, and enemies, all of which merge in a "panorama," which fills up his pit. The self represented thus becomes a landscape, which, through the metaphor of the hole, merges with the place of confinement.

Like Avvakum's pit, the camp is transformed into a figure of the dissolution of the writer's self, which is crowded out by his surroundings: "It was no longer a human being, but an avalanche or a mountain of chips of rock, not a prisoner, but a camp, rearing up, primordial, like chaos, a camp in which the lives of others already occupied, very likely, more space than his own first-person story and character, as when wood is being floated down river, and still water or a logjam occurs, from which the logs stand up, like hair on the head—just like that was I gathered into a heap and thrown as carrion—not as a reproach to someone, but, rather, to be looked at" (566). The passage that follows elaborates on the same idea: "A second life is superimposed on the ribbon of my daily life, the images of which in the process of all these departures for work, going to bed, reveille, seem unreal. There arises a feeling opposite to solipsistic principles, when everything around me is more persuasive than I am myself. It's easier for me to assume that I don't exist, while life is in full swing" (566). The author's perception of himself—which, because it is embodied in the text, is inseparable from its representation—becomes a surrender of self, an absorption into the landscape of confinement and into the others who populate it. Thus, the author looks within himself and finds others: "They say—character. I don't know what character is. And in myself I sense more not myself, but my father, my mother, you, Egor [Sinyavsky's son], Pushkin, Gogol. A whole crowd. They are superimposed on perception, participate in my fate and go where we are taken, making their presence felt hourly, and if one is to portray a human being really [*real'no*], then this will take the shape of a space—a landscape, an ocean, rather than character" (625).

As I pointed out earlier, the textual relationship between the voice and the chorus evolves in the course of the work. *A Voice from the Chorus* begins with the voice of another contrasted, by contiguity, with the voice of the author. The interplay between voice and chorus, initiated by this confrontation, disappears in the sixth and penultimate chapter of the book. In his afterword to the original Russian edition of *A Voice from the Chorus*, Igor Golomshtok suggests that the chorus disappears in the concluding sections because the author's

interest in, and curiosity about, those around him wanes as he tires
of the constant and distracting presence of others:

> In the course of the book the Choir gathers force and in the
> third chapter literally drowns out the Voice, composing more
> than half of its text. By that time the carrier of the Voice is
> tired. Not so much from the exhausting physical labor and the
> constant severe undernourishment as from the impossibility
> of remaining for a minute alone in private with his thoughts
> and a blank sheet of paper. That which earlier had been inter-
> esting has exhausted itself and turned into a nightmare of
> enforced collective existence. "I want to be deaf in order to
> read and write . . . In these years I have grown so tired of
> people" (p. 245). After the third chapter the Chorus subsides,
> and finally it disappears in the last two chapters. The Voice
> seemingly distances itself from its surroundings, retreats into
> itself, and the intonation of curiosity is replaced by a different
> one—tired, drawn-out, self-absorbed.[23]

While the chorus does predominate in the third section of the book,
and while the author does occasionally lament his lack of privacy in
the later sections, I would argue that the chorus does not disappear.
Rather, as the author's "I" dissolves in the camp, as he looks into
the empty pit of his soul, the boundaries between self and other collapse. The self is transformed in representation and contemplation
into a multiplicity of voices. The author's voice merges with those of
the chorus.

Two images in particular which support such a reading appear
toward the end of the fifth section, that is, the last section that incorporates the voices of other camp inmates. The first is elaborated in
the section's penultimate passage:

> It always seemed to me that our existence is an island,
> but now I see it as—a mainland, a continent, and the people
> who visit here, coming or going, living and dying, enter into
> its composition, and so this island grows and snatches more
> spaces and distances, so open to contemplation that for all the
> immobility of life you begin to notice how the epic was cre-
> ated—always tied to a place, to some island-bound people and
> tribe, from which, however, numerous streams of journeys,
> caravan routes, and fates branched off, in their turn flowing

into what was already a mainland zone. The link by place of birth, by intersection of destiny, imparted to scattered persons and thoughts a kinship owing to which a single unit, which incorporated the memory of many, could become the center (as happened with Odysseus) of a vast epic mainland and story. (638)

Here the author, by implication again casting himself as a latter-day Odysseus, redefines the meaning of the epic center.[24] The center becomes not what defines, but what serves as a locus of intersection, what contains and remembers, the single individual who is the repository of the many. The epic text is an island that branches out into a mainland, a place of meeting for those coming and going, an expanse that unites people through a kinship of place and fate. By the same token, the author of *A Voice from the Chorus* becomes the mainland on which voice and chorus, memories of the past, books, and art merge in the landscape of the represented self.

While the analogy with Odysseus pictures the represented self projected into a body of land, the body of the text, the second model for the author's project proposed four passages earlier expresses the desire to escape the body:

In youth I imagined a confessor to be a person overburdened with the sins of others. So much does he hear, so much does he remember of it all—from this spectacle one could not help but grow cold toward people. In reality—he does not hear, does not remember. In reality—the consciousness that would hold back evidence in his sieve and keep it for his own use is absent. Not an ear, but a conduit, a passageway into the dark sky. A chink. As if with a vacuum cleaner, he draws through the chink litter that has lain for years, compressed, now breaking off in lumps, with a droning—as if a wind were blowing into the exit, into the expanse, into the open gates sucking so greedily that, following your sins, it seems, you yourself will fly away. There is no person in the confessor, and therefore the shame that would hold back the admissions of those confessing is also seemingly obliterated; on the contrary, you hasten not to forget anything, to scrape yourself clean—and the rare responses of the witness who leaves no trace, his light sighs and questions help you to liberate yourself, will carry you away. His visible image in that night is spectral as if disappearing, growing thin, present more as a voice, like an ancient chorus, as a weak moan, accompanying the act of a confessed and forgiven life. And now you in your very self no longer distinguish either name or personality, but only a faceless chorus, which creates the semblance of a background against which the soul that has thrown off the skin coils in tangles—carried by that wind, by that rain of voices. (637)

The confessing priest represents the negation of conscious self in the presence of which voice and chorus merge, the difference between self and other, inside and outside, disappears. By the same token, the person in the act of confessing is also sucked clean of self, finding within only a "faceless chorus" which accompanies the soul's liberation. Echoing the author's earlier statement that "art is always more or less an improvised prayer," confession becomes a metaphor for art as an offering up, a shedding, of accumulated sins, a surrender of the self to God, which promises the transcendence of difference that accompanies the release of the soul from the body.

The merger of the voice and the chorus prefigured in these two paradigmatic instances metaphorically transpires in the penultimate section of *A Voice from the Chorus*. The structural role played by the voices of the chorus interspersed throughout the first five sections is taken over in the sixth section by the cycle of Chechen songs about the prophet Kunta-Khadzhi, which, like the voices of the chorus earlier, alternate with the authorial voice. An analogy is clearly suggested between the imprisoned prophet and the imprisoned writer, an analogy underscored particularly by the blurring of identities that occurs between the concluding passage of the sixth section and the opening passage of the seventh and final section concerning the author's release from the camp. The former reads: "These are the last tidings of Kishi-Khadzhi. However, there exists a legend that to this day he has not died and will still return, because he was granted the age of four human lives" (662). The latter bears the date of the author's return home from imprisonment and is the only dated entry that breaks chronology: "I walk about the house like a ghost. Not the one who lived here once. But the one who is yet to come" (662). This textual echo reinforces the patent resonances not only between the situations of Khadzhi and the writer, but also with the vision of art and the writer that runs throughout *A Voice from the Chorus* and the other Tertz writings.

Khadzhi, as a prophet of Allah, receives words from a divine source outside of himself. He is both an outsider persecuted by the Russian authorities and one placed on trial by scholars of his own nation and religion, who challenge the authority of the words he claims to have been given by Allah. Most important, in the cycle of songs revolving around Khadzhi the images of chorus, song, and prayer come together. The author observes: "Songs about Kunta-Khadzhi usually conclude with colophons in which a choral principle predominates. They can change, pass from one song to another, from legend to legend, like common exclamations or winged incantations" (641). The songs thus root the text's lack of fixed form in the "choral principle," the mutability and communality of the voices that sing of the prophet. Finally, the two excerpts from songs about Khadzhi that frame the sixth section, making up its first and penultimate passages, both conclude with the "circular prayer" or "fast prayer", which Khadzhi passed on from Allah to his people and for which he was put on trial.[25] "The meaning of the words," the author observes, "was, evidently, not understood by the participants in the circular prayer themselves" (641). The circular prayer suggests an ideal text, joining human voices in a refrain granted to them by God, through the vessel of his prophet, and offered back up to God. While the human celebrants can combine their voices in the singing of the words, the meaning of the words is understood only by God.

At the center of the complex structural and conceptual framework of *A Voice from the Chorus* stands the fundamental distinction that Sinyavsky drew at his trial between literature and law, art and reality. On at least two occasions the author explicitly contrasts legal form with the basic principles of his vision of art. The first instance occurs in a discussion of Leskov's writing. The author's remarks are prompted by Leskov's statement "I am afraid that I will not be able to sketch his portrait at all precisely because I see him very well and clearly" (521). The author comments:

> This sentence sounds the death knell of all premeditated precision and, perhaps, provides the basis for a general psychology of creation, which always works, in essence, on unfamiliar material that strikes and arouses the imagination. It—the imagination—having reared up on its haunches, actually stumbles over the "resemblance to nature." That which is too familiar does not amaze and therefore does not lend itself to being copied. Art always first transforms reality into the exotic and only then undertakes to depict it.

Taking off from here with his discourse, Leskov first of all creates a sense of confusion and inability to tell about what happened and sticks words in helter-skelter, with a coarse clumsiness, hoping that this discourse rushing about in blind perplexity in the end will inadvertently run up against the object and revive it and raise it up in its tongue-tiedness— in its "impetuous and dense disharmony." How does one describe a suicide so that it does not come out as a police report, but conveys the whole horror and senselessness of the occurrence? Evidently, to begin with, one must chuck the very task of describing it precisely. And so he [Leskov], stepping back, spreads words wide, like fingers, and waves them, so that, as a result, this renunciation of the story becomes the best means of acquainting us with the facts and of grasping what happened through a helpless piling up of discourse, which does not even try to represent anything. (521)

By contrasting a literary text with a legal document (*protokol'nyi otschet*), the author suggests the basic principles of his understanding of how language works in literature. He opposes precise description to transformation—the transmutation of the everyday into the exotic, the other. The writer accomplishes this transformation by "stepping back," by changing his angle of vision, a contextual dislocation that, echoing the author's earlier comments on *Gulliver's Travels*, entails a loss of the ability to name, a breakdown of the relationship between word and object on which the legal document rests.

As in *Thoughts Unawares*, Russian culture is portrayed as exemplary, its impulses here explicitly related to art.[26] The author contrasts "Western comfortable form, legality" (614) with Russian "formlessness," which he associates with the centrality of the Holy Spirit in Russian Orthodox belief:

Our Russian sensuality in relation to miracle, icons, relics, rituals is fed by a perception of the Holy Spirit, of the life-creating Lord that is tangible to the point of magical impulses. . . .

The Religion of the Holy Spirit somehow corresponds to the traits of our national physiognomy—to our natural formlessness (which outsiders erroneously take for savagery or for the youth of the nation), to our fluidity, amorphousness, readiness to assume any form (come and rule over us), to our vices, or talents to think and live artistically while unable to organize everyday life, to take it completely seriously (Why bother? Who needs it? Life's too short. I'm fed up! It will take care of itself!). (613)

As manifestations of this formlessness in art, the author adduces "the striking absence of sculpture (perhaps more than the other arts presupposing a realization of form)," a "gap" that he suggests is filled "by the overflow of song and painting (it flows)," as well as the "violation of the hierarchy of genres" in literature (613–14). Just as Russian art seeks to escape the confines of matter and formal structure, so Russian nationality is endlessly permeable: "From the spirit—we are sensitive to all ideological trends to such an extent that at some moment we lose language and face and become Germans, Frenchmen, Jews" (613). Russianness is identified as an emptiness that can be filled up with anything, and Russian formlessness manifests itself as a resistance to "legal" identity, an aspiration to escape the confines of the body and of language through constant transformation, to become ever other than oneself and thereby elude definition.

This basic dichotomy between "formlessness" and "legality" underlies the author's attacks on realism in art—"Realism in the bad sense (an interest in indelibly etching the exterior)" (558)—and his comments on character in literature. He assails the "feeling of no appeal, of a wall" which is "so unbidden, unbroachable in portraits of the realist school, where the living face is aimed at you, like a gun, loaded with an unneeded acquaintance pressed on you by force" (464). This "resemblance to the person" is an "obstacle" over which "you stumble": "How the gaze of the self-satisfied nineteenth century crowds you out, where each portrait cries: 'Go away, it is I,' or 'Look, it is I,' one way or the other detaining you, not letting you pass" (464). In copying external appearance, realism intrinsically equates the self with the body, which, by demanding attention to itself, does not allow the viewer to look beyond it to the soul. The author argues that "character in literature, evidently, is an attempt to derive the movements of the soul and fate from immanent characteristics of the person, gathered into a psychological cliché [which is] more or less clear-cut, immutable, and self-enclosed, on the model of the body" (565). Thus the illusion of the integrity of the self is derived by analogy with the physical unity of the body and is sustainable "only in a strict system of historical coordinates" (565). Removed from the defining context, character is exposed as a fiction.

Just as he dismisses character as a formal convention, so also the author rejects plot:

> Paper is necessary so that one can forget oneself in its whiteness. When you write, you dive into the page and emerge with some thought, with some word. Blank paper disposes one to immersion—in the depths of the unpretentious space of the sheet. A writer is something of a fisherman. He sits and tries to catch something. Without understanding anything, without thinking—put a blank sheet in front of me, and I will unfailingly fish something out of it.
>
> But that is why plots are dangerous. A plot imposes obligations. You no longer obey the paper, but the unfolding of the action. There is something false in a plot. On the other hand, what freedom and immediacy there are in an essay, in "sketches," "notes" from this or the other world. An essay— you simply outline and spin out on paper. An essay is a lake, a blot on an empty space. (668)

Plot and character are both impositions of convention on language. Both are formal structures that express a single point of view, necessarily bound to specific coordinates of time and space and, therefore, relative. All form in the conventional sense becomes an assertion of a defining center, of the fiction of a unitary "I." In contrast, the author maintains that just as the text aspires to the silence of the pauses between words, so it emerges from the empty space of the page. The self is a void that can be filled up by language. "In order to write anything worth the trouble," the author maintains, "it is necessary to be absolutely empty" (630).

Thus, throughout *A Voice from the Chorus,* the author repeatedly portrays writing as a sloughing of the conscious self, a submission to language. Rather than being subordinated to a subject to be depicted, language should itself be treated as a substance whose qualities must be respected: "One must trust in language, which will lead you by the hand, just as a sculptor carves wood in accord with its fibre, without knowing what will come out in the process, what knot or word will bulge out and turn, and yield a shape and structure" (489). Drawing on the images of water, flowing, and formlessness that recur throughout the text, the author compares the sentence to a river and underscores the analogy through the form of the passage itself, which is made up—with the exception of a brief coda at its end—of a single twisting sentence from which both writer and reader emerge gasping for air:

> How pleasant (how terrible) it is, having taken in as much air as possible and not knowing clearly where to begin, to dive into the sentence which scorches at the first strokes, which opens up and closes behind you, like water, and has no relation to you until you enter into it completely and, having felt a sudden aid, flowing from inside, from this discourse whither you imprudently leapt, until you trust in the course, the channel you share with it, running the risk of choking and never emerging from the river, which, having shown pity and taken you quietly in its hands, already, it seems, prods you toward the object about which you undertook to write, except that you suddenly notice that it is now no longer the same, and it is already getting toward evening, and you must swim, without being capricious, silently obeying the mother still ready to humor you, and, whether you want to or not, to keep your manners and plunge to the very bottom, where having almost lost consciousness of what you are talking about, you finally say something equivalent to that force which in casting you out on the surface bears witness to its goodness rather than to the swimmer's experience. You come out of the sentence somewhat ashamed and dumbfounded by what was said. (558)

Writing is expressed as a relinquishment of self to the flow, to the force of language, which, while seeming to push the writer toward the object about which he consciously intends to speak, transforms the subject of discourse itself.

A similarly syntactically complex passage takes us to the heart of the understanding of language—suggested in the sentence-river above—out of which the structured formlessness of the text originates:

> I repeat myself and beat the air. In justification I will note that the text as a spatial problem can be neither a static platform nor a tape moving in one direction. Antinomies—like "winter," "sun," "island," "woman," "book," and so forth—force the words to scatter along radiuses, repeating and excluding one another, producing a rotation of discourse, its return to old riddles, seemingly succumbing to an effort, an influx of meaning, but then to an ebb-tide in the impotence to solve off-

hand reversible paradoxes, which without such reversibility would be a tribute to form and nothing more. In this lies the role of irony, which does not allow the world to congeal with the bulging eyes of unambiguous [*odnoznachnoi*], vociferous lifelessness, but which introduces vacillation into discourse, like modulation of the voice, which, moving away, ceaselessly returns to its beginning, until we guess that this is not a torrent of words, not a voice, but the horizon itself which is rotating and reversing, granting and drawing the force to live on and on. (479–80)

I would suggest that the central thrust of this complicated passage lies in an affirmation that while language embodies the ability to name, to distinguish one entity from another, it does not intrinsically contain a defining point of view that would render the relationship between word and referent stable, "univocal." The writer's surrender of self, his refusal to impose his own defining point of view on language, opens him up to the plurality of perspective inscribed in this text in the voices of the chorus. Irony and riddle are invoked here as tropes that a priori correspond to language's multivocal potential. They are rhetorical stances that originate in the writer's ability to submit simultaneously to disparate perspectives of definition. It is in this ability that the vision of art elaborated throughout *A Voice from the Chorus* is rooted: art not as the attempt to represent "precisely," but rather as an embodiment of the transformative potential of language.

The author in fact repeatedly describes riddle and metaphor as means of transformation. In one brief and particularly significant passage he claims: "Metaphor is the memory of that golden age when everything was everything. A fragment of metamorphosis" (576). This postulation of metaphor as a vestige of a golden age harks back to Tertz's interpretation of the fall in *The Trial Begins* as a fall into difference. Here, in viewing the "golden age" as a time when "everything was everything," he makes explicit the genesis of riddle and metaphor—both of which have their roots in analogy, in the collapsing of boundaries between distinct objects—in an inevitably doomed aspiration to return to this pristine, ideal state.

In a lengthy discussion of riddles, which follows close on the statement about metaphor cited above, the author expands on this point. He launches his discussion by citing the "Logomachy of the youth Pippin, the son of Charlemagne, with his mentor Alcuin (or Albinus the Scholastic)" (578). The citation begins:

Pippin: What is faith?

Alcuin: Certitude in that which you do not understand and which you consider miraculous.

Pippin: What is the miraculous?

Alcuin: I saw, for example, a person on legs, a strolling dead man who never existed.

Pippin: How is that possible, explain to me!

Alcuin: It is a reflection in water. (578)

We can easily see from this single example that the riddle is constructed on the same estrangement, on the same dislocation of an object from its name that the author illustrates elsewhere by adducing the Lilliputians and Leskov.

While taking pains to point out that just as word is not deed, so riddle is not miracle, the author nonetheless insists, taking his cue from Alcuin, that "the origin of riddles, we see, is directly linked with miracles," that riddles are a "manifestation of the miraculous in life" (579). He goes on to argue that we can, "explaining the riddle, genetically deduce it from miracle in roughly the same way as the magic trick, the circus stunt, came out of miracle, making up for the lack of magic through deception and dexterity of the fingers. The riddle fills in for the miraculous through dexterity of language, the play of thought. The word, which once called forth and conjured fire, chose here the roundabout manuever of the figurative description of flame, where instead of a literal blazing up of brushwood under the pressure of the magic word, as a result of mental efforts a click is felt in the head and the flame of the solution to the riddle blazes up" (579). What miracle in an earlier time made happen in reality, the riddle now accomplishes in the reader's or listener's mind. Deception takes the place of magic and also, by implication, of realistic representation. Riddle, as a paradigm for the artistic text, seeks not to copy reality, but to turn one object into another, in the process collapsing the boundaries between them. Its "miraculousness," moreover, hinges precisely on its revelation of its own deception. The solution to the riddle is the "blazing up" of the metaphorical fire as the one who guesses the answer apprehends simultaneously the equivalence the riddle poses and the illusion on which the equation rests.

The author brings his discussion of Alcuin's and Pippin's riddles to a close by explicitly linking them to the genesis of art:

The world was still sufficiently metamorphic to toss and turn, turning one thing into another and giving the word a shove toward the production of allegory-riddles. We are seemingly present at the acting out of the birth of art, when the folkloric soil was still hot and smoking and swollen with the sprouts of metaphor, when the life of the language, remembering the miracle of its origin, still performed magic tricks, with which, like riddles, like every sort of knavery and deceit, fiction and artfulness, the fairy tale is filled and foams. Here we understand that all of world art is moved by the insatiable craving for the miraculous that is concealed in us. Here it becomes clear that the poet, even in the new, contemporary sense of the word, is a failed magician-miracleworker, who replaced metamorphosis with metaphor, act—with word play. (580)

Here, harking back to "At the Circus" and looking forward to *In the Shadow of Gogol*, Tertz invokes one of his favorite figures of the writer. Metaphor is the tool of the writer-magician's sleight-of-hand. He is a "failed" magician, because his "word play" is "knavery and deceit," illusion.

The "criminality" of the writer's deception is underscored by the equivalence Tertz draws between the writer as magician and the writer as thief: "in general, almost all that remains of the fairy tale is now found in the circus. Sorcerer—magician—thief: the evolution of an image" (577). This takes us back to the third section of *A Voice from the Chorus*, in which, as Golomshtok points out, a higher percentage of the text is occupied by the voices of the chorus than elsewhere and in which the constituent passages arguably exhibit the greatest degree of thematic coherence—revolving around crime, escape, spectacle, laughter, and play. The section's centrality, both literal and figurative, is marked by its concluding passage:

> When the stoolpigeons put Pushkin on a sheet of iron and began to roast him over the bonfire, he shouted a sentence to the onlookers standing in the distance. I could not choose anything better for my epigraph if only I considered myself worthy of repeating it:
> "Hey, suckers! Tell people I died a thief!" (550)

The author's placement of his epigraph—or the epigraph he would use if he considered himself "worthy"—at roughly the midpoint of his book rather than at the beginning accentuates the disruption of conventional structure that informs the entire text. More important, the Pushkin who figures in this anecdote is not Aleksandr Sergeevich Pushkin, the poet, but rather a thief nicknamed "Pushkin." The thief thus incarnates art as imposture, the transformation of the self: "As if we wanted to not resemble ourselves and to find out—at least that way—what the miracle of the Transfiguration is. All theater comes from this, all costumes: Look, I am not I" (443).

The image of the thief embodies the assertion reiterated throughout *A Voice from the Chorus* that art is brighter, more colorful, than everyday reality, that it is created "not at all by analogy with life—on the contrary, by contrast, against its colorless background" (550). Tertz observes in his 1979 article, "The Fatherland. A Thieves' Song":

> Look how much space is allotted here [in the thieves' song] to attire, to costume—by contrast with the surrounding poverty. In this the pungent psychology of the clan can be discerned: a thief at work must look respectable, while easy enrichment and the transitoriness, the ephemerality of free existence give birth to the need at least once in life, if one has got lucky, to flash like a count, to splurge in a princely fashion, to dress a dear slut up in finery. But the other side of this also (a violin joins in) testifies to the artistic nature, which seeks to touch "something lofty."[27]

The thief steals gold, a recurring image for art throughout *A Voice from the Chorus*, not to "accumulate," but rather, to shed his identity, to squander what he has taken from the other on a theatrical self-transformation, an imposture, which at the same time represents an impulse to escape the grayness of life, the confines of the body, and to strive toward "something lofty." The author maintains: "Almost as among poets, in the etiquette of thieves pride of place is allotted to spectacle and to an understanding of the personality and fate of a person as spectacle" (543). Echoing his persistent contention that art lies outside conventional moral systems, the author expands on the idea of a thieves' "etiquette" or "law": "Nevertheless, sometimes thieves are evaluated extremely negatively. Evidently, both this and the other [positive] evaluation correspond to reality and to the concept of the thief as part of a moral code which took shape in conditions of the absence of morality. In the place of moral gaps appeared humps of morality: order, caste, etiquette, hierarchy—there where normally reigned arbitrariness and limitlessness. A thief in the precise sense is not at all an amoral subject, but a person adhering to elite principles of morality (544).[28] These "elite principles of

morality" are, again, inextricably linked to the "conception of personality as spectacle" rooted in the centrality of "spirit" to the thieves'
code:

> In this light, that same "law" presented itself to me as
> an order of knights (inside out, but precisely of knights), in
> which, along with the strictest regulations, was maintained
> *spirit*, inextinguishable and employed in a particular sense.
> "To be strung up you have to have the spirit."
> "If you have the spirit, I say, take a knife and go ram it in."
> (545)

Spirit is thus the impetus of the "theatrical feat and gesture, the
effective death" (543). The theatricalization of the self becomes an
attempt to incarnate spirit, a metaphor for the literary text, which,
trapped in the fallen world, emulates the liberation of the soul by
asserting its own imposture.

"In principle," the author observes, "only miracle is worthy of
being written about" (621). In the following passage, he cites a tale
from Paulus Diaconus's *History of the Langobards* that encapsulates
the vision of artistic creation at the heart of *A Voice from the Chorus*.
In the story the king of the Franks, left alone in the forest with
one faithful follower, falls asleep. A lizard crawls out of his mouth,
and the retainer follows it as it crosses a stream, enters a chink in
a mountain, and then comes out and goes back into the sleeping
king's mouth. When the king awakes, he relates a dream in which he
has crossed a river and found an enormous pile of gold in a mountain. Guided by the man who followed the lizard, they find the gold,
which the king orders be made into a chalice decorated with precious stones and placed on the tomb of the sainted martyr Marcellus.
The author comments:

> Let us follow the outline of the plot of the creation of
> the precious unique object: it glides, like a lizard, describ-
> ing a complex but precise figure, returning exactly there from
> whence it came. The miracle, already somewhat shading over
> into anecdote, into a strange and amazing event connected
> with some ancient, pagan perhaps, archetypal nature of the
> soul which slips out of the body in a dream in the guise of
> a lizard, is resolved by the creation of the marvelous chalice,
> which, like a flower on a stem, crowns the event, immortalizes
> it, and returns to the proper quarter—to God, to the other

world, through the Holy Sepulchre or the nearby tomb of
Saint Marcellus. (623)

In the author's interpretation, the story of the lizard and the gold
clearly represents a paradigm both for the work of art and for the
process of creation. The process is initiated when the soul leaves the
sleeping body, apparently in response to a summons from outside.
The shedding of the self is portrayed as a miraculous transformation, an imposture: the soul adopts the exotic guise of the lizard.
And, like the lizard, the story returns "from whence it came"; the
gold obtained from its circular journey is also sent back to its source,
fashioned into a work of art and offered up to God. By the same
token, the author, who at the beginning of *A Voice from the Chorus*
finds himself on a "naked point" (440), after journeying through
a series of metaphorical transformations, is left a "naked point of
view" (664) at the end. The gold of the text remains, offered up to
God in prayer.

A Voice from the Chorus, like *Thoughts Unawares*, is an experiment in writing as it is "forbidden" to write in order to challenge
conventional conceptions of narrative and of self-representation. If,
however, *Thoughts Unawares* makes a point of its own failure, of the
impossibility of capturing the self in art, *A Voice from the Chorus*
recognizes the genesis of art out of this very impossibility. Anticipating the metaphors of imposture and magic that are elaborated
at greater length in the other two works of Tertz's "middle" period,
Strolls with Pushkin and *In the Shadow of Gogol*, *A Voice from the
Chorus* denies that art should try to copy reality: "Art is not the
representation, but the transformation of life. The image itself arises
from the requirement of transformation: the image is shifted from
the object, pushing it toward change into another, transformed aspect. We notice the 'image' only in the overcoming of that which it
makes an effort to represent. A table or forest is not an image. A
golden table is an image. A green forest is not an image: it must
be—green noise" (587). By the same token, the self, represented,
translated into images, is transformed and, in becoming other than
itself, becomes worthy of being looked at, of being art.

Chapter Seven

. . . .

Decanonizing the Classics: *Strolls with Pushkin* and *In the Shadow of Gogol*

Pushkin is our all.

—APOLLON GRIGOREV

The eternal companion of our life, Pushkin is especially near and dear to all of us. A great patriot of his motherland, he gave the fullest expression to the spiritual powers of the Russian people. . . .

In the history of Russian literature Gogol and Pushkin stand together as the founders of realism. . . . With Gogol, Russian literature, developing the traditions of Griboedov and Pushkin, became a rigorous exposer of the feudal system of serfdom, of the parasitism and moral decay of the ruling classes.

—SOVIET GRADE SCHOOL TEXTBOOK

Throughout the writings of Tertz the image of the writer as criminal is threatened by the specter of the writer canonized, turned into a figure of authority, a prescription for how one must write. In "Pkhents" the narrator is terrified by his own imaginings of being transformed into the center of a cult, while in "Graphomaniacs" Straustin is oppressed by the overbearing presence of the classics, which haunt him in the names of streets throughout Moscow, in the preserved tubercular spittle of Chekhov and the fingernail parings of Tolstoy, and, most of all, in this injunction: " 'Read Chekhov, read Chekhov,' they've repeated to me my whole life, tactlessly hinting that Chekhov wrote better than I do' " (176). In *What Is Socialist Realism* Chekhov is invoked as an authoritative standard that seduces with the lure of fame: "Ch-ch-ch-chekhov. This ruined us. We immediately wanted to become famous, to write like Chekhov" (456). In *The Trial Begins*, on the other hand, the ironist Karlinsky fantasizes about blowing up the Opekushin Pushkin monument in Moscow. In essence, that is precisely what Tertz sets out to do in *Strolls with Pushkin* and *In the Shadow of Gogol*. In the two works he casts the two authors as opposite models for the writer—Pushkin as the pure artist and Gogol as the artist who strives for authority. Ultimately, however, he aims to rescue both from canonicity, not so much by offering an alternative reading of their lives and works as by subverting the equation of the body of the writer with the body of the text on which that canonicity rests.

Tertz's immediate target in *Strolls with Pushkin* and *In the Shadow of Gogol* is the Soviet tradition, which traces its lineage back to Belinsky and the nineteenth-century radical critics, to "critical realism," a tradition that claims Pushkin and Gogol as its founding fathers and its primary sources of legitimacy. Tertz treats realism in his Pushkin and Gogol books, as elsewhere in his works, first and foremost as a prescription for how one must write, entailing an obligation on the part of the writer to serve utilitarian aims. One depicts reality in order to change it by "enlightening" the reader, by imposing the author's supposedly "objective" vision of reality on the reader. Both literature and the writer are subordinated to "reality," but this reality, as Tertz continually suggests, is either—or both—a system of literary conventions or an ideological framework. Thus, in *Strolls with Pushkin* and *In the Shadow of Gogol* he seeks to subvert the Russian tradition of the writer as political, social, or moral critic by impugning the concept of realism itself, counterposing to it the inherent difference between reality and its representation, rooted in the role of the reader, from which the uncontrollability of the text, the multivalence of the literary sign, springs.

Like *A Voice from the Chorus*, *Strolls with Pushkin* and *In the Shadow of Gogol* challenge conventional genre classifications. Here we can see both the polemical strategy behind the writer's attribution of certain of his works to Sinyavsky and others to Tertz and the formal and stylistic distinctions between the two sets of writings. The Sinyavsky signature affixed to *V. V. Rozanov's "Fallen Leaves"* corresponds to and confirms the scholarly format of the work, which is designed to legitimate the rebellion against convention of a notoriously controversial writer. The Tertz books on Pushkin and Gogol, on the other hand, adopt a deliberately unconventional form and style in order to wrest the two pillars of tradition from the tradition.[1] Sinyavsky himself has designated the works "fantastic literary scholarship" (*fantasticheskoe literaturovedenie*), explaining:

When a person takes up the study of art, he can write an academic work or he can act just as he would in fantastic realism. After all art is the same objective reality as reality is. That means that it can be portrayed in different ways, emphasizing some things, exaggerating, sometimes turning them upside down. By the way, that's why people say that everything is wrong in those works. But sometimes it's done wrong consciously. It was simply amusing to write a scholarly monograph on Pushkin while in a labor camp. But some things I simply broke first, the way you break a toy, and glued them back together a new way. Take *The Bronze Horseman* for example. I present the hypothesis that Peter is a poet, and Evgeny—an ordinary man. That is the root of their conflict. But it's only a hypothesis. I don't insist on that reading and I never suggested *Strolls with Pushkin* be used as a textbook for the study of Pushkin. Or elsewhere in the work I take up the hypothesis that Tatyana was in fact in love with Pushkin, and not with Evgeny Onegin. I don't assert this in absolute seriousness. I simply took it and turned it upside down.[2]

Strolls with Pushkin and *In the Shadow of Gogol* are both exercises in writing as "it is forbidden to write," in deliberately violating convention and taxonomy. Behind—or rather embodied in—the whimsical hypotheses and dazzling strings of metaphors out of which the works grow, however, lies a complex vision of the workings of verbal art, which eludes definition, but endlessly generates meaning.

    Strolls with Pushkin has been, as we have seen, its author's most controversial work, provoking numerous attacks when it first appeared in the emigré community in the West in 1975 and serving as the focus of a political uproar when an excerpt was published in the Soviet Union in 1989.[3] On the surface of it, it would appear to be an unlikely book to have unleashed such a furor. Emigré and Soviet critics alike rather improbably took *Strolls with Pushkin* as an attack on Pushkin. What was really at issue, however, was the particular vision of Pushkin as the father of Russian realism, elevated into a cult protected by ritualized language and canonic interpretations of the poet's work. The fetishized Pushkin is indeed Tertz's target in *Strolls with Pushkin*, and the outraged response to the work testifies to the deep roots in Russian culture of the traditional vision of the role of the writer and literature that the official Pushkin has been called on to validate. As a subversion of the conventional attributes of the

Pushkin cult, *Strolls with Pushkin* recalls, perhaps more than any other of Tertz's works, *What Is Socialist Realism,* his argument there against purposeful art transmuted here into the central metaphor of aimless strolling. Also like the early essay, *Strolls with Pushkin* is constructed out of an interplay of polarities and boundary crossings, which destablizes the borders between words and exposes the complex interrelationship of sign and referent.

Tertz opens his text by stating his project precisely in terms of the problem of transcending dichotomy. Asking why Russians consider Pushkin "such a genius and why Pushkin and no one else always comes in first in Russian literature," the narrator poses the enigma of Pushkin in terms of an apparently unbridgeable bipolarity: "the difficulty lies in the fact that he is absolutely accessible and at the same time inscrutable, enigmatic in the obvious accessibility of the truths he enunciated."[4] The problem is thus presented from the outset as an attempt to solve the riddle of Pushkin's simultaneous "accessibility" and "inscrutability," to find what lies beyond the boundaries of words. The narrator proposes to set out in search of the "beautiful original" (342) of Pushkin "not through the front hall, which is crammed with wreaths and busts that have an expression of uncompromising nobility on their brows, but rather with the help of the anecdotal caricatures of Pushkin that were sent back to the poet by the street, apparently in response to and in revenge for his great fame" (341). He thus again sets up a polarity between the Pushkin of the official cult, of "wreaths and busts," and the Pushkin of jokes and popular sayings. The latter, Pushkin's "caricature double," is linked with the metaphor of strolling: he is "fond of jokes and pranks and therefore more or less suited to accompany us on our excursions through the sacred verses of the poet—to keep them from immediately transposing us into an exalted key and leading us by a direct route to the Pushkin Academy of Sciences and Arts with the aforementioned wreaths and busts on every paragraph" (341). The caricature Pushkin thus is liberated from goal-directed action, which is in turn equated with the ritualized diction of the Pushkin cult, just as strolling becomes, first of all, a mandate for discourse that violates convention. The wreaths and busts emblematizing the Pushkin cult come to signify the claim to define which rests on the subordination of meaning to teleology. As in *What Is Socialist Realism,* this claim lies at the root of bipolar oppositions, since everything that does not submit to it is stigmatized as other.

The joke-Pushkin represents that which subverts the possibility of definition by eluding purposefulness. The idea of transgression is at the heart of the strategy of the text and is implicit in its central metaphor. If one strolls—by definition wandering aimlessly, not following a prescribed route—one runs the risk of violating boundaries, in this case the boundaries erected by the canonic representation of Pushkin. In choosing the caricature Pushkin as his companion on his strolls over the "sacred verses" of the poet—by employing slang, vulgarisms, and whimsical hypotheses instead of formulaic language and a conventional scholarly approach in writing about the sacralized texts and figure of the poet—the narrator metaphorically crosses the boundary between sacred and profane cultural space, thereby again challenging the bipolarity between the acceptable and the unacceptable erected by the canonization of one particular representation of Pushkin and his works. The postulation of Pushkin's simultaneous "accessibility" and "inscrutability" and the proposal to stroll over the "sacred verses" of the poet in the company of the anecdotal Pushkin are thus two sides of the same coin and together serve as a paradigm for the basic strategy of the text, which subverts bipolarity by counterposing to it the union of opposites and the violation of boundaries.

The metaphor of the caricature-Pushkin, moreover, serves to pose the basic problem of identity and representation that this challenge to the integrity of the sign, its ability to mean unambiguously, entails. Mimicking the process to which he will subject the "real" Pushkin later in the text, Tertz begins by stripping this caricature double down to essentials. Asking himself "What will be left of the generally known jokes about Pushkin if we clean them up a bit, getting rid of the scabrous trash?" he answers first of all: "What will remain are those same indestructible sidewhiskers (he'll never get away from them), a walking stick, a hat, flying coattails, sociability, lightmindedness, a talent for getting into scrapes, and a ready tongue for parrying right and left with the dexterity of a magician—in flickering flashes, like the frames of a silent film—the sidewhiskers, the walking stick, the frockcoat" (342). He then adds:

> What will be left is Pushkin's fidgetiness and a kind of omnipresence, along with his ability to evaporate and suddenly reappear, buttoning himself up on the run, taking on himself the role of recipient and dispenser of impromptu kicks, the mission of scapegoat, of everybody's solicitor and wellwisher, who pokes his nose into everything, of the elusive

and ubiquitous universal No Man [*universal'nogo cheloveka Nikto*], whom everyone knows, who'll put up with anything, who settles up for everyone.

"Who'll pay?" "Pushkin!"

"Who do you take me for—Pushkin—that I'm supposed to be responsible for everything?"

"Pushkinspieler [*Pushkinshuler*]! Pushkinstein [*Push-kinzon*]!"

(342)

Irina Reyfman, in her *Vasilii Trediakovsky: The Fool of the "New" Russian Literature,* describes the linguistic manifestations of Push-kin as a figure of popular discourse: "Pushkin is frequently evoked by Russians as a comical figure. Thus, he is the hero of numerous anecdotes, most of them obscene. . . . It is noteworthy that Push-kin, like Trediakovsky, can appear in the role of an uncle. His name frequently serves as a substitue for a word *uncle* in expressions of the type 'Who will do that, someone's uncle?'—meaning that there is no one but the addressee to take up some burdensome task—and 'Who did that, perhaps someone's uncle?'—meaning that one's guilt is clear beyond any doubt, so there is no point in denying it."[5] The narrator, in invoking the popular image of Pushkin, plays not only on its essential vulgarity—here primarily in the sense of being a spontaneous manifestation of the popular consciousness—but on its semantic emptiness, on the use of the name Pushkin as a linguistic filler. The popular Pushkin—the narrator's companion on his strolls and the point of departure for his wanderings—epitomizes the central problem of language, representation, and identity addressed in the text. Pushkin becomes an empty linguistic sign, a word with no fixed referent, the identity of the signified changing with every context of utterance. Everyone and no one at the same time, this Pushkin is a deceiver—a *shuler,* or cardsharp—who can become the other, a Jew, as suggested in the Russian by the distortion of his surname into "Pushkinzon," as well as by the reference to Pushkin as a "scapegoat" (*kozla otpushcheniya*).[6] Thus the paradox inherent in the project announced at the beginning of *Strolls with Pushkin* is ultimately resolved. It is, after all, a contradiction in terms to go strolling—once again, wandering aimlessly—in search of some-thing. The narrator, in effect, however, finds himself at the end back where he started. He begins with "nothing," with an empty linguistic sign—bearing, however, unmistakable "Pushkinian features" (sidewhiskers, walking stick, frockcoat)—the very emptiness of which opens it up to virtually endless permutations of meaning. He will at the conclusion of his strolls, once he has "dissected" Pushkin, find himself left with the same "nothing," which in turn becomes a metaphor not only for the Pushkinian text, but for the text of *Strolls with Pushkin* as well, which in affirming its inability to define opens itself up to the free play of meaning.

The entire text of *Strolls with Pushkin*, then, is nothing but a series of variations on the paradigm introduced on its opening pages. In this context, if there can be said to be a key to a verbal construct as complex as *Strolls with Pushkin* it lies in the realization that the flesh-and-blood Pushkin, Pushkin as a historical figure in real historical surroundings, has at most a tangential relationship to the Pushkin of Tertz's text. He is the body whose imprint lies on his texts, yet which it is impossible to recover, because the reader "strolls" in the gap between the real Pushkin, which lies beyond the text, and his representation in the text.

From the beginning the narrator deploys a series of metaphors pitting Pushkin against the writer as a figure of authority, the occupant of an official post. Opposing the "lightness" (342) of Pushkin's verse to the "weighty tasks that were being pressed on him from all sides" (344), the narrator traces that "lightness" to "the deliberately unserious speech" of the students at the Tsarskoe Selo Lycée, "which committed [Pushkin] to nothing and was entertaining primarily because of the spontaneity of the tone with which conversation curled around insignificant and empty subjects" (343). Schooled on this training ground, "instead of striving for poetic mastery as it was understood at the time, [Pushkin] learned to write badly, any old way, worrying not about perfecting his 'winged epistles' but only about writing them on air—thoughtlessly and fast, without exerting himself. His concentration on *unpolished* verse was a consequence of this 'careless' and 'frisky' (favorite epithets of Pushkin at the time) manner of speech, attained by means of an open disregard for the status and authority of the poet" (343).

Life, Tertz argues, saved Pushkin from the traditional demands placed on the artist. From the very beginning of his career it supplied him—in "empty" conversations with lycée classmates and in flirtations with women—with an alternative model of discourse and alternative outlets for his verse: his poetry "lowered itself to the level of after-dinner toasts, love notes, and the other stuff and nonsense of the prose of daily life. Instead of laboriously hatching a *Rossiad*,

Pushkin's poetry squandered its talents on trifles and was dispensed cheaply in his circle of friends—in albums and witticisms" (344). Pushkin's verse was thus freed from "grand programs and majestic goals" (344), "from all possible fetters and obligations, from the binding necessity—even!—to be called *poetry*, to dream of eternity, to strive for fame" (344), or, as Tertz puts it later in the text of *Strolls with Pushkin:* "Pushkin hid in the embraces of women from the eyes of authority, from the didactic tradition of the eighteenth century" (432). Tertz proposes that

> while others crawled up the steps of lofty tradition onto a pedestal and never thought of taking up the pen without mentally arraying themselves in full-dress coats or togas, Pushkin, without stopping to think, tumbled down on his bed and there —"in pleasant oblivion, his head inclining toward the pillow," "with a slightly drowsy hand"—jotted down something or other that demanded neither concentration nor effort. That's how his manner, so striking in its freedom of thought and language, was worked out, and with it came a freedom of the word hitherto unprecedented in our literature. It turned out that it was easier for him to become Pushkin when he was lying on his side. (344)

To his vision of Pushkin's laziness, Tertz opposes the research of scholars: "Later biographers, with the polite smile of police augurs accustomed to turning a blind eye to the escapades of the big bosses, explain to readers that of course Pushkin was not nearly the loafer he is for some reason considered to be. Informers turned up who had peeped through the keyhole while Pushkin panted for long hours over drafts" (345). Tertz's response to those who would look beyond Pushkin's poetry to the supposed facts of his life asserts the most basic premise of the text: "We aren't interested in such gossip. We're not concerned with evidence—whether it be the truth [*pravdoi*] or the invention of learned pedants—that lies beyond the boundaries of the truth [*istiny*] as the poet presented it, even more so that contradicts the version adhering to which he managed to endow us with a whole universe. If Pushkin (let's assume) was only pretending to loaf, it means that he needed that pretense to free his tongue, that it suited him as the plot motivation for the unfolding of his destiny, and without it he couldn't have written anything good" (345). This statement speaks to the very heart of Tertz's project and, even more than that, to the most fundamental assumption about the relationship between art and reality that *Strolls with Pushkin* enacts. Pushkin throughout is the artist not as representor, but as represented, the writer who vanishes into his texts, whose life is transmuted into art. The "evidence," as Tertz points out, is irrelevant, for it is impossible to equate the sign with its referent. Pushkin thus merges with his texts, becoming a multivalent metaphor for the uncontrollability of the sign, for art itself.

It may therefore be best to view *Strolls with Pushkin*—which Mariya Rozanova has termed a "novel-metaphor"[7]—as above all an enactment of the drama of meaning in which attempts to define art are discredited, just as the author discovers in the course of his text that the "beautiful original" of Pushkin lies beyond our grasp. Just as from the very beginning he offers up a challenge to the "wreaths and busts" of the official Pushkin cult, so the author throughout opposes his Pushkin to historical attempts to ground art in a purportedly stable relationship between word and referent. He portrays Pushkin as reacting in his own time against the tendentious tradition of eighteenth-century literature, which was implictly rooted in an assumption of the controllability of the sign, and opposes his Pushkin to *post factum* attempts to coopt the poet's works to realism's contention that art should reproduce life, that the sign is a mirror held up to the referent. He equates claims to define with the subordination of art to some "purpose" outside itself (echoing the conceptual grid established in *What Is Socialist Realism*) and subsumes them under the metaphor of art as *dolzhnost'*, the occupying of an official post. The claim to define becomes equivalent to an arrogation of the authority of rank. The metaphor of art as *dolzhnost'* dovetails with the evocation in the text, which echoes Pushkin in *Mozart and Salieri*, of the figure of Salieri and "all Pushkin's antipodes" (412–13) as "villains," "because villainy, the hallmark and weapon of the untalented failure, originates in vain attempts to correct fate arbitrarily, to impose the principle of envy on fate through blood and deception" (356).[8] The attempt to control fate implicitly becomes equivalent to the attempt to control meaning.

To art as a mode of public discourse, implicit in the equation of art and official rank, in the figure of his Pushkin Tertz postulates a countermodel for the relationship between text and reader based on intimate intercourse among friends: "The form of epistles to friends became the content of Pushkin's poetry as a whole, which unequivocally lets us into the private life of the bard, who flaunted his accessibility—through his mimicry of true-to-life features, through details that bore a resemblance to his day-to-day life and his portraits. The reading public, little by little, learned to be voyeurs spying on the author's adventures, trysts, banquets, misfortunes, and squabbles on the most private occasions—all of Russia looked on in admiration to see what trick Pushkin would come up with next" (402). Thus Pushkin's "accessibility" is a by-product of his introduction of his own biography into the text (an innovation that, as we shall discuss further below, the author is careful to describe as a form of "mimicry"):

> Pushkin's name is always associated—and this, to everyone's surprise, makes him new, fresh, up-to-date, and interesting—with the sense of physical presence, of unmediated closeness, that he produces under the pretense of being a good fellow, one of us, our kind of guy, accessible to everyone, acquainted with everyone, the one who was casting his pearls here just yesterday. His appearance as a private person who depended on no one and represented no one but simply strolled along on his own, striking up conversations with his readers right there on the boulevard—"Hello, I'm Pushkin!"—was like a bolt from the blue after all the circumlocutions, ranks, and official posts of the eighteenth century. Pushkin was the first civilian to attract attention to himself in Russian literature. A civilian in the fullest sense of the word—not a diplomat, not a secretary, a nobody. A goldbrick. A deadbeat. But he made more noise than any military man. He was the first poet who had a biography instead of a service record. (398)

In one of several daring and pointed anachronisms in the text, the author, putting Nekrasov's words into Lomonosov's mouth and with characteristic Tertzian irony giving voice to the viewpoint of the opposition, levels at Pushkin an accusation of "treason": "This was tantamount to throwing down the gauntlet to society—to decline a post, to renounce active service for the sake of poetry. It was desertion, treason. Even Lomonosov insisted: 'You don't have to be a poet, but you must be a citizen!' But Pushkin, who didn't give a damn about the civic rights and duties of his time, became a poet the way some people become tramps" (399). The point of this anachronism is clear and rests, as we have seen before with Tertz's irony, on the drawing of an analogy that annihilates a boundary between two apparently distinct ideological stances, between the official patronage of eighteenth-century poets and the demands by nineteenth-century civic poets and radical critics that literature be subordinated to sociopolitical aims, again, between the tradition against which he portrays Pushkin as reacting and the later tradition that either dismissed Pushkin or tried to co-opt his poetry to the demands of social relevance. Both constitute attempts to define poetry as *dolzhnost'*. Both, moreover, cast poetry as goal-directed action, a movement in a single direction, while Pushkin "strolls," becomes a poet by chance, "the way some people become tramps." Viewed from the point of view that demands civic responsibility, purposefulness, from art, Pushkin's refusal of *dolzhnost'* is tantamount to treason and therefore criminal.

So the "lazy genius of Pushkin-Mozart" is counterposed to the "vain attempts to correct fate arbitrarily" of Salieri and his ilk. "Laziness" becomes "a type of humility, the grateful receptivity of the genius to whatever happens to fall into his mouth (with the concomitant danger of drinking poison given to him by an untalented villain)" (356–57). Laziness—that is, the pose of laziness which, as the author takes pains to point out, Pushkin adopts in his works—is a form of humility, because it entails a submission of the self to fate, to chance, rather than an imposition of the will, an assertion of the self. This subordination of the self to a higher power, moreover, is a liberation: "Despite dissensions and preventative measures, Pushkin had a sense of fellowship with fate, which liberated him from fear, suffering, and vanity. *Volya* (freedom) and *dolya* (fate) are synonymous rhymes in his works. The more we trust in Providence, the more freely we live, and complete submission is as happy as a lark" (363–64). Here we see the point of contact between the metaphor of strolling and creation—as it is depicted throughout *Strolls with Pushkin*—as a surrender of self (echoing the equation of freedom and negation in *Thoughts Unawares*). The poet, giving himself up to fate, renounces any single goal and allows himself to be carried in different directions.

The author crystallizes the link between strolling, representation, and self in two models for Pushkin's works proposed early in the text: "Perhaps only the noisy ball, which occupies just as honorable a place in his poetry, can compete with the gypsy camp as a symbol of the collected works of Pushkin" (365). The gypsy camp—counterposed to the rebellious Aleko (the protagonist of Pushkin's narrative poem *The Gypsies*) and, we might add, to the Salieris who try to "correct fate"—becomes an incarnation of freedom as humility, of aimless wandering:

> Despite the common opinion that freedom is proud and recalcitrant, in *The Gypsies* Pushkin clothed it in robes of humility. Humility and freedom are one when fate becomes our home and trust in it spreads out like the steppe into the summer night. In this case ethnography coincided felicitously with the predilections of the author, who, being Russian and being Pushkin, was not indifferent to the gypsy way of life. To the wretched nomad tents of the gypsies— "those humble adherents of pristine freedom," "the children of humble freedom"—Pushkin harnessed his nomadic soul, filled with laziness, carefreeness, passions, idle reverie, vast horizons, wanderings—and all this under the care of fate, not weighted down by rebellion and grumbling, under the light of the moon, soaring up in the clouds. (364)

The submission of the rebellious self to fate allows the poet to "stroll" over boundaries, to see from a higher point of view:

> The moon and fate as well, which stroll about the universe filling everything they encounter with their radiance, are both the pledge and the nature of Pushkin's universalism, of Pushkin's adaptability and imitativeness. Humility in the face of the inscrutability of providence and an identification with it opened up the way to a broad mental outlook. Pushkin's gift for understanding and penetrating everything owed much to this inclination to shift obligations onto fate, assuming that it knew better. From its position you really can see farther.
> In *The Gypsies* Pushkin looked at reality from the height of the soaring moon. (365)

Looking on from this height, Pushkin rises above polarities of antagonism and opposition:

> The dramatic poet—Pushkin demanded—must be impartial, like fate. But that's true only within the boundaries of the whole work (put in parentheses); but while the action is going on, he is partial at every step and takes care by turns now of one, now of the other side, so that we don't always know

whom we are supposed to prefer: with Pushkin's assent we manage to become friendly with both warring sides. The tsar and Evgeny in *The Bronze Horseman*, the father and the son in *The Covetous Knight*, the father and the daughter in "The Stationmaster," the count and Silvio in "The Shot"—and we get confused and exert ourselves trying to figure out whom the obliging author favors. But he favors everyone. (370)

Here, as implied in the identification of Pushkin's viewpoint with that of the "strolling" moon, the poet's ability to transcend any necessarily limited individual point of view is explicitly equated with the adoption of an angle of vision that is above difference precisely because it comprehends difference: "But from which vantage point is Pushkin looking? From both sides at the same time, from their camp or ours? Or perhaps from above, from the side, from some third point of view, equally distant from 'them' and from 'us'? In any case he plays up to both sides with relish . . . , as if setting them on each other to test their equal forces in action as fast as possible" (370). The narrator thus suggests that Pushkin's "vantage point" is simultaneously transcendent and multiple, above each separate term of a bipolarity precisely because it is immersed in both at the same time.

While the gypsy camp roaming over space becomes an embodiment of the equation of freedom with the yielding of the self to fate, chance, aimlessness, the ball serves as a metaphor for the text as a space that embraces diversity over which the gaze of the author, like the moon, glides: "the image of lightly and freely intersected space filled with a motley confusion of figures, clothing, dialects, and fortunes over which the condescending gaze of the poet glides, waltzing, lighting up with momentary attention now one, now another, tableau" (365). Pushkin's texts become an ever-expanding ball, violating and thereby transcending boundaries: "Pushkin's mobility, his life on wheels, allowed him to clear the most difficult national and historical hurdles without delays. Lightmindedness became a means of communication with other peoples; the traveler accepted the relay baton from the ballroom show-off. There was a war going on. He was dispatched into exile, sent on missions on the bloody trails of Paskevich, Ermolov, Pugachev, Peter, and the ball got bigger and bigger and the number of guests, attires, and of tribes and fortresses smashed to dust grew" (366). Tertz suggests that Pushkin's ability to cross borders, to go off in many different directions, to inscribe difference in the space of his texts, to "stroll," is the source of his accessibility and is rooted in the poet's propensity for impersonating the other:

> Pushkin loved to dress up in foreign costumes both on the street and in his verses. "Just look—Pushkin is a Serb or a Moldavian; women of his acquaintance gave him the clothing. . . . Look again—and Pushkin is a Turk, Pushkin is a Jew, he talks just like a Jew." These girlhood reminiscences about the poet's escapades in Kishinev could pass for literary scholarship. "Adaptable and sociable in its relations with foreign languages,"—that's what the Russian language was like according to Pushkin, and that's what Pushkin himself was like, for he knew how to make himself at home in any idea or language. Sociable, on a first-name basis with the whole world, tolerant "sometimes even to a fault," he, according to the testimony of his acquaintances, chatted with equal willingness with fools and clever people, with scoundrels and vulgarians. Pushkin's ability to communicate knew no bounds. (366)

Here—playing, as he does throughout the text, on such clichés of traditional Pushkin lore as the poet's proteanism and universalism, rooted, in Dostoevsky's messianic vision, in Pushkin's ability to incarnate other nationalities—Tertz brings together strolling with what, as we shall see below, functions as the other key metaphor of *Strolls with Pushkin:* imposture. Aimless strolling, as I have suggested, is identified with a surrender of self, which concomitantly makes possible the adoption of alternative points of view—of alternative identities, impersonations that implicitly entail the violation of forbidden boundaries: between Russian and Jew, between genders ("women of his acquaintance gave him the clothing").

Tertz locates the sources of Pushkin's wanderlust, of his creativity, in eros (or desire) and death. Drawing his model first from the poet's pose as a philanderer in his early love lyrics, he suggests the paradigm, reiterated throughout the text, of the artist drawn in many directions and therefore not resting in any single place for long:

> Pushkin's amorousness—precisely because of the breadth and inflammability of the feeling—takes on the dimensions of

a life devoted solely to a single occupation, practiced around the clock, an eternal circulation among feminine charms. But the size of the collection and the abundance of the hero's love do not allow him to concentrate exclusively on a single object nor to go farther than simple flirtation, which in essence exhausts his relations with these enchantresses. His readiness to chase after every skirt endows the ventures of the womanizer with traits of disinterestedness, selflessness, renunciation of personal needs, satisfied in his spare moments, on the run, constantly digressing from the goal and letting his attention wander. It was as if Pushkin had made up his mind to indulge and humor all women, bypassing in his bustling nary a single fleeting beauty, and he was dazzled, and he didn't have enough hands to go around, and there was neither the time nor the money to take care of himself. Contemplating so many perspectives, captivated by impressions that made his head spin and plunged him into prostration, he ceases to be a lover and becomes an admirer, an erudite of the science of love, and as usual the best dishes go to others. (348)

Pushkin's "amorousness," then, has so many goals that it has no goal, so many objects that none can claim exclusivity. The erotic attraction, moreover, is so all-encompassing that it inevitably entails a forgetfulness of self.

The outward draw of desire—which shades over into the "benevolence" Pushkin extends to all objects and characters depicted in his works—is fed by an absence within Pushkin himself. Here the author takes as his point of departure an accusation made by E. A. Engelhardt, the director of the Tsarskoe Selo Lycée—"an old fogy, a Salieri, who failed to recognize the new Mozart"—that "perhaps [Pushkin's heart] is as empty as ever a youthful heart has been" (372): "But perhaps Engelhardt's confusion in the face of that 'as ever has been' is worthy of serving as a prologue to the enormity of Pushkin, who himself was quite willing to sigh over the inadequacy of his heart and gobbled up distances as if he wanted to sate his empty belly, which demanded nothing less than—the whole world, lacking the strength to stop, having no reason to linger for long on any one thing" (372). Turning Engelhardt-Salieri's incomprehension of Pushkin's "enormity" on its head, Tertz thus appropriates the director's words into one of the key—and most controversial—metaphors in the text:

Emptiness was Pushkin's content. Without it he wouldn't have been full, he couldn't have existed, just as there can be no fire without air, no inhalation without exhalation. It more than anything else ensured the poet's receptivity, which yielded to the fascination of every caprice and to the colors of pictures that he hastily devoured and let fly like glossy postcards: How natural! Absolutely true to life! Let us remember Gogol, restlessly, nightmarishly preoccupied with himself, painting everything in the perverse light of his own crooked nose. Pushkin had nothing to worry about; Pushkin was sufficiently empty to see things as they were, without foisting himself off on us as a willful daydreamer, but filling himself up with things to the brim and reacting almost mechanically . . . —benevolent and indifferent. (372–73)

Because Pushkin, unlike Gogol, is empty, he is able, rather than imposing his own vision, his own definition, his own self on reality, to "fill himself up," to become or impersonate what he is depicting. Thus, Tertz maintains:

Loving everyone, [Pushkin] loved no one, and this "no one" gave him the freedom to nod to all and sundry—every nod an oath of loyalty, an intoxicating rendezvous. He winds the spring of these obeisances tight in Don Juan, who puts all of himself (not much is needed when there's nothing to put!) into each new passion—ever ready to be transfigured into the image of the person being seduced, so that at any given moment our betrayer is truthful and sincere, in accordance with the astonishing change that has taken place in him. He all the more industriously and truthfully devours the souls of others because he doesn't have enough stuffing of his own, because for him impersonation is a way of life and subsistence." (373)

While impersonation is thus rooted in desire—"passion transformed Juan into an angel and Pushkin into Pushkin's creation" (373)—it is desire allied with death:

But don't get too carried away: what we see before us is a vampire.

Something of the vampire was hidden in so heightened a susceptibility. That's why Pushkin's images have such a luster of eternal youth, of fresh blood, high color, that's why the present manifests itself in his works with such unprecedented force: the whole fullness of existence is crammed into the moment when blood is transfused from random victims into the empty vessel of the one who in essence is no one, remembers nothing, does not love, but only declares to the moment: "You're beautiful! (You're full of blood!) stop!"—guzzling until he slides off. (373–74)

Tertz's Pushkin is exposed as an "empty vessel," an image of the sources of creativity in an absence of self, equated with death, drawn by desire to "steal" the self of the other. The vampire becomes an angel, Pushkin becomes the text, precisely by transcending the boundaries between self and other and embodying this transcendence in the "empty vessel," the dead body, of the sign.[9]

So Tertz asks, "Isn't it strange that so much space is devoted in Pushkin's works to unburied bodies smuggled in between the lines?" (374), maintaining that "miraculously—the appearance of these corpses energizes Pushkin's text, just as if an armload of birchwood had been thrown into a burning stove" (376). These corpses, like the "empty vessel" of the vampire, serve as a metaphor for the figurative and literal interconnection between art, creativity, and death: "Reasoning hypothetically, we come to the conclusion that corpses in Pushkinian usage represent the prototype of the inexhaustible spiritual vacuum, which pushed the author into making more and more pictures and served as a photo negative in the creative process of the genius. Therefore, more specifically, his corpses are not at all phantasmal, not sepulchral, but are repulsively corporeal, being the empty casing of someone who is in essence absent" (376). Precisely because they are so "repulsively corporeal," Pushkin's corpses point to the absence, to the missing soul.

Pushkin's *Feast in Time of Plague* exemplifies the intensified vitality of life in the face of death: "Feast in time of plague!—that's Pushkin's formula for life, served up in the best possible way and crowned with its flowering before death: poetry" (378). The orgy in the plague city, where conventional morality disintegrates before the imminence of death, figures life "inspired" (378), transformed paradoxically through the debauches of the body into prayer: "On the threshold of destruction all the forces of instinct for existence produce this upsurge, which is marked by a creative act that resembles an outpouring in prayer" (378). Earlier in the text, Tertz, writing of Pushkin's eroticism, points to the inherent duality of desire: "The erotic element in Pushkin's verses is free to dissipate, to grow thin, reaching the distant pinnacles of the spirit as a quivering echo (continuing on its way to produce and nurture ribald creatures of the lower order)" (347). Desire aspires to the spirit, dwindling almost to silence, while simultaneously taking form in the body, "the ribald creatures of the lower order." By the same token, Tertz proposes the Chairman in *Feast in Time of Plague*—who is torn between the pure souls of the dead women in heaven, "whither my fallen spirit/Can no longer attain" (379) and the pleasures of the flesh—as a model for the fallen state of the poet: "Yes, fallen. Yes, cannot attain. But gazes, sounds, rays to and from—intersect; aeriness of thought is achieved thanks to fall, shame, disgrace; he who has condemned himself to art can no longer escape them" (379). Reiterating the motif that recurs throughout the Tertz writings, the writer—the writer incarnated in his text—is fallen, confined to the body of the sign: "Judging by Pushkin's standards, art clings to life through death, sin, lawlessness. Art itself is complete lawlessness, called forth by the emptiness of the dead house, of the walking corpse" (379). Yet by surrendering to its own fallen nature, art holds forth the possibility of redemption: "To console the artist, who has been condemned and damned, let us cite Michael Psellus, a medieval scholastic: 'Brilliant speeches wash the dirt from the soul and impart to it a pure and ethereal nature'" (379).

At this point in the discussion, extrapolating from the metaphors developed in what is roughly the first half of the text of *Strolls with Pushkin*, I would venture to suggest what art's surrender to its own fallen nature means, what constitutes the essence of the "lawlessness" of the text. In the simplest terms, just as the soul is trapped in the body, so meaning is trapped in the word. The oneness of the body, the distinctness of the boundaries of the physical person, serves as a model for the illusion of the oneness of the self, of a direct and unambiguous relationship between name and self, between word and referent. Again, this conception of artist and word is inscribed in the text in the metaphor of art as *dolzhnost'*. The metaphor of strolling proposes an alternative model for the relationship between representation and self that entails transgressing the bounds of "legal" identity. Art can only hope to transcend the limits of its material embodiment, to point beyond the substance of the text, by embracing multiple points of view, multiple selves. In other words, the poet transmuted into the text, by continually becoming the other, points to the absence of the self, to the emptiness of body and word, and thereby to what lies beyond, the soul. This portrayal of representation as a rejection of the "legal" bounds of identity is figured in the central metaphor of the latter half of *Strolls with Pushkin*, that of the artist as impostor.

Taking his cue from Pushkin's 1827 lyric poem "The Poet"—in which the poet in a state of inspiration is distinguished from the poet as ordinary person, who "among the insignificant [*nichtozhnykh*] children of the world" is "perhaps, the most insignificant"—Tertz claims that Pushkin

> split the single whole of man-poet in two, into Poet and man, and, giving all the advantages to the former, he left the man with nothing, without even a ghost of his elegant profession, but in all his petty and undemanding simplicity. He turned them into his right and left hands, and with them he embraced reality from all sides as if they were tentacles; he worked them together and separately, like a juggler—for example, while the right hand was writing poetry, the left might be picking his nose—like Indian sculptures, in a storm of gestures, a many-handed idol running, *figaro-figaro-figaro*, raging along two keyboards. He knocked their heads together: while the Poet majestically sauntered, the man was forced to squeal and weep. (404)

"Pushkin's Poet," Tertz maintains, "is not human at all, but something so wild and inexplicable that people don't know what to make of him, and they, together with his empty shell, swarm in the world below like ants, and looking at them, you understand both the degree of separation and the height to which the Poet ascended when he shed his human appearance" (405). Tertz here reprises the image of the "empty vessel" as an absence of self incarnated in the metaphors of the vampire and the corpse, invoking another of Pushkin's most famous lyric poems: "A similar story is set forth in Pushkin's 'Prophet,' where the man is struck down and dissected like a corpse, so that when he arises as a Poet, he can no longer find anything of *himself* left in him" (406). The man becomes like a "saint" who "in his heart's contrition proclaims himself the worst of sinners—'and among the insignificant children of the world, he, perhaps, is the most insignificant.' Or even more direct—without the 'perhaps.' This is neither modesty nor hyperbole, but a real touch of sanctity, which no longer belongs to the man, who has realized the insignificance of the vessel into which it has been poured" (407–08).

Harkening back to the riddle postulated in the opening paragraph of *Strolls with Pushkin*, the Poet becomes the antithesis of accessibility, the source of "inscrutability":

> Pushkin's Poet (in his most extreme and, I repeat, loftiest manifestation) has no face—and this is very important. What happened to all the grimaces, the fidgetiness, and the chatter to which we've grown so accustomed? Where has all trace of Pushkin gone, leaving behind this figure that can't even be called a personality, to such an extent has all personality been trampled out of it along with everything human? If *this* is a state, then what we see before us is some sort of idol; if *this* is movement, then we are observing a tempest, a flood, madness. Just try to approach the Poet—Hello, Aleksander Sergeevich!—he won't answer, he won't even understand that you are talking to him—to him, to this effigy that sees no one, hears nothing, holding a stone lyre in his hands. (408).

All attempts, whether Tertz's or Pushkin's (who "fidgets and fusses and suffers and knows the beautiful and frightening secret of his connection with the Poet, and he wants to name it in human language, to find an approximate synonym" [409]), to describe the Poet—by analogy with an idol or a tempest or Ibrahim Hannibal or Peter the Great—remain metaphorical approximations, recalling the extraterrestrial narrator's attempts to translate the terms of his lost planet into human language in "Pkhents." The Poet represents the inaccessible ideal of art, that which exists beyond language: "Allegories and cold conventionalities are necessary to mark, even if only through ellipsis, this sojourn in the spirit of Poetry, which is inaccessible to language. We have reached the highest point we can attain in describing it, here all life ends, and only muted symbols try to convey the message that it is better to remain silent at these heights" (408). As in *A Voice from the Chorus* the loftiest aspiration of the verbal text paradoxically becomes silence. The Poet is that which lies beyond the difference inscribed in language.

While the metaphor of the Poet as idol or monument echoes the "wreaths and busts" of the canonized Pushkin invoked in the opening pages of *Strolls with Pushkin*, the man, as the author finds him in Pushkin's poetry, recalls the joke Pushkin:

> If we compare Onegin with Pushkin (and they are compared in the novel), the first thing that jumps out at us is the "difference," seizing on which the author muddles everything by

giving us clues like "I was embittered, he was morose," or for
a long time I couldn't get used to "his caustic arguments, his
jokes, mixed with equal parts of gall, and the malice of his
grim epigrams" (at least as far as epigrams are concerned,
Pushkin could have given Onegin a run for his money!). All
this covers the traces of the true alignment of forces. Taken
as a relatively whole image (although in essence he really
isn't), as he is seen from a distance, as a literary type, Onegin
bears no resemblance to Pushkin (what could someone who
hasn't a grain of poetry in him possibly have in common with
Pushkin?), while in specifics and trivial details, he coincides
with Pushkin so closely that it seems as if the author had
looked in the mirror and copied himself feature by feature:
superficiality, good breeding, laziness, impiety, the attention
he devotes to care of his fingernails, et cetera. The result was
a human parody of the poet, a zero without a 1 in front of it
(the 1 was the poet), and, having lost it, all of Pushkin's natural qualities were transformed beyond recognition, turned so
sour that it was disgusting even to contemplate it (thus the
magnificent laziness of the poet became the ordinary idleness
of an untalented good-for-nothing, the fullness of love was
emasculated and became the sexless "science of the tender
passion," and whereas the poet Pushkin was killed in a duel,
the man Onegin himself had no qualms about killing a poet
friend as trivial as himself). Everything loses its meaning and
content, and perhaps only the outline of the respectable form
of Nulin, who is clever enough by the standards of everyday
life and who knows how to behave, remains. (420–21)

Thus Onegin—his emptiness underscored by the play on Nulin's
name (*nul'* means "zero" in Russian)—becomes a figure of the man
divorced from the Poet and left nothing but an empty shell constructed out of features—like the "indestructible sidewhiskers" and
walkingstick of the joke-Pushkin—of Pushkin's physiognomy and
biography. Also like the joke Pushkin, Onegin is so empty that he
can become anything: "so that ultimately you can make of him anything you want—a 'superfluous man,' a petty demon, a carbonaro, or
simply a minor [the reference is to Fonvizin's play *The Minor*]" (421).
Onegin is "like some rented 'I,' borrowed from [Pushkin's] human
contemporaries because, after all, a poet had to live somehow, because, after all, he was still human" (421).

"No," Tertz concludes, "you can't throw a bridge to Pushkin over Onegin with his blurred face and gaping lack of spirituality. A different sort of character is needed here, someone who, even if he is bogged down in the masses, all the same elbows his way into history as a pretender to a higher post, someone who, even if he has been deprived of his rights or is marked by the shameful stigma of the scoundrel, is all the same a king (the king is naked!) vain, loud, aspiring to make his way out of the crowd into the ranks of the poets, someone with more bite than Onegin, what we need here is— Khlestakov!" (421). One cannot get to Pushkin from Onegin, from the writer embodied in his art to the flesh-and-blood writer, from the sign to the referent, because the relationship between what is represented and its representation is one not of *dolzhnost'* but of imposture. Khlestakov, the protagonist of Gogol's *Inspector General* (whose words serve as the epigraph to *Strolls with Pushkin,*) thus becomes a metaphor for the imposture of the sign:

> It's no accident that Khlestakov "is on friendly terms with Pushkin." Like Pushkin, he mixes with the crowd and plays the Frenchie, and, like Pushkin, he is nimble, talkative, free-and-easy, empty, universal, and sincere: he lies and believes his own lies, as Gogol puts it, "aimlessly."
>
> Isn't he the spitting image of Pushkin? "He presents himself as a private person," but is really a "damned incognito" "with secret instructions," "he is wearing civilian clothes and walks like this around the room and has such a serious expression on his face." (421–22)

To art as a claim to an official position, Tertz counterposes Khlestakov, who "lies aimlessly," who is a "damned incognito" who walks about in "civilian clothes" presenting himself as a "private person" but is erroneously taken by all around him as an official personage, the inspector general.

By the same token, the man Pushkin is an impostor in relation to the Poet. Tertz expands on the implications of this imposture in his discussions of the pretenders in Pushkin's works: Pugachev and the False Dmitry. Like the pretenders, the man lays a claim to the title of tsar: "Pushkin solved the vital problem of the relationship between 'the poet and the tsar,' which tormented him for so long, with the equation: the poet is a tsar" (411). The tsar, and specifically Peter the Great, serves as a metaphor for the transcendent Poet, and Pushkin, like Pugachev, pretends to the status of Peter's god-son (in Pushkin's case, notably, through his "otherness," through his black great-grandfather Hannibal). The pretenders' attempts—those of the man and Pugachev and the False Dmitry—to usurp the status of tsar become a figure of the sign's aspiration to reach beyond its own limits.

These attempts, however, remain not legal claims to official identity but "criminal" imposture. What is most important here is not the actual ascension to royal status, but the playing of a role, the creation of deception: "But Pushkin's impostors are more than just tsars—they are artists as well, and he is particularly fond of that aspect of them. . . . For impostors also create deception by instinct and inspiration; they bear within themselves and enact their human fate as if it were a work of art" (424). The point is that the imposture is more interesting than the *dolzhnost'* to which the pretenders aspire: "By the way, that's why they [the pretenders] don't particularly insist on the literal authenticity of their royal origins. The story of the impostor is much more striking and entertaining from an artistic point of view. Dmitry assures Marina that he is offering her his hand and heart not as a tsarevich but as a fugitive monk. The personage and prestige of the artist are dearer to him than the high post—what a brilliant conception, what wonderful acting! what power of art!" (425). By the same token, "Pugachev will play not the tsar whose title he covets, but the black-bearded muzhik, the impostor tsar, the tsar Emelyan Grinev sees in his dream. This once again reveals the poetic nature of Pushkin's staging. In his works imposture lives, like art, not as a reflection of something else, but by its own wits and ardor" (425–26). Pugachev "is even more captivating in his other role, in his own skin, that of a *royal thief,* author of his own terrible and entertaining life" (427, my emphasis).

Here, as implicitly in *A Voice from the Chorus,* the metaphors of the artist as thief and of the artist as impostor converge. The impostor/thief attempts to "steal" an identity, yet it is precisely the role of thief, rather than the status to which he aspires, that is the essence of art. This is the nature of the Pushkinian sign: "In his texts pulses the primeval joy of the simple naming of things, which are transformed into poetry simply by the magical summons alone. Isn't that why many of his stanzas resemble catalogues—of the articles and rubrics most popular at the time? The idea was that a fashionable word found in a line of poetry would provoke amazement: How

authentic!" (380). The amazement—"How authentic!"—derives precisely from the artistry of the imposture, the sign for its own sake,
rather than the sign as a reflection of something else.

The essence of art therefore lies in spectacle: "After all, poetry
by its very nature is extraordinary, and it is predestined to awe and
amaze. Poetry in and of itself is an uncommon spectacle" (404). In
the drama of the pretender the ultimate spectacle is the revelation of
the imposture embodied in the execution: "For [Pugachev], the main
spectacle is still to come, and the gallows that accompanies the advance of the impostor guides us there, to the final act of the tragedy.
Barely having begun his ascent, the impostor already knows what
will happen in the finale and moves toward it without hesitating,
knowing it is a denouement necessary to the plot, to his final spectacle" (427–28). In the drama of Pushkin the man as an impostor in
relation to the Poet, the "final spectacle" becomes the duel, which
the author casts as a confrontation between the man and the Poet,
the inevitable result of Pushkin having brought his own biography
into his poetry: "Oh, how risky it is to let your biography into poetry,
to show your face on the stage. This is imposture!" (429). The duel is
thus transformed into a metaphor for the spectacle of poetry which
derives from the exposure of the imposture of the sign. Spectacle—
which, as in *A Voice from the Chorus*, lies in the revelation of the
transmutation of the "I" into the "not-I"—is the death of the author.

In this spectacle, then, the flesh-and-blood man dies, leaving behind only his "empty shell" embodied in poetry—and the Poet: "But
there was one other, whom all the shooting, the fuss, all the laughter and moaning didn't reach. As he had stood in prostration, so he
remained. He is always what is left, beyond death, beyond life, beyond spectacle" (430–31). It is the "silent presence" of the Poet that
"injects discordancies into the compositions of the author, whose
personality, as soon as it remembers him, begins to deny itself and
contradict itself at almost every turn. Discrepancies begin to crop
up" (431). Harking back to the terms of the riddle of Pushkin invoked
in the opening paragraph of *Strolls with Pushkin*, the Poet is exposed
as the source of Pushkin's "inaccessibility," which runs counter to
the "accessibility" of the man:

> The most accessible writer in the world, understandable
> even to a child, suddenly introduces himself as "not under-
> stood by anyone." The most companionable, the most sociable
> Pushkin suddenly turns to stone: "live alone." The most fun-

loving and talkative of authors announces that he has taken
an oath of silence: "despondent and mute." The most ardent
and eccentric of people declares—"but you remain steadfast,
calm, and grim."

What's going on here? What was the name? We don't know.
"A damned incognito." (431)

So we find ourselves back where we began, with the "damned incognito" Khlestakov, the archetypal impostor, in whom imposture has
taken the place of identity. Man and Poet cannot be dissected. When
we try, all we are left with are the "wreaths and busts" of the canonic
Pushkin and the empty sign of the joke-Pushkin.

The ideal of art, figured in the metaphor of the Poet, resides beyond language, difference, and purpose: "Strictly speaking, the dei-
fied creation feeds on itself, suffices unto itself and is an end in itself,
being defined as a deity to a large extent negatively: it needs nothing,
shines from within, and is pure and purposeless" (434). Here Tertz,
as the text of *Strolls with Pushkin* draws to its close, echoes the basic
terms of his argument in *What Is Socialist Realism*. Art becomes
akin to "the final goal of everything that is and that is not and the
endless (and, probably, goalless) end in itself."[10] Hence Tertz's assertion that "pure art bears a remote resemblance to religion, which
it, viewed in the broader perspective, succeeds" (433). Yet he further
maintains, invoking to ironic effect Zhdanov's scurrilous 1946 attack
on Akhmatova: "Besides religious emotions, there is always a hint
of depravity in pure art. The ungracious formula, applied in passing
to Akhmatova: 'a spoiled gentlewoman, rushing back and forth between chapel and boudoir,' aptly defines the nature of poetry, poetry
in general, as such, conveying the unstable essence of art as a whole.
Pushkin's muse was just such a gentlewoman" (434). The aspiration
of art to the transcendent must be embodied in the substance of the
word, and in this embodiment religion and eroticism meet.

Just as in *What Is Socialist Realism* Tertz challenges attempts to
define the final "goalless goal" by characterizing them as the doomed
striving to name what cannot be named, so in *Strolls with Pushkin* he discredits all attempts to define art on essentially the same
basis. Here, as throughout the text, Pushkin, proposing many "goals"
for his creation in order to elude the ascendancy of any one, is
exemplary: "We see how, by substituting some motives for others
(women for service to society, money for women, amusement for
lofty tasks, entrepreneurship for amusement), Pushkin gradually re-

nounced, without exception, all the conceivable purposes that are generally imposed on art, and opened up the way to an understanding of poetry—negative to its very core—according to which it 'by its nature lofty and free, must have no other aim but poetry itself'" (433). Following the paradigm established by the image of Pushkin's imposture as the dissolution of the self in multiple impersonations, the negation of any single direction in a dashing in many directions, the pursuit of many goals becomes no goal at all:

> Just try to find a place here for some purpose, to limit the process or make it conditional . . . But precisely because this art is free and obeys only "the movement of momentary, free feeling" (as Pushkin called inspiration), it has a habit of slipping through fingers that embrace it too tenaciously, even if they are the fingers of those who worship the beautiful, and it does not fit into its own pure definitions. Pushkin's nods and bows to the good of the fatherland, virtue, mercy, etc., are neither concessions nor a betrayal of his principles of freedom, but a consistent and vital application of them. His art is so purposeless that it pokes its nose into every nook and cranny it happens to come across on its way and doesn't shrink from asking questions about things that are none of its business, but which for some reason attract the author's attention. He is free enough to allow himself to write about anything that comes into his head without turning into a doctrinaire of any single idea—even a purposeless one. (435)

Tertz thus concludes: "In the broad sense Pushkin's road embodies the mobility and elusiveness of art, which is inclined to shift and therefore is not subject to strict rules with regard to where to go and why. Your way today, ours tomorrow. Art strolls" (436). All art strolls. All art is imposture. All attempts to turn Pushkin—or art—into a lifeless bust, to define him once and for all, are doomed to failure.

Yet there remains one final and essential term to the vision of the elusiveness of art and the artistic sign elaborated in *Strolls with Pushkin*, and that is the role of the narrator-reader who strolls with Pushkin throughout the text. As he writes relatively early on: Pushkin "became the Russian Virgil, and in this role of teacher-guide he accompanies us in no matter which direction of history, culture, or life we go. When you go strolling today with Pushkin, you meet yourself as well" (367). Just as the empty sign of the joke-Pushkin can become anyone, so the reader inevitably finds himself in Pushkin's poetry, filling up the void left by the absent Pushkin. Here Tatyana's letter to Onegin provides a model for the interaction between text and reader. Invoking Pushkin's narrator's assertion in *Evgeny Onegin* that he gives only a translation of Tatyana's letter, Tertz elaborates it into a figure of the shortfall between the ideal text and the text embodied:

> But if this is only a pale copy, then what is the beautiful original like and what could be more complete or more original than the document we have here?! . . . The reader is given the right to think what he wants, filling in the empty spaces that have been formed with surmises and groping his way among the incongruities. Pushkin obstinately insists that his "translation" is inspired by Tatyana's "foreign words," and assigns them a place above his own creation. The letter cooling down in front of us is only a weak imprint of a previous relationship between the poet and Tatyana, which remains outside the boundaries of the text—where Pushkin keeps the inaccessible original of her letter, which he reads eternally without ever tiring of it. (354)

The ideal text remains "inaccessible," "outside the boundaries of the text," and the reader wanders—or, perhaps better—strolls, in the region of difference that stretches between the original and the translation, between the ideal and its realization. Here we are again reminded of the dilemma of the narrator of "Pkhents," who in attempting to bridge, at least approximately, the gap between his lost homeland and human language is forced to resort to metaphor. The reader-narrator, by the same token, strolling, finds himself in the text and has no recourse but metaphor to reach from the self he finds to the original he seeks. The final imposture thus becomes that of the reader-narrator Tertz for Pushkin, embodied in the metaphors out of which the text is woven, leading him in many directions and leaving him at the end exactly where he started. *Strolls with Pushkin* itself incarnates the purposelessness of art, which exhausts itself in the spectacle of the revelation of its own imposture.

Sinyavsky has described *In the Shadow of Gogol* as being more "fundamental" in its approach to its subject than *Strolls with Pushkin*.[11] This description makes sense not only in terms of its significantly greater length, but also as regards the extensive incorporation of Gogol's works and of secondary sources into the text. Here we should remember that although Sinyavsky began the first chapter of *In the Shadow of Gogol* while still incarcerated in Dubrovlag, he completed the bulk of the book after his release, therefore when freed of the external constraints that informed the composition of its predecessor. Most important, perhaps, the greater scope of *In the Shadow of Gogol* allows the writer, in the course of his polemic with earlier interpretations of Gogol, to elaborate more comprehensively than in any earlier work his own vision of the creative process. In this sense, *In the Shadow of Gogol* serves as a conceptual bridge between Tertz's earlier writings and those he has written later, in emigration.

Despite the evident differences in compass between the writer's books on Pushkin and Gogol, there remains a distinct resonance between them, which is underscored by the comparisons between the two writers adduced periodically in both works. The title of *In the Shadow of Gogol*, for example, echoes a passage in *Strolls with Pushkin:* "Let us remember Gogol, restlessly, nightmarishly preoccupied with himself, painting everything in the perverse light of his own crooked nose" (373). The shadow cast by Gogol's nose in *Strolls with Pushkin* becomes the image of Gogol's shadow which recurs throughout the text of *In the Shadow of Gogol*. The contrast between the cliché of the "bright Pushkin" (*svetlyi Pushkin*) and the dark Gogol on which the author plays in *In the Shadow of Gogol* is emblematic of the underlying counterposition of Pushkin to Gogol in the text of the later work. Gogol does appear in *In the Shadow of Gogol* as Pushkin's "antipode," a "willful daydreamer" (373) who tries to "correct fate," and while Pushkin the man is murdered by the Poet, the man Gogol sacrifices art to life, burning the manuscript of *Dead Souls* while the Genius stands by weeping. Yet as much as Tertz in *Strolls with Pushkin* and *In the Shadow of Gogol* portrays his two subjects as two very different types of writers, he also in the two works essentially approaches the same issue from opposite, but complementary points of view. In *Strolls with Pushkin* Pushkin becomes, above all, a figure for the artist represented, the writer transformed in his own works into an empty sign that can be filled up with meaning by any reader. In *In the Shadow of Gogol*, Gogol appears as the flip side of the same coin, as the artist representing, who is ultimately destroyed by his inability to control his own works, to control the reader. Both works, then, play out the same drama of the uncontrollability of the sign in which the writer as a living body falls victim to his own art.

Tertz divides *In the Shadow of Gogol* into five chapters, outlining the basic structure of the book from the outset: "Perhaps it is more correct to trace [Gogol's] development beginning with the epilogue, with the grave, moving backwards against the current of our author's life, which with some luck will bring us closer, more surely, to its roots, which would accord with our instinctive sense of *Gogol* as something rounded, curved, disappearing from under our feet. To move, not forward, but back: back to his birth or, as I would allow his mission in the world to be expressed: forward to the sources!"[12] In conformity with this scheme, the first and last chapters of *In the Shadow of Gogol* are entitled respectively "The Epilogue" and "The Dead Are Resurrected: Forward to the Sources," and the text runs roughly backwards through the chronology of Gogol's life and works. The "backwards" composition of the book mirrors Tertz's underlying contention that the late Gogol is not a break from, but rather the logical continuation of, the early Gogol, that the tendentious writings Gogol produced toward the end of his career had their "sources" in the same primeval link between art and magic that fueled Gogol's earlier fiction.

Tertz opens *In the Shadow of Gogol* by posing the question: "You don't by any chance know how Gogol was buried?" (5). Realizing metaphorically Gogol's own fears of being buried alive, he suggests that that scenario rings true. He remarks that his own interest in the question

> began when an old man heard somewhere and remembered and in a conversation with me expressed interest in whether or not it was true that Gogol was buried alive, prematurely, and that this had been made public only later, almost in our time, when the grave was opened. They say he was lying on his side.
>
> I'd never heard this. And suddenly I was struck that it had all really happened as the old man said, and I had always known it, had known, without having any ideas on that score, any factual information, but somehow I had suspected, assumed it, for it agreed with my general conclusion from Gogol's image and works. It could have happened to *him*. It does ring true. (5)

The issue here, of course, is not really whether or not Gogol was buried alive. Rather the hypothesis serves as a whimsical provocation to metaphor: "Sometimes it seems as if Gogol was dying all his life, and everyone was already sick of it. He specialized in this occupation, and comparisons with those who had been buried alive escaped from his lips as often as if the thought of them was eating away at him and tormenting him relentlessly. Not just the thought of death, but precisely of the living dead [*zhivom mertvetse*], doomed to the physical horror of forced burial" (6). Haunted by this image all his life, Gogol himself, according to the narrator, became one of the "living dead" in the last decade of his life: "Long before his death Gogol had occasion to experience the state he so feared to suffer in the grave" (7).

Following from imagery initiated on the opening pages of *In the Shadow of Gogol,* Tertz casts Gogol's *Selected Passages from Correspondence with Friends* [13] as the public moaning accompanying the writer's death agony: "Ugly! . . . Uninspired! . . . Well, are the appearance and wheezing of a dying man very decorous? Are [Gogol's] yells for help, preparations for departure, fears, complaints—beautiful, logical? Gogol was a dying man, about whom it is appropriate to recall that he was dying at his writing desk, and his agony was much too long and drawn out. If, unable to bear this spectacle, they buried him prematurely, then in some sense he had died much earlier, many years before the formal date, if he had not carried death in himself from his very birth" (10). This moaning, the substance of his text, becomes equivalent to Gogol's corpse: "Just as in antiquity a quick-tempered general, bleeding profusely, gave the order that when he had died a catapult should be loaded with his corpse and fired at the enemy, counting on at least thus being of use [*pol'zu*] to the fatherland, so Gogol, sensing that his life was lost, issued into the world his decayed, almost lifeless body. So appeared the book *Selected Passages from Correspondence with Friends*" (13–14).

The image of the text as the corpse of the author pressed into service to the cause ties Gogol's metaphorical death to the desire to be of use. Echoing the system of metaphors he elaborates in *Strolls with Pushkin,* Tertz here maintains that in *Selected Passages* "Two words play . . . a paramount role: 'utility' [*pol'za*] and 'official post' [*dolzhnost'*]" (14). He links Gogol's "desire to be of use" with his aspiration to state service: "From childhood, it turns out, he was enticed by a career in service, and only writing, which diverted him by chance, prevented him from occupying the post of a state official [*gosudarstvennogo chinovnika*] which would have corresponded better to his talent and character, until finally this craving for practical good, fed by spiritual experience, by an awareness of Christian and civic duties, having come to fruition, forced its way through into this book of advice and exhortation, which meddles in every chink of private and social life in order to extract some use [*pol'za*] from everything" (14). Tertz cites Gogol's own expressed hope "that my field of endeavor is just as honest, that I serve like you, that I am not some empty buffoon [*skomorokh*], created for the amusement of empty people, but an honest clerk [*chinovnik*] of God's great state" (18). Tertz then comments: "I repeat: let us not be put out of countenance by the antiquated word '*chinovnik.*' It is for Gogol just as much a synonym for the designation of the common good [*obshchei pol'zy*] as any 'shoemaker' or 'ascetic.' 'Production,' 'the radiant kingdom of good,' or anything else good can also easily be substituted for 'God's state.' And everything will become understandable" (18). Gogol's own stated vocation as "clerk," his desire to occupy an official post, is explicitly equated with a desire to be of use. The antithesis of the artist as *chinovnik*, by Gogol's own account, is the artist as "empty" buffoon or mummer (*skomorokh*), an entertainer of "empty people." It is precisely this image of the *skomorokh* with which Tertz, turning Gogol's own image on its head, will bring *In the Shadow of Gogol* to its close.

Tertz thus places Gogol in—or rather at the start of—the Russian tradition that pits "art" against "utility": "All we need do is remember such disparate figures as Pisarev, Tolstoy, Mayakovsky, without having recourse to a longer list of literary names, to realize that Gogol is not so alone in his iconoclasm, in the holy war against aesthetics incited under the banner of utility" (16). Echoing again his argument in *What Is Socialist Realism*—here specifically that each attempt to define the Goal is inevitably hostile to every other one—the author points to the "difference and often even polarity of the conceptions of what is useful [*polezno*] and in the names of which virtues beauty should be ignored (which is why the nihilist, say, cannot find a common language with the orthodox believer or the Tolstoyan with the adherent of LEF)" (16). All, however, raise the same question: "They all unexpectedly converge in posing the question in its sharpest and most threatening form: what is more important—art or living goodness, and in what, consequently, consists the rank and utility [*dolzhnost' i pol'za*] of the artist?" (16). The issue then becomes, as in *Strolls with Pushkin*, the disposition to define art in relation to some extraliterary use or "goal."

The problem lies precisely in the investment of the writer with authority: "Writer is a name so important in its moral content that, once one has called himself that, it seems that he must constantly justify the fact that he is a writer, as if it were something suspicious, inauthentic, and he strives to prove in words and in deeds that he is just as honest and legitimate [*zakonnyi*] a person on the earth as, say, a doctor, an engineer, a teacher, a soldier, a clerk, a worker, a sower, a horsebreeder, a water-carrier—whomever you like, but not a writer" (18). Paradoxically, in "demanding milk from a goat, a clerk from a writer, utility from art," we are motivated, Tertz claims, by the soul's craving for beauty:

> It's crazy! Not for utility? Not for good? And not even for the salvation of humanity by means of useful [*poleznykh*] prescriptions? No. For beauty. For that beauty which will resurrect the world. Which is perfect, all-powerful, and therefore radiates, like the sun, truth and good, certifying and satisfying everything with itself. And therefore the ordinary, ineffective beauty exalted by aestheticians, which gives neither warmth nor cold, which doesn't feed you, with which you can't sew boots, cure diseases or death—this incomplete, insufficient beauty is offensive and insulting to us, making us in turn take offense at writers and artists, who are incapable of making us happy on the scale our soul, yearning for perfect beauty, expects. (18–19)

The reformulation here of Dostoevsky's axiom "Beauty will save the world" contains an important key to reading the central metaphor of *In the Shadow of Gogol*. "Resurrection" is equated by implication with "salvation." The ideal of beauty promises the overcoming of death through the resurrection. Yet art, trapped in the substance, the body, of the fallen world, can never achieve the incorporeal ideal of perfect beauty, must always fall short when measured in relation to that ideal, and therein lies its frustrating inadequacy. The writer who, like Gogol, tries to dictate how his texts must be read in order to resurrect himself in the body of his reader transforms his writing into a corpse and commits himself to a living death.

Tertz thus locates the source of Gogol's repudiation of his past works, the renunciation of literature embodied in *Selected Passages*, precisely in his faith in the beautiful: "As regards Gogol, at the height of his moralizing—perhaps more than ever before—faith in the beautiful prevailed over him. It was what forced him to reject his literary past, which had not justified his excessive hopes" (19). Here, as so often in *In the Shadow of Gogol*, Tertz deploys Gogol's own words against him, citing passages from an early essay in *Selected Passages*,

"Woman in Society." There Gogol affirms a beautiful woman's power to influence those around her by her beauty alone. Commenting on Gogol's argument, the narrator points out: "But in expecting utility from a woman, Gogol demands nothing from her except that which she already possesses as a woman—neither moral admonitions nor social activism. Her good task is to be herself, showing everyone for their edification her beauty, more persuasive than any educational method, making use of which she would have spoiled everything with this foreign note, which is inconsistent with her image (just as Gogol spoiled the second volume of *Dead Souls*)" (25). Gogol's beautiful woman becomes an "image of the ideal work" (25), which is inherently self-justifying: "Apparently the beautiful woman, as [Gogol] sees it, needs no confirmation either from politics or from religion; she herself is both politics and religion, she is sufficient unto herself, justified by the very fact of her existence in the world. . . . 'You owe! Owe!'—the hammer knocks at our brain as a reminder of the acts, of the utility with which we must pay off the sin and satisfaction of being born on the earth. Only the beautiful woman owes no one anything. She is" (27). The artwork, as exemplified by Gogol's beautiful woman, is independent from its creator, as it is from everything outside itself: "Is that not also the significance of creation? The author is not the issue. The author will vanish, will go off his head, like Gogol (that's where the road goes). But the image, but beauty! . . . How comforting, beautiful, it is to be a woman, not a person—a landscape, to be a fresco, the Giaconda, Khlestakov, Gogol's 'troika' (the bell jingles). To make everyone laugh, to amaze. Oh, I believe: art will be saved. Not the artist—art. Coming dry out of the water. In debt to no one. Simply being itself, residing in its own light, allowing itself to be admired as a favor" (27).

In the first passage from "Woman in Society" cited in *In the Shadow of Gogol*, however, Gogol speculates: "If the senseless caprices of beauties alone have already been the cause of world-wide upheavals and have forced the most intelligent people into folly, what would happen if this caprice were given a meaning and directed toward good?" (252). Rather than allowing beauty simply to be beautiful, Gogol wants to turn it into a means to his own salvation, to the salvation of Russia, to the resurrection of the dead: "But Gogol took the business of Russia, the business of converting perfect beauty into the flesh of the word, to heart, literally" (27).

To accomplish this, to turn beauty into word, word into deed, Gogol needs Chichikov, the protagonist of *Dead Souls:* "Chichikov, only Chichikov is capable of moving and pulling out the cart of history" (30). He represents the "energy potential of the country" (31); he is a "zero" capable of being multiplied into "millions": "moreover, precisely the lack of a human face, completely eaten away by a utilitarian attitude, the unicellarity of the whole being and makeup, capable, however, of colossal proliferation ever of one and the same utter zero reproduced in millions turned out to be the guarantee that he and no one else would serve as the generator of historical progress" (30). It is Chichikov who is to provide the impetus for the realization of Gogol's utopian vision: "All this need of Russia for a motive force, for a tough businessman, which had accumulated for centuries and grew in the course of the poem, leads unwaveringly to Chichikov, who, in truth, would pull out Gogol's carriage, which had gotten stuck in soft stuff halfway to the ideal" (31). Just as in both *Strolls with Pushkin* and *In the Shadow of Gogol* Tertz musters Gogol's own character, Khlestakov, into a metaphor for the imposture of the sign, so here he turns Chichikov into a figure for the reader, the energy source to turn word into deed, the zero that can be multiplied into millions. While the "zero" Khlestakov figures the emptiness of the sign, the "zero" Chichikov figures Gogol's reliance on the malleability of the reader, on whom he can impose his own meaning, in whom he can resurrect himself, multiplying himself into millions, into the Russian readership, which can thereby serve as the motive force transforming word into deed—Gogol's vision into the salvation of Russia.

Following from this, Gogol's inability to complete the last two volumes of the projected trilogy *Dead Souls*, in which Chichikov's spiritual rebirth was to be chronicled, becomes a figure of the uncontrollability of the reader embodied in Chichikov. Claiming whimsically that Chichikov is not riding in, but is harnessed to, the bird-troika flying into an unknown distance at the end of the first volume of *Dead Souls*, Tertz proposes the rushing troika as an image of Chichikov's resistance to Gogol's attempts to "resurrect" him, to force him to drive the troika in a straight line to the goal. Chichikov will drive the troika for the sake of his own satisfaction, for a love of speed. The question, however, remains: "But would [Chichikov], having reformed, toil with the same ardor—for the sake of toiling in the sweat of his brow alone?" (34). The artistic failure of the tendentious second volume of *Dead Souls*, which Gogol dramatically acknowledged by burning the manuscript, provides the answer to the question. Beauty subordinated to utility loses its potency.

Gogol's failure to remake Chichikov, the reader, to bring about the "expected Resurrection of the Dead" (20), precipitated a crisis in Gogol, the profundity of which was in direct proportion to the grandiosity of the hopes that Gogol had invested in his project: "When the miracle did not come to pass and the dead—even in the manuscript, in a figurative sense—were not resurrected, Gogol considered himself guilty of a catastrophe on a world scale. However, the degree of the fall gave an indication of the height to which he almost ascended, the hyperboles in his evaluation of his guilt spoke of the creative will that, having broken free of the bridle, collapsed on the ill-fated author, who, like the careless sorcerer's apprentice, could not find the right word to subdue the elements he had brought to life" (20). Gogol was confronted by his inability to resurrect himself in his readers, to control his own creations. This inability, Tertz argues, was all the more horrible for Gogol because of the power he believed was invested in them, a power which, if not turned to practical use, became sinful, criminal.

In the wake of the failure of the second volume of *Dead Souls*, Gogol's abandonment of literature, his attempt to address his readers directly in *Selected Passages*, "served as a monastic haven, where the artist temporarily sequestered himself in order hastily to pray for forgiveness for the sin of his past sorcery" (20). Gogol, Tertz argues, sought to write the "ideal book": "To Gogol the ideal seemed to be a book, having read which the world would begin to radiate the beauty of perfection, and an eternal, sinless tribe would be established on a renewed earth. In its contemplated light all that had been created by him earlier, as artistic exercises obligating to nothing, lost its value, appeared bankrupt, harmful, requiring cancellation, prohibition. Not having written it only because it is granted to no one to write such a great book, Gogol was nonetheless guided, directed, by it" (20). *Selected Passages* bears the distant imprint of this guiding ideal: "Spurred by this realization of the perishability and irremediability of what he had done, *Selected Passages from Correspondence with Friends* came out as a final, desperate, and once again unsuccessful gesture to grasp at a straw. But the reflected light of the other, great, periodically burned book, unwritten, inaccessible, lay on its pages, and by them we can judge Gogol's goal and purpose, for the sake of which, strictly speaking, he both lived and wrote" (20). Gogol's renunciation of literature, graphically represented on the postcard the narrator remembers from childhood of the writer burning the manuscript of the second volume of *Dead Souls* while the Genius looks on weeping, is therefore fueled, paradoxically, by the desire to embody the ideal work.

Selected Passages becomes an attempt to write "the total book [*kniga total'naya*], the final book, an apocalyptic book" (51), a book that claims to speak with absolute authority, that aims "to recreate reality on the model of Utopia" (28). Gogol, Tertz maintains, wanted, through this "total book," to restore the world to its original, prelapsarian state, "to return society to the primary source of beatific unity with the Lord" (40). He desired to combine the uncombinable: the eternal with the temporal, earth with heaven, matter with that which lies beyond matter, Christ with a *chinovnik*. Playing on the image of the ladder invoked in the last essay in *Selected Passages*, "Radiant Resurrection," and echoed in Gogol's own dying words—"A ladder, as fast as you can, give me a ladder" (57)—Tertz portrays Gogol's project as an attempt to turn Russia into a ladder to heaven, a link between the transcendent and the fallen earth erected through the designation of *dolzhnost'*, finding everyone and everything its proper place in the hierarchy: "The ladder, running through all of Gogol's worldview, is presented, among other things, as a form of official ranks and departments, along which with a firm step society rushes toward identity with the Heavenly Kingdom" (49). If the ultimate definition for everything could be established, difference would be abolished, and the breach between word and deed, heaven and earth, transcendent God and fallen humanity would be closed. Thus, the "total book" represents an arrogation by its author of the right of absolute definition, of control over meaning, of the right to speak with the voice of God.

The inherent flaw in Gogol's scheme lies in his "search for the mean, for unity, given the fatal fragmentation and disparateness of the elements he is trying to combine (the police and religion, morality and economy, the church and the theater, a primordial idyll and European enlightenment), his attempts to reestablish a truce resting on a multiplicity of points of consciousness which has been scattered throughout the universe" (37). Just as Gogol strove to create unity out of the disparate impulses of his own heterogeneous personality by subordinating them all to a single, higher calling, so he sought to overcome the fragmentation of the world by ordering it, "by finding each thing its legal mean and place" (37), by turning individuals into *dolzhnosti*: "Therefore all persons and roles are presented by him in official [*dolzhnostnoi*] packing—[sorted] not by person, but by full-dress coat, by the place made ready for them by God, from time immemorial" (40). In reducing human beings to *dolzhnosti*, Gogol denies the uniqueness of human individuality, just as in repudiating the "great multitude" (11) within him he transformed himself into the "living dead," the corpse of *Selected Passages* catapulted into space in a final, desperate attempt to be of use.

Gogol's actual death and his metaphorical death merge at the end of the first chapter of *In the Shadow of Gogol:*

> Gogol, in the end, deliberately starved himself, having refused to take nourishment, because, having lost his talent as a writer, he already considered life useless. If that is really so, then his death was a tactical step, a final military maneuver continuing *Selected Passages from Correspondence with Friends* and his condemned efforts to force himself to write under compulsion—an attempt this time entirely given over to God to fulfill. Only a miracle could save him, and Gogol embraced death in order to call forth a miracle. No, he didn't commit suicide, but, as it were, proposed that the Creator Himself make the final choice: either—or. (Then he was buried alive.) (63)

The figure of Gogol being buried alive, which culminates here in his real death, becomes a metaphor for the artist's inability to resurrect himself in the body of his own works, to control the images he himself has created. Gogol's recognition of the inevitability of his own physical death is a realization of the limitations of his own powers as an artist, of the impossibility of turning word into deed, of remaking the reader in his own image. He has no recourse but to demand the miracle he himself is incapable of performing from the final arbiter of all meaning—God.

In the course of the first chapter, Tertz makes certain assumptions: "That the late Gogol is not some other, altered or shaken, author, but exactly the same one, only revealed from his reverse, shadowy [*tenevoi*] side (or having come finally into the light out of the darkness of his previous works). That both antipodes counterbalance and complement each other as well as could be, forming the single plot of the completed fate of a man who paid in life—on the second half of the path—for the guilt (or blessing) of his first half" (38). Following from Gogol's famous words about laughter and tears in *Dead Souls*,[14] the narrator counterposes the bright and laughing Gogol to the dark and tearful Gogol of the late works. If the Gogol of *Selected Passages* is the "shadowy" Gogol, the Gogol of *The Inspector*

234   **Decanonizing the Classics**

General marks the culminating point of the "bright" Gogol. *The Inspector General* is presented as an exemplary work, inspiring a paean to laughter, which "in its broadest sense is the true symptom or impulse of art, its original definition" (82). Laughter corresponds to the nature of all art, because the illusion of resemblance between representation and reality is inherently comic: "In the very teetering of art on the border of likeness and identity there is already something comic, parodic, buffoonish" (83).

The principal image of the chapter is suggested in the title: "Two Turns of the Silver Key in *The Inspector General.*" As a metaphor for the workings of the play, Tertz proposes a music box "with little doll-like figures, which came alive [*ozhivavshimi*] suddenly to the chirping of a marvelous spring and danced, a well-structured contredanse on silver tacks, as if real, faster and faster, moving elegantly, so that the stylized character of their poses is barely discernible and everything soars, almost as in life, only more gracefully, more distinctly" (68). The characters in the play thus appear as artificial figures *brought alive,* made to appear real, while nonetheless remaining dolls, representations. These animated figurines dance, that is, engage in a form of "useless" play, and this "goallessness" is reflected in the very structure of the play: "The action stops, begun by an inspector general and concluded by an Inspector General, having gone the distance, while at the same time seemingly having returned to its point of departure, whence, if you like, you can wind it up again and play the same music, word for word, through from the beginning" (68). The play as music box thus embodies dance for the sake of dance, ever returning to the beginning, leading nowhere. The key that winds up the music box, that sets the whole mechanism in motion is the "imaginary inspector general" (70), whose appearance brings into the play "not simply an important boss and dexterous old fox, but the very personification of theater—unintentional and mutual deception" (70–71).

Taking off from this metaphor, Tertz arranges the remainder of the chapter around discussions of what he terms the "two turns of the silver key in *The Inspector General*" in order to answer the question of why a play that seemingly contains no positive characters and nothing to laugh about, nonetheless makes us laugh: "Stop! Let us try to listen to this box in a more scholarly fashion, more comprehensibly, so to speak, in order to grasp the mechanism that fills us with gaiety, unconstraint, when everything in this work should, on the contrary, arouse in us, it would seem, inexhaustible disgust and anger" (71). In the simplest terms, the first "turn" of the key comprehends the resemblance of the characters in the play to reality, while the second comprehends their manifest imposture, personified, as in *Strolls with Pushkin*, in the figure of Khlestakov.

The core of the narrator's argument in his discussion of the "first turn" lies in the appeal of the characters' individuality, which calls forth the reader's or viewer's fellow feeling: "for all their vices and defects, these embezzlers of state property and bribetakers, to tell the truth, inspire sympathy in us" (72). "In *The Inspector General*," Tertz maintains, "we are free to love, to sympathize, . . . the character invites us to enter into his position as a partner who laughs precisely because he is imbued with the state of his neighbor" (74). The viewer's or reader's perception of the characters in *The Inspector General*—the sympathy those characters for all their faults evoke— is rooted in a recognition of common humanity. "In *The Inspector General*," Tertz argues, "every character utters mentally or aloud: 'I am a human being, too!'" (75).

What elicits the reader's or viewer's feeling of fellowship, which gives rise to love and laughter, is the illusion of individuality created in the play's characters. Each character is endowed with some "trivial detail, trifle," some trait that is peculiarly his own, even if it is only "the simple assertion of his name" (76). It is precisely the affirmation of each character's particularity, of what makes him unique, that evokes in the reader or viewer a sense of shared humanity, allowing him (the audience) to place himself in the position of the other (the characters):

> We experience in our heart the shock of discovering a doorway into the mystery of the mysterious relationships between our heroes and freeze for a moment before the miracle of our sympathetic presence in a home that is completely alien [*chuzhom*] and yet suddenly to our excited gaze completely our own [*rodnom*]. Laughter becomes a means of bringing to light and turning over an insignificant speck of dust, which is suddenly rendered in its own way huge and attractive through this friendly attention of the author to its modest persona, compelling us to experience in that moment of transfiguration something like love toward it, so big and so insignificant, something like a trembling, a vibration of the soul, in which love and laughter merge in a single amazement in the face of the fact of its mysterious, glimmering life, which is both the

same and not the same, familiar and unrecognizable, truthful and fantastic, common and unique. We, as it were, rush about and, within our consciousness, are torn between the opposite feelings that arise in us; we are breathless from the abundance of meaning pouring on us from everywhere and, trying to bring ourselves into equilibrium, we laugh and laugh. (78–79)

Here, perhaps more directly than anywhere else in his works, Tertz explicates his vision of the profusion of meaning that results from the coming together of reader and text. The "moment of transformation" becomes a simultaneous identification with the other and consciousness of the self as different. Echoing the portrayal of love between husband and wife as the transcendence of the difference between self and other in *A Voice from the Chorus* and foreshadowing the interpretation of love as the basis of communication in *Goodnight*, Tertz portrays the reader here as experiencing something akin to love as well, which makes possible meaning and laughter by breaching the boundary between self and other.

The bringing alive of the figures in *The Inspector General* results from a collaboration between writer and reader. By drawing attention to the ordinary and insignificant, Gogol makes it extraordinary. He becomes "like God, creating the world with peals of laughter.... There is something magical, wonderworking in his ability to extract with the help of laughter wondrous sounds and amusing grimaces from inert matter, which, if you only wink at it, sticks out its tongue in response, shows its nose, becomes animated and begins to act on the footing of an independent personality" (84–85). The "inert matter," given the illusion of individuality through the tics with which the writer endows it, takes on an independent existence no longer under the writer's control. It is the audience, whose sympathy and laughter are evoked by the images created by the writer, who animate the figures, recognizing themselves in them: "in this play, as in a mirror, we, quaking with laughter, see our own face, and the whole world turns into laughter at itself" (81).

While our recognition of ourselves in the characters, the "first turn of the silver key," makes us laugh at *The Inspector General,* the opposite pole of laughter in the play is rooted in the obvious deception the animated figurines of the music box embody. In this "second turn of the key"—which does not contradict, but rather complements the first—we laugh not because of the resemblance to reality, but because we recognize the patent fictionality of the characters:

"and our laughter intensifies, no longer creating anything, not building any towns, but to mark the illusory nature of both the town and the inspector general. Everything is always capable of turning into something else. Who is Khlestakov? The mayor? We don't know. They are figments of imagination, specters, leading one another by the nose. It is difficult to believe in their real existence" (99). The laughter inspired by the manifest fictionality, the imposture, of the characters is, moreover, "filled with holiness and gratitude to God for the happiness granted. . . . This laughter, like prayer, is inspired by goodness and love" (101).

The laughter called forth by *The Inspector General* is akin to prayer because it rests on the realization of the illusory nature of evil:

> As evil reveals its absence, its imaginary nature, our hearts grow lighter, and our souls are inspired with a consciousness of good and beauty, which constitute the true fullness of being, darkened by nothing, losing nothing from the deviations and violations that have taken place here, for they are invalid, as *The Inspector General,* operating with pure figments of imagination and semblances, makes clear to us. There is no evil. It only seems that it exists. (100)

By revealing evil as deception, *The Inspector General* performs a "miracle" (101) and thereby makes us laugh, and, laughing, we are freed from the fetters of the body: "Laughter in Gogol is a similar ecstatic, marvelous state, which does not allow life to harden, the soul to come to a halt, a state that overturns the law of gravity, beckoning us with space and freedom. Laughter is the disappearance of matter. Laughing, we do not simply shake, but also, at times, soar, are carried away, leap out of the body" (110). Laughter promises liberation: "Heaven is the natural boundary of laughter. Not because it is impossible, forbidden to laugh at heaven (what won't a Russian laugh at? and what for him are the boundaries of what is permitted?). But because there, where there is no matter, there is nothing to shake off and nothing to disappear. If heaven is fullness itself, height itself, freedom itself (and, perhaps, laughter itself), what is there for our laughter to do there? Nothing but to rush there. In laughter we break loose from place—toward heaven" (111). Tertz thus equates evil with matter, with confinement in the body, in the substance of the fallen world. When we laugh at the characters in

The Inspector General, we laugh at ourselves, at the illusory nature of our material existence and are, at least for the moment, set free.

"Art," Tertz maintains, "begins with miracle, but, in the absence of such, it begins with deception, forgery, betrayal, loss, and crime" (82). In the fallen world, trapped in matter, deception becomes the only means of exposing deception. We laugh, on the one hand, because we sympathize and love, because we recognize our shared humanity with the other embodied in the characters of the play, and in laughing at them, we laugh at ourselves. On the other hand, we laugh because the characters announce their own fictiveness, which becomes a figure of the imaginary nature of all substance, of all evil, of our own bodies. In laughing at them, and at ourselves, we are vouchsafed a vision of the transcendent reality that lies beyond the body of the text and the body of the earth, and, for a moment, our souls are set free.

"After *The Inspector General,*" the narrator claims, "Gogol could not laugh" (90). In the third chapter of *In the Shadow of Gogol,* entitled "The Dead Suffocate: Relief of a Portrait," the narrator largely elaborates the argument outlined in the book's first chapter.[15] He explores the process of "disintegration" that Gogol purportedly underwent while writing *Dead Souls,* as he tried to dissect himself and subordinate all the conflicting aspects of his complex personality to a single goal. As a result, Tertz argues, Gogol became a "caricature" (171) and lost the ability to laugh, to love, and to create.

Gogol's downfall lay in his attempt to turn the writing of *Dead Souls* into a religious "feat" (*podvig*), a means to the salvation of his soul. Here Tertz draws on Gogol's own description of the process of creation: "the author imagined an All-saving hand stretched out to him, guiding the labor of his life to its cherished goal. One of the miraculous revelations, as became known from Gogol's quite open acknowledgments, was that he endow his characters with his own vices and free himself of them in the course of his literary work. Two birds were thereby immediately killed by one stone: the writer equipped and manured his work with material well known to him, taken from his soul, and himself gradually became better and purer, making short work of his own sins. The creative process was thereby directly merged with his efforts to remake his own personality" (122). Here we see Gogol's project as an attempt to rid himself of his own otherness, to purge his soul of its vices, its plurality, in the belief that only by himself becoming good could he create good, could he bring forth the "ideal book" that would resurrect the dead.

His enterprise, however, inevitably backfired: "As a result *Dead Souls* turns into a battlefield between the author and his base characteristics, brought outside, into the artistic flesh of the poem" (123). The author thus finds himself confronted in the body of his writing with precisely those parts of himself that he wished to repudiate.

Gogol's attempt, embodied in *Dead Souls*, to purge himself of alterity results in an inability either to love or to laugh:

> The drying up of laughter in Gogol's works runs parallel to and is somehow synonymous with, identical to, the drying up of love. His barrenness is marked by the disappearance of both. He somehow unwittingly overlooked or lost love, while working on *Dead Souls*, driving out of himself vices and deficiencies, persecuting them with whatever came to hand, rising above them, and at the same time above humanity, which had become debased in the same sins, developing morally, exhibiting miracles of abstemiousness, forbearance, diligence—in a word, surpassing everything, and without as a result finding love in his heart. The cross he bore of spiritual callousness, the cross of the inability to love— therein, most likely, consisted the most profound flaw in his soul, out of which an incurable disease spread through all of his task and his text, and it is possible that there was in him no other vice except this screaming lovelessness. (187)

In renouncing his own vices, Gogol denies his own individuality, as well as that of others: "Like some distant god, Gogol looks at the earth and sees from on high only mass expenditures—sorts, classes and types, herds and categories of banality" (185). Thus the "incurable disease" from which Gogol metaphorically dies is the inability to love, which is rooted in his reduction of people to categories, in his obsessive desire to subordinate everything and everyone to utility and *dolzhnost'*.

Tertz imagines Gogol, his "human image gradually being extinguished because of lack of love" (192), trapped in "a cruel crust, through which it becomes ever more difficult to let us know he's in there" (192). He discerns an analogous reification in the text of *Dead Souls*, which confronts Gogol with an image of his own incarceration in matter, cutting him off from everything living: "The same thing happened with his writing: as the work slowed down and the energy of inspiration ebbed, it froze in motion into a sinister mask of laughter entitled *Dead Souls*, which no longer excited laughter, but rather ennui and horror. How could he, having finished the first volume, again force himself to produce caricatures (besides, he could no longer really produce anything), if all of them, not having completely separated themselves from him in his recent creation, seemed to him his own exaggerated image—the image of a soul buried under a crust of matter" (192–93). Hence the significance of the chapter's title: Gogol is suffocated by the deadness of his own text. Citing the description of Sobakevich in *Dead Souls*— "It seemed as if there was no soul at all in that body" (193)—the narrator claims:

> This is about Sobakevich. But indeed about Gogol as well. Not in the sense that Sobakevich is a masked Gogol or one of his personified and hideously exaggerated vices, of which he wanted to rid himself by shoving it off onto his character. It's not so easy to get rid of what Gogol captured here, having touched voluntarily or involuntarily on his own fate as well, his own personality as a writer who had retreated into himself, as into the grave, hardened in cold disdain, living as if under the burden of his strange formations, under a layer of this sticky and hermetically congealed magma, which he here piles up with mountains of things, with a cathedral of monsters, himself already grabbed by the throat by the hand of merciless old age. So like the earth's crust, the crust of *Dead Souls*, whose artistic density and power seem so inimitable to our outside, reader's gaze, the crust that forces us to admire it, to discuss the new cosmos created by Gogol, the "geography of prose," that crust from within, from the interior, weighed down on him and crushed him. (193)

Gogol is crushed by the substance of his own text, trapped in a seemingly soulless body under the accumulation of his own creations.

The fourth chapter of *In the Shadow of Gogol* takes its title from the above passage: "The Geography of Prose." At the core of the narrator's discussion of the "landscape" of *Dead Souls* in this chapter stands his contention that "In his literary experience per se Gogol reached a boundary beyond which there was nowhere to go—the senseless and objectless pouring out of words" (278). The text of *Dead Souls* becomes an apotheosis of the corporeality of the word, existing for its own sake, divorced from meaning.

Animated objects, Tertz contends, take the place of living characters in *Dead Souls*, and the characters, Chichikov foremost among

them, are defined by their acquisitiveness, by their preoccupation
with the accumulation of material goods: "Is it not marvelous that all
the major characters in *Dead Souls*—including Plyushkin, Nozdrev,
Manilov, Korobochka, and Sobakevich—are acquirers and accumulators. This is some sort of common generic trait of Gogol's characters, which consolidates, unifies [them], which is linked with the
author's intention to present in the poem diverse forms and stages
of the accumulation of things. . . . One way or another descrip-
tions of supplies and storehouses form the core of the characters
depicted in the poem. And among all the accumulators a grasping
man who turned acquisition into a feat [*podvig*], the buyer-up of
dead souls—Chichikov—follows his path full of temptations" (226).
Chichikov's purchasing of dead souls, acquisition transformed into
a "feat" (echoing Gogol's attempt to turn his writing into a "feat"),
serves as an analogy for Gogol's style, personified in the characters
of the poem. Gogol's language becomes, above all, the "accumulation of words" just as his characters are "accumulation[s] of traits
and objects of a suitable model and category" (227). Just as in the
preceding chapter the author envisaged the late Gogol trapped in
a shell of dead matter, so his "soulless" characters become matter
incarnate, chthonic deities, emanations of the crust of the earth: "Indeed, they aren't really just landowners, and if types, then not just of
people—types of the elements and essences that make up the body
of the earth" (248).

The "acquisitiveness" of Gogol's language, the piling up of things
for the sake of things, information for the sake of information, words
for the sake of words, amounts to a "means of violating the semantic links and communicative functions of language" (283). Language
itself becomes an object: "It is evident that Gogol derives enjoyment from the very process of giving an account of things [*veshchei*]
everyone knows, because when he does so the accent shifts from the
object of discourse to language as a process of objectless designation, which is interesting in itself and suffices unto itself. Deliberately contentless discourse diverts attention from the material to the
method of its verbal organization; discourse about unnecessary objects [*veshchi*] itself enters the consciousness as an object [*veshch'*],
as a ponderable mass" (278–79). The limit that Gogol reaches in
Dead Souls, "beyond which there was nowhere to go," is the epitome
of the sign as body, to all intents and purposes divorced from any
referent, becoming an end in itself.

The narrator proposes two images of Chichikov as reader that give figurative shape to the aspirations and limitations of Gogol's project in *Dead Souls*. Both are linked inextricably with Chichikov's box, the "double bottom" (262) of which epitomizes the two poles of *Dead Souls:* "[The box] is presented in detail by the author twice: once in the light of his 'prose,' the second time—in the light of his 'poetry,' once through a deliberately humdrum, factographically precise and boring description of its colorless, uninteresting disposition and contents, the second time—through the miraculous extraction from its interior of the file of specters coming to life" (259). The box's latter appearance serves as the impetus to Chichikov's perusal of the lists of the names of the dead souls he has bought. Inspired by the distinctiveness of their names to imagine the details of their lives, he endows them through his own flights of fancy as reader with an illusion of life which, as critical cliché would have it, is never achieved by the living characters in the poem. As Tertz observes: "That over which Gogol labored self-sacrificingly for many years, which absorbed him more than anything else, which consumed him, sent him off his head and drove him to the grave—the resurrection of the dead—Chichikov in a burst of fantasy brings about easily and simply, like a magician, bending over the fabulous box with the priceless merchandise hidden there" (261–62). Thus it is precisely the unfettered imagination of the reader, inspired by the names as the viewer is by the individualized traits in *The Inspector General*, who brings the dead alive.

At the opposite pole of "prose" lies Chichikov's perusal of the playbill he happens to pick up while walking through the town. Before putting it away in his box he studiously reads through it. The playbill embodies language as the accumulation of dead matter, which transforms reading into a senseless and automatic process:

> Just to reproduce Chichikov's reading of this unneeded playbill it was necessary to possess a similar interest, divorced from meaning and object, in the reading and description of things, in prosaic language as a self-sufficient process. Any scene as described by Gogol, any page of *Dead Souls* is, in principle, equivalent to the playbill as read by Chichikov: the author will also take care to remember to track down the whole inventory of colorless names, to specify the price, date, and place of publication, and even to turn the picture every which way in his mind, looking to see whether or not there is something on the other side and, having made sure that there

is nothing there and, as it were, having exhausted the topic of the composition with what demonstrably comes to naught, to put the next page-playbill neatly into his world-embracing box entitled *Dead Souls*. (284)

Thus the playbill comes to represent language for the sake of language, words piled on words, matter devoid of meaning. The role of the reader is reduced to the "monotonous, announcer's voice" of Chichikov's servant Petrushka, "who reads indiscriminately whatever happens to fall before his eyes in the open book of life, for the sake of the satisfaction derived from the very process of forming the verbal string" (284). Only the reader can bring alive the images of the text, can resurrect the dead souls. Yet reading nonetheless remains a collaborative act between text and reader. The text as conventional form, dead matter, epitomized by the playbill, automatizes the process of reading, the reader is transformed into a sort of robot mechanically parroting meaningless words. The text, like the list of dead souls that violates the expected, drawing attention to the uniqueness of the individual, inspires sympathy, even love, and thereby engages the imagination of the reader, who alone is capable of bringing alive the dead word.

Chichikov's "imagined resurrection of the dead" (289), Tertz maintains as the chapter draws to a close, reveals the "magic of the name, which has for Gogol a secret power, attractive force, and charm" (289). He proposes as a model for Gogol's project in *Dead Souls* "an old legend that says that as soon as all the names of God are named and counted, the universe will be extinguished, for the whole contents of the historical process will then be exhausted, yielding its place to Eternity or the new day of Creation" (290). Gogol, he maintains, seeks to enact this process:

If Gogol could have, instead of this prolix, drawn-out narration, he would have pronounced only one world-creating name in order in the twinkling of an eye to restore truth to life, bypassing the mediation of ideas and writings. That possibility was not open to him, but to make up for this deficiency his creation breathes the striving to name in detail everything there is in the world and thereby to exhaust this world once and for all, calling it quits with dead, spectral existence. His poem is a deed of purchase, concluded for the liberation of humanity from death, for control of the world with the help of the word. Too bad the transaction didn't come off. As always in literature, it was relegated to the category of fantasy, metaphor, and parody of once sacred speech. (290–91)

Deprived of the magic word, the unnameable name of God, Gogol's attempt to resurrect the dead, to call forth a new creation, remains trapped, like the author himself, in the dead matter of the word and of the world. The only recourse lies in illusion, in deception that can bring forth life in the mind of the reader.

In the final chapter, "The Dead Are Resurrected: Forward to the Sources," Tertz focuses on the image of Gogol as a sorcerer destroyed by his belief in the magic power of his words. The core of his thesis, evoked throughout the text of *In the Shadow of Gogol,* lies in his affirmation of the "consistency with regard to the word of Gogol the artist and Gogol the censor, of Gogol the fantast and Gogol the purist" (292), of the early Gogol, the writer of what the author terms "magic realism," and the late Gogol who repudiated, or tried to dictate the interpretations of, his early works, who called on the public to " 'Believe my words!' " (291). For both the early and the late Gogol the word

> is magical, wonder-working, fraught with real, tangible consequences, whether Gogol calls on us to believe and submit to his words blindly or warns against the disorders that can occur as a result of the irresponsible use of the word. The circumstances attendant on his biography, complicated by acute crises, discord and struggle with himself, correction, explanation and destruction of what he had done, have as their basis the same magical root, from which Gogol took his departure in his work as a writer, being always in a state of persecution by the word, of which he was master and from which he fled, which he tried ceaselessly to explain and recarve, falling into trances and into despair, imagining himself sometimes a great saint, sometimes an irredeemable sinner, from whom a shadow [*ten'*] spread over the whole earth. (292)

Gogol thus falls victim to the power of his own talent, to his ability to invest the dead matter of the sign with the illusion of life, to the magic power of the word, which he both fears and seeks to harness to his own end.

Tertz terms Gogol's ability to create through "hyperbole, or the grotesque, or laughter, or the living detail, noticed and put into a descriptive frame. . . . the illusion of the presence among us of a dead person coming alive" (297) "magic realism," which "has the goal of turning literature into a physically real and palpable body" (298). Drawing on the imagery of Gogol's early stories, Tertz proposes the metaphor of the artist cutting eyes in dead matter: "To look is to vanish. Because to look, to see (let alone, to represent) means to cut eyes in unseeing, dead matter and to allow them to see you, to overtake, to kill: 'It's looking!' In the artist (in every artist—take a good look) there is some doom ('it's looking!')" (300). The "doom" that overhangs Gogol—and, as Tertz suggests, every artist—is that in cutting eyes in the metaphorical corpse of the sign, in investing himself in the images of his work, he is forced to confront himself as other. His creations become like "portraits, which come alive at the expense of the death of the original" in which "an alien [*chuzhoi*], strange soul" (317) takes up residence. That "soul" is the soul of the reader, who, like Chichikov filling the dead souls with life and meaning, looks back at the author through the eyes of his creations.

The efforts of the late Gogol and of other writers in Russian literature to control their own words, to turn word into deed, by subordinating them to "utility," by ascribing to them absolute meaning in relation to a goal, Tertz argues here, constitute an attempt to return to the sources of art in magic: "It is not given to us to return to those times and secrets, but the will to 'action,' to 'morality,' to a 'social' role, and 'utility' resounds in art as a burning nostalgia for paradise lost. . . . The artist wants again to be a magician, and he cripples and disfigures himself, takes it upon himself to 'serve' the state and society, endeavoring to go back—to magic" (335). The attempt to deny difference in a world fallen into difference inevitably "cripples and disfigures," just as Gogol, renouncing art for the sake of an unattainable ideal, consigns himself to a living death.

At the end of *In the Shadow of Gogol*, Tertz echoes the concluding paragraphs of *What Is Socialist Realism*, proposing the fantastic as the only recourse left to the artist in the fallen world:

> The fantastic! What an absurd, what a stupid whimsy to invent what does not exist and to make do with blind illusions?! . . . However, the fantastic dimly remembers that art once belonged to magic and wants in an illegal, stolen [*nezakonnym, vorovannym*] way—stealthily and by guesswork—to experience in the imagination that which humanity had in fact at its sources. The fantastic is an attempt by the alien-

ated soul to make up for the experience lost by society. The
fantastic fumbles about where nothing remains and there is
no hope of saving and returning to life the paradise lost in
the progress of civilization. The fantastic is despair, which
flings itself to disinter with its hands long extinguished coals,
even without any hope of uncovering and fanning the forgotten fire. Oh, the fantastic, green envy, a plague upon your
house! A shadow [*ten'*] fallen on the earth from a once beatific
light. The light has not existed for thousands of years, but the
shadow, it seems, remains. (327)

Resolving the play of light and dark that runs throughout *In the
Shadow of Gogol,* Gogol's shadow here metamorphoses into the
shadow of the fantastic cast by the light of the lost and unattainable
ideal. The darkness of the shadow can only exist because of the light
that casts it; darkness becomes an intimation of light, just as the
fantastic, revealing its own deception—its own criminality—vouch-
safes us a glimpse beyond the body of the sign, the substance of the
fallen world to a higher reality.

"What would happen," Tertz asks as his book draws to a close, "if
the powers of the artist, the doer, the saint had been united in Gogol
in the lost magical synthesis, then in what form, in what inspired
image would he have risen before us?" (335). He finds his answer
in the singing of mummers (*skomorokhi*): "Only with them is Gogol
saved. Only with them will Russian art be saved. . . . This is the artist,
become saint, whose sanctity is reckoned in terms of the light and
maturity of art. This is the doer whose deeds are exhausted in play
and music" (336). The ending of *In the Shadow of Gogol* calls to mind
Gogol's own words cited toward the beginning of the text: "I am
not some empty buffoon [*skomorokh*], created for the amusement of
empty people, but an honest clerk [*chinovnik*]" (18).[16] The sanctity of
art lies precisely in the confrontation between the artist transformed
into the empty sign of the text and the reader who recognizes his
own emptiness in the illusion of the text. Reading, like writing, holds
the promise of transcendence of self, of liberation from the body, of
magical transformation—if only on paper and in the imagination.
In the Shadow of Gogol thus ends up in the same place as does *Strolls
with Pushkin*—in an affirmation of art's independence from reality.
Like Gogol's "woman in society" art cannot teach, but it does hold
the possibility of salvation, of liberation—simply by being itself.

The basic premise of both *Strolls with Pushkin* and *In the Shadow of Gogol* is inscribed in the stance adopted by Tertz in the two works. Here the writer is also a reader, creating his own text by reading other texts. Tertz as reader plays the role of Chichikov bringing alive in his imagination the lists of the dead souls he has purchased as he reads. The "dead souls" here are the texts of the lives and works of Pushkin and Gogol, brought alive in the metaphors of the narrator as he strolls through the gap between himself and the "beautiful originals," creating plays of meaning to pass along to the readers who stroll with him.

Chapter Eight

. . . .

Literature and Morality:
Little Tsores and *Goodnight*

What after all does the Marxist worship of a corpse, artfully preserved and placed at the center of existence, at the foundation of the universe, which is what Lenin's mausoleum is, signify? What is the symbolic meaning if the symbol is devoid of content and retains only the dead casing of the pharoah reposing beneath the glass? What are they trying to say with this? That Lenin died, but his body and the letter [of his writings] are imperishable? That this worship *is* the religion of victorious materialism, with all the murderous consequences that flow out of this?
—ANDREI SINYAVSKY, "On the Night After Battle" (*"V noch' posle bitvy"*)

For now we see through a glass, darkly.
—1 CORINTHIANS 13:12

For we know that if the earthly house of this tabernacle were dissolved, we have a building of God, an house not made with hands, eternal in the heavens.
—2 CORINTHIANS 5:1

Sinyavsky has written two pseudonymous works published separately in book form during the third period of his Tertz career, dating from his emigration to France in 1973: the novella *Little Tsores* (*Kroshka Tsores*) and the much-longer *Goodnight* (*Spokoinoi nochi*), to which the writer refers in the text alternately as a "novel" and "memoirs."[1] *Little Tsores* was originally conceived as part of *Goodnight*, outgrowing its original frame and emerging as an autonomous work only in the course of its writing. It therefore, hardly surprisingly, shares a certain affinity in imagery and concerns with its "parent" text. Both are hybrid works straddling the line between fiction and autobiography, and in both Andrei Sinyavsky appears as a character, in a work attributed to Tertz. Both incorporate responses to the writer's critics and trace the origins of his literary career to the Stalin years, confronting in the "night" of Stalin's dictatorship and its aftermath the ethical dilemmas raised by Tertz's vision of literature. While in his books on Pushkin and Gogol he challenged the canonization of the poet and the pretensions of the writer who seeks to remake the world in the image of his own ideal text, in these later works he comes face to face, on the open field of his own autobiography, with the issues of the writer demonized and of the artist's implication in the horrors he depicts. While Tertz's Pushkin and Gogol are destroyed by the clash between life and art, in *Little Tsores* and *Goodnight* the author seeks, and apparently achieves, a resolution of his own duality, a reconciliation between Sinyavsky and Tertz.

Little Tsores is the most enigmatic of the writer's works, partially perhaps because it remains so deeply rooted in *Goodnight* and partially because it so hermetically interweaves the private imagery of the writer's autobiography with historical allegory to create a parable of sin, guilt, writer, and text.[2] The apparent conflation of writer with character, of the fallen state of humanity with the uncontrollability of the text, and of writing with expiation renders the novella particularly resistant to schematic readings. Yet it would seem appropriate that a work so concerned with misunderstanding, conflicting interpretations, and riddles of identity should challenge the reader with images that are particularly open to multiple meanings precisely because they defy reduction to any single one.

Little Tsores is dedicated to E. T. A. Hoffmann, who is whimsically reincarnated in a cabinet filled with books that is presented to the title character toward the end of the novella. To use the imagery of the text itself, *Little Tsores* is, in a sense, "fathered" by Hoffmann, for, as the references to the German writer and the similarity between the titles attest, *Little Tsores* is an inverted rewrite of Hoffmann's story "Little Zaches" (*Klein Zaches,* translated into Russian as *Kroshka Zaches*).[3]

The title character of "Little Zaches" is a repulsive dwarf with no redeeming qualities. The story takes place in a kingdom where all fairies have been banished by the ruler in the interests of enlightenment and progress. At the beginning of the tale, the one remaining fairy, named Rosabelverde, casts a spell on the monstrous child Zaches so that he is given credit for the talents of those around him and for all the good deeds performed by others in his proximity. Basking in the light of the noble actions of others, Zaches, under the name Zinnober, achieves political success and rises steadily in rank, still, however, remaining his repugnant self. In the end, the story's hero, aided by the local wizard, breaks the spell. Deprived of Rosabelverde's protection, Zaches drowns in his own chamberpot. Most important to an interpretation of Tertz's use of the Hoffman tale is the fact that those around Zaches—as well as Zaches himself—confuse his true self with the mask of the virtuous and pseudonymous Zinnober. Tsores/Sinyavsky, as we shall see, falls victim to the same misconception in reverse.

Tsores (which echoes both Zaches and Tertz), who is both the title character and the first-person narrator of Tertz's novella, takes his name from the Yiddish word for "sorrow" or "trouble."[4] While he claims to have been "born and raised as a perfectly normal child" (612), the narrator from an early age develops a stutter from overhearing "the moans of the half-crazy old alcoholic Polina Mikhailovna Glinka, who was dying long and hard behind our communal wall" (612). At the age of five, in answer to his prayers, Tsores is visited by a fairy in the guise of a pediatrician named Dora Aleksandrovna. In exchange for her curing of his speech defect, he agrees to give up love: "Not knowing what love meant, I sacrificed it. I renounced good, fame, wealth, everything beautiful on earth. I sold myself, never suspecting what I was doing, to the devil" (613). In the wake of the fairy's visit, Tsores's life begins to follow a pattern opposite to that of his fictional predecessor, Zaches. Despite his good intentions, he is again and again assigned blame for the evil that transpires in his presence. He unwittingly causes the deaths, one by one, of his five half-brothers by another father, each of whom bears the distinctly Russian surname Likhosherst and each of whom occupies a responsible position in Soviet society. Spurned by his mother, haunted by guilt, Tsores retreats into the outcast status inherent in his name. Toward the end of the novella, Tsores, apparently just having returned from a stint in a labor camp (one of the numerous autobiographical references interspersed throughout the work), again meets the ageless Dora Aleksandrovna, now working as a saleswoman in the grocery section of a Moscow department store. Dora indicates her willingness to marry Tsores and accompanies him home. Their wedding celebration, however, turns into a wake when the narrator's dead brothers materialize in the empty chairs set out for the feast. Listening in on their conversation, himself invisible and inaudible to them, Tsores learns that it is not they, but he, who is dead. "You died," Dora Aleksandrovna tells him. "You died, you died a very long time ago. And you don't exist, do you understand? Before you were born." (651). Having asked for his old stutter back, "so that I can just live, like all normal people, without causing anyone particular unpleasantness" (644), the narrator finds himself at the close of Little Tsores "a shattered, jaded, stuttering old man—to some extent evil and to some extent good. Neither father nor mother, whom, all things considered, I had sent to her grave. No dog. And only my five brothers, like five fingers, shown dark on my hand, when I covered the ream of pages written during the night" (654).

The chronology of the events of the plot of Little Tsores points to the historical allegory that overlays the deeper issues of good and evil, representation and death, that stand at the center of the text. The deaths of each of Tsores' half-brothers correspond to crucial moments in Soviet history. Nikolai, a naval officer, drowns in 1936, and Pavel, an agronomist on a collective farm, is arrested and sent to Vorkuta, from which he never returns, in 1938. The dates of their deaths thus coincide with Stalin's purges, to which Pavel's fate is explicitly linked. The third brother, Vasily, serves in the army during World War II and is killed at the front in 1943.[5] While the dates of the deaths of the last two brothers are not given, their associations with historical events are evident. The demise of Yakov, a surgeon with a markedly Jewish name, alludes to the Doctors' Plot, while Volodya, an official of unspecified high rank, appears figuratively to be a casualty of the aftermath of the thaw, perhaps even Khrushchev himself.[6] Most important, the narrator loses his stutter in 1934, the year in which the first congress of the Soviet Writers' Union, at which the hegemony of Socialist Realism over Soviet letters was officially proclaimed, was convened. In this context Tsores's stutter—which keeps speech from "flowing unhindered, soaring out of my mouth in perfect octaves" (613)—suggests a veiled reference to Isaac Babel's plea, in his speech at the writers' congress, for the right to write "badly." Tsores's renunciation of love for the ability to speak well— for "the words and talent of an orator, a writer, a fabulist" (613)—appears as a condemnation of Soviet literature fallen under the sway of the "classicist" aesthetic of Socialist Realism, just as the ills he brings on his half-brothers suggest the downfall of the writer who tries to do good. The more assiduously Tsores strives to save each remaining brother, the more surely he brings down destruction on each of them in turn. The writer's intentions inevitably and repeatedly reveal their fallacy.

The crux of Little Tsores lies in the complex relationship between

Tsores's guilt, the possibility of assigning blame, and his vocation as writer, between his parallel quests for the origin of evil and for the identity of his father, about whom we learn only that he was a writer whose destiny his son seems doomed to replay. Tsores's mother passes judgment on him from the very first death, branding him with the mark of Cain:

> "You are guilty of everything! You killed your brother!"
> True, she never actually said this again later. But the words had been said and marked me for life. . . (619)[7]

This passage suggests that the answer to the riddle of his father's identity, which torments him throughout—"It seemed to me that the source of my and my mother's misfortunes and discords was hidden somewhere in the darkness of my origin" (628)—may be solved metaphorically. If the narrator is Cain, then his father is Adam, and the mystery that confronts him is the horror of the fallen world:

> Since that time no matter what I do—it's all bad. In the final analysis, you turn out to be guilty of everything. Oh, Little Tsores! Little Tsores! How I weep for you! Yet, probably even you, like everyone, wanted only to be good and useful. What have you done? Why did you give rise to so much sorrow? . . .
> Or is it that sometime—a very, very long time ago—we shamelessly sinned? And we ourselves don't know how guilty we are. If we weren't evil, if we weren't guilty, neither Hitler nor Stalin would have floated out of us to the surface. There would be no death. "Look back in anger!" said a nameless author. And I repeat after him: "Look back in anger and you will see yourself!" (619)

The enigma with which the narrator grapples throughout *Little Tsores* is the problem of original sin, which he as Tsores incarnates, but in which all human beings are implicated.

What most torments the narrator in his meditations on evil is its apparent pointlessness, its genesis in unfortunate circumstances or even good intentions. In illustration he adduces, at roughly the midpoint of the novella, episodes of abused children drawn from his "archive." This passage recalls Ivan Karamazov's catalogue of tormented children, which prompts him, in the *Brothers Karazamov*, to return to God his entrance ticket to paradise. Like Ivan, Tsores proposes to present his tales of innocent suffering at the Last Judgment, yet there is a marked difference here. In the stories related by

Ivan to his brother Alesha the brutality is intentional and malicious. In the examples tendered by the narrator in *Little Tsores* it is random, the result of unforeseeable circumstance: "I beat my head against the wall when I hear such stories, and I can't find an answer. Everything, absolutely everything involves some trifle, some stupidity, some kind of mistake of nature, an invisible little-*tsores* [*kroshka-tsores*]" (632). "Besides, evil in its pure form doesn't interest us, doesn't make us glad. Evil is only the side effect of the good we expect" (633).

Marked by his name as the source of evil, the narrator is stigmatized by others and by his own mother as alien (*chuzhoi*, 628). In one of the dream visions he has in the novella, he imagines his mother demonizing him and in effect accepts the guilt she assigns him: " 'Devil! Devil! Devil!' she yelled, jealous and raging, with each new word beating me back, into the blackness whence I had come, and which I was fleeing and feared, knowing my trait and ill-luck to vex and torment by my presence alone" (639). Tsores incarnates the Jew as scapegoat, about which Tertz writes in "The Literary Process in Russia":

> In short, the Jew in the popular understanding is a demon. He is a devil that has penetrated by illegal means into the righteous body of Russia and made everything not as it should be. The Jew is an objectification of Russia's original sin, of which it constantly tries to purge itself and cannot. . . .
> It is, if you will, the metaphysics of the Russian soul, which tries for the umpteenth time (and the revolution occurred because of this) to return to its original, paradisiacal state. And it just keeps not working—some "yid" just keeps interfering and spoiling the game. "Yid"—he is somewhere among us, behind us and, it sometimes happens, inside us ourselves. The "yid" itches in our midst, he screws himself in everywhere and spoils everything. "Don't play the yid!"—this is said testily, with the consciousness that a Russian should not, cannot, be bad.[8]

Later in the same article, Tertz, revealing the conceptual roots of the image of the writer as Jew incarnated in the title character of *Little Tsores*, maintains: "Every Russian writer (of Russian origin)[9] who does not want at the present time to write by decree is a Jew. He is a monster and an enemy of the people. I think that if now (finally) they were to begin to slaughter Jews in Russia, first of all they would massacre writers, members of the intelligentsia not of Jewish origin, who somehow do not fall under the rubric of 'one of us' [*svoi chelo-vek*].[10] Tsores's outcast status, his mother's[11] assignation of guilt for all ills to her pariah son thus represents the impulse to externalize evil, to deny humanity's common fallen state by creating a bipolarity of *svoi* (us, the unambiguously good), opposed to *chuzhoi* (them, the incarnation of evil).

The source of the writer's otherness, his status as the only semi-legitimate son in the family (metaphorically the national family), lies precisely in his vocation to serve as a reminder of humanity's fallen state, thereby challenging attempts to deny the moral ambiguity of the individual by objectifying evil in the other. Lamenting the fact that he has crossed his half-brothers' paths like a black cat, the narrator is even more greatly distressed by the realization that such is the nature of his calling: "But what am I to do, tell me, when one can tell not in retrospect, but in advance: everything that I do, write, think—all will be incorrect and not as it should be. And I will be exposed, accused! Will this be useful to writing like mine, which cuts against the grain? Perhaps that's the only reason I write—counting on again and again crossing someone's path" (630–31). Just as Tsores cannot avert his brothers' deaths, so the writer cannot control his texts, which leave him open to anathema and opprobrium.

Yet by embodying the evil within, the shared guilt of humanity— "Look back in anger and you will see yourself!"—the writer transformed into his text, Sinyavsky as Tsores/Tertz, holds the possibility of redemption: "To whom have I brought at least some good? Never and no one. And the world would be better off without me—without my intervention, without my secret sympathy and compassion for it, which act like a sting. Prophylaxis? An inoculation with guilt of humanity, which knows nothing but how to justify itself? All of us dream of justifying ourselves somehow—with works, children, books. But when you look at a human being in sum—before death he's left with nothing. Only with fear in his soul and with a single hope—for mercy: I've sinned" (630). Following from this, the narrator invokes the Russian Orthodox belief in "sin for the sake of salvation": "We try to justify ourselves, we strive, while the evil committed by us keeps growing and growing. Would it not be better to repent to begin with? To say honestly, looking truth in the eye: I have never met anyone worse than myself. Would not then the long-sought 'sin for the sake of salvation' [*grekh vo spasenie*], at which people have so laughed, appear like a guiding light? Would not the ascent to the light begin?" (630)[12] The crux of "sin for the sake of salvation" lies in acceptance of one's fallen condition, of the inevitability of sinning.[13] According to the logic of this belief, attempts to achieve human perfection are inherently flawed because they are incompatible with humanity's postlapsarian state. The recognition of the inevitability of sin paradoxically becomes the only means to redemption.[14] "Sin for the sake of salvation," moreover, takes its genesis from "lying for the sake of salvation" (*lozh' vo spasenie*), the practice of taking the sin of falsehood on one's own soul in order to spare the feelings of another. The writer's "sin," which holds the promise of salvation, is thus deception.

Just as Tsores's posthumous existence—"You died. . . . Before you were born"—suggests the death of self the writer undergoes in transforming himself into the text, so "sin for the sake of salvation" serves as a complex metaphor for the ontology of the work of art. Recognizing its own uncontrollability, the inevitable shortfall between intention and realization, art nonetheless holds forth the possibility of salvation. Thus, counterbalancing his dream about his mother rejecting him, Tsores has another dream which promises liberation:

> I saw the likeness of a merry forest clearing, along which was strolling either a slender maiden, or, strange as it might seem, a dog of lofty breed and at the same time a rare beauty. In a long, shaggy dress, in a collar and on a chain, she toiled slowly along in front of a fantastic *muzhik* in a fur coat, bearded, with a fat face, at the sight of whom you immediately remembered that there are still villains on the earth prepared to order about a creature singular in its nobility and gracefulness. He shouted at her rudely, tugged at the chain, and threatened her with a whip-handle, probably for some offense against him, and she began to rush about and suddenly tore herself away from the leash and darted up the tree, like an ermine speeding away from the pursuit of a hunter. But what was even more incomprehensible, as she ran up the branches as if up a ladder, she threw off like a whirlwind the dress spinning around her and—flashing a desperate, sunny nakedness—in an instant reached the summit, whence she soared aloft, flapping her wings, as a bird. This lasted several moments in all, and the bird, which had slipped away into the sky, was a natural continuation of the whirlwind with which the fugitive extricated herself from the clothing that flew from her body and also—

the crown of the tree, high, sharp-tipped, and seemingly foreordained to serve as take-off strip. The *muzhik*, cursing, tried
to rush after the maiden and agilely crawled up the trunk, also
throwing off on the way the inconvenient caftan, but he was
more uncertain and heavier in his movements, and got stuck
halfway—as the bird took off from the branch. (639)

While the imagery of the dream evokes the oppression of art by
the state, in a broader sense it suggests the very nature of art as
Tertz understands it, art which issues from sin and death, the conditions of humanity's fallen nature, and aspires to the release of the
soul. Literature, tacitly through acknowledging the fallen nature of
its medium, the difference that precludes the author's control over
his own text, finds its true moral worth in the redemptive power
of beauty, in the possibiity of self-forgetfulness. Thus, the saleswoman Dora, who "resembles the bird that flew away in my dream"
(643), performs a hypnotic dance as she serves her customers: "Yes, I
thought, in dance, in song every person is purified, shedding himself,
leaving the body, decay, for somewhere higher, as they did in ancient
times. The cleansing significance of rhythm was known to Dora,
who, distributing salable goods throughout Moscow, remembered
poetry and in precise accord with it through flowing movements removed charms and fears. Charms of death, fears of life, of my own
unendurable, original face" (646–47). Art holds the promise of the
liberation of the soul from the *tsores* that plagues the earth.

    Meditating on his dream about the release of the chained woman-
dog transfigured into a bird, the narrator concludes: "How glad I
was for her! So, I thought in the morning, we also, God willing, will
be rid of slavery, of the fetters of evil that we cyclically cause, ourselves not wishing it—I and mama and Volodya and the dog . . .
What purpose is served by these private scores, searches for the one
who is guilty? Everyone deserves to be repudiated. And everyone—
to be embraced" (639–40). This realization anticipates the epiphany
he experiences in the concluding scene of the novel. When Tsores
learns that his half-brothers are in fact alive, he asks Dora if that
exonerates him:

    "So they are alive?" I whispered. "Alive, and not killed?
And, that means, I'm not guilty? . ."
    "What does it matter?" she answered. "Guilty, not guilty?
Everyone is guilty of something." (650)

Tsores's recognition that he, like everyone else, is "to some extent evil and to some extent good" constitutes an acceptance of his common humanity. In recovering his stutter—the emblem of his flawed nature and of his fragmented, "incorrect" discourse as well—he also assumedly regains the ability to love. He is made whole as the gulf between himself and his half-brothers is bridged when they merge in a single body.

Sinyavsky has suggested that Tsores "becomes a writer when he stops being a human being."[15] Seen in this light, Tsores's simultaneous rejection of his own defect—his stutter—and of love recalls Gogol's transformation into a corpse, the reification of his works into dead signs, when he loses the ability to accept his own and others' imperfections, thereby forfeiting the capacity to love, in *In the Shadow of Gogol.* If, however, Tsores's renunciation of love for writing looks backwards to *In the Shadow of Gogol,* his reclaiming of love looks forward to *Goodnight.* There the author confronts the duality of the writer—as representor and represented, as the flesh-and-blood human being Andrei Sinyavsky and his metaphorical double Abram Tertz—and finds the point of reconciliation between the writer's two selves in love, which holds the possibility of trust as the basis of meaning.

Echoing the recurring image of the writer scribbling through the night in *Little Tsores,* in *Goodnight*[16] the author traces the origins of his literary persona back to the "night" of Stalinism:

> But, speaking philosophically, as an author linked with a definite epoch (the end of the '40s-the beginning of the '50s), the epoch of mature, late and flourishing Stalinism, I cannot help remembering *my time* with a certain satisfaction and feeling of filial gratitude. Yes, I am unashamed to say: I am a child of that hellish epoch. All those petty intrigues, bits of madness, little horrors that I am describing so knowledgeably here, which permeated everyday life with the electricity of an impending end of the world, all those warlocks, vampires that to this day do not allow me to go peacefully [*spokoino*] to sleep, created at that time a sort of universal radioactive stream or, better, shroud to which I was—like it or not—attached. That time is dear to me for the sole reason that in it and only in it, and not somewhere in another place, did I understand something opposite to it and, gritting my teeth, chipped myself off

from society, bared my teeth, shut myself up in a shell[17] and
recoiled in horror in order to live and think at my own risk.[18]

The title of the work—which means literally "have a peaceful night,"
the Russian equivalent of the English expression "goodnight"—is
thus simultaneously ironic and cathartic. Night in the Stalin years
was a time of terror presided over by the insomniac dictator, as
people fearing arrest lay awake into the wee hours. Night, however,
is also a time of stolen pleasures, shared confidences, and intimacy,
transmuted in the end into the release of peaceful slumber under the
open sky. *Goodnight* is thus, in a sense, Sinyavsky/Tertz's "journey
to the end of the night," an attempt, through the medium of the text,
to subdue the demons and make peace with the night.[19]

Goodnight is divided into five chapters, which, roughly speaking, move chronologically backwards in time, to the point of origin of the author's surreptitious literary career, the birth of Abram
Tertz. However, as even a cursory overview demonstrates, the work
is constructed out of a complex interweaving of temporal strata.
Thus the first chapter, "Turncoat" (*Perevertysh*), beginning with the
author's arrest and ending with his transport to Dubrovlag, focuses
on his interrogation and trial, yet includes an interpolated text on the
author's release from prison. The second chapter, "House of Assignation" (*Dom svidanii*), intertwines a narrative of Mariya Rozanova's
conjugal visits with her husband during his term in the camps with
reminiscences of the authorities' hunt for Abram Tertz, which ended
in Sinyavsky's arrest. The third and central chapter, titled simply
"Father" (*Otets*), traces the author's relations with his father, beginning in childhood and culminating in a conversation between father
and son in the woods after the elder Sinyavsky's release in 1952 from
nine months of imprisonment. The fourth chapter, "Dangerous Liaisons" (*Opasnye svyazi*), centers on Stalin's death in March 1953[20] and
therefore comes chronologically later than the main episode of the
preceding chapter. The final chapter, "In the Belly of the Whale" (*Vo
chreve kitovom*) again takes the main stream of the narrative back
in time, focusing first on the author's friendship, beginning in adolescence, with the character called alternately S. and Serezha and
then on Sinyavsky's relationship between 1947 and 1952 with Hélène
Peltier, the daughter of the French naval attaché assigned to Moscow. The latter part of the chapter chronicles MGB attempts to coerce
Sinyavsky into participating in a provocation aimed at his foreign
friend. References to the narrator's distance from the events he is

relating from the vantage of his subsequent emigration to France add a further temporal layer to the narrative.

Toward the beginning of the first chapter, the narrator explains the vagaries of the work's complex temporal structure as an attempt to reproduce the workings of memory:

> My narration, I see, moves away from me with the leaps of a kangaroo and returns in its tracks, falling at my feet, like a boomerang. It must be that this is inherent in its character, which has its basis in the efforts of memory to reduce hero and author to a meaningful unity, to make ends meet in an orderly causal chain, where development in time is not so obligatory. Do we not all, when sorting through the past in our souls, leap backwards and forwards along a segment that has been measured off, trying to grasp with the eyes the space allotted to the person simultaneously from several points of a life still in motion? Or do we not mentally return to an event, to ourselves, to those close to us, to our enemies, to the same dreams, at their old address, each time anew? The past is incomprehensible without these displacements. It slips through our fingers as soon as we set out to build it a monument. In the desire to tell in order, year by year, day by day, everything that happened to us in our lifetimes, we unintentionally dissemble against the factual truth, to which in the given case we would all the same be better off sticking. All the more so when the circumstances are somewhat extraordinary. . . . I add in justification that in skipping from place to place on my biographical canvas I was guided not by a weakness for being entertaining nor by an innate tendency to natural disorder, but, on the contrary, by an insatiable desire to write as precisely, rigorously, and sober-mindedly as possible. Even more the experiment in reconstructing one's own literary fate demands from an author what is termed in science precision and purity of analysis. While not promising a linear narrative, I am striving all the same not to deviate by one iota from the original sketch of events and collisions that reality bestowed upon me. (351–52)

Here the author[21] articulates a fundamental premise of his conception of and approach to literature. While the sign, once written, is fixed, the representing self remains constantly in flux, changing over time, ever becoming different from itself, frustrating the writer's attempts to build himself a "monument," to set himself in stone. The disruption of conventional form becomes the sole means of somehow approximating the "truth," of reducing "hero and author"—Tertz and Sinyavsky—"to a meaningful unity."

Toward the end of *Goodnight*, the author, meditating on the effects on himself, when in emigration, of surveying the French—therefore foreign, other—countryside, writes: "You notice that you are not simply looking to the right and to the left, but are drinking in, absorbing the landscape and becoming gradually different because of these visions. You are not the same as you were yesterday because you looked" (578). The writer carries his memories with him into the landscape: "We are rooted in what we have seen. We grow into the landscape. And we are no longer ourselves, but rocks and trees, all it takes is to look. And we bring the dead, who still waft over us, after us, in dreams, into its soft outlines. Look! Remember! . . So that we all will go to rest sooner or later in the contours of these hills" (578). Invoking here images of the merging of self and landscape and of the transmutation of living beings into stone which figure prominently throughout *Goodnight*, the author elaborates on the plurality of the self, which carries with it—like the narrator of *Icy Weather*—the people and events that go on living in the author's mind, changing with him as he, moving through new landscapes, continues his mental conversations with those who are dead or absent, bringing the past into the present, which is constantly slipping away. The dislocation of time in the novel-memoir thus becomes an attempt perhaps not so much to bridge the difference between the fixed sign and the mutable self—between the author and his hero, between the representing self and the self represented,—as to render the difference, to expose the imposture of the sign, which is the essence of Tertz's fantastic realism. The author, somewhat disingenuously, sets apart certain passages in the text, which in the Russian edition are printed in red ink,[22] of which he writes: "The author, at times, is free to depart from the facts for the sake of their fuller and more powerful presentation, each time, however, specially stipulating these rare incursions of the creative will into the natural order of things" (341). Despite this disclaimer, these inserted texts are less departures from the narrative as a whole than the logical extension of its basic premise. They thereby underscore the key issue addressed in *Goodnight*: the ethical implications of the relationship between the representing subject and what is represented, between reality and art.

The possibility of communication, questioned in one form or

another throughout the Tertz writings, is pivotal to this exploration of the interconnection between meaning and morality. Throughout *Goodnight*, memory frequently takes the form of dialogue, and conversations—failed, hindered, surreptitiously intercepted, and, in crucial instances, successful—are integral to the narrative's central concern. This concern, limned in the distinction Sinyavsky drew at his trial between the language of literature and the language of the law, is rooted in the assertion of an intrinsic ethical distinction between the workings of the literary sign and the function of language in everyday life. In "The Fatherland: A Thieves' Song." Tertz discourses on the theatricality of the description of a robbery in a thieves' song: "And the whole comical situation (a rich cavalier suddenly becomes naked and pitiful) is resolved exclusively by means of the spectacular effect, which gives the performers above all artistic satisfaction—not because they so deftly fixed a smart fellow, but strictly by the theatrical eccentricity and picturesqueness of what happened." Tertz then contrasts the "artistic satisfaction" provided by spectacle with the same text read as a straightforward account of an actual occurrence:

> People will say gloatingly: you would sing a different tune if you were in the place of the victim. I agree. I would sing a different tune. But it would no longer be a song, but a sad fact of my biography or, more broadly, a "social calamity," "morality," "the police," "the struggle with crime," a "special juridical case," and so on and so on, which has no direct relation to poetry, and sometimes even irresolvably contradicts it. This does not mean at all that art is "asocial" or "amoral." It's simply that its social and moral criteria are evidently somewhat different than in normal life, perhaps broader.[23]

In *Goodnight* the author directly confronts the ethical distinction between art and life by charting the genesis of his literary persona out of a society where everyday life has run amok, crossing over the boundary into art with horrific results. The text itself becomes an act of restitution and reintegration, an attempt to return the artistic sign to its proper context and, in so doing, to return reality to reality.

The first chapter, "Turncoat," draws its title from the scurrilous article by Dmitry Eremin published in *Izvestiya* some three weeks before Sinyavsky's trial. As discussed earlier, Eremin's diatribe accuses Sinyavsky of being a double-dealer who masqueraded as a loyal Soviet man of letters—that is, *svoi*—while in fact being something quite different—an "internal emigré," a degenerate, other, *chu-zhoi*. While the author's use of the title in *Goodnight* is clearly ironic, it nonetheless serves to focus the issues of self and representation, body and metaphor, on which the chapter and the book as a whole turn. The question of identity is raised from the outset, in the description of Sinyavsky's arrest with which *Goodnight* opens:

> It was at the Nikitsky Gate when they took me. I was late for a lecture at the studio-school of the Moscow Art Theater and was hanging around at a trolley stop, watching to see if a trolley was coming when suddenly, behind my back, I heard an interrogative and seemingly familiar exclamation: "Andrei Donatovich?!."
>
> As if someone doubted whether or not it was I, in the joyful impatience of meeting. (339)

The writer's name, who he really is, is called into doubt by the very terms of his arrest. Yet if the chapter begins with a questioning of identity, it ends with a recognition.

The question of whether Andrei Donatovich Sinyavsky is Abram Tertz, of what relationship the author's legal identity bears to his literary persona, is the focal issue addressed in the chapter. In the car on the way to the Lubyanka, the author realizes the irony of his situation: "It resembled what I had written ten years before my arrest in the novella *The Trial Begins*" (340). The writer finds himself transported into his own plot. This is not an absurd coincidence, he suggests, but rather the logical consequence of his own writings:

> Then, still in the car, while they were driving me, in that decisive moment of face-to-face confrontation with myself, no one helped me—not my wife, . . . , nor my friends, . . . , nor, all the more so, I myself, Sinyavsky, who just by this flourish and shove into the car had been decisively crossed out. But only he, he, my black hero, for greater nonsensicality, for fun, even if just to make things more interesting and funnier beforehand, nicknamed like an old buddy "Abram," with the cutting appendage "Tertz," only he whispered then that everything was going right, as it should, according to the intended plot, which required realization, as has happened many times in literature—the taking to the end, to the truth, of all those similes, metaphors for which it behooves the author to pay with his head. (346)

The author then claims that he was able to stand up to the Soviet authorities not because he was better than others: "What am I— better than others? More courageous? Stronger? Not at all; I've been more badly burned. Many things have helped me and proved useful to me in life, about which I will tell later, if you will allow it. But for the time being, to begin with, I will render my gratitude to Abram Tertz, my dark [*temnomu*] double, who, perhaps, will even be the death of me, but who rescued me then and got me through, me, the bright [*svetlogo*] person, Sinyavsky, shamefully caught and delivered to the Lubyanka" (345). What the author means by crediting his literary alter ego with having saved him becomes clear in the course of the chapter, as he demonstrates how the manipulation of language by Soviet officialdom transforms reality into a literary text, where the "absurd intellectual" (340) Sinyavsky is helpless, but where his metaphorical double is in his element.

The author draws a vivid contrast between his own "bright" legal self and his "dark" alter ego. He imagines Tertz:

> I see him as if it were now, a robber, gambler, son of a bitch, hands in his trousers, moustache like a thread, in a cap flattened to his eyebrows, propelled by a light, rather shuffling gait, with tender interjections of an indecent character on his withered lips, his emaciated body honed in many years of polemics and stylistic contradictions. Intense, irrefutable. He'd slit your throat at the drop of a hat. He'll steal. He'll croak, but he won't betray you. A businesslike man. Capable of writing with a pen (on paper)—*with a pen* [*perom*], which in thieves' language is a *knife*, dear children. In a word—a *knife*. (345)

To this metaphorical, knife-wielding description of his own creation the author counterposes the respectable literary scholar Andrei Sinyavsky, implicitly raising the question of which of his two personae is truly a mask: "For some reason people, even among my close acquaintances, like Andrei Sinyavsky and don't like Abram Tertz. And I'm used to it; let me hold onto Sinyavsky as an accomplice, as a cover for Tertz, as a playbill. We all need a modest and noble appearance in life" (345).

Had it not been for his arrest and trial, the author moreover maintains, Sinyavsky and Tertz would simply have "peacefully cohabited":

And if they had not then tied us together—in one person [*v odnom litse*], in the heated trial, which to this day I deeply regret—we would even have peacefully cohabited, troubling no one, each working in his profession, each in his own branch, without going public, sheltered in the burrow of Soviet hard times, in the solitary semi-basement on Khlebny Street. And Abram Tertz—impudent, fabulous Abram Tertz—you can be sure, would have acted on the sly, not going too far, to the end of Sinyavsky's days, in no way discrediting or clouding his commonplace biography. He would have enjoyed in secret the pungency of the plot, the impudent fellow, drawing satisfaction from the mere fact that he, a real thief and castoff, was hobnobbing like a member of the family with an honest intellectual, inclined to compromise, to a retiring and contemplative life, and who only to pay off God knows when and God knows what inferiority complex simmering in his soul hatched this astringent villain by the name of Abram Tertz, a clown, a jester, a rogue in the bazaar of writing, saying to him one day: "Go ahead, go ahead! If not, I can't answer for myself!" (345–46)

Here the author acknowledges and accepts his own duality, manifested in his legal and literary personae. While he considers it possible to live with this plurality, the Soviet authorities do not:

Perhaps we will pause again on the causes of this personality split as the drama unfolds,[24] when no longer engineers[25] but surgeons of human souls set to work on the personality, the surgeons who opened up this whole malignant abscess or dislocation of the psyche and, word by word, presented to the compliant, respected Andrei Donatovich a memorandum to the effect that he was now being called by his pleasant name and patronymic exclusively out of politeness, out of the goodness of our harmless organs,[26] which for a long time, since the Twentieth Party Congress, had no longer beaten anyone, but he, a hireling of imperialism, a doubledealer, a turncoat [*perevertysh*], should himself understand that he is not a bit respected, not Andrei and not Donatovich, but the proven and sworn traitor Abram Tertz. (346)

The author claims that the authorities cannot accept his duality, the coexistence of Sinyavsky and Tertz, and that they therefore realize him into his own metaphor: they turn Andrei Donatovich Sinyavsky into Abram Tertz.

The revelation of the horror of the transformation of human beings into empty signs is the most damning indictment that *Goodnight* levels against the Soviet system. In the first chapter the author explores the mechanisms by which the "surgeons of human souls" effect this transformation, as revealed by his own interrogation and trial. In the same chapter, however, he exposes the malfunctioning of the system, which, ironically, gives birth to the very duality, incarnated in Abram Tertz, that it seeks to repress.

The author points immediately to the theatricality of his situation in prison: "In general, it is difficult to comprehend where in prison theater ends and reality begins, especially for a new arrival, who right away, right from the street, still at full steam, is drawn into the intrigue of investigation by a striking play of chiaroscuro" (340). One of the new prisoner's first experiences of the workings of language in his new surroundings—a few kind words uttered to him in passing by an old warder who is searching his clothing—is emblematic: "'It's all right, it will all work out, maybe they'll still let you go . . .'—I didn't understand and am not certain to this day whether he wanted at a suitable price to bolster me with a word of sympathy, whether he thought to mitigate his own awkward role, or whether he with his soul-saving response was already taken into account and consideration in the system of prison countermeasures, which played on the nerves of those under investigation. Forgive me, old man, if I have sinned against you!" (341). This episode exposes from the outset the system's reliance on the erosion of trust in language. Any possibility of a stable relationship between sign and referent is undermined by the sowing of suspicion.

The prisoner's isolation from those near and dear to him, including particularly the author's separation from his co-defendant Daniel, places language entirely in the control of the authorities, who manipulate it to their own ends. The abuse here is such that, by the end of his interrogation and trial, the author learns to assume that his interrogator's words mean exactly the opposite of what he literally says. Life, as orchestrated by the author's captors, becomes theater, where everyone plays roles and where the linguistic sign, as in the literary text, loses the more or less direct relationship with reality rooted in trust necessary for communication in everyday life. The author evinces a particular fascination for his persecutors' manifestations of blatantly inappropriate laughter and tears prompted by their victims' sufferings. These expressions of emotion become masks, the masks of tragedy and comedy, symbols of the theater into which they have transformed life and into which they have themselves been absorbed through the destruction of the integrity of the sign. They laugh and cry incongruously, become masks, because their words are, for them, completely divorced from their consequences to the bodies of those they are persecuting.

The author's vision of the subversion of language on which the system rests is crystallized in the two inserted texts, set off in red ink, "The Mirror" (*Zerkalo*) and "Eyeglasses" (*Ochki*), which are integrated into the text of the first chapter. Taken together they define the underlying malfunction of language with which the author grapples throughout *Goodnight*.

The author prefaces the first of several excerpts from what he terms the "fairy-play" (*feeriya*) "The Mirror," interspersed in five segments through his account of his interrogation, with the following remarks:

> It seems to me that it is impossible to comprehend the gigantic laws of prison without projecting its walls into some sort of other, theatrical mechanisms and symbols, into the stylized realms of the stage, which are undoubtedly inaccessible to us as a tangible reality and which exist only in the image of surmises or the author's dreams. The author, at times, is free to depart from the facts for the sake of their fuller and more powerful illumination, each time, however, specially stipulating these rare incursions of the creative will into the natural order of things. I subsequently undertook a lofty attempt of this sort to interpret what had happened to me in drafts for the fairy-play "The Mirror," which as it happens remained unfinished. I ask that you not confuse them with the real story of my arrest, which I am relating concurrently. (341)

As suggested by the genre designation of "The Mirror," the five "scenes" of the purportedly unfinished text incorporated into *Goodnight* are presented in the form of a play, complete with stage directions, lighting and sound effects, dialogue allotted to characters— foremost among them Sinyavsky and his interrogator Pakhomov —and props—most notably the mirror of the title. The "mirrors"— both the prop mirror, which does not accurately reflect what transpires before it, but rather distorts and at times serves as a window to a reality behind the scenes, and the fairy-play of that name—lay bare the theatricality of the events being staged, of reality turned into spectacle. The mirror becomes a means not of reflecting reality, but of creating a mask, of entering into a role: "People in the know, involved in this matter (who themselves suffered later), explained to me that the laughter of the interrogator, like the mastery of an actor, was worked out through years of labor and training in front of a mirror and was included in the program of his practical instruction" (343).

In *Soviet Civilization* Sinyavsky outlines what he considers the basic features of the "bureaucratized language" of Soviet official-dom: "This language has two essential aspects. First, it is estranged from normal human discourse. It is a word divorced from its origi-nal meaning. It is an emasculated language, in which words do not denote things but symbols or conventions, accepted by the state but often without any relation to reality. Second, it is an extremely standardized language, its norm or basis being the handful of stock words and locutions most often used in Party propaganda and politi-cal agitation."[27] This is the language that the author finds himself up against during his interrogation and trial and which he ironizes in "The Mirror." At the basis of this perversion of language lies a com-plete inability on the part of the speaker to see from any point of view but his own. The speaker is simultaneously the defining center and a slave to the empty sign. The result is a complete breakdown of dialogue, as the author illustrates with particularly black humor in a segment of "The Mirror" in which he conflates the later attacks on him for *Strolls with Pushkin* with his pre-trial interrogation, thereby suggesting the continuities between the tactics of his interrogator and his later emigre detractors.

The fifth and final segment of "The Mirror" raises the issues of definition and taste, the possibility of differing points of view:

> *He [the interrogator]:* Fear God, Andrei Donatovich! What kind of writer are you? Consider appearances. Judge for yourself. To no matter which page I open up your so-called "opuses": it makes me sick! Is this really language? Nothing but obscenity! . .
>
> *I [Sinyavsky]:* Perhaps we simply have different literary tastes? . .
>
> *He:* Oho. You mean to say that I have bad taste? So be it. But we gave it to a commission of experts. Scholars, writers . . . Sergei Antonov, Idashkin. Academician Vinogradov. Re-

spected names. And all say in one voice (he reads from his papers): "obvious anti-Sovietism, semi-concealed pornography, and formalism devoid of principles!"

I: Well I don't consider Idashkin a writer . . .

He: (with spite). And Chekhov? Do you consider Chekhov a writer? (371)

What is at issue here is the interrelationship between language and authority. The interrogator, backed up by "respected names," claims the authority to define who is a writer and who is not, dismissing the possibility of differing interpretations and thereby frustrating all possibility of dialogue. Words become a means not of bridging but of exorcising difference, as the increasingly absurd conversation reveals:

I: Yes, your Chekhov . . . Always with respect—Chekhov, *Uncle Vanya* . . .

He: There you see—"*your* Chekhov"! That means "our" Chekhov is not yours? "Ours" and "yours"? Nothing more need be said. What a viper—excuse the sharp expression—they bred in the Institute of World Literature. (*He stands up.*) Yes, Andrei Donatovich, yes! You are right! Chekhov is ours. We love Chekhov. We will allow no one to trample *our* Chekhov with their feet! The people [*narod*] will not allow it, Andrei Donatovich! The people are watching us! The people! (371–72)

The people (*narod*) serve to legitimize the authorities' right to define. Yet, as becomes clear, this *narod* is merely an empty symbol, which has no relationship to the real people the author will encounter when he is sent to the camps.

Just as the interrogator has worked himself into a frenzy over Chekhov, however—"Maybe I shed blood for Chekhov!" (377)— voices are heard, apparently coming from the mirror: "The cassette. It's the wrong cassette! You bungled everything again, Pashka! It's Pushkin! Pushkin, I tell you!" (377). The interrogator immediately loses all interest in Chekhov and redirects his outrage to a defense of Pushkin:

He: Come on, there's no Chekhov now! I don't give a damn [for Chekhov]! Chekhov is small change. A misprint. Rubbish. Simply under the cover of Chekhov you were trying to force

through much more far-ranging plans and perspectives on
Pushkin. Pushkin—that's the point. . . . And we will not permit you to offend Pushkin. We love Pushkin. Everyone agrees
on Pushkin. Pushkin is dear to everyone as a national heritage. And it's here, my dear man, with your permission, that
we'll rap you on the paws! On the claws! Don't set foot in our
garden! And don't go strolling arm in arm with unknown soul
experts from foreign embassies around our Monument not
made by hands! (380–81)

The interrogator's invocation of the first line of Pushkin's famous
1836 poem "I raised myself a monument not made by hands" is
self-subverting. The authorities' claim to exclusive right to control
Pushkin's words, to Pushkin as "monument," is undercut by the
words themselves. The epithet *nerukotvornyi* ("not made by hands")
refers to the genesis of the icon as sacred image from the imprint
of Christ's face left on St. Veronica's veil, that is, created without
human intervention. As we have seen in the discussion of "Pkhents,"
the image "not made by hands" suggests the ideal image, which lies
beyond the boundaries of language. The usurpation of the divine
right to define, the attempt to suppress difference by denying the
possibility of diverging interpretations ("Everyone agrees on Pushkin"), thereby creating the bipolarity of "we" versus "you," results
in a linguistic nightmare, in which Pushkin becomes interchangeable with Chekhov, the actors become their roles, translated into
the world of the self-validating text, where words are divorced from
their referents, utterances from their consequences.

This dystopia of linguistic neurosis necessarily depends on the
silencing of the other, the crushing of any challenge to the authorities' hegemony over the power to define. In "Eyeglasses"[28] the author
confronts the horror of this silence. In this inserted text he conveys
the experience of his release and return to freedom. Just as the segments of "The Mirror" are interspersed with what are purportedly
more straightforward—for lack of a better word—accounts of the
same events, so "Eyeglasses" follows the author's narrative of his
return to Moscow from Dubrovlag. As in the case of "The Mirror,"
he prefaces "Eyeglasses" with a brief explication: "Sometime during
this last lap my eyes failed me. For information's sake I am append-
ing a sketch [*ocherk*] of an unimportant episode, useful primarily as
a repetition of what was laid out above—from a different angle or
with a somewhat different focus. Perhaps, its exaggerated precision

will allow me to grasp, finally, the elusive thread of meaning, which one so fears to lose as life becomes crueler. I'll try" (356).

"Eyeglasses" is ostensibly concerned with the question of when in the course of his unexpected, premature release from prison the author's eyesight markedly degenerated, forcing him finally to acquire glasses. The glasses, however, become a metaphor for the bifurcation of the writer, caught between the worlds of the dead and the living, between the conventionality of the sign and the heterogeneity of the self.

Before he learns he is to be freed, the author finds himself in a cell in Potma Transit Prison. He is surprised to learn that "the papers on me had not been drawn up and in general they didn't know who I was. . . . that they did not have any clear idea what to do with me and where to send me, that I was no one, no one's and seemingly outside the law" (357). He accepts this legal anonymity as a "blessing from above" and savors the thought of perhaps spending some days there "in peaceful [*spokoinoi*] solitary confinement" (357). Automatically searching the walls of his cell for marks left behind by earlier prisoners, however, he "marveled at the somber art of the builders. . . . The cell from top to bottom was eaten away by a shallow relief, as if flooded by a sea of rearing stone waves. It was impossible to write on this crust. The sharp, flinty crests would break any pencil, devoured drawings and symbols. One could not draw a cross, nor a curseword, nor a name, nor the date of a supposed departure, an execution" (358). This wall becomes for the author an incarnation of hell: "With what could it be compared, with what architecture? It excluded the faintest hint of the presence here of a human being. . . . It seemed that I had somehow managed to get to that very hell that I had dreamed of seeing" (358–59). The author thus equates hell with the eradication of tokens of human presence embodied in the wall—which precludes all communication, the recording and preservation of any vestiges of life. The infernal wall, moreover, serves as the prototype of images of human beings translated into stone that recur throughout *Goodnight*. Yet the same wall, transformed by art, becomes the means of asserting the very right of the individual self to leave its trace in language that it was constructed to suppress.

Just as the author responds to his interrogator's and the court's denial that he is a writer by writing—which is, after all, the only true confirmation of his vocation—so, confronted by the wall, "I composed, I wrote, understanding perfectly well that that is not the way to write." In this place where writing is forbidden he manages

to write with a pencil on a copy of *Izvestiya*, both of which he—
now a seasoned *zek* [prisoner]—has managed to smuggle through
the search: "On the newspaper, more precisely in the margins of the
newspaper and here and there between the lines of the unanimous
headlines, without letting out of my sight the round peephole in the
door and the thick cave-like [*peshchernye*][29] deposits along the walls,
I undertook with an uneven hand to mark down fleeting signs." The
author claims that he no longer remembers what he wrote and that
it hardly could have been anything "serious" (358). The point here
lies not in the product, but rather in the act of writing itself. This
scrawling in the margins—that is, challenging the symbolic center—
and "between the lines" of the "unanimous" official discourse of *Izvestiya*, with an eye to the danger of being caught and an eye to
the intractable wall, constitutes a prototypical image of writing as
crime.

As the writer writes, he hears the sounds of the prison around
him, living traces of the human presence the wall is designed to
negate. Then, through the force of metaphor, the hellish wall becomes a representation of the very voices it was designed to silence:

> But sitting in the compartment of the remote transit prison,
> I already regarded myself as a cell, a molecule of an enor-
> mous Leviathan, floating into the distance of history, without
> lights on the sides, but with lights inside, in the hold, with
> crowds of prisoners who had been gulped down, swallowed,
> and yet still rejoiced. The squeals of women, laughter, singing,
> women's merry exchanges with men who held their own and
> were establishing contact with transient girlfriends by ear, by
> skirts (flashing through the mind), inaccessible to memory,
> swearing, the sounds of games or fights beginning, whither
> our foreman rushed, like a lion to mass in order to gape at the
> show and then to punish the fighters, who were coupled in a
> wet tangle, in order to avoid fatal outcomes—all of this con-
> stituted the regular, slight quivering, running along the stone,
> as if along the skin of a monstrous animal. (359)

The writer, through metaphor, which springs from his openness
to the sounds of others, brings the dead wall alive, transforming it
into the hide of a beast and the corrosion on the wall into the sounds
of the prison shivering along that hide.

When the author returns to Moscow after his release, he discovers that, although his eyesight had been fine only a few days

before, he now needs glasses, which become for him a symbol of his bisection:

> And I wept—not over my blindness, which, I repeat, was no reason to get upset. And not for my prematurely ended youth, of which, to tell the truth, there wasn't much anyway. But for the *saddle*, as I called it, that had suddenly arisen in my consciousness, dividing me into two halves, into *before* and *after* my exit from behind the barbed wire—as if having a presentiment of how difficult it would be to return from there to people and what a gulf ran between us and them. I cried and I saw the *saddle* in the image and form of the glasses that I would put on as a sign of the impassable boundary, in memory of the gas-like wall streaming with letters, wailing tirelessly—and always about the sea, about the sea. (361)

Having imagined the glasses as an image of division, he finds, when they do finally arrive from friends in England, that they seem to have a strange effect on his vision: "My eyes did not fit into the target chamber and doubled reality in a disturbed and distorted image. With the right eye, it seemed, I rummaged for my lighter, which was always getting lost, blending into the relief of the carpet-textured couch. But with the left eye . . . But is it necessary to specify what visions at the same time I saw on the left? Laughter, singing, women's merry exchanges with men, hardened deposits of lime along the walls, from which, however, I was torn away, fenced off, thrown into the world from my native menagerie like godless spit, like excrement from under a dog grown wild" (363). The writer thus finds himself caught between automatized reality—the cigarette lighter that blends into the pattern of the couch—and the voices of the living dead he carries with him.

The narrative of the author's transport to Dubrovlag with which the first chapter of *Goodnight* closes resonates with both "The Mirror" and "Eyeglasses." In a final conversation the interrogator Pakhomov strongly advises the author to shave his beard. "You'll be just like new" (395), he remarks, revealing the symbolic significance of this attempt to eradicate the physical mark of otherness embodied in the beard, to remake the author into a new man by destroying his alterity. He moreover warns the author that the beard will draw unnecessary attention to him, perhaps provoking the thieves and criminals with whom he will be transported to set it on fire. The author, however, resists the suggestion:

Funny as it seems, at that moment removing my beard seemed like throwing in the towel.

I didn't impute any significance to my appearance, to my portrait. I didn't care a rap about any beard! But they were trying so hard, insisting . . . Repentance? Betrayal of myself? Loss of face? Why should this Pakhomov, with all his important affairs, keep harping on my beard? . . No, bastards! I won't give in. In short, little by little I was becoming a criminal, as they themselves called me, a spiteful and mistrustful *zek*, calculating my every move by the opposite. Exactly the opposite! (395)

This apparently trivial interchange encapsulates the irony inherent in the chapter's title: *Perevertysh*. In response to Pakhomov's attempts to remake him, to destroy the traces of his otherness, the author becomes the opposite, becomes a criminal, which is both what the system has named him and the realization of his own metaphor. The attempt to eradicate alterity thus creates alterity: the mild-mannered, conventional Sinyavsky becomes the hardened criminal Tertz.

The crowning irony, however, comes at the very end of the chapter. On the train carrying him to Potma, when he is taken past the other prisoners, common criminals being transported with him, the author suddenly hears his own name called out: "Sinyavsky! Sinyavsky!" (397). Despite his distrust of Pakhomov he is concerned for his own safety and suspects that the guards (their chief a man-monument with "a marble face," 397) have leaked his identity to the other prisoners. When the transport arrives at its destination, the author, who has up to then been segregated as a "political," finds himself together with the others. Learning that he has been held at Lefortovo Prison, they ask if he saw Sinyavsky there, and he, his fears notwithstanding, admits that he is himself Sinyavsky: "I stood, resting on my feet, waiting for the blow. And something went wrong. Instead of beating me, they were embracing me, shaking my hands" (398). The system has backfired: "In the thieves' world notoriety is valued. But there is one thing more, which I grasped then: in defiance! In defiance of the newspapers, the prison, the government. In defiance of sense. They considered the fact that I was reviled on the radio, at meetings, and in the press an honor. I was considered worthy! . . And the fact that I had smuggled something to the West, had not confessed, not bowed and scraped before the court made me grow into some sort of altogether unrecognizable image. Not of a human being. Not of an author. No, most likely, of some sort of Thief with a figurative capital 'T'" (399). Most ironic of all, as he learns from the man who had yelled "Sinyavsky" in the train, it is his beard that served as the mark of recognition:

> "But how did you guess? Then, who told you I was Sinyavsky?"
>
> "But I didn't guess. I saw them leading a funny man with a beard. Well, so I yelled 'Sinyavsky!' Just like that, as a joke . . . Forgive me, we didn't think that it was you." (400).

The beard thus becomes a symbol of the failure of the authorities' attempts to manipulate meaning, to suppress otherness, and the author exults that he in the end has won his argument with Pakhomov; he has been accepted by his "people" [*narod*]—thieves, hooligans, bandits—who have ceased to believe in the powers that be. He attributes this acceptance precisely to those who tried to suppress him: "To what do you think I owed this success, Viktor Aleksandrovich [Pakhomov]? To my good disposition? To my beautiful eyes, as you liked to say? No, simply to the foul reputation of a writer who disagreed with you, who turned a *salto-mortale* several times and landed on his feet, on equal ground with thieves" (400–401).

The author closes the chapter with a final comment on the farewell called to him by his fellow prisoners:

> "Goodbye, Andrei Donatovich . ."
>
> After all, Pakhomov, they certainly had nothing to gain by uttering my unusual name and patronymic so coordinatedly, collectively from their cages, in the stuffy air, blindly. Besides, the affectionate, joyous "Goodbye" was not appropriate to the circumstances, Viktor Aleksandrovich, was not appropriate to those leprous lips. That's not your theater. What would you say now in continuation of your interrogation? I, for my part, know one thing:
>
> "The sea accepted me! The sea accepted me, Pakhomov!"
> (401)

Here, first of all, the author turns the bureaucratized language of Soviet propaganda, the sign emptied of referent and transformed into symbol, on its head. Just as above he identified the true "people," invoked by Pakhomov as the source of his authority to define, as these outcasts of society, so in this instance he cites a true, spontaneous example of collective action, the recognition embodied in the calling of his real name and patronymic. This, he maintains, is not theater; these are the actual referents of the words manipulated by the authorities. This is the "sea," the voices of the silenced that the author carries within him, brought alive in the text through metaphor and memory.

In the first chapter, the author establishes the fundamental opposition between the authorities' attempts to control language, to transform human beings into empty signs, and the affirmation of the possibility of communication "in defiance of" those attempts. The four remaining chapters of *Goodnight* elaborate this opposition in a rich series of images and confrontations that traces the evolution of the writer back to what we might metaphorically term the birth of Abram Tertz.

The second chapter, "The House of Assignation," intertwines the "one illuminated night"—"all meetings run together into one illuminated night" (430)—of the author's visits with his wife while in prison with the "detective story," told from the fugitive's point of view, of the authorities' pursuit of Abram Tertz: "It's strange that these conversations from so many years ago slipped into the House of Assignation. Exactly as if we had here the denouement of the plot of a detective story, a mock-up of a table game of cops and robbers" (415). The chapter's two main time strata are linked by memory— the author's memories in prison of how he got there—and by the information that his wife brings him from outside, which ties up the loose ends of the "detective" story in which they were accomplices. The two time layers juxtapose analogous situations in both of which husband and wife are allied in their deception of their pursuers and oppressors and in which their own resorts to fiction and theater in retaliation for the authorities' attempts to suppress their words are counterposed to the communication and communion they achieve between themselves.

The basic counterpoint of frustrated versus successful communication is inherent in the situation of the House of Assignation. The couple must assume that they are under invisible surveillance, that what sounds like the scurrying of mice is in fact the rustling of a tape on which their conversations are being recorded. The game of deception and manipulation that the author and his wife play with the invisible tape recorder–mouse parallels in its theatricality, in its attempts to turn the methods of the captors back on them, the game of hide-and-seek (*pryatki,* 420) they earlier played with Tertz's pursuers.

The author presents the hunt for the "incognito" (419), for the "nameless" writer who hides under the "cap of invisibility" of Abram Tertz as a black comedy played out by disembodied signs. The fugitive catches only fleeting glimpses of his bodiless pursuers: "Someone was running, running, and disappeared as if through the asphalt. And a cigarette still glimmers . . . A fire not from a human being . . . And now all at once, the whole horizon surrounding you began to speak with unfamiliar, guttural voices. Really, what's the matter? Nothing. Take a step and you'll run into a plain-clothes man. You glance back—not a soul. Are you imagining things again? No, they are here! At the door! Beyond the window! In the air! You're not the only clever one. A whole world of invisible beings" (421–22). Tertz, the "invisible man" (412) whose tracks in the snow these "specters" (409) are trailing, engages his pursuers in their own game, setting them off in search of a fiction. He plants false clues about his biography, sending his hunters off on wild-goose chases. The main red herring, the essence of the author's metaphorical alter ego, is, however, his style, his translation of himself into text. One of his colleagues, not suspecting that he is in fact talking to the man behind the pseudonym, speculates on the possibility of finding Abram Tertz by running his writings through a computer: "In our time, Andrei, it's nothing to figure out a person by his style, by his language. The frequency of vocabulary, indices, probability theory. The machine swallows examples of the literary production and delivers up a ready answer" (412–13). The author, however, dismisses this equation of writer's identity with style, this reduction of self to the calculations of a machine: "Style, thank God, is not fingerprints. Not even character. Nor way of life. Often the man and the writer are completely incompatible personalities. Different handwriting. They won't be able to calculate it" (413). Here the author draws a clear distinction between man and writer, fingerprints and style, body and language. Both the invisible Abram Tertz and his invisible hunters are human beings transmuted into signs. There is, however, an obvious and essential difference here between the hunters and the hunted: the former are actual people, while the latter is a metaphor.

Like the disembodied pursuers of Tertz, whose presence is marked only by fleetingly glimpsed signs, so the sole trace of the tape recorder running in the House of Assignation is the telltale sound of the mouse.[30] Like the language of the author's interrogator and the court, the constantly running tape presents an image of discourse that frustrates dialogue: it records, but does not respond. By the same token, just as the author tries to beat the interrogator of "The Mirror" at his own game, so here he manipulates language to his own ends, in effect staging a play for those listening in: "And we'll say, my friend, only what we choose and what in the given situation it is advantageous to us that they should record" (437). Speaking for the benefit of the tape, the spouses use other methods to communicate between themselves. The body itself becomes a means of communication, and husband and wife convey their true meanings in a pantomime that runs counter to the words they are speaking: "How do you do it, you'll ask—write without paper? . . . In essence, all of our face and body is letters. The nose, for example. Or the eye. And if we should run out of names, can't we use our fingers? After all there are ten of them. Counting the toes—twenty. Isn't it just like an ABC book? And the whole person is one interjection! All the punctuation marks, the whole alphabet is in us. Write not with words, not with ink, write—with gestures. Like deaf-mutes. Write, finally, with saliva on your palm. With fruit juice on your brow. With a bird in the head. With two in the bush. Just write. And someone will get it" (438–39).

At the beginning of the chapter the author explains what the House of Assignation is:

> Here on the prison grounds, once a year—for three days in the best case, for one whole day, for one night—the lost family of the prisoner reestablishes its legal rights and duties as best it can through a muddle of kisses and a fount of tears. Therefore this institution is called, as in old times, the House of Assignation, and all these nuances of meaning are correct, reader. A bordello, an inn, an orphans' shelter, a final farewell . . . The prison, you know, infuses its false, sarcastic meaning into everything. But there is also no abode on earth more beautiful and sacred nor, at the same time, a higher and more distant Mountain from which we might contemplate dales and valleys, rivers and ravines scattered over the earth. Here demons come together with angels once a year, with the authorization of the authorities, husbands with wives, children with fathers, the living with the dead. (402)

The House of Assignation, literally "the House of Meetings," echoes the image of the work of art as a place of meeting in *A Voice from the Chorus*; it stands as an archetype of the multivalence of the sign, of the relationship of word to reality, defined at its two poles by the "sarcastic meaning" interjected into everything by the prison and the "sacred" intimacy of the coming together of loving beings.

These poles are pictured most forcefully in passages juxtaposed to one another at the end of the chapter. Opening the door of their room to air it out, the author looks into the corridor and finds the guard on duty peering into their neighbors' keyhole, spying, unbeknownst to the young couple inside, on their lovemaking. Overcome with disgust, the author asks himself whether he should warn the unwitting spouses, whether he should "tear away the veil of chastity from the conjugal chamber, reminding them that they were being observed, and everything that they were up to on the bed in their room was only cinema and only circus?!" (448–49). The guard's voyeurism transforms reality into spectacle, cheapening—introducing the "sarcastic meaning" of the prison into—the chaste intimacy of the young lovers. Like the tape recorder, which surreptitiously records words without allowing dialogue, the guard who sees without being seen figures the ultimate violation of the trust on which the possibility of communication rests. Most important, this violation constitutes a transgression of the boundary between life and art. What should remain private and intimate becomes cheap spectacle. Life is transformed into art.

The author's own conjugal relations with his wife are sheltered from the guard's prying eyes by the forethought of previous inhabitants of their room, who stuffed the keyhole with wadding. The significance of this segment of the text is signaled from the outset by the invocation in its first sentence of the title words (the single instance in the entire narrative of *Goodnight*): "There are times when you would come dragging yourself along to your wife to say goodnight, and she was already falling asleep. 'You're funny,' you would say, tucking in the blanket on her back, as if she were a child. 'And why am I funny?' she would ask in her sleep, without, however, waiting for a reply. I would think: because I love you. With sadness. Who, dearest, will tuck in your back when I'm not there? That's the whole explanation" (450). The simple, everyday phrase "goodnight" thus becomes emblematic of the intimacy of souls bound by love, an intimacy that countervails the dehumanizing surveillance of the camp regime and holds forth the possibility of communication rooted in and yet overcoming the fragility of existence.

This communication is figured in a counterpoint of words and body, convention and transcendence. As the author paces like a beast in his cage, he opens himself to thoughts "from the air, from the cosmic, if you will, space, which quivers in the summer lightning of as yet ungrasped words" (451). What comes to him is the melody of a thieves' song to which he cannot remember the words. Because, as he claims, he has no talent for singing, he tries to "express with his fingers" (451) to his wife the song he has in mind, and "she reads his thoughts" (451), realizing which song he means and prompting him with the words. Just as the spouses have been united in their creation of fictions to deceive the authorities, so here they collaborate in bringing that which comes "from the air," that which exists before words, a melody, into words. Significantly, the song that they together "resurrect" is, by definition, "criminal," composed and sung by criminals about a crime. The basis of communication thus becomes a shared otherness, which originates beyond the verbal, but can be translated into art.

The song itself, as the author—who merges with the composer-narrator-murderer of the song—interprets it, presents a model for the potential of art. While others weep at his girlfriend's death, the murderer himself looks at her photograph, in which she appears " 'as if she were alive' " (453). The image of his dead love holds for the author the promise of resurrection: "Everyone wept, was sorrowful. But I rejoiced: she is coming back to life! I was touched by a premonition: she is saved! . . . Her soul craved to return posthumously to the bosom of original innocence" (453). The photograph of the dead woman—her representation—becomes a pledge of her resurrection, the release of her pure soul in death from the sins of her life. In the song the murderer, himself about to be executed for his crime, looks forward to being reunited in death with his beloved. Thus this song about betrayal, crime, and death holds the promise of resurrection and purification; art transforms sin into the promise of salvation.

The two lovers in the song, who are separated by crime and reunited by death, serve as a symbolic bridge between the "crime" of art and the "sins" of the body. Mariya likens her meeting with her husband to a lover's tryst in a morgue: "We are meeting in a morgue. Do you understand? And we are taking advantage of the conditions" (453). Standing on the threshold of separation and death, the body becomes a final, desperate means of communication, "a means of saying what has remained unsaid in words, in life, to your sole accomplice and proxy on earth—for the whole remaining term allotted to her by God. . . . It is necessary to transfer all the eloquence concentrated in you, for lack of other analogies, into the language of *gestures*, performed, moreover, in the main by the lower, unseeing, and voiceless half of the torso. This would be improbable were it not for the momentary instinct for self-preservation that hurls us to grasp at straws in moments of extreme danger" (454).

Echoing *Little Tsores,* the author likens this desperate attempt to communicate through the body in the face of death to redemptive sin: "And if death, they say, is born of sin, then here, in the vicinity of death, the scales are suddenly tipped in favor of sin, as if this were sin for the sake of salvation [*grekh vo spasenie*], for the sake of helping you, a prayer for aid, a confession and an incantation combined" (454). This "pantomime" in which the two bodies engage becomes a "dialogue," which can only be "approximately and schematically" translated into words: "Know me and forgive me. There is no one in the world. Nowhere and never. You understand. Commit this to memory before the end. To the end. Remember. Remember. Understand and remember" (454). The act of lovemaking on the threshold of extinction, which is simultaneously a metaphor for the creation of art "in defiance of" the dead sign, embodies the aspiration to overcome difference while trapped in conditions of difference, to transform transgression into salvation, mortality into memory. It is the attempt of one self, before death, to convey itself in all its fullness to the beloved other, in a paradoxical "dialogue" that resists translation from the language of gestures into the language of words precisely because the boundaries between pronouns, between selves, disappear: "Here there are no divisions into 'he' and 'she,' into questions and answers. The question is the answer. And sin is on an equal footing with death. Finally! . . . I was always waiting for this. And now it has fallen into place. Not laughter, but death opens my mouth: to begin to speak about what is forbidden" (455). Death, which threatens separation, also betokens resurrection and reunion of souls purged of difference. The transgressions of the body and of the text, sin for the sake of salvation, are earthly surrogates for the posthumous return to innocence. Birth, the author suggests at the end of the chapter, is the fruit of this communication of self: "To make up for it as a result it then became clearer to me, where children come from and what in general conception [*zachatie*] in and of itself means. Your wife has concealed you. Committed you to memory. Trusted you. Understood you. And conceived. It's not genes at all. Not molecules. But understanding and memory" (456). Thus, transgression—engaging in the "sin" of sexual relations or, by analogy, violating linguistic convention in the work of verbal art— becomes the sole means of committing the mortal self to memory and thereby allowing it to be born into a new body, be it child or text. This birth into a new body, moreover, approximates in the substance of the fallen world the release and resurrection of the soul, which simultaneously results from and overcomes death.

The House of Assignation, then, becomes the locus of a complex metaphor for art, for the writer's confinement in the conventionality of the sign, which is analogous to the soul's entrapment in the body. Earlier in the chapter the author invokes his memories of the Alps, seen much later in emigration, echoing his conception of the "ideal book" that ever beckons the author and always remains immanent, beyond realization. He sees in the image of the trees struggling up the slopes of the mountains, unable to reach the inclement, ice-covered, summit, an image of the aspiration of the text:

> As once in the House of Assignation, here the paths of our innumerable accomplices and brothers-in-arms, after having come together, came abruptly to an end. They drag themselves along, one after the other, to the height of the sepulchre, some crawling. Some slightly bending. And look, this one turned a somersault, roots up, when it reached the ice. What a rush toward the impossible, and a commensurate readiness to come to nothing in order to attain flight, ascent. There was something religious in this stern demolition work . . . But, as if it were my sadness, the impudence and inconclusiveness of speech, on which every authorial intention hangs, is built and perishes for nothing, was immediately revealed to me. And that which we, from force of habit, take for style, for artistic features, is only one more attempt, doomed to failure, to go beyond the limits of the language and space allotted to us and in the head or by a roundabout maneuver to speak, finally, about things not subject to being divulged. It is a question of the inaccessible. . . . We are born, as it turns out, for prison. But all we think about is freedom, flight. . . . The soul is a fugitive . . . How many prison legends, woven into the pattern of a carpet, teach us the technology and poetics of flight [*poetiku pobegov*]. (425–26)

Thus style is precisely the transgression of limits, not an expression of self reducible to the calculations of a computer, but the attempt to escape the limits of body and convention. Authorship, again, is not an affirmation of self, but "self-elimination," a flight from "the limits of language and space allotted to us."

Having concluded the second chapter by postulating a link between birth and memory, the author devotes the third and middle-most chapter of *Goodnight* to his own father, of whose memory he is the corporeal incarnation. The problem played out in the chapter entitled simply "Father" is thus intrinsically that of translating the self as living memory into the text. As in the first two chapters, this attempt to transmute memory into representation is couched in terms of self and other, similarity and difference, art and reality, and the possibility as opposed to the frustration of communication.

The author begins the chapter by recognizing himself as a bodily facsimile of his father: "Every time I walk up stairs I commemorate my father. . . . Walking up stairs, I repeat myself. All of this already happened—both the shortness of breath and the heartburn. Not to me—to my father. He walked on these steps before me and bequeathed me this groaning, panting, in commemoration of old age" (456). This legacy of the body, realized in growing old, is an experience of both resurrection and communication: "True, I began to grow old early. . . . That's why my father and I found a common language. But I am only now beginning to understand my father. Now, in France? What difference does it make whether we understand our fathers in Russia or in France! And there is no task more pressing. I would like to have the time, to live long enough. Through groaning, through spitting. Through snoring in my sleep—to resurrect him" (457). As in the preceding chapter, true understanding comes not through words but through the body. The author comprehends his father—and "resurrects" him—to the extent that his body repeats him, erasing the experiential difference between them. This repetition threatens the boundaries of the self: "Sometimes I become frightened: to such an extent am I not there [*menya net*]. He crowds me out, replaces me—in the curve of the back or the neck, in walking upstairs. Nothing is independent. I lose myself, disappear. But the moment I recollect myself, come to my senses—then thanks be to the Lord—it means, you're alive, father? You're alive?!" (457). The body itself thus becomes a living memory, a continuation of the dead. It does not, however, finally erase the bounds between discrete selves. Rather it serves as a point of contact which allows communication and comprehension despite difference.

Thus, the author, as he traces his relationship with his father back to childhood, makes it clear that the bond between them rests on the ability of each to accept and respect the other's point of view. As he points out, "My father had a different point of reference—

from the year 1909. The point of reference is terribly important in all of our fates" (470). He goes on to affirm his acceptance of differing angles of vision: "No, I had no intention of remaking my father. He grew from the year 1909 as I did from 1948. Each person has his point of reference" (471). By the same token, his father, as he was dying, asked his son about his book on Picasso: "What were Picasso, painting, to him? He didn't know much about art. He just sensed that for some reason it was important and trusted" (474). The basis of communication here, as elsewhere in *Goodnight*, is the trust that makes possible the acceptance of otherness.

Just as the first chapter of *Goodnight* is constructed around the author's conversations with the interrogator Pakhomov and the second chapter around his conversations with his wife, so this chapter revolves around the author's conversations with his father in the forest. On their hunting excursions into the woods in the author's boyhood, his father repeatedly adjured his son to remain silent: "All I had to do was to embark on extensive discussions for papa to cut me short: 'No talking in the forest!' And it's true, behind a bush, perhaps, a beast lurked, or perhaps—a human being. It's better not to run into a stranger in the forest" (469). His father's rule suppressing dialogue, however, seems honored more in the breach, giving way, significantly, to the force of memory: "Under the influence of the flow of recollections, my father on occasion would violate the precept 'no talking in the forest'" (470). In fact, "It was in the forest that he spoke to me the most freely. Here, in the forest, no one would listen in" (473). The forest, like the House of Assignation, becomes emblematic of opposing poles of communication: the hunters must remain silent so as not to frighten off their prey or be overheard by someone "alien," while at the same time they can speak freely because the forest holds forth the possibility of unsullied intimacy, security against unwelcome eavesdroppers. This counterpoint between communication and its hindrance coalesces in the chapter's focal episode: the author's reunion with his father and their walk in the Rameno woods after his father's release from prison.[31]

Sinyavsky's father, whose left Socialist Revolutionary sympathies predated the revolution, was arrested in 1951. In the course of nine months of incarceration he managed to prove—somewhat miraculously given the times—his innocence of the charges against him and was released to five years of exile at Rameno. The father's experience of arrest and imprisonment is one that, like his laboring up the stairs, the son is doomed to repeat, but at which he will arrive by a different route, from a different reference point. Thus the author comes to Rameno to see his recently liberated father directly from the train journey with which *Goodnight* ends. This journey will come, by the end of the novel-memoir, to mark the moment of decision, the symbolic birth of Abram Tertz, the choice of action that will finally send the son to prison in his father's footsteps. The author eagerly anticipates telling his father, "the only listener who would understand me" (482), of the change he has undergone in his absence. In the course of their walk in the woods, however, he learns that as a result of the changes worked in his father by his stint in prison, he can no longer tell the one person capable of understanding what has become most important to him. So the chapter ends in an acknowledgment of silence: "Need I add that neither in the forest nor after we had returned home did I breathe a word of this to my father?" (498). The walk in the woods becomes a drama of the need to communicate and its frustration, finally "sublimated" in the text.

From the beginning of their walk, while the son is bursting to hear about his father's experiences and to tell him of his own, his father avoids conversation. Despite his father's reticence, the author persists in talking, recounting details of the search of their apartment following his arrest. When he tries to raise the issue most important to him, however—"Papa, I must tell you in secret one serious thing. Just before my trip to visit you, a week before"—his father stops him dead: "I had not seen my father in such a rage for a long time" (483). This reference to his father's anger, which prompts him to silence his son, serves as a bridge to an episode from the author's childhood: the "one time in twenty-six years that he gave me a real scolding, and shouted so that I will always remember" (483).

His father's earlier anger was provoked by his son's "acquisition of his first independent book in life" (483), *The Headless Horseman* by Mayne Reid, which the child bought with money given him by his aunt. As the author relates, this purchase incensed his father on two counts. First, while his parents had to scrimp to survive, "I had allowed myself to spend five rubles for my own complete enjoyment. . . . What does *my* money mean, if for the sake of my subsistence my mother and father were breaking off the last crumbs? What was I—a bourgeois, a proprietor, a thief?! . ." (484). Second, and more serious, his father considers the tome in question "an empty, stupid little book. . . . If I'd bought with that money, let's say, water-color paints, or a drawing compass, or even a book, but a book that was useful, indispensable to life, then there would have been no scandal" (484). Shamed by his father into disposing of this useless, fantastic work—which so ill-accorded with his father's own utilitarian principles—without reading it, the author was left with a sense of deprivation: "But thanks to this rationalistic education I grew up, speaking frankly, with a defect. It always seems as if I missed what is most important, what is most beautiful in life, let it slip, looking the other way sometime still in childhood, and the unread *Headless Horseman* gallops ahead, without me. Perhaps therefore, in the final analysis, that's why—I missed something—I became a writer" (485). The image of the Headless Horseman ever galloping ahead of him, always beyond his reach, evokes the inaccessible "ideal book" of which the author's works always fall short, just as, when he finally later reads *The Headless Horseman*, the book disappoints his expectations. This is, moreover, the single instance reported in the narrative in which the father attempts to suppress his son's alterity. Significantly the father's attempt to control his son's taste yields a result diametrically opposed to that intended, leading the son to assert his otherness, to become a writer, to follow a vocation that originated in what his father terms a "theft." This foray into the more distant past thus becomes a necessary prelude to the much delayed, culminating conversation between father and son.

Having avoided speaking for so long, the father finally reaches a place in the forest where he is prepared to sit and talk: "Like an experienced hunter, he selected a remote, but rather naked spot, with good visibility on all sides: no one could sneak up unnoticed." As the author soon learns, however, while his father has indeed been waiting for an opportunity to speak to him alone, to "tell you everything, only you," it is a question not of place but of time: "I was waiting for the right *time*, to speak to you without witnesses, calmly [*spokoino*]. Especially the first time." As he tells his initially skeptical son, the father believes that while imprisoned he was the subject of psychological experiments performed "with the aid of equipment, brought back from conquered Germany," that some form of surveillance had been technologically implanted in his brain, and "now [his jailers] themselves were sorry that they could not completely disconnect this strange, two-way link [*svyaz'*] with their object of study." The father has been waiting for a time when those listening in, not in the forest but in his brain, have temporarily tuned out (489–93).

In the end both father and son accept the possibility of two explanations: either the elder Sinyavsky is in fact hooked up to a surveillance device and is mentally receiving signals from outside himself

or, as a result of the psychological pressures applied during his interrogation and imprisonment, "One half of the brain is conversing
with the other." What is clear is that the author's father, subjected to
the "surgeons of human souls" with whom his son sparred earlier in
the narrative, has in some sense bifurcated and can no longer guarantee his son the bond of trust that makes confidences possible: "So
for the time being don't tell me anything you don't have to. Do you
hear? I must not know. Must not! Is that clear to you?" Just as the
spouses in chapter two resorted to body language to foil the tape
recorder in the House of Assignation, so the author's father signs
to him that the "two-way connection" has been turned back on, but
here the "language of gestures" puts an end to communication: "He
raised his hand and made a sign with his fingers which resembled
a soundless click. They've tuned in! Attention: they've tuned in! . .
Somewhere in Lefortovo the generator had begun to work. Strange:
we were alone, alone as before in the huge empty forest, but invisible
guests were already hovering over us." The son realizes that despite
his joy at his meeting with his father, "having met with him, I had
lost something forever" (495–96).

Son and father in effect find themselves in analogous situations.
Just as the father has been bisected by his experience in Lefortovo,
so the son has conceived his secret life, has undergone the split into
Sinyavsky and Tertz. Like his father, the son receives signals from
outside. The forest comes alive with signs: "Looking at this ruffled
settlement, scattered over the whole wasteland, it seemed as if it was
also raving madly—under a volley of signals sent from everywhere.
As if a horde of demons was raging in the foliage, amidst the silence
of the forest, and cats were jumping along the feeble trunks, and
squirrels and deer, ciphered through morse code into a frantic roll
of tiny drums" (493). If, however, the author sees no way out for his
father from the signals, real or imagined, invading his father's head,
these signs from outside herald a means of escape for himself: "It
seemed to me suddenly that the way out had been found: not for
him—for me. That the path was open, the signals heard, and nothing and no one could stop me any longer . . . The seal of a curse and
of happiness lay on my brow" (497).

The forest come alive with signals, like a "localized whirlwind,"
becomes an illustration of the author's vision of literature as he for-
mulates his argument to imagined opponents: "this is *reality*, which
you disregard, scornfully calling it the 'fantastic,'—here it is! And it
is unnecessary to fantasize—it's enough just to see, and it doesn't

matter at all what it's called. It can be called a tree or—a human
being. Whatever you like! A tree is me in my imagined dream. A
tree is my father." The writer's apparent distortion of reality thus derives not from fantasizing, inventing, but from *seeing*. He becomes
a medium open to signals from outside, disappearing in the process
of translating himself into the text:

> Since then, when I suddenly found myself close to it, I have
> understood that a writer—retiring to work and truly to write
> —without fail withdraws into the forest. So that no one will
> see or hear. Only one thing on his mind: 'it's time to transfer
> me onto paper,' the forest says, and becomes a text.
>
> God, what a fabulous kingdom there is here! You can't tear
> yourself away—you just keep looking. Communication? With
> whom? With a human being? With readers? I don't believe it.
> They'll catch you up on every word and prove that everything
> is wrong. I know them! The only refuge is the text. Not too
> dense, not very sparse . . . But remember, there will be no way
> back, no way back from the text. We are in the forest.
>
> It's also important to find the time to remark that when
> you write you must not think. You must turn yourself off.
> When you write, you lose yourself, stray, but the main thing is
> that you forget yourself and live without thinking about any-
> thing. And how beautiful that is! Finally you are not [*tebya
> net*], you are dead. All there is is the forest. And we retire into
> the forest. We retire into the text. (497)

Looking back to *Little Tsores* and ahead to the concluding chapters of
Goodnight, the writer portrays writing not as a form of self-assertion
or an attempt at communication, but as refuge, self-oblivion, and
death. The writer becomes the locus where self and other meet,
where the forest turns into text, reality into metaphor. The writer
who sees loses himself in what is seen and suffers the death of
translation into the text. In the final two chapters of *Goodnight* the
inversion of reality into art and art into reality—which culminates
here in the artist's flight into the text—is traced back to the interplay between reality and representation in Stalinist culture and to
the realizations that have led the author to the forest.

The fourth chapter of *Goodnight*, "Dangerous Liaisons,"[32] falls
into two parts, which are roughly linked by their common focus on
events surrounding Stalin's death. On a deeper level, however, they
are united by the imagery of "dangerous liaisons," which proposes

the writer as intermediary between the living world and the dead sign and identifies the horror of Stalinism as the reduction of living people to dead signs.

The seance as a model for the process of artistic creation figures as the central metaphor of the chapter from the outset. The dangerous liaisons of the title become the links between the worlds of the living and the dead, between reality and art, the medium—an archetype of the writer. The opening section revolves around an actress with psychic powers, called alternately A. and Alla. This alternation between initials and names in referring to A. and other characters, as we shall see, both derives from and elaborates the implications of the seance as metaphor.

The seances described from the beginning of the chapter operate on the principle of a ouija board. The dead, responding to the receptive powers of the medium, guide the saucer to letters, spelling out for the living their identities and messages letter by letter. The incorporeal dead are thus reduced to signs as their only means of embodying themselves, of creating a "material liaison [*svyaz'*] between this world and the other" (501). Here the author employs the seance as a metaphor for the translation of the self into text to illustrate, first of all, the distinction that recurs throughout his works between word and act. He thus relates one instance in which during a seance a spirit moves the saucer, identifying himself as a dead relative of the medium:

> A. B. C. . . . The saucer spins and spins. And what next? Next, following the alphabet—D. No matter what you do. The pointer, as if it were the needle of a compass, will remain on the letter D.—without any doubt. Turn the picture over, and again the pointer, as if to order, returns to the sought-for point. You can't get away from it.
>
> "Is it you, D.?" asked the amazed A.
>
> "And he repeated to her in letters: "Yes, it is I. Yes, A. It is D." (502)

To prove that he is really Dmitry Sergeevich, that this is not a "dirty trick, the intrusion of a charlatan," the disembodied spirit calls A. by her childhood nicknames. The full name, as opposed to the "dead" initial, thus becomes a means of recognition, a token of the possibility of establishing a bond of communication. As the seance progresses, however, the putative Dmitry Sergeevich makes it clear that

he wants to return to the body, that he has been conducting experiments with that end in view, and that he believes he is already
capable of moving physical objects in the world of the living. Yet
when he claims that he has moved a vase, the participants in the
seance see nothing budge. A. informs him, "Dima, you are mis-
taken. It all just seems that way to you. Your achievements are not
yet reflected on this plane. The telekinesis failed" (503). After repeated unsuccessful attempts, the spirit turns against his audience
and threatens to report them to the police. A., realizing he is not her
relative after all, places the pointer on the sign of the cross, and "the
demon flew away" (504). The dead sign cannot be transformed into
action; all endeavors to make word into deed become intrinsically
"demonic."

Yet the possibility of communication between dead and living,
of influencing the material world through the sign, does exist—the
key lying, it would seem, in the particular nature of the medium's
powers, in the medium's ability to empty him- or herself and to be
open to voices from outside. A. has a dream in which the recently
deceased young husband of an acquaintance appears to her and informs her that the shoes in which he was buried are too tight and
asks for comfortable slippers to be brought for him to a certain address. The widow, B., refuses to believe in the dream, so A. herself
takes the slippers to the address specified, where she does indeed
find a succession of mourners and a corpse in an open coffin, into
which she surreptitiously slips the footwear. The medium is thus one
who truly sees and believes the other, one who is receptive—like the
writer in the forest—to signals from outside and therefore is able
to serve as an intermediary between the worlds of the dead and of
the living. The medium's very talent is a form of self-effacement, the
ability simultaneously to draw the other's presence and to submit to
the external power guiding the saucer. The author, to clarify the "liaison" (*svyaz'*, 501) embodied in the medium, adduces the analogy of
a man married to a widow who continues to love her dead husband:

> The newly-made widow, imagine, while loyal and attentive to
> you, nonetheless maintains a liaison [*svyaz'*] with her former
> better half, with the unforgettable Benik. . . . You are an inter-
> mediary, a medium between her and Benik. You are a system
> of digressing similes. And you do not contradict them. Your
> round face serves as a television screen from which Benik
> nods and smiles sadly. You are like a saucer, which in itself

means nothing, running inoffensively along the circle with its handwritten ABC primer. (501–02)

As earlier in *Goodnight*, the body becomes a sort of alphabet, but here it is a "system of similes" pointing beyond itself, transcending the line between life and death. The medium becomes the text, which has meaning only because it points beyond itself.

The metaphor of the writer as medium suggested here is realized in A., to whose "fairy tales" the author claims he always listens "avidly" (504). The author employs his own narrative of A.'s stories as a means of defining the essential distinction between literature and life. As he comments on an incident in which A. apparently catches sight of a ghost of a dead acquaintance in broad daylight on a Moscow street: "There is nothing more interesting than ghost stories told in a cozy company. But there is nothing more unpleasant than to meet up with this kind of thing in real life" (499). This observation echoes the passage cited above from "The Fatherland: A Thieves' Song" in which the writer distinguishes between crime in literature and crime in reality. The author goes on to explore this crucial distinction further in his retelling of Alla's "fairy tale" of her confrontation with Stalin's ghost in which the role of the writer as medium is directly contrasted to the dehumanization of the real person transformed into an empty sign.

Alla relates that on the night before the official announcement of his death, Stalin appeared to her at her place of exile in Vorkuta. "But how did you guess that it was Stalin in front of you?" the author asks, "Did he look like himself? Like his photographs, his statues?" (505). Alla responds that, on the contrary, the dead Stalin was devoid of all recognizable features, a column of cold reminiscent of Dante's Satan frozen in the ninth circle of hell: "He had neither a moustache, however, nor an image, nor a likeness. It was, I would say, the definitive *no*, uttered in the affirmative. In the darkness of the room he towered like a column weighing many *poods* [1 *pood* = 36.113 lbs.], his head disappearing into the ceiling, made not out of stone, not out of bronze, not out of any other normal substance, but out of cold alone, perhaps out of some methane or nitrogen taken to the absolute, which all the same did not harden, did not freeze into ice, but retained, having congealed, its gaslike state" (506). Stalin thus represents absolute death, the negation of self embodied in the empty sign.

Stalin, it seems, has come to A. seeking forgiveness for his sins, but even his bid for repentance mirrors his transgressions. Apparently he was drawn to Alla because "A.—the first letter of the alphabet—served him as a magnet, a pure test-case personification of a victim" (506). In other words, the specter of Stalin comes to A. as to a dead sign, a symbol divorced in the most profound sense from any living referent. By the same token, he cannot bring himself to make his request outright, but resorts to a play of names and initials:

> "Listen, what is it to you?" he repeated capriciously, as if he were ashamed of manifesting a momentary weakness. "I'm telling you in plain Russian: give back my debts! Do you understand? To me. I'll spell it out letter by letter." And he immediately uttered in code:
> "Mikoyan. Onegin. The opera—*Evgeny Onegin*. I . . .—Ilych [Lenin].
> "Gamarnik. Radek. Enukidze. Khrushchev. Ibarruri (Dolores Ibarruri).
> "Understood? No? I'll repeat the initials.
> "Gorky. (Come on, there was a writer—Maksim Gorky, what—don't you know him?) Rykov. Ezhov. Khasan (Lake Khasan). Ilych.
> "Period. Stalin." (507)

The first letters of the names the apparition invokes spell out the Russian for "my sins": *moi grekhi*. Mimicking the dead communicating with the living through letters at a seance, Stalin, unable to speak the words, adduces names to stand for letters. His means of reluctantly seeking absolution thus evokes the essence of his sin: the reduction of individuals, living and dead (significantly equated in his list with fictional characters and geographical landmarks) to disembodied signs.

The dead Stalin's appearance before Alla is, moreover, construed as "the Last Judgment" (509). He selects her as judge and spokesperson for all his victims in terms that simultaneously evoke and, because of their inappropriateness to the situation, reveal the essential vacuity of the relationship between language and person in Stalinist society: "Let her speak for all! We elect her to the Soviet. Who is against? As a plenipotentiary deputy to the All-Union Congress of People's Prisoners" (510). Just as Stalin conceives Alla as a letter of the alphabet, an empty sign, so in trying to manipulate her into playing out an empty linguistic farce, he reveals the nature of his sins. She is to act as a false, meaningless representative for others. Alla, however, refuses to play her assigned role:

> "To forgive you for others, for all the *zeks?* The Lord has not given me the right. And besides people would not forgive this. But all that you are due me, that you brought on me, me alone—take it. I absolve you" . . .
>
> "And now—go around to all! To each one, in order—to whomever you owe. Living and dead. And let each one forgive you separately. Implore in the name of our Lord." (511)

While Stalin—here the incarnation of the empty rhetoric, the theatricality of the culture over which he presided—tries to suppress the diversity of individual voices and transform people into abstract signs, just as the dead are reduced to letters on a ouija board, Alla confronts him with the task of facing each individual person's right to judge, turning letters back into full names, empty signs into human beings. Apparently overwhelmed by the enormity of the charge laid on him, the glacial Stalin—like the demon routed by the sign of the cross at the seance—vanishes.

The second part of the chapter picks up chronologically at the point where Alla's fairy tale ends. On the day of Stalin's death, the author goes to the Lenin Library to read, as he has "all these anxious days while Stalin was dying" (514). This retreat to the library, when the rest of the country is held in thrall by the dictator's death throes and the library itself is virtually empty, bears witness to the author's otherness. His status as an outsider within his own time and culture is further underscored by his reading: *Foreigners' Stories of the Time of Troubles, in Five Volumes.*[33] The author seeks refuge from contemporary events in the voices of those who stand outside the immediate temporal and cultural frame of reference, in the depths of history: "These facts relax me. They take me away from the news of the day"[34] (515). The author's resort to the "emergency exit" (515) provided by books turns out, however, to be not so much a repudiation of what is going on around him in the world outside the library as a means of access to a broader, estranging perspective, which allows the writer, like a medium, to serve as a bridge between the dead letters of the past and the world of the living.

The library in *Goodnight*—like such recurring images as the museum in *The Trial Begins* and the archaeological dig in *Lyubimov*—represents a spatial locus where different time periods co-

exist and jostle one another on equal terms, challenging the hegemony of any single epoch over the right to define:

> I went out to smoke. Along the way the chipped shelves,
> as usual. Dictionaries. Portraits of Lomonosov, Molotov. The
> back room. Catalogues. The great encyclopedia, the small en-
> cyclopedia. Marx-Engels-Lenin-Stalin. Garnets . . . The true
> books were located not here, on the surface, but in the bowels,
> in compartments, making themselves known latently, unpre-
> meditatedly, through the suspicion that only in a library do
> we truly walk the earth.
>
> They say, humus. I'm not sure. It would of course be
> good. For those who follow. But history isn't soil. It's rockier.
> Hazardous to life. Fundamental, however. Serious. An accu-
> mulation of volumes like heavy, deep geological deposits.
> The mezozoic era. Here you'll find everything. Cockle-shells.
> Snails. The Babel of peoples. Belemnite. The imprint of a
> wondrous bird—the archeopterix. The stories of foreigners.
> The earth. (518)

The danger inherent in the library is the same danger with which
the seance is fraught, the peril of crossing the line between living
and dead. Like the letters in which the dead attempt to communicate
on the ouija board, into which they are reduced by the death of the
body, so the library's card catalogue becomes a repository of dead
signs ready to be called forth by the living:

> In the book depository, deserted today, empty, it was as
> quiet as in a church. But history was invisibly being packaged
> and ripening here. Here, in the library, it takes its sources,
> draws its reserves. Everything is to hand—the renegade son
> and the reactionary ancestor are lined up according to indexes
> in ranks. It would be inconceivable to read it all—there are not
> enough human lives; it suffices to glance over the even surf of
> bindings, receding under the earth like a fund dead before its
> time, where all of us are to stand like a card catalogue, some
> by name, others by subject listing. Where every alpha and
> beta is fraught with shocks. Where is Lenin? Where is Stalin?
> Where is Hitler? Where are the best minds of humanity? Like
> labeled jars—here. Not a cemetery. An arsenal. Huge hangars.
> Reserves. When the spirits rebel, break away, there is a revo-
> lution above, and then quickly back to the shelf, until a new

summons comes. Famusov was right to be worried: "All books should be gathered together and burned . ." The trouble is that he himself is also already sealed up in the collecting department. You'll easily find him in any index. Under the letter "G" (Griboedov). Under the letter "F" (Famusov). Under the letter "B" (Books). (519–20)

Just as death awaits all of us, just as we will all become disembodied signs at a seance, so will we all end up in the card catalogue of the library, where the line between fiction and reality—between the early nineteenth-century playwright Griboedov and his character Famusov—is blurred, where history waits in reserve to rise up when summoned and engulf the world beyond. The uncontrollability of the text suggested by the image of the rebellion of books holds forth the possibility of challenging the reign of empty symbols embodied in the figure of Stalin.

Thus, while the author claims that he has taken refuge from current events in the library, he in fact finds himself at their source, and his sojourn at the library serves as the impetus to a complex interplay of historical analogy. Just as "The Mirror" and "Eyeglasses" lay bare the fundamental disfunction of language underlying the author's experiences, so passages of text set off in red ink in this section take the reader out of the immediate historical context in order to expose its basic workings by looking on from outside, first from a human and then from a divine vantage point. In the counterpoint between these interpolated passages and the narrative concerned with the events surrounding Stalin's death, the writer as medium serves as a locus of intersection for the forces shaping history. These passages apparently incorporate, moreover, the author's earliest attempts at writing, on which he comments later in the chapter:

All of this coincided with an oppressive remoteness from my environment, from life, from current literature, with every passing day, it seemed to me, of an ever more hopelessly low standard, backward, and with attempts, as is usual, to write something of "my own," "special," for the drawer, confiding in no one, like notes on the Russian Time of Troubles, about the Pretender, or drafts of the later novella *The Trial Begins*. For all that, I confess, by no means was this a repudiation of the time, of the age, which had fallen to my lot like a winning card and which was sucking me ever farther, ever more horribly into its global jaws. This being swallowed up was, however, accompanied by a realization of myself finally as an insubordinate quantity, a pea, an incalculable maggot with its own small, skewed, dissenting view, which made this whole process doubly painful and extremely interesting. (536)

The red passages in chapter four of *Goodnight*, which are apparently drawn from the writer's notes on the Time of Troubles mentioned here, thus become emblematic of the author's realization of self as a dissenting voice forged, like the talent of the medium, out of the ability to be open to the voices of others.

The first series of inserted texts takes the reader back to the time about which the writer is reading, to the events surrounding the death of the Tsarevich Dmitry, as the author, in attempting to create something of "his own," tries to reanimate the voices and motivations of others long dead. The first inserted text pictures the tsarevich's bloody corpse and the reaction of the boy's mother to his death. She prays to Christ, the Virgin, and John the Baptist, thus creating a link with the chapter's concluding series of red texts, in which the three figures appear as an icon brought to life. The question of divine intervention raised in those later sections is here tied to the issues of death, identity, and imposture. The mother does not recognize her son's body: "Omnipresent flies scurried over the face, and the Tsarina did not recognize the tsarevich. No! For the fear of God! What heir? It was a dream . . . Was it because all those who have died—even children—resemble dead people more than they do themselves? Or was this already the result of someone's benign intervention? God's speedy aid? . . . An alien [*chuzhoi*], supercilious youth, with an unnaturally opened mouth and piercing eyelashes, was stretched out on the carpet runner. Not the right one [*Ne tot*]! Thank God—false, spurious" (517). The dead body, from which the soul has fled, is no longer recognizable as the living person—even by his own mother. As the events that follow demonstrate—the pretender appears, and despite his lack of physical resemblance, the tsaritsa recognizes him as her son—the tsarevich has become an empty sign the place of whose referent can be usurped by any living body. The transformation of a person into an empty sign, a symbol of power, thus rests on the denial of death, in which personhood, the individuality of the self, is rooted. Resurrection in the body of an impostor becomes a parody of the immortality of the soul, the distortion undergone by the transcendent when translated into corporeal terms.

The second red text takes author and reader into the head of the executioner who carries out the purges that follow the tsarevich's murder. He has been delegated the task of reducing to silence, cutting out the tongues, of those who might bear witness to the facts of the crime, which differ from the official account. The executioner equates unrestrained speech with thievery, crime run rampant, and the destruction of authority: "There are almost fifty of them here! You barely manage to have done with one . . . Move quickly, hangman! If you don't, a magic word [*petushinoe slovo*] will fly out and, you'll see, the kingdom will vanish, the treasury will be squandered, and elaborate thievery will go swaggering through the world" (521). The reign of the dead sign is ushered in by the silencing of voices that might challenge its claim to legal identity.

Here it is important to remember the ambivalent status of the author's relationship to these inserted texts. On the one hand, he presents himself as a reader perusing the texts of others, while, on the other, he suggests he himself has written these passages. The boundary between writer and reader collapses. He is, moreover, reading the writings of foreigners, outsiders, writings that differ among themselves and question official accounts: "The foreign writers, like Trotskyites, doubted: was he authentic or imaginary?" (518). The conjunction of dissenting voices with embedded historical analogy—the equation of the foreign writers speculating on the Time of Troubles with Trotskyites challenging Stalin's right to authority—validates and defines the nature of the author's own alterity, his criminality in relation to the powers that be. Again invoking the "dangerous liaisons" of the chapter's title, the author suggests that the coexistence of discrepant views affords the possibility of "linking": "Not like in our country. So what if the versions in the chronicles differ. So what if the Pretender reveals himself to one foreigner as the true Achilles. To another—as the opposite. This can be linked [*Eto mozhno svyazat'*], it can be imagined. There is logic here, and Divine Providence is discernible. This is History for you and not a way station. History clad in Eternity (as befits it), Eternity—in fabulous images. History, which today we so lack" (516). A multiplicity of differing views makes possible linking and representation, opens the channel, so to speak, for the writer as medium. The linking here, as the context makes clear, is the possibility of drawing historical analogy, of applying the heterogeneous voices of the past to the situation of the present. The source of the writer's estranging vision lies in the ability to place the present within larger historical patterns, thereby subverting its pretensions to authority.

"All sorts of things come into your head in the nighttime" (524), the author writes. "In my brain swept past pictures, each one more picturesque, more marvelous, and more godless than the last, pictures which corresponded, as it seemed to me, to the true spirit of the moment" (525). These "pictures" constitute a grotesque fantasy in which the events of the Time of Troubles are updated and reprised in the wake of Stalin's demise. The author imagines a plot to deny Stalin's death and engineer the appearance of a False Stalin, on the order of the False Dmitry, giving rise to new purges, the cutting out of more tongues. He further envisages the emergence of other pretenders—a False Tsarevich Aleksei, a False Kirov, and even a False Lenin—all staking rival claims to legitimacy and authority. "It's not my fault," the author maintains, "that history at that time did not take the course projected for it. . . . So that my pictures, for all their absurdity in the literal realization on the historical canvas, are not far from the truth in its concealed sense" (527, 528). Their truth, underscored by the author's interpretation of the Time of Troubles, lies in their exposure of the horrific potential of the person reduced to a sign, which constitutes a living death.

As the author reiterates on several occasions, he is not concerned with Stalin as an individual human being: "My interest was aroused not by Stalin per se, but by his consequences" (514), and "However, I was agitated at that time not by facts, but by [Stalin's] imagined portrait, deposited in future generations" (533). Stalin has ceased to be a human being and has become a symbol: "They could put a doll in his place! A double! Isn't it all the same who is Stalin?" (515). As an image of Stalin's "consequences," the author again invokes the figure of the seance:

And although, I repeat, the general secretary himself, personally, locked up somewhere in a fortress, behind seven seals, little interested me in his obvious, barracks-like ordinariness, an unhealthy interest was aroused in me by the atmosphere of black masses, dogs' weddings, and howling from beyond the grave incited by him or granted him for his pleasure and support, which made up, in my view, the true fabric of that unique reign. History for the first time revealed itself to me as a field of activity and an opportunity for figuring out certain supernatural forces. And the more coarsely and clumsily the obvious results of hypnosis manifested themselves, the more irrational, it seemed, the principle secretly guiding this general intrigue. And people became like instruments of sorcery, flying broomsticks, revolving tables and plates, mumbling not their own, but someone else's speeches, inspired from above, memorized, by rote, translated by interpreters into the most primitive language just for the sake of appearance, for general accessibility. (537)

In this fantastic reality everyone up to and including Stalin himself plays a role, parrots the words of others. The Stalinist world becomes an artistic text. Life becomes art.

The author parodies Stalin as a symbol devoid of personhood in the figure of a Georgian who enjoys success with women because of his superficial resemblance to the dictator. While he claims to be tired of his situation, the man balks at ridding himself of the trademark pipe, moustache, and accent—the physical marks on which his imposture rests. This leads the author to speculate:

But meanwhile behind his accent I discerned rustling past the shade of another man, even more tired of the burden of love, power, and glory. The other one after all had also been sucked in and did not have the right to get rid either of the pensive pipe or of the confectionery moustache, which it's a sin to laugh at, because even if he'd wanted to, he could no longer shave it off. Not a man—a portrait. How difficult it must be to be turned into one's own portrait while still alive and to do everything that is prescribed to the heaven dweller by his worshippers. It's like that wretched saucer, which runs servilely in circles under the influence of our fingers. They summon Napoleon—you must become Napoleon. You dream of Stalin? You get—Stalin. Who turns it? Perhaps we ourselves, we ourselves without noticing it, just can't wait and keep asking that he kill some of us periodically in order to maintain the portrait likeness. If he were to try to be good—we'd be thrown into confusion. We'd lose our faith in the truth of the image. Is it we who need this? Not he, but we?! (540).

Stalin becomes the ultimate horror: a living being transformed into —and thus trapped by—his own representation. In the metaphor of history as a seance, the dead letter merges with the saucer, which moves, the author suggests, perhaps less in response to the prompting of the dead than in response to the summons of the living.

To this image of Stalinist history, in which the living are locked into a futile and fatal communication mediated by the living death incarnated in the empty sign, the author counterposes a vision that places a kenotic model for the individual at the center of the forces driving historical events: "History, I'm convinced, does not act by itself. Not according to its own independent laws and channels. But under surveillance—alas, not always benevolent. Both from above, from heaven, and from below, from under the stage, from everywhere, from all sides, floodlights beat down, coming together and intersecting at a shining, alive, burning point: 'Behold the man!'" (543). Pilate's words, "Ecce homo," heralding the appearance before him of Christ identify personhood with the model of Golgotha, the suffering of the body "emptied" of divinity. Resurrection awaits, but only after the death of the body: "Among plants, stone: behold the man. Neither angel nor beast, fish nor fowl. No matter where you rush—ridiculous, pitiful, sinful, the last—a human being. Weeping and laughter. You'll make it to death. You'll rise: 'I believe in the One God! I expect the resurrection of the dead!' This exhausts it: 'Behold the man.' It's not understanding I want. But to escape perdition. But how, tell me, is one to make the connection and endure this cross on one's back: 'Behold the man'?" (543). Life becomes the bearing of the cross to death, beyond which, however, lies the promise of resurrection, the release of the soul from the illusion of the "I": "Maybe [God] has your true, original soul lying on a shelf, until the time comes, like a diamond at a pawnbroker's. When you die—then they'll show you: who you were in fact, had you not kept yelling: 'I,' 'I'" (542). Thus the empty sign, capable of being resurrected in the bodies of impostors who deny the death of the body, becomes a parody of the true immortality of the soul, freed at death from both the body and the illusion of individuality. Stalinism, incarnated in the depersonalized symbol of the dictator, becomes the quintessential illustration of the horror of human attempts to create the ideal on earth, denying the intrinsic shortfall between the soul liberated from the body and humanity's corporeal, fallen state.

In the following series of red texts, the last of which closes the chapter, the author employs ekphrasis to underscore the unbridgeable gap between representation and ideal, human and transcendent. He animates an icon depicting Christ Pantocrator (the ruler of the universe), the Virgin Mary, and John the Baptist.[35] The three fig-

ures represent the divine vantage point on the human events acted
out in the preceding red passages, and the juxtaposition of the two
series of interpolated texts emphasizes the discordancy between
eternity and the tempo of human history. Christ, Mary, and John
deliberate over various alternatives for intervention in human affairs. The scars left by their sojourn in the body remain evident.
John's severed head, speaking from the plate that he holds in his
hands, tries to persuade Christ, still suffering pain from the wounds
of the crucifixion, to wreak vengeance against humanity for the murder of the "legitimate ruler" (543), while Mary pleads for mercy, for
an answer to the prayer of the dead tsarevich's mother: "Be merciful,
Master. Lay Your Hand on the mother of the murdered boy. She,
Mary, beats her head against the damp earth in Uglich [the town
where the Tsarevich Dmitry was murdered]. She calls You to sit in
judgment, Me to bear witness. She believes, as I believed: my son
is alive and God is not dead! Return the lost tsarevich to the poor
woman, at least for a time" (544). Her Son acquiesces as the chapter
draws to a close: "I will do as you ask. But what is the use? . . Her
unworthy son will be resurrected and will stir up Russia. Much, oh
so much blood will be shed because of that child" (544). The irony, of
course, lies in the fact that the divine forces must act through human
agency. The Tsarevich Dmitry is not in truth resurrected; his place,
his empty sign, has been usurped by an impostor. The drama of
the resurrection of Mary's divine son, played out, in response to the
pleading of another Mary, by earthly actors, ends not in salvation,
but in blood.

The author's use of ekphrasis, his translation of the icon—an
image, according to Orthodox belief, "not made by hands"—into
words, emblematizes the shortfall between human and transcendent: "We will depict [the icon] in an overblown, stylized manner, as
befits a Manuscript Illuminator. We will not, however, set ourselves
the impossible and seductive task of representing naturally, as if
we were eyewitnesses, that Celestial Light which our saintly fathers
and intercessors were the only ones to contemplate from the earth
and of which we, in our folly, are lucky if we grasp the reflection,
which has fallen mentally into this fleshly world, in a cloudy, smoke-
blackened glass" (541). By exposing the imposture of the sign in the
text, by pointing to its artifice, the writer attempts to transcend difference by exploiting it: "In this case, I dare say, the back of the
reader's head, from its reverse, concave side will serve us as a Mirror. Concave? But what do you want—a direct Mirror of heaven? I

don't have one. Rays, however, unbearably hit truth in the eye and, passing through the whole cerebral tangle of vessels, finally reach the shaded screen, on, I repeat, the back, disenfranchised side of the question. Even so, even distorted, isn't it still possible through binoculars, through a telescope, with a certain effort, for something to be made out?" (541). The interaction between reader and text thus becomes a sort of inverse distorting mirror, which, invoking the metaphor of criminality, approaches the problem from the "disenfranchised side": the text, acknowledging the difference between itself and the ideal, holds forth the possibility of correcting, at least to a small extent, the gap between sign and referent, of allowing some hint of the transcendent to be transmitted in words.

This interpretation presents a partial resolution to the ethical dilemma the author poses himself in the chapter. In a burst of self-flagellation, he laments the "pathology" of aesthetizing history: "That's the trouble with aesthetics. It messes with your head, plucking gilded strings with the illusion of the reality of an existence that is, in its essence, inadmissable and unworthy. You rejoice, like a little boy: Maestro, a catastrophe? And the smell of history suddenly becomes distinct and sweet. Aesthetics on the brain! It abstracts itself from reality, keeps hostilely aloof from the very object of study and at the very same moment is drawn back as if on elastic to the mother, besottedly scrutinizes, shuddering, the dear, disgusting features that gave birth to it" (536). The author, tracing his own genesis as a writer to the night of Stalinism, raises the ethical problem of the implication of art in the horrors out of which it originates, pitting the voyeurism of the artist, revelling in the monster of his historical epoch, against the apparent moral imperative to take action: "All it wants is to amuse itself. How it moves, on tentacles, an armored miracle! What greedy eyes it, the miracle, has! It's interesting, what does it think about—whom to eat? Don't worry, it will guzzle down everyone, myself included. But I, a worm, while I remain intact, wiggle. And instead of plotting against the viper I dream of painting it" (536). Does not the artist, having recognized the horror of his time, have an obligation to act against that horror, and if he does not act, are not he and his art, his aesthetic aloofness, tainted by their passive complicity?

This question resides intrinsically in the vision of art as crime on which the Tertz writings rest, but nowhere does the writer address the moral issue inherent in his affirmation of the uncontrollability of the text, of the distinction between word and deed, and of the independence of art from ethical and legal constraints placed on "reality" more forcefully than he does here. While in *Goodnight*, as elsewhere in his works, the author resists offering any simple resolution to this ethical dilemma, his suggestion that the text's acknowledgment of difference can allow it to convey an intimation of the transcendent—that the preservation of differing voices can provide the "liaison" between history and eternity—prepares the way for the author's epiphany in the fifth and concluding chapter. As a prelude to our discussion of that chapter, however, we should remember a small, yet possibly lifesaving, detail the author provides toward the beginning of the second segment of "Dangerous Liaisons." When the library closes, upon the official announcement of Stalin's death, the author is sent from his refuge into the crowd surging through the streets to view the dictator's body. He is carried along for a time by the press of people and his own curiosity, but he is finally forced to turn back by the books he is carrying in his briefcase: "I was held back by the briefcase in my hand. Weighted down with books. How could I push in with such a load? . . . It would be interesting to have a look. But—the briefcase! . . . And they might not even let me in with the briefcase. They'll think it's a bomb. . . . So right at Pushkin Street I turned back, toward home, without even entering the funeral hall, without becoming one of the witnesses of the great events. It was disappointing. If it weren't for the books, for the briefcase, I would already have been on Trubnaya Street, at the corpse" (522–23). As the writer acknowledges, the events that followed, the deaths of the people—the victims Stalin "took with him"—trampled by the crowd of mourners, have gone down in history: "I will not relate what became of those who at that time turned out to be quicker than I was, more devoted or braver. That's already history" (523). The fact remains that the writer's life is saved by books—books that, on a more profound symbolic level, deflect him from the general herd and from the corpse to which it is drawn. These books, representing the dissenting voices of history, are, not a literal, but a metaphorical bomb, holding the potential to explode the imposture of the dead sign.

The final chapter of *Goodnight* is entitled "In the Belly of the Whale," which—as in "Graphomaniacs"—invokes the story of Jonah and, more broadly, the image of the prophet as an "empty vessel" who, like a medium, becomes a conduit for words from outside. More particularly, it refers to the time that Jonah spent within the "great fish" that swallowed him up after he fled from God's call to be His prophet and from which he emerged ready to accept the divine summons. The title thus suggests a metaphor for the writer, engulfed by the monster of Stalinism, who, after a period of false belief and incubation finally accepts his vocation. The three days Jonah passes in the belly of the whale are as well a figura for Christ's descent into hell during the three days between the Crucifixion and Resurrection and thus point to the writer's "conversion" as a rebirth and to the promise of resurrection he finds inscribed in the true work of art.[36]

The chapter opens with yet another image that reprises the figures of monuments and stone running throughout *Goodnight* and forming the symbolic background against which the drama that finds its metaphorical denouement in the birth of Abram Tertz unfolds. The author describes the renowned collection of Assyrian bas-reliefs, which he first saw reproduced in pictures in his youth and later, after his emigration, in the original in the British Museum in London:

> On the pitted slabs of Assyria the lions snarled, dying, with the authenticity of human speech. While the people, as if they were dolls, with the impenetrability of battering-rams, in profile, feet in step, with muscle joints strained, to the roll of drums, in divisions, walked and walked, absolutely not budging from the stone. Perhaps they are not people, but gods, I began to suspect—so elevated were they in rank, so abstracted in ritual from our nature and consciousness—except that below, in the second tier, in the stone twists and turns of the river, along the Euphrates bodies floated, turning somersaults, chopped up by butchers, and that voracious fish hastily gnawed at the chopped-off legs and heads of those who used to trod the upper path, but now, among the stones, were drowning, beginning with the flood, including you and me, in the current of bas-reliefs, archers, tsars, gods and dancers. It was death's business to sum up the procession of hosts, from Noah to the defeated lion in its final frenzy. And the roar of the lion hung like a wall, like the crown of history, proclaiming the spectacle of systematically triumphing death, of agony experienced in various poses, competently, naturally, agony which evidently afforded the hunters the utmost pleasure. Next we too, as if on a leash, as if in a dry sketch of our convulsions, would become intertwined in the alien [*chuzhuyu*] entourage of incorruptible guards and pointsmen, in the nation of professional executioners—may the furious seed perish, may it

be forever annihilated—except that we ourselves are already floating down the river as disfigured bodies and are striding in wall on wall in the ceremony of courtiers, except for these fire-breathing lions, dying like us and before our eyes. Here, above this arena, the suspicion may arise that only on their deathbeds will one human being understand another, and understand the lion, and every creature oppressed, because the movement of time is impartial, merciless, embracing in passing both you and those who left the stage five thousand years ago, and this beast, left to die slowly for our edification, disgorging curses at the stone flow of history. (544–545)

The tiers of the bas-reliefs representing the royal hunt graphically capture the opposition between hunter and hunted that runs throughout *Goodnight*. The hunters, the "nation of executioners," appear like gods, marching in unison along the upper level, seemingly immune and oblivious to their own death, while deriving enjoyment from the "spectacle" of their victims' death agony. In the guise of these hunters "absolutely not budging from the stone," the author condemns all of the hunters of his own day—the police spies, interrogators, jailers—the living statues who recur throughout his narrative. The tiers of the bas-reliefs echo the image of the archaeological dig exposing diverse geological and historical strata reiterated throughout the writer's works as a metaphor for the possibility of drawing historical analogy. Here the message of history is given in its most direct and concentrated form: all life ends in death. Thus the hunters in the first tier join their victims in death, becoming, in the second tier, dismembered bodies foundering in the river of history. The viewer/reader is saved from being drawn into the hunters' pretensions to divinity and self-delusion by seeing their oblivious arrogance spatially juxtaposed to the fate that awaits us all: "only on their deathbeds will one human being understand another." The image of the writer "reading" the bas-reliefs thus becomes a metaphor for the workings of art, whose otherness lies in its reminder of the origins of our common personhood in death.

The figure of living creatures turned to stone, like the metaphor of people transformed into dead letters at a seance, also addresses the intrinsic disparity between artistic representation and life. While the description of the Assyrian bas-reliefs opens with the author's assertion that the dying lions seem to roar "with the authenticity of human speech," the human beings marching arrogantly in step on the upper tier are dehumanized, become "like gods." The animals, in other words, appear more human than the humans. All are transformed into stone—undergo a form of death—by art. The core dissimilarity, however, lies in those who turn to stone in life—like Stalin, transformed into his own portrait while still alive—and the power of artistic representation to immortalize mortal flesh, to preserve images in stone of those who passed out of life millennia before. Consequently, only the dying lions call forth the writer's sympathy, and particularly "one lioness. Struck in the back by arrows, her spine broken at the sacrum, she, bleeding to death, spewed blasphemies on the whole procession of bearded swindlers" (545). The "blasphemies" of the expiring lioness become perhaps the writer's most forceful metaphor for the criminality of art. True realism, he maintains, is death: in the image of the lioness "you witness death. Death *is* realism, without the shrouds and canopies under which they raise to the heavens impervious kings, until they themselves are hurled into the netherworld, on the model of the lion, with hind legs paralyzed, with an indignant, bloody flame issuing from the mouth—through all of the floors of the merciless universe. Fiend. Curse. O flood of History, which sends us like a waterfall over the stones of Mesopotamia! The perishability of times and the eternity of stones" (545). Art's power lies in its ability to elicit the viewer/reader's identification through the realization that our shared fate lies in death.

The analogy with his own time implicit in the author's description of the Assyrian bas-reliefs is amplified in the second major metaphor of water and stone incorporated into "In the Belly of the Whale." The author introduces the image with his most straightforward explication of the significance of the "night" invoked in the title: "I see my epoch in images of a thick, thick August night. It dropped on our heads neither today nor yesterday, but sometime as far back as the neolithic age—as a starry meteorite shower on the flinty, kremlin earth. And each falling crystal playing in the sky above said of itself: 'stalin,' 'kirov,' 'hitler,' 'zhdanov'" (551). Several pages later he elaborates: "I cannot speak for others, but I never cease to rejoice in my own horoscope. I was born under the constellation: 'Stalin-Kirov-Zhdanov-Hitler-Stalin.' And nothing else. No big or little bears. The millennial sun itself—'Lenin'—having dried up, had become the barely noticeable, unmalicious little Octobrist star"[37] (553).

The author's portrayal of his own epoch as a night with the

constellation "Stalin-Kirov-Zhdanov-Hitler-Stalin" in the ascendant takes on its full significance only in the context of his visit as an emigré to a cave—called both the "Cave of the Maimed" and the "Cave of Cut-Off Hands"—in the foothills of the Pyrenees. Along with other sightseers, the author follows the guide down into the cave and finds that under the surface of the earth "everything is as in life" (552). In this "emptiness the size of Europe," which was "all made by water," the tourists are surrounded by "waterfalls of stone," stalactites that suggest towers of Babel reaching toward the "stone sky" (552). At the bottom they find "tracks of brontosauruses" and, further along on their trek, they come across traces of ancient human habitation: "In the sunbeam-flashlight we notice imprints. I realized I didn't have a camera. And, besides, taking pictures was no longer allowed. More and more red, white, black imprints, with the phalanges of the fingers half chopped off, grew on the walls as we got used to the darkness. It would be good to stay here. To bury oneself. To find salvation [*Spastis'*] . . . But no—you crawl upwards" (552). The author, who entered the cave standing erect, comes out of the darkness into the light on his hands and knees: "I crawled out of the shelter like a primordial man and, on honest all fours, looked in amazement into the sky. It's bombing. It's bombing so hard! I understand: they're trying to frighten us. There's another kind of life on the planets. But it is all filtered through the network of stone rain, through the grid: 'stalin,' 'lenin,' 'hitler,' 'zhdanov'" (552–53).

The cave in *Goodnight* echoes the cave from which the philosopher emerges into the sun of direct apprehension of the forms in Plato's *Republic*. The prehistoric "Cave of the Maimed" merges with the night of Stalinism, casting the epoch as a period entrapped within representation, cut off from the sun by a stone sky. Yet if Plato's myth of the cave resonates with his condemnation of literature as illusion in the *Republic*, the author here employs the metaphor of the cave to vindicate literature and the writer. Within the cave, as within the cell in "Eyeglasses," the author finds evidence— fingerprints—of a former human presence, marks left by persons on the seemingly unyielding stone. When he leaves the cave, resisting its seductive promise of salvation, he finds himself bombarded by the deities bred by the "stone sky" of the cave. Playing on Plato's images of illusion versus truth, the darkness of the cave versus the sunlight that awaits outside, the author in the course of the concluding section of his narrative affirms the potential of art to save residing in the very deception Plato condemned.

Against the background of the stone Assyrian hunters and the dying lion, of the cave and the sun, the author unfolds the chapter's focal drama: KGB attempts to recruit Sinyavsky in 1948 and 1952 to participate in provocations directed at his fellow student at Moscow University, Hélène Peltier, the daughter of a French naval attaché, mentioned earlier. This drama—or "melodrama"—has three major players: the author, Hélène, and the author's acquaintance— alternately called S. and Serezha in the narrative. In simple terms, S. and Hélène come to represent the two poles to which the author is drawn—and between which he must choose—in his journey of self-discovery as a writer and as a human being.

S., as the author puts it, "was my Virgil" (547), taking him through museums and introducing him to the art of different times and places: "He led me through Egypt, through Assyria and Babylon, pointing out for the first time the dying lion on the stone, which is why even today, over this burning slab, I remember him with a shudder of gratitude" (547). Most important, however, S. was the first to give the author, tutored on the realism of the *Peredvizhniki* (the Wanderers), an appreciation of the "semi-forbidden" (547), sunlit works of the European Impressionists: "But, most important, he inherited, like a family estate, the new European painting, with the Impressionists, Cézanne, Gauguin, who at that time had still not been aired out of Moscow, into which he solemnly initiated me as well, a neophyte from the barge-hauling *Peredvizhniki*, forced me to breathe in and taste, casting off shame, the hurried canvas—like an infuriated hedgehog, like nothing I'd ever seen—which was truly closer to the solar source, to the air, to the fragrant brushstroke, than the old jades and hearses of our black Tretyakov [Gallery]" (546–47). Invoking the image of the sun to which one emerges from the darkness of the cave, the author identifies these paintings "resembling nothing," the illusion of light created by impressionist technique, as being "closer to the solar source" than the realism from which S. weans him: "S. helped me to rid myself of realism, of Pisarev, of utility [*pol'zy*], of lofty ideological content [*ideinosti*] and didacticism in aesthetics" (548). Yet just as Virgil, by leading Dante through the inferno, helps him to attain the summit of paradise but is himself denied the true light, so S. leads the author to the light of the Impressionists, of art, in the hell of Stalinism, while he himself remains a creature of that horrific netherworld.

As the author's periodic references to S. as Serezha show, his use of the initial to designate his mentor is not an attempt to disguise his

identity. The character S. is recognizably based on Sergei Khmelnitsky, who, years after the events related in "In the Belly of the Whale,"
served as a witness for the prosecution at Sinyavsky's trial.[38] The reduction of the character's name to a single letter again invokes the
imagery of the letters on the ouija board. S. exemplifies the human
being transformed into an empty sign, personifying what the author
considers the essence of Stalinism: the transgression of the line between life and art.

Just as the author casts S. as Virgil to his Dante, so also he invokes
Pushkin's *Mozart and Salieri* as a paradigm for their relationship.
S. is Mozart, a "born artist," while the author takes the part of Salieri:
"We studied in the same 'A' class from the second to the eighth grades
and argued a lot in adolescence about where in the world abilities
and talents came from. From birth, as he insisted unwaveringly, dar-
ingly affirming himself? Or, as it seemed to me, through the difficult
p~th of life, equally open to all who labor, with the help of persistent
work. And he turned out to be right. Despite my criticism, based on
Pisarev, with whom I was intoxicated in the fifth grade, on the purest
sociological statistics, no matter how much I worked on myself, he,
Serezha, was the firstborn from birth." Yet the author's concession
of his rival's superiority contains more than a hint of irony, for, as
he learns "to my horror," this "truly born artist" is an "artist of life"
(546).

Thus, S., an incarnation of the "pure artist," becomes an informer, thereby undermining the trust necessary for communication. Yet the author suggests that S.'s treachery is rooted in the very
qualities which give rise to his exquisite poetry—his apoliticalness,
disdain for the crowd, his "sense of squeamishness, or aestheticism,"
which, evidently, was incredibly developed in him, to excess, to the
point of disgust at everything ugly, pitiful, and ridiculous in our life"
(559). Yet his perfidy also arises out of a desire to wield power over
those around him. S. is a "true Assyrian" (550), who "translated aesthetics into practice" (347): "Oh, if only all [S.'s poetry] had remained
on paper! It's not art, but the link [*svyaz'*] between art and reality
that does us in" (549).

S. oversteps the line separating reality from art and transforms
life into spectacle:

> You remember Meyerhold's effacement of the boundary be-
> tween stage and audience? Besides, how many generations
> of artists, writers, musicians dreamed of and strove to trans-

form the world through the magical power of play? What's the harm if one of them achieved his aim? And not in blood-less verses, which no one reads, but, let's say, on a crowded square, while paying a visit, at a tea-table, he conducts himself inimitably, unpredictably, his character unrestrained, coming before your eyes, suddenly, out of the ethereal swaying suf-fering in nonexistence incarnated at last as something com-pletely concrete, corporeal, and at the same time worthy of amazement. (569)

The "harm" lies precisely in the transformation of life into theater, which, for the author, is the essence of Stalinist society.

The author provides a number of examples of S.'s antics which illustrate his complete disregard for the consequences of his ac-tions—rooted as they are in purely aesthetic considerations—for other people. The most telling instance of S.'s "aesthetics of provo-cation" (557) occurs during S.'s first visit to the author's home. As the author relates it, he "raised his hand against Stalin. Yes, liter-ally, stretched out his index finger, like a revolver, slowly aimed and formed his lips into a soft 'pu,' as small children do to signify a gunshot. And in triumph, appraisingly, looked sideways at me: as much as to say, what will you say? What'll you do now?! . . I re-mained silent, depressed by the stupid blasphemy. Then he made a 'pu' sound out of his finger at the harmless poster a second time, en-joying my embarrassment" (556–57). This "empty game, eye to eye, with no risk, at what should not be played with" (557) exposes the link between S.'s transformation of life into art and Stalinism. S.'s act is one of pure representation: there is no revolver—just a finger; no Stalin—just a poster; no shot—just an empty sound. Yet the per-formance, acted out in a context where metaphors are realized, is fraught with danger: "It's clear that the innocent shot at our paper screen mocked the diversions that mottled our newspapers. People, it seemed, were shooting from behind corners with their fingers, and afterwards those who were caught were shot for real" (557). S. per-sonifies the essence of Stalinism: representation takes the place of life.

The author's friends object to his insistence on S.'s artistic bril-liance: "Have you read *Mozart and Salieri?* 'Genius and villainy are two incompatible things'" (565). To this the author responds: "I don't agree. In my childhood dreams [S.] reigns, like Mozart. Whence then those features that violated his harmonious image with secret and

obvious treachery? Was it not from birth, we ask? Was it not precisely from his brilliant gifts, inclined to turn everything around him,
as it suited him, into a poetic workshop, as well? Into, as it were, an
experimental aesthetics, even if second-rate? But then, that means
that even his 'villainies' did not contradict his 'genius,' but flowed out
of it and irrepressibly merged with it in ecstasy, as a matter of complete compatibility. Pushkin must have got it all wrong" (565–66).
At this, however, the author revises the basic premise, asserting, "Indeed [S.], I fear, was never a villain. Not for a single minute—that's
the rub. . . . He harbored nothing evil, dark, perfidious, demonic in
himself. Nor, on the other hand, anything like good, conscience, or
honor. All of these concepts of yours simply did not relate to him.
As if in childhood he had had them amputated like an unnecessary
organ. Like an appendix. A dead man, if you will. A visitor from the
other world. But a genius, none the less. A sinless genius!" (566).

In labeling S. a "dead man," the author directly invokes the imagery of the disembodied letters at a seance. He then surmises that S. is
one of the living dead, a human being born without a soul: "There
are among us, say specialists, the gynecologists of the occult sciences, particular beings—with a different index. If memory serves,
they are called in science 'shells.' From the word *shell:* an empty shell
in the image of a human being. They were born that way—without
a soul, and it's not their fault" (566). S.—who is one of these "frauds,
brought to perfect resemblance [with]," (566–67), totally indistin-
guishable from, "full-fledged, standard creatures like you and me"
(567)—appears as the obverse of the man as the "empty shell," the
embodiment of the poet in *Strolls with Pushkin*. S. is a literary sign
come alive, an empty body, acting by all the rules of pure art and
thereby wreaking havoc in reality.

In a key passage following the image of the cave, the author
echoes the Grand Inquisitor's assertion in *The Brothers Karamazov* that people must be ruled by miracle, mystery, and authority:
" 'Stalin,' in a cluster ('molotov,' 'kaganovich'), shone over the whole
horizon and grinned enigmatically. And with him, like a fiery hoop,
mystery, the moustached Mystery, spread over us into that romantic
night. We underwent a great, unforgettable temptation—by miracle.
Only the Antichrist promises us something of the sort, even more
entertaining in the future. What is power without mystery, without
miracle?" (553). Through his memories of S., the author explores
the impulses behind the mystery, the temptation of miracle, reality's
transformation into spectacle. Just as the Grand Inquisitor proposes

to "correct" Christ's mistakes, to create the kingdom of God on earth in the body, so also, by transforming reality into a series of self-validating signs—attempting to overcome the difference between sign and referent by denying the referent—Stalinism, in the author's reading, seeks to create paradise. Both attempts, because they misconstrue the fallen state of humanity, result in dystopias that rest on the dehumanization of all who find themselves under their sway.

Hélène appears as the absolute antithesis of S., as underscored by the parallels between the portrayals of the two characters. While S. introduces the author to the sunlight of the Impressionists and to the art of other lands, Hélène brings him art books containing reproductions of those paintings. She is a foreigner in the flesh, a Frenchwoman incarnate, a living representative of the land of light and color captured in the paintings. Confronted by S.'s dark soulless "shell," the author adduces the proverb "The human soul is a mystery [*chuzhaya dusha potemki*]" (572). His relationship with Hélène, however, teaches him, "That's not true. Another's [*chuzhaya*] soul, if it, of course, exists, is, with rare exceptions, pure as glass. I'm not talking about the personality—but about the soul, which, perhaps, is not even involved in the human being. He commits murders, deceives, while his soul remains pure" (588). Thus, just as the author fashions a myth of Stalinism as the reign of the empty sign out of his relationship with S., so, through a complex web of images and associations, he makes Hélène into a figural locus of intersection for art, light, foreignness, death, and the possibility of escape from the cave into the sunlight.

The first of the two key narrative incidents that define Hélène's symbolic function has nothing to do with the flesh-and-blood woman herself. The author sees in a dream a fellow student disabled in the war, who tells the author that he has seen him in his own dreams: "And I, Andrei, have of late frequently encountered you in dreams, and always in the same company. You are always walking through Moscow at night with a girl in a blue dress. And other guys from our invalid group have also seen you with her: on the Sofia Embankment, by the Kremlin, on the Stone Bridge . . . After midnight, and even after one in the morning. You stroll about with her a bit late." (583–84). The author realizes that the "girl in the blue dress" is Hélène. Yet he maintains that he never goes out late at night "either with this girl, or with any other," (584), but often wanders the city alone, composing poetry. When the invalid, still in the dream, insists on his vision, the author for a moment sees himself "from outside, on

the Sofia Embankment, and then on the bridge, as if it were yesterday and as if through his eyes, objectively, in the company of a blue,
phosphorescent and undoubtedly young creature. But I was in no
condition to make out who it was precisely. Because I myself, as
such, at that moment on the bridge, did not notice anyone next to
me. They see her, my blue female friend, and I do not. I go my way
imperturbably and mumble verses" (584).

The author experiences himself simultaneously as see-er and
seen. This instance of "double vision" reflects the duality incarnated
in the author's poetry, which "in no way corresponded, if you please,
to my person" (585): "In what followed it became clear that much
earlier somewhere behind the wall, behind the wall of my soul (?!), a
double had apparently taken up residence, a double who was entering all of my ideological decay into his inflexible protocol" (585). The
image of the author's double—implicitly Abram Tertz, the author as
represented in his works—merges with the fleeting vision of himself
through the eyes of the other, a vision in which—standing outside
himself, seeing himself through the eyes of the other—he is able to
see more, to catch a glimpse of a reality otherwise hidden from him.

When the author awakens in the morning, he mulls over the
dream's significance, particularly the invalid's comment. " 'Watch
out!,' he said, 'you'll stroll too far with your foreign woman. It's your
death that's strolling about arm in arm with you' " (586). The vision
represents not only his poetry, which, after all, is what does accompany him on his strolls through Moscow, but also his death: "Death,
perhaps, is a girl, is our young female friend, which our whole life
long walks arm in arm next to us, softly warning, prompting: Don't
stumble! Wait! It's not time yet!" (586). Thus, in the dream-figure of
Hélène, the author's death and his art become one.

The author is summoned to a series of conversations with a man
who is apparently a state security official at which he is pressured to
betray Hélène by luring her into marriage with him. The main question deployed against him in these "dialogues" is "Are you a Soviet
person, or are you not a Soviet person?" (407)—are you with us, or
against us? He is thus asked to define himself in terms of a simple
bipolarity; there is, in the eyes of this representative of the system,
no third alternative, no more complex vision of the self. There is only
the demand "if the Motherland requires it" (587).

The author is finally coerced into meeting Hélène at Sokolniki
Park, where he is to play out the role assigned him by the authorities. He finds himself, however, directly confronted by her soul: "And

here, it seemed to me, I saw it, the soul, for the first time. It appeared in Hélène like a little oval body or a small cloud, resembling a white infant, swaddled until the time came, situated, however, unlike a child in the womb, directly head upwards, and not in the stomach, but in the chest, in the middle, stretching up to the face. The soul shone out of her . . .[39] You can't discern this in yourself. No. You are all dark. But there, in the depths of matter . . . That little image . . . That last candle lit before the Lord God" (589). Under the influence of this vision, the author reveals the entire plot to Hélène. Instead of running from him in disgust, as the author had expected, Hélène continues to walk with him: "Oh, Lenka! When I remember all of that now, I think that at that moment only a miracle saved me, the miracle of your trust in me and in what I said" (590). Trust, rooted in recognition of the soul, becomes the basis of communication.

Just as the author and his wife—later in time and earlier in the narrative—played the authorities at their own game—staging their own fictions to elude surveillance—so the author and Hélène act out a scenario of their own devising to foil the intrigue into which the powers that be would draw them. The author dictates to Hélène the script they must perform "on stage, publicly" (591): she is to pretend to be outraged at the author's crude attempt to force her into marriage and to break with him once and for all. The author worries about Hélène's apparent inability to dissemble and feels guilty at making her practice deceit: "She was still seeking truth. The ray of light in the dark kingdom [*Luch sveta v temnom tsarstve*[40]]! And I taught her deception, only deception" (592). Yet the two manage to pull the wool over the authorities' eyes and escape from the plot unscathed.

They succeed, the author would have it, because of the "saving role [*spasitel'nuyu rol'*]" (589) Serezha is tricked into playing in their drama: "I used him. Yes, I used him—as an informer, and that . . . saved me" (570). While the trust between the author and Hélène allows them to transcend theatrical pretense and communicate, it is precisely S.'s role as an informer, his violation of the trust on which the link between sign and referent is based, that allows them to draw him into their script, turning his deception to their advantage. Knowing that he will inform on them, Hélène confides her pretended dismay at the author's treachery. He passes this conversation on and thereby authenticates the scenario constructed by the author. He has been "transformed into a mechanism, into an instrument, like a bassoon or a clarinet, on which, sad as it may be, it was still necessary to play, pressing now on one or another familiar stop, like fear or laughter, and coldly observing how he immediately began to play" (571). This theatrical production acted out in life thus parodies literature as "sin for the sake of salvation," with S. as an empty sign turned, against his volition, into a means of redemption.

This drama, moreover, has an "Epilogue". In 1952, while his father is in prison, the author is once again coerced into participating in a provocation aimed at Hélène. He sends her a telegram asking her to meet him in Vienna. Though he manages to insert a word warning her not to come, she, having forgotten the code they had agreed upon earlier, follows the literal meaning of his words and travels to the rendezvous. Despite the author's misgivings about his "mission," the goal of which remains unclear to him both before and after the fact, the two friends again get away with no ill effects. Ironically, moreover, under the watching eyes of the author's "stone escorts" (603), Hélène agrees to help the author smuggle his works to the West: "Is it not for this that we went [to Vienna]? Was it not for a new literature?" (605). Hélène thus comes to represent literally as well as symbolically the possibility of escape, the flight of the author's works out of the "enchanted circle" of Stalinism to the sun-filled world outside: "That's how my long path from Sokolniki ended. 'Let's get out of here! Let's get out of here, Andryushka'" (597).

While in Vienna, the author manages to convince his "companions," who are far more interested in shop windows, to let him visit a museum. The tapestries he sees there prompt him to musings that, in a sense, summarize the vision of art to which his journey through the night has led him:

> There's one thing I don't understand: how did the old masters one way or another manage to convert their bad epoch, which was probably also cruel and, perhaps, very debased, into the magnificent superiority of art? Whence was given to them this sense of fresco on tapestry, which by the wave of an eye transports us from art into life and back? After all, what, we ask ourselves, are tapestries? Are they not magic power which has passed over into playful embroidery? A merry shuttle slips back and forth. And here the sufferings of Christ become so artistic and different from real torture that we admire the holiday instead of experiencing shame or pain at the horrifying villainy being perpetrated before our eyes. Is it not because the tapestry masters remembered that behind the scenes of

torture and death there is something different that follows
after? Does not the hope of resurrection get mixed into art,
little by little, no matter what it's relating? Or its pledge? Its
promise? And is it not through this, primarily, that it conquers
reality? It is stronger and more lasting, and, if you will, it is
more vital than destructive life. It is precisely for that reason
that it is healing and always moral [*nravstvenno*], independent of stupid morality [*morali*] . . . There is no art without
love. Love is inherent in the principles of art. That's why it
strives upwards. And death, why death is only a condition for
creation. You can't do without it. But how splendid, as a result, is Christ woven, under his burden, and right here, on the
tapestry, resurrected during his procession to death. (598–99)

Here the author responds directly to Ippolit's horror in *The Idiot*—
invoked, as we have seen, in "You and I"—at the Holbein painting depicting Christ's crucifixion. The realism of the painting, its graphic
portrayal of his bodily sufferings, precipitates a crisis of faith by riv-
eting the viewer's attention on the death of the body, on the physical
presence of the representation. The author counters by evoking the
image of art as imposture, an imposture that by openly displaying
its difference from physical reality can convey to the reader/viewer
an intimation of the transcendent: "Even so, even distorted, isn't it
still possible through binoculars, through a telescope, with a certain
effort, for something to be made out?" Thus, the final condemnation
of S., of all the stone figures of authority that populate the narrative
of *Goodnight*, of the totalitarian system that transforms reality into
representation is that they take the dead body, emptied of divinity,
for the final reality. Art, on the other hand, by pointing to the emptiness, the imposture of the body for the soul, can become a form of
"sin for the sake of salvation," transforming the dead letter into the
promise of resurrection, the horrific cave of the night of Stalinism
into the peaceful night—shared with loved ones, sleeping under the
open sky—with which *Goodnight* ends.

The author's revelation that love is the foundation of art clearly
confirms the fatal error into which the narrator of *Little Tsores*
stumbles in renouncing love for art. Tsores dies "before he is even
born," because, in a sense, he exists only on paper, finds refuge by
hiding in his own representation. As in the case of Gogol in *In the
Shadow of Gogol*, Tsores's loss of ability to love goes hand in hand
with his apparent inability to distinguish between himself and his

writing. Viewing writing as sin, he accepts his mother's condemnation of him as an incarnation of sin, of "tsores." Only by recognizing that he is not evil personified, but both good and evil like everyone else, does he achieve wholeness. The author in *Goodnight* achieves a similar epiphany toward the end of the text. As he is walking back from his meeting with Hélène at Sokolniki, he imagines people pointing their fingers at him: "An enemy of the people, there—look— there goes an enemy of the people."[41] He experiences a "sense of being torn away from people, from society, once and for all, a state of passionate disenfranchisement, as happens in inveterate criminals." He is bifurcated between two irreconcilable poles: "Half of my consciousness persistently asked me: but aren't you after all a Soviet man? While the other snarled out: leave me in peace, I am just a human being, or no one, or an enemy of the people." It is only many years later, he maintains, that he escapes this bipolarity, when a priest addresses him as "servant of God." Echoing Tsores's realization that he is no more guilty than anyone else, the author experiences a revelation and a release: "That means—me too? Me too? Like all people? Like everyone else? . . A servant of God, and nothing more on my slate. And we don't need any other ranks [*dolzhnostei*]. Like the call of freedom: servant of God . . . For there is no better title, no more precise designation . . . At long last. No one's servant. Only God's." The author finally achieves integration by understanding that he can only be named in relation to God (591).

As we have seen from Tertz's invocation of Tolstoy's *The Death of Ivan Ilych* in *The Trial Begins* and from Sinyavsky's discussion of Rozanov in *V. V. Rozanov's "Fallen Leaves"*, the dismissal of law, system, and convention as dead forms which hinder the realization and expression of the true self has deep roots in Russian thought. The early twentieth-century religious philosopher Nikolai Berdyaev gives a pained rendition of the dilemma of the artist forced to objectify the creative impulse in the substance of the world:

> Art is subject to law and is not an interaction of freedom and grace, as the primary creative act is. In realizing his creative intuition man is limited by the world, by his material, by other people; all this weighs on him and damps the fire of inspiration. There is always a tragic discrepancy between the burning heat of the creative fire in which the artistic image is conceived, and the cold of its formal realization. Every book, pic-

ture, statue, good work, social institution is an instance of this cooling down of the original flame. Probably some creators never find expression; they have the inner fire and inspiration but fail to give it form. And yet people generally think that creativeness consists in producing concrete, definite things. Classic art requires the greatest possible adherence to the cold formal laws of technique.[42]

Tertz, as a metaphor for the transgression of these "cold formal laws of technique," is clearly both a product of and a response to this tradition.

Born out of the practical necessity dictated by Sinyavsky's "criminal" violation of Soviet borders, both geographical and linguistic, from the beginning of the writer's career Tertz was an image— and has continued to grow into an increasingly rich image—for the writer's "crime" in transforming himself into text. While this book has attempted to trace the continuities in Tertz's "poetics of crime," it has also tried to chart the evolution of the writer's views as exemplified in his ever more radical departures from convention. Thus, Tertz's early works, for all their fantastic premises and experiments with language, are relatively easily classifiable by genre and have recognizable characters and plots. In almost all of them the prospect that the text will reach its desired reader, or any reader at all, is left in doubt. At its most extreme, in "Pkhents"—which is arguably about the writer's inevitable failure to find his ideal reader, someone exactly like himself—Tertz seems to express a despair akin to that of Berdyaev: the creative self can evade the cold, formal structures of the law and society only by self-immolation of body and text.

In his 1976 article " 'I' and 'They': An Essay on Extreme Forms of Communication under Conditions of Human Isolation" (" 'Ya' i 'oni': O Krainikh formakh obshcheniya v usloviyakh odinochestva"), Tertz[43] expresses the desperate situation of the writer in an authoritarian state—and, to an extent, of all writers—confronted by a hostile and unreceptive readership by analogy with the breakdown of language between authorities and prisoners in the camps: "In attempts to start a dialogue here [in prison], the natural interaction of 'I' and 'you' is replaced by the relationship 'I' and 'they.' 'They' are the people to whom 'you' are not 'you' (and not 'I') but simply another cipher from the impersonal, alien category 'they.' Communication takes the form of challenge, insult, mockery and ridicule."[44] Prisoners respond to this denial of their personhood by turning their

bodies themselves into a mode of communication *in extremis,* and he
adduces gut-wrenching examples of their self-mutilation to support
his argument. Tertz then concludes that these acts may be viewed as
an analogy for the literature of our time

> when the creative author stands sharply aloof from society
> and regards it with suspicion, in a situation, as it were, of
> extreme solitude and extreme want of understanding and con-
> tact. Here too, confronted by a public or a readership which,
> as well as the friendly 'you,' also bears the stamp of the hostile,
> blank 'they,' art too sometimes resorts to extreme methods
> to obtain its effect—*épatage,* the grotesque, the absurd, the
> fantastic and various kinds of eccentricity, which may be gen-
> erally described as forms of intensely expressive, aggressive
> and at the same time communicative 'speech.' (282)

Abram Tertz is just such a mutilation of the body of the sign in a
desperate attempt to reestablish dialogue, to demolish the "blank
wall" of dehumanizing, dead form that frustrates the free interaction
between reader and text.

Yet in Tertz's more recent writings, dating from the years spent
in the camps and in emigration, the hopelessness of the plight of the
writer trapped in his text is mitigated by the potential for communication rooted in love, trust, and the shared experience of death.
Mariya Rozanova as ideal reader in *A Voice from the Chorus* and
as beloved accomplice in *Goodnight,* along with Hélène and the
writer's father in the latter work, provide models for the possibility
of bridging the separation between selves and achieving communion. These ideal models of communication on the basis of intimacy
remain, however, expressions of the text's aspiration to transcend
difference, a transcendence that it, sent forth into the world and left
to the mercy of "random" readers, can never achieve. The images—
both from *Goodnight*—of the dying lioness carved in stone on the
Assyrian bas-reliefs and of the tapestry masters' representation of
Christ's crucifixion suggest, on the other hand, that text and reader
may find common ground in the shared experience of death and
resurrection, in the reminder of the transience of the body and the
eternity of the soul. Thus, in Tertz's later works, the criminality of
the text becomes its saving grace as well. Through the spectacle of
the exposure of its own imposture, art becomes redemptive sin, just
as, in the Viennese tapestry, the representation of Christ's corporeal death exposes the emptiness of the body, thereby redirecting

the reader/viewer's attention to the resurrection that lies beyond. Thus, art strives not to change the world, to turn word into deed, but rather to expose the "insubstantiality" of the matter of the physical world and to provide a glimpse "through a glass, darkly" of the true reality of the soul that lies beyond the body.

Although Berdyaev maintains that art as law is not "an interaction of freedom and grace," Tertz suggests that writing as crime holds forth the possibility of liberation. The writer, recognizing his death in the text, is freed of the delusion that he can control his own words, and is able to reconcile his own duality by realizing that he is neither angel, nor demon, but an empty vessel, a slave of God, "to some extent evil and to some extent good." The highest sense of the ethics of the poetics of crime, however, lies in the liberation of the reader, in the freeing of the reader's imagination to bring alive the images of the text, and in opening him or her up to the free play of meaning, which promises an intimation of the true self, the soul, set free from the dead body.

Notes

Chapter 1. The Trials of Abram Tertz

1. The concept of fantastic realism can be traced back to Dostoevsky, although Sinyavsky claims to have arrived at the term independently. In the third chapter of *Diary of a Writer* for 1876, Dostoevsky writes: "It is always said that reality is boring, monotone; in order to divert themselves people have recourse to art, to fantasy, read novels. For me, on the contrary: what could be more fantastic and unexpected than reality? What could be even more improbable sometimes than reality?" (Dostoevskii, *Polnoe sobranie* 22: 91. For a discussion of the concept in Dostoevsky's works, see the editor's note on this passage [22:363].) In the foreword to his "fantastic story" "The Gentle One," also published in *Diary of a Writer*, Dostoevsky explicates the story's subtitle in similar terms: "I titled it 'fantastic' although I myself consider it in the highest degree real. But the fantastic really is present here and precisely in the very form of the story, which I find necessary to explain in advance" (*Polnoe sobranie* 24:5). I would like to thank Deborah Martinsen and Slava Yastremski for having directed me to these references.

I have been unable to trace Sinyavsky's earliest application of the term *fantastic realism* in relation to his own works. In conversation with me, he claimed to have used it first in the essay "Chto takoe sotsialisticheskii realizm" (What is Socialist Realism). While he does explicate the concept for the first time in the concluding paragraphs of that essay, he employs there the term *phantasmagoric art*. Curiously, the first mention of the term I have been able to locate in Sinyavsky's "vicinity" is connected with an article that his wife, Mariya Rozanova, wrote and published in the journal *Dekorativnoe iskusstvo* while Sinyavsky was imprisoned in a labor camp. Although the article is about Russian folk art, its title, "Fantasticheskii realizm" (Fantastic realism), may be taken as a rather daring reference to her imprisoned husband's approach to literature. Sinyavsky himself titled an officially published article on Soviet science fiction "Realizm fantastiki" (The realism of the fantastic).

Sinyavsky defines "fantastic literary scholarship" as the application of the principles of "fantastic realism" to the study of literature. (See, for example, [Nepomnyashchy], "Interview," 10.) He has employed the term *exaggerated prose* to place his Tertz writings in the Russian literary tradition: "Speaking provisionally, on the one hand, [there is] particularly realistic prose, following the line: Turgenev, Lev Tolstoy, Chekhov. This tradition has been the stronger even in our day. The other tradition, which is more congenial to me, to which I give the conditional name *exaggerated prose* [*utrirovannaya proza*], is Gogol, Dostoevsky, Leskov. This tradition was subsequently picked up by the modernist literature of the beginning of the twentieth century (let us name here at least Andrei Bely)" ([Glad], "Antizapadnichestvo," 147).

2. Mariya Rozanova suggests that the Sinyavsky-Daniel trial and the two public uproars over *Strolls with Pushkin* be viewed as the three "trials" of Abram Tertz in her article defending *Strolls with Pushkin*, "K istorii i geografii etoi knigi," translated as "On the History and Geography of This Book." Rozanova's article originally was published in *Voprosy literatury*, following a discussion in the same issue of *Strolls with Pushkin*. Olga Matich points out in an article that appeared before the first Soviet publication of *Strolls with Pushkin* that Sinyavsky's "supporters commonly refer to the Puškin scandal as 'the second trial of Abram Terc'" (Matich, *"Spokojnoj noči,"* 60). Sinyavsky himself refers to the emigre attacks on *Strolls with Pushkin* as "the second trial of Abram Tertz" in "Sinyavskii o sebe" (108).

3. The edition of Pasternak came out a month before Sinyavsky's arrest and was later confiscated and reissued with a new introduction. A listing of Sinyavsky's writings published under his own name in the Soviet Union before his arrest appears in the bibliography of this book. For discussions of Sinyavsky's pre-trial critical works, see Kolonosky, "Andrej Sinjavskij as a Literary Critic"; Kolonosky, "Andrei Siniavskii: Chorus and Critic"; and Lourie, *Letters to the Future*, 171–94. Rufus W. Mathewson, Jr., discusses the full spectrum of Sinyavsky/Tertz's "voices," ranging from the criticism and scholarship published in the Soviet Union before Sinyavsky's arrest to the writer's tamizdat publications, in the (unfortunately) unpublished study, "Trapped in History: The Mind of Andrei Sinyavsky." I would like to thank Ruth Mathewson for having given me a copy of the manuscript.

4. Tvardovskii, "Po sluchayu yubileya," 17.

5. In an interview with *Time Magazine* published in February 1987, Yevgeny Yevtushenko related the curious story that during his 1966 visit to the United States, Robert Kennedy had informed him (while the two men were locked in the bathroom of Kennedy's hotel suite with the shower running!) that the identities of Sinyavsky and Daniel had been revealed to the KGB by none other than agents of the CIA, who supposedly hoped that the suppression of the dissident writers would deflect attention from the unpopular war in Vietnam. A week after Yevtushenko's "revelation" appeared in *Time*, an article reporting the account and citing the episode as proof that "our enemies need an unfree Soviet Union" appeared in *Moscow News* (Simonov, "Vid iz okna," 3). That article contains the first mention I have been able to find of Sinyavsky's name in the Soviet press during the glasnost period. In May of 1989, Yevtushenko published in the popular magazine *Ogonek* his own rather self-serving account of the incident, setting it within the context of his attendance at the trial of Sinyavsky and Daniel and his apparent attempts to mitigate their punishment (Yevtushenko, "Kontramarka na

protsess"). A condensed English translation of the article was subsequently published in *Soviet Life* ("A Pass to the Trial"). Sinyavsky and his wife also believe that the CIA was responsible for his arrest (see [Maksimov], "Russkaya emigratsiya"). A former CIA employee, on the other hand, denied Yevtushenko's charges, claiming that the CIA did not learn Tertz's true identity until after Sinyavsky's arrest (Jameson, "What Yevgeny Knew").

For the purposes of this study, most interesting are the responses to Yevtushenko's claim in the emigre community in that they shade over into the other controversies that have dogged Sinyavsky in emigration. See, for example, Kozlovskii, "Vydalo li TsRU Sinyavskogo i Danielya?"; Efimov, "Vymysel demagoga"; Gorbanevskaya, "Kto na chei kryuchok klyunul?"

6. In all Sinyavsky helped three other writers send their works abroad for publication. According to Sinyavsky, aside from Daniel, he aided Andrei Remizov (pseudonym: Ivanov), who served as a witness for the prosecution at the trial, and Yury Pavlovsky, whose identity was not uncovered by the Soviet authorities.

7. For a brief overview of the events surrounding the Sinyavsky-Daniel trial and their significance, see Galina Belaya, "Da budet vedemo vsem . . ." in Eremina, *Tsena metafory*. An English translation of this article, entitled "Yea, So Shall It Be Known to All . . . ," was published in Nepomnyashchy, "Return of Abram Tertz," a special edition of *Russian Studies in Literature*, 12–24.

8. For a collection of documents related to the Sinyavsky-Daniel affair, including a transcript of the trial, Western and Soviet press accounts, letters and articles, and commentary, see Ginzburg, *Belaya kniga;* and "Rossiiskie dokumenty." For an English translation of most of these materials, see Hayward, *On Trial.* A small selection of protest letters can also be found in Eremina, *Tsena metafory.* Many of those who openly supported the two defendants later suffered reprisals. Aleksandr Ginzburg, the compiler of the "white book" (*belaya kniga*) on the trial, was arrested, tried, and sent to the camps.

9. Although the publication of *One Day in the Life of Ivan Denisovich* was an exceptional case, since it was facilitated by Khrushchev himself in the belief that the work would aid his policy of de-Stalinization, later events bear out the contention that the "realism" of Solzhenitsyn's work made it more acceptable to the Soviet authorities. Sinyavsky himself points out that "typically, the first salvos against Solzhenitsyn's *One Day in the Life of Ivan Denisovich* (1962) were fired at the language. Too crude, they claimed, though everyone knows what sort of language is used in a labor camp" (Sinyavsky, *Soviet Civilization,* 208). In her book *Russian Experimental Fiction,* which unfortunately came to my attention only after this book essentially was completed, Edith W. Clowes takes the following premise as her starting point for the exploration of what she terms "meta-utopian" works of the post-Stalin period: "This book explores the challenge that literary play poses to ideological fixation. Since the death of Stalin experimental fiction has been more openly contested and its authors more severely punished than so-called realist fiction and its authors" (ix).

10. Eremin, "Perevertyshi." Page numbers will henceforth be given in

parentheses in the text from the reprint of the article in Ginzburg, *Belaya kniga*.

11. Olga Matich observes, "Originally meaning *werewolf*, *Perevertyš* in the sense of *turncoat* was the term used for Sinjavskij and Daniel' in the Soviet press during the Sinjavskij-Daniel' affair (Eremin). In both meanings it connotes rebirth, but in a negative, demonic sense" (Matich, *"Spokojnoj noči,"* 57). Harriet Murav makes a similar point in her excellent article "The Case Against Andrei Siniavskii." My argument dovetails with hers on a number of points, and I am grateful to her for having given me a copy of her article before publication.

12. Stephanie Sandler discusses this passage in her insightful article on the underlying sexual dimension of the discourse in the *Strolls with Pushkin* "scandal" ("Sex, Death and Nation," 295).

13. Eremin does not identify which work he is talking about, but he would seem to be referring to Sinyavsky's portrayal of Lenin baying at the moon in *Lyubimov* (translated as *The Makepeace Experiment*).

14. Z. Gulbis, "Ikh udel—prezrenie," *Izvestiya*, 18 January 1966. Page numbers cited in text are from the reprint of the letter in Ginzburg, *Belaya kniga*. Given the undercurrent of nationalist rhetoric in the campaign against Sinyavsky and Daniel, from the point of view of Soviet multinationalism, it is convenient, to say the least, that this letter was written by a Latvian.

15. The brief argument leading up to this statement is explicitly directed against Daniel-Arzhak, who ostensibly wrote about "our women" with "terrible cynicism," which, since after all "he was given birth by a woman" constitutes, following the tortured logic of the letter writer, a betrayal of his mother. In fact, in the course of the trial, the accusation of betraying motherhood was leveled not against Daniel, but against Sinyavsky, suggesting that there is a confusion of the two writers here. Moreover, since there is no mention of this accusation in Eremin's article, and the letter writer almost certainly had never seen works by either Sinyavsky or Daniel, this tirade suggests that the letter was written "to order," perhaps not even by the person who signed it.

16. Kedrina, "Nasledniki Smerdyakova." Page numbers to Kedrina's article in the text are from its reprinting in *Belaya kniga*. The consistent invocation throughout of Western commentators who identified Sinyavsky's and Daniel's works as being anti-Soviet as proof of the anti-Soviet nature of the works—aside from the grotesque illogic of the tactic—also demonstrates how Western cold war appropriations of literature dovetailed with Soviet ones, a topic that is interesting in itself but lies beyond the bounds of this study.

17. Sheila Fitzpatrick's observations on the link between "unmasking" and the instability of class identity during the period of the New Economic Policy (NEP) resonate with Kedrina's argument, suggesting that the paradigm evoked here has deep roots in Soviet culture:

"Unmasking" of concealed or fraudulently claimed class identity was a great preoccupation of Communists in the 1920s and, as a result, a constant anxiety for some segments of the population. . . .

The proletarian writers' slogan "Tear off the masks!" ostensibly

referred to a literary technique by which the real person was revealed behind the social persona. In reality, however, the young Communists of RAPP [Russian Association of Proletarian Writers] tore
off the masks in order to reveal class enemies. It was this instinct
that brought them success in the Communist milieu of NEP and lent
credibility to their dubious claims to be proletarian. Fear of hidden
enemies and habitual suspicion that people might not be what they
seemed were already basic components of Soviet political culture in
the NEP period.

. . . One source of anxiety was fear that the more cultured class
enemy might hoodwink and manipulate them. (Fitzpatrick, "Problem
of Class Identity," 27, 28)

Two points are of particular interest here. First, I would draw attention to
Fitzpatrick's contention that "unmasking" the "other" served to legitimate
the identity of the unmasker. Second, her suggestion that the desire to un-
mask was prompted by the fear of being "hoodwink[ed]" by a "more cultured
class enemy" anticipates the similar anxiety implied in Kedrina's article.

18. In the last paragraph of her article, Kedrina refers to Sinyavsky as an
"internal emigre," thus echoing Eremin's rhetorical expulsion of the writer
from the community of Soviet citizens.

19. Here it is worth noting that although Sinyavsky's Tertz works must
seem quite tame, especially in terms of overt portrayals of sexual activities, to the Western reader, against the background of Socialist Realism,
which still dominated Soviet literature at the time of the trial, the gallery of
psychological misfits that populate his writings and his portrayals of malfunctions of the family and of sexual relations did represent excursions into
the darker side of the human psyche that had so long been "repressed" in
Soviet literature.

20. Kedrina deploys this phrase in the course of making the argument
that Sinyavsky's works are anti-Semitic. In this context it is worth noting
that Sinyavsky's use of a Jewish pseudonym, when it was mentioned at all,
seems to have caused Soviet commentators particular difficulty. As a rule
the chorus of attacks against the writer was generally repetitive to the point
of monotony, yet in this area there was apparently no comfortable party
line. Thus, for example, another Soviet journalist saw the pseudonym as a
suggestion that there was anti-Semitism in the USSR. That a non-Jewish
Russian should identify himself as a Jew is so discordant within the mythology of Russian and Soviet culture that it arguably becomes unreadable,
or, rather, elicits multiple readings.

21. We must consider *public* something of a relative concept here, since
entrance to the trial was rigorously restricted, and with few exceptions the
audience was packed with "plants" from the security services. The press suppressed virtually completely any direct reporting of Sinyavsky's or Daniel's
testimony. Mariya Rozanova along with Daniel's wife, Larisa Bogoraz, and
the Leningrad writer Boris Vakhtin managed to produce a transcript of the
trial. Page numbers in parentheses refer to the transcript of the trial as it
appears in Ginzburg, *Belaya kniga.*

22. The issue of the appropriate "juridical" use of language figured

prominently in protests and commentaries on the trial. Thus, Aleksandr Ginzburg, in his commentary in the *Belaya kniga*, suggested that the defendants should not have simply assented to the terms of the indictment: "An affirmative answer in the given case is one of the defendants' mistakes. If they had left it to the court to explain the meaning of the term 'anti-Soviet propaganda,' referring to that explanation, the defendants could have avoided a broader interpretation of the term" (174). In the same vein, the dissident Aleksandr Esenin-Volpin, forced to write an "explanation" of his own activities with regard to the trial questioned the propriety of the two terms that figured most prominently in accusations against the defendants reported in the press. He first disputed the charge of "slander," referring to the terms in which that crime is defined in the Soviet criminal code:

> However, I first of all do not see from the newspapers proof that these works could not be the product of sincere creative writers, which should have exonerated them from the accusation of slander [*kleveta*]. After all what is called slander in the juridical sense of that word (see article 130 of the Criminal Code of the RSFSR) is the dissemination of deliberately false fabrications of a defamatory character, and this point of view on the conception of slander, judging by the newspaper accounts, was expressed at the trial by Smirnov, who presided over the trial. The subjective, deliberate character of the crime of slander— i.e., the necessary consciousness on the part of the criminal that what he is disseminating is false—is clearly indicated in Soviet juridical literature; it was also mentioned in the newspapers in connection with the trial. Therefore, sincerity, even in error, excludes the possibility of indictment for slander. (Ginzburg, *Belaya kniga*, 399–400)

Esenin-Volpin then goes on to comment on the complete inappropriateness of the term "blasphemy" [*koshchunstvo*] as a juridical concept:

> The newspapers with revulsion called excerpts from the works of the accused blasphemous, and judging by the newspapers the prosecutors at the trial were agitated by such blasphemy as well. This accusation of blasphemy could be made only in the interests of supporting the accusation of anti-Soviet slander, otherwise it would have no relationship to the essence of the trial and should have been suppressed by the court in the interests of objectivity. "Blasphemy" is a term of the Inquisition and not of Soviet justice, and can be brought to bear (and only in particular cases) under the juridical concept of insult [*oskorbleniya*], and not of slander. Article 70 of the Criminal Code of the RSFSR speaks of agitation or propaganda of a slanderous, and not of an insulting character for Soviet power. (400)

Esenin-Volpin's statements here in particular are examples of the sort of "language games" that became popular among Soviet political dissidents in the years following the trial, accepting the basic terms of the Soviet legal code in an attempt to force the authorities to adhere to the letter of their own laws.

23. Krymov, "Sud prodolzhaetsya," cited from its reprinting in Ginzburg, *Belaya kniga*, 268.

24. Sinyavsky was apparently misinformed about when he would have his last word and expected to have more time to prepare.

25. Murav, "Case Against Andrei Siniavskii," 550.

26. Harriet Murav in "Case Against Andrei Siniavskii" makes a similar argument, basing it on Lotman and Uspenskii, "Role of Dual Models."

27. Barbara Johnson, in her reading of *Billy Budd*, draws a distinction between literary, legal, and political language that is somewhat similar to Sinyavsky's: "Judgment, then, would seem to ground itself in a suspension of the opposition between textuality and referentiality, just as politics can be seen as that which makes it impossible to draw the line between 'language' and 'life'" ("The Execution of *Billy Budd*," in Johnson, *Critical Difference*, 104–05). She, moreover, maintains: "It would seem, then, that the maintenance of political authority requires that the law function as a set of rules for the regular, predictable misreading of the 'difference within' as a 'difference between.' . . . law is thus defined in terms of its repression of ambiguity" (106).

28. During his questioning, Sinyavsky commented on the horrors that could be unleashed by the transgression of the linguistic boundary between art and reality: "If we realize metaphors, it will be the end of the world. We say 'it is raining cats and dogs [*dozhd' idet*],' 'stars fall,' and so forth. Stalin realized [Lenin's] metaphors, and the horrors of 1937 began. Stalin turned metaphors inside out. But Lenin is not responsible for Stalin, just as language is not responsible for the realization of metaphor" (239).

29. Nikodim Troekurov, "O 'samovyrazhenie' i mezhdunarodnom polozhenii," *Agitator*, no. 6 (1966). Page numbers in the text are from its reprinting in Ginzburg, *Belaya kniga*.

30. Sholokhov's address was designed apparently as a response to a letter signed by sixty-two Moscow writers requesting that Sinyavsky and Daniel be released to their keeping. (For the text of the letter, see Ginzburg, *Belaya kniga*, 385–87.) Sholokhov may have had something of a personal stake in the affair. News of the arrest of Sinyavsky and Daniel reached the West only shortly before he went to Stockholm to receive the 1965 Nobel Prize for Literature, and he received Western requests that he intercede on their behalf. Page numbers in the text are from the reprint of an excerpt from Sholokhov's speech in Ginzburg, *Belaya kniga*.

31. While Sholokhov is probably referring specifically to avant-garde art (*iskusstvo*), the context of his speech shows that he imputes the same power to language in the works of Sinyavsky and Daniel.

32. In fact Sholokhov never once refers to either of the two writers by his proper name, confining himself to pejorative epithets.

33. For details of Sinyavsky's release and of the controversy involving continuing accusations that he in some way collaborated with the Soviet authorities, see Rozanova, "Abram da Mar'ya."

34. For a listing of the articles that Sinyavsky has published both under his own name and his pseudonym in emigration, see the bibliography of this book. Sinyavsky has on a number of occasions told me that in deciding to

which of his personae to attribute an emigré work he has sometimes been influenced by the concern that he might be accused of hiding behind the "mask" of Abram Tertz. This consideration would seem to relate primarily to his most overtly political writings.

35. Sinyavsky's original support of *Kontinent* is reflected in his defense of the journal in an exchange of letters with Günter Grass in 1974 before the first issue of the journal had even appeared (Sinyavsky and Grass, "Letters," 94–95). In 1978, he explained his departure from *Kontinent* as the result of "theoretical and stylistic differences," deploring the Russian reflex "which angrily sees words as deeds and tends to make of every controversy a cold or even civil war" and maintaining, "Style makes the man, and I am surprised by the inappropriateness of the style by which *Kontinent* demonstrates its tolerance" (Sinyavsky, "Emigré," 79–80). Sinyavsky discussed his views on Maksimov within the context of the polarization of the Russian emigre community in an interview with John Glad in 1986 ("Antizapadnichestvo," 149). The ongoing animosity between Sinyavsky, Maksimov, and *Kontinent* came to a head in 1992 when *Kontinent* reprinted materials from the journal *Dvadtsat dva* along with an editorial note accusing Sinyavsky and Rozanova of collaboration with the KGB ("Spetsial'noe prilozhenie," *Kontinent* no. 71 [1992], 307–50). For more on the controversy over Sergei Khmelnitsky with which this publication was concerned, see chapter 8.) Two issues later *Kontinent* published a letter from Sinyavsky and Rozanova threatening legal action unless the journal retracted its slanderous statements along with a letter from the new Moscow editor of the journal disclaiming responsibility and a letter from Maksimov reaffirming the charges ("Raznoe," *Kontinent* no. 73 [1992], 308–313.) Sinyavsky and Rozanova retaliated by bringing a lawsuit against the journal in Moscow, to which *Kontinent* had moved its base of operations with no. 72. For a sample of the controversy generated by this act in the emigre press, see Amurskii, "Igra v 'durachka'"; Shturman, "Spokoinoi nochi . . ."; Gurvich, "Tol'ko li gipoteza?". Dora Shturman's angry tirade against Sinyavsky is perhaps the most interesting, not only because it demonstrates the confusion of the various different controversies surrounding Sinyavsky in emigration, but also because, certainly unwittingly, it echoes Sinyavsky's own repeated claim that his differences with his detractors are "stylistic." The core of Shturman's argument is that Sinyavsky continually fires controversies about himself, because otherwise no one would pay any attention to his writing, that he is an envious "Salieri" in relation to Solzhenitsyn. Solzhenitsyn, Shturman claims, "is always occupied with the meaning of what he creates and not with originality as an end in itself. In this he is subordinated to the fullest and most precise disclosure of meaning, and not to draping it in the garb of multiple significance [*mnogoznachitel'nosti*]." Sinyavsky, on the other hand, "often consciously obscures meaning." This suggests the extent to which discomfort with figurative language lies at the heart of the various political accusations that have over the years been leveled at Sinyavsky.

In the wake of the bombing of the Russian White House in October 1993, Sinyavsky and Maksimov apparently came at least to a temporary reconciliation. Together with a third party they signed a letter calling for Yeltsin's resignation. It was originally published under the title "Pod sen' nadezhnuyu zakona . . ." in *Nezavisimaya gazeta* (16 October 1993) and was reprinted in *Sintaksis* under the same title and in *Novoe russkoe slovo* under the title "El'tsin—v otstavku!" (20 October 1993), 5. See also Rozanova, "Abram da Mar'ya."

36. On the subject of the controversy over *Strolls with Pushkin*, see Nepomnyashchy, "Andrei Sinyavsky's 'Return'"; and idem, introduction to Tertz, *Strolls with Pushkin*. See also idem, introduction to "Return of Abram Tertz"; and Stephanie Sandler's excellent article "Sex, Death and Nation."

37. Gul', "Progulki khama s Pushkinym," 117. Page numbers will henceforth be given in parentheses in the text.

38. Gul lists several people he exempts from this boorification, notably including Solzhenitsyn and Igor Shafavevich.

39. The role of the Pushkin cult in Russian and Soviet society is a key issue in understanding the controversy over *Strolls with Pushkin*. On the history of Pushkin's "sacralization" see Levitt, *Russian Literary Politics;* Gasparov et al., *Cultural Myths of Russian Modernism;* Debreczeny, "Zhitie Aleksandra Boldinskogo";* Terras, "Some Observations on Puškin's Image"; Brooks, "Russian Nationalism and Russian Literature"; idem, "Readers and Reading at the End of the Tsarist Era"; and idem, *When Russia Learned to Read*. On the Pushkin cult specifically in relation to the *Strolls with Pushkin* controversy, see Nepomnyashchy, introduction in Tertz, *Strolls with Pushkin*.

40. Gul's use of the adverb *naglo* here echoes Ham's father's "nakedness" [*nagota*] invoked at the very beginning of the article.

41. Solzhenitsyn, ". . . Koleblet tvoi trenozhnik." Page numbers will be given in parentheses in the text.

42. A more literal translation of the Russian here (*rezvost'*) would be "friskiness." I have taken the liberty of translating it "playfulness" to underscore Solzhenitsyn's discomfort with the idea of literature as play.

43. Among the main statements in the public polemic between the two writers, apart from the article presently being discussed, are Sinyavsky's interview by Olga Carlisle, "Solzhenitsyn and Russian Nationalism"; and his articles published under his own name in *Sintaksis:* "Solzhenitsyn kak ustroitel' novogo edinomysliya," "Chtenie v serdtsakh," and "Russkii natsionalizm." The latter article is a response to an article by Solzhenitsyn titled "Nashi plyuralisty," in which he attacks Sinyavsky and other emigre liberals. (The article is available in English as "Our Pluralists.") In that essay, Solzhenitsyn argues against the very principle of pluralism as an end in itself: "Of course, variety adds colour to life. We yearn for it. We cannot imagine life without it. But if diversity becomes the highest principle, then there can be no universal human values, and making one's own values the yardstick of another person's opinions is ignorant and brutal. If there is no right and wrong, what restraints remain? If there is no universal basis for it there can be no morality. . . . That is why the Western world today is defenceless; paralysed by its inability any longer to distinguish between true and false positions, between manifest Good and manifest Evil. . . . In the whole universal flux there is one truth—God's truth" (English edition, 2). For an analysis

of Solzhenitsyn and Sinyavsky as polar models of the Russian writer, see Fanger, "Conflicting Imperatives"; and Cohen and Fanger, "Abram Tertz." See also Numano, "Iz knigi 'Za odnu ostanovku do vechnosti.'"

44. See also Stephanie Sandler's ingenious analysis of the underlying sexual connotations of Solzhenitsyn's argument ("Sex, Death and Nation," 302–04).

45. Tellingly, even Leonid Batkin in his article on *Strolls with Pushkin,* which is to date the lengthiest defense of the work to have appeared in Russia, stumbles over the same dead bodies. For example, he writes: "I must say that what follows is the only argument in Sinyavsky's book that shocks me and which I cannot accept: about Pushkin's 'vampirism' as not only a general, but even a concrete feature of his poetics, i.e., as a particular passion for the provocative and ambivalent presence of corpses in Pushkin's works" (Batkin, "Sinyavskii, Pushkin—i my," 177). Batkin's tendency to read metaphor literally is more obvious in his comment on Tertz's use of Pushkin's sleeping tsarevna: "In this case there simply is no dead body, just as there was no vampire; poor Vanya only imagined it" (179).

46. And also—as Sylvie Richards astutely pointed out in commenting on the manuscript of this book—to the body politic.

47. In phrases quoted in this paragraph Solzhenitsyn cites Pushkin and Father Aleksandr Schmemann to support his point. "The writer should employ . . ." and "passion for novelty" are Pushkin's words. "Russian literature as a whole . . ." are Schmemann's.

48. Solzhenitsyn expresses similar views in "The Relentless Cult of Novelty and How It Wrecked the Century." The Russian text was published later in *Novyi mir* (Solzhenitsyn, "Otvetnoe slovo").

49. Daniel died 31 December 1988. Sinyavsky did not receive a visa in time to attend the funeral.

50. Antonov, Klykov, and Shafarevich, "Pis'mo v sekretariat."

51. "Russophobia" first appeared in the emigre journal *Veche,* no. 32 (11 December 1988), and no. 33 (March 1989). The latter issue of the journal is dedicated "to Aleksander Isaevich Solzhenitsyn on the occasion of his seventieth birthday." An abbreviated version of the essay appeared in *Nash sovremennik,* no. 6 (1989), 167–92. Purportedly at the request of readers, *Nash sovremennik* published the sections of the article that had been cut from the June issue in November, at the height of the campaign against Sinyavsky (*Nash sovremennik,* no. 11 [1989], 162–72). Page references in this text are from the Soviet edition of Shafarevich's essay.

52. Citations in the text are to the English translation.

53. See Nepomnyashchy, "Perestroika and the Soviet Creative Unions."

54. Vozdvizhenskii, "Progulki s Shafarevichem," 167. According to Vozdvizhensky this article was published in an emigre journal rather than in the USSR because no Soviet publication would agree to print his defense of *Strolls with Pushkin.*

55. "Pushkin is one of the last saints . . ." is from Vladimir Gusev on the television program "Vesy," aired 31 January 1990.

56. The Safonov passage is translated from a taped transcript of a meeting held at Columbia University on 10 May 1990. A group of seven Soviet

writers and critics, all of them associated more or less closely with the Russophile camp, participated in a roundtable discussion. They were visiting the United States under the auspices of the U.S. Information Agency.

57. Rozanova, "K istorii i geografii etoi knigi" (Eng. version: "On the History and Geography of This Book"). Text citations are to the English edition.

58. Sandler, "Sex, Death and Nation," 296.

59. Sinyavskii, "Stilistichestskie raznoglasiya."

60. Solzhenitsyn's insistence on the oneness of genius thus emerges as a defense of the referentiality of language.

61. When I asked Sinyavsky (some decades after the fact) whether he had Benya Krik in mind when he chose *Abram Tertz* as his pseudonym, he said that he had never consciously thought of the Babel character.

62. Vladimir Novikov cites these lines in his excellent discussion of the distinction between Sinyavsky and Tertz published as the introduction to the two-volume edition of Tertz's works that came out in Russia in 1992 ("Sinyavskii i Terts," in Tertz, *Sobranie sochinenii* 1:5).

63. Mandel'shtam, "Chetvertaya proza," in idem, *Sobranie sochinenii* 2:182. Tertz uses this passage as the epigraph to his first article published in emigration: Tertz, "Literaturnyi protsess v Rossii." This essay, which as a literary manifesto stands on a par with the concluding paragraphs of *What Is Socialist Realism*, constitutes Tertz's most sustained discussion of the metaphors of the writer as thief and Jew and their realization in Soviet society. For an examination of this article within the context of Tertz's other emigre writings, see Nepomnyashchy, "Sinyavsky/Tertz."

64. See Barthes, "The Death of the Author," in idem, *Image—Music—Text;* Foucault, "What Is an Author?" in idem, *Language, Counter-Memory, Practice;* and idem, *Archaeology of Knowledge*, 92–96.

65. Barthes, "Death of the Author," 148 and 147. For Derrida, see Derrida, "Difference," in idem, *Speech and Phenomena*.

66. See Derrida, "Structure, Sign, and Play in the Discourse of the Human Sciences," in idem, *Writing and Difference*.

67. Barthes, *S/Z*, 4. Page numbers to the English edition will be given in the text. See also Johnson, "Critical Difference: BartheS/BalZac," in idem, *Critical Difference*, 3–12. Barthes's, as well as Tertz's, conception of a distinction between texts that dictate how they are to be read and texts that elicit the reader's collaboration in the act of creation may also be related to Umberto Eco's distinction between "open" and "closed" texts (Eco, *Role of the Reader*) and Mikhail Bakhtin's categories of the "dialogic" and the "monologic" (Bakhtin, *Problems of Dostoevsky's Poetics*). The convergences between Sinyavsky's and Bakhtin's visions of the interrelationship between reader and text are interesting and worthy of further study. Sinyavsky did read Bakhtin's *Problems of Dostoevsky's Poetics* before his arrest, and, after his release from the camps, he met Bakhtin. Several critics have commented in passing on Bakhtin in relation to Tertz's writings. See Cohen and Fanger, "Abram Tertz," 170; Aucouturier, "Writer and Text," 4; Holmgren, "Transfiguring of Context," 968. I have discussed Sinyavsky in relation to Bakhtin in an unpublished paper, "Anachronism in Sinjavskij's Prose." I have chosen

not to address this issue in this book primarily because I believe the connections between the two figures to be primarily the result of their common context, rather than of "influence."

Chapter 2. Subversion from Within

1. *Tamizdat,* from the Russian word *tam* ("there") and the root *izdat-* ("publish"), signifies publication abroad, implicitly without official authorization.

What Is Socialist Realism first appeared anonymously and with what the editor's introduction terms "very brief cuts" in French translation in the journal *Esprit* (Anon., "Le réalisme socialiste," *Esprit,* no. 2 [February 1959], 335–67). The first Russian version of the Essay to be published was in fact translated back into Russian from the *Esprit* text. It appeared, attributed to an 'unknown Soviet writer,' under the title 'Sotsrealizm; 'tsel, 'trans. E. Neledinskii, in *Mosty,* no. 2 (1959), 269–302." *The Trial Begins,* released under the name Abram Tertz, was first published in Polish translation in the same year in the *Kultura* Library series together with a Polish translation of *What Is Socialist Realism,* again attributed only to an anonymous writer, (*Abram Terc, Sad idzie [and] Anonim, Co to jest realizm socjalistyczny?* translated by Jozef Lobodowski [Paris: Instytut Literacki, 1959].) *The Trial Begins* first appeared in Russian in a special issue ("devoted to Polish-Russian relations") of the Paris-based Polish emigre journal *Kultura* (Russian issue, May 1960). The foreword [*predislovie*] notes that "Tertz's novella should be read simultaneously with the excellent essay by an anonymous Soviet [writer], *What Is Socialist Realism,* also published by *Kultura*" (Gustav Gerling-Grudzinskii, "Predislovie," 63.) A note on the author accompanying the first English translation of *The Trial Begins* in *Encounter* maintains: "Abram Tertz's story would almost appear to be a practical illustration of the theoretical critique which has been written in Russia under the title, 'What is Socialist Realism?'" ("Authors," *Encounter* 76 [January 1960], 95.)

2. As indicated in the previous note, critics generally have recognized the two works as being in some sense companion pieces. Thus, Robert Maguire maintains that *What Is Socialist Realism* and *The Trial Begins* "together form a single eloquent dialogue" (Maguire, [Review of *On Socialist Realism* and *The Trial Begins*], 193). Richard Lourie also points to the close link between the essay and the novella: "It is best to speak of the novel as a continuation of the essay in a different genre, the artistic concerns of the essay having given the novel its shape, and the philosophical concerns having become the characters and the plot" (Lourie, *Letters to the Future,* 75). Margaret Dalton has referred to *The Trial Begins* as a "fictional 'pendant'" to *What Is Socialist Realism* (Dalton, *Andrei Siniavskii and Julii Daniel',* 34), and W. J. Leatherbarrow's article "The Sense of Purpose and Socialist Realism in Tertz's *The Trial Begins,*" as the title suggests, examines the novella specifically as an illustration of the views expounded in the essay. Hardly surprisingly, given the context in which the works appeared, virtually all critics who have written on the two works have explored them primarily as political and historical documents. Dalton even suggests that

Tertz's claim to be analyzing "aesthetic and psychological premises" in the first part of the essay is merely a blind: "But it probably seemed safer to Tertz to pretend to be speaking about aesthetics and psychology rather than about Communism and Marxism" (22–23). Hugh McLean, in his scathing attack on the translators of *What Is Socialist Realism*, provides a refreshing exception to this tendency. Opining that the essay "far surpasses in literary quality the same author's fictional pieces," he maintains: "From beginning to end it is so charged with semantic electricity, so loaded with meanings and double meanings, that it actually seems to radiate intellectual energy. It is not only an important 'document of our times,' as it has so often been called; it is a major work of literature" (McLean, "Abram Tertz and His Translators, 434.)

On *What Is Socialist Realism*, see also Pevear, "Sinyavsky in Two Worlds," 385–91; Clardy, "Andrei Sinyavsky's 'On Socialist Realism'"; and Alla Marchenko's preface to one of the first Soviet publications of the work during the glasnost period, Marchenko, "Opyt raznomysliya vnutri inakomysliya."

3. The existing English translation of the essay renders the title as *On Socialist Realism* (see translation by George Dennis [New York: Pantheon Books, 1960]). I have chosen to use the more literal translation of the Russian in order to underscore the work's association with the earlier Russian critical tradition discussed in the text.

4. Dalton makes this connection as well. However, rather than viewing *What Is Socialist Realism* as subverting the tradition, she claims that "it follows the tradition of Russian 19th century polemical writings which had combined literary criticism with critique of social conditions, or with exposition of radical ideas" (Dalton, *Andrei Siniavskii and Julii Daniel'*, 27).

5. Quote from Terts, "Chto takoe sotsialisticheskii realizm," in his *Fantasticheskii mir Abrama Tertsa*, 446. Henceforth page numbers from this edition will be given in parentheses in the text.

6. In fact, the title of *What is Socialist Realism* (which might also be translated as "What Socialist Realism Is") does not "pose a question," since, unlike its predecessors listed above, it does not end in a question mark. Thus, Tertz's polemic with the tradition that claims to be able to define art begins with his initial punctuation.

7. I am grateful to Caryl Emerson for pointing out that this observation actually belongs to Dmitry Karamazov. Its implicit attribution to Dostoevsky here thus underscores the blurring of the line between author and character on which this whole section of the argument hinges.

8. These two paragraphs were written later than the rest of the essay and were smuggled out of Russia by Andrei Remizov sometime after the rest of the essay was already in the West.

9. I use here the title as it is literally rendered in the existing English translation. The Russian title of the novella—*Sud idet*—could also, and perhaps more appropriately, be rendered "Court Is in Session," since this phrase in fact opens Russian court proceedings.

10. As Margaret Dalton has written: "While Globov stamps Rabinovich a 'child murderer,' he himself becomes, ironically, a child-murderer when Katia is trampled to death in a stampede at Stalin's funeral" (Dalton, *Andrei*

Siniavskii and Julii Daniel', 38). For other substantive discussions of *The Trial Begins*, see Lourie, *Letters to the Future*, 75–96; Leatherbarrow, "Sense of Purpose and Socialist Realism"; and Chapple, "Bible and Zoo."

11. Terts, "Sud idet," in idem, *Sobranie sochinenii*1:251. Page numbers from this edition will henceforth be given in parentheses in the text.

12. In his article "The Bible and the Zoo in Andrey Sinyavsky's *The Trial Begins*," Richard L. Chapple explores the biblical imagery in the novella, maintaining that the text is structured around a tension between Old Testament and New Testament motifs. Although much of his argument is strained, his suggestion that the image of the Master appearing on high echoes God giving the law to Moses from the top of Mt. Sinai resonates with the theme of law and criminality played out in the text. As we shall see, the image of the writer as a prophet, a vessel transmitting words that emanate from outside himself, recurs throughout the Tertz writings. In this context, W. J. Leatherbarrow points out that "the whole Prologue" of *The Trial Begins* "is a thinly disguised parody of Pushkin's famous poem *The Prophet* (*Prorok*)" ("Sense of Purpose and Socialist Realism," 276). In *Strolls with Pushkin*, Tertz explicitly invokes this 1826 lyric poem, which is generally considered the genesis of the image of the writer as prophet in the Russian tradition.

13. Rabinovich is a stock character in Russian jokes, as are the "two men in civilian clothes." On Tertz's view of jokes as transgressions of taboos and a fertile source for literature, see Terts, "Anekdot v anekdote."

14. I am grateful to Richard Borden for pointing out to me the irony that it is an abortion that "gives birth" to both Globov's plot and the writer's text.

15. Richard Lourie, who generally finds *The Trial Begins* an unsatisfying work, locates one of its deficiencies in apparent inconsistencies in the narrative stance: "The device of the first person narrative, which Sinyavsky puts to good use in his subsequent works, in this tale is weak and not fully developed. The narrator, for example, recounts events (dreams within dreams) that could not be known to him and would seem the rightful property of a third person narrator" (Lourie, *Letters to the Future*, 81–82). He concludes that, "we find [*The Trial Begins*] restless, erratic, *not flowing from a single, stable center*, reflecting the author's difficulty in finding a unified relationship to his fable" (95–96, my emphasis). As I argue below, it is precisely "decentering" that motivates the work's narrative structure.

16. Underscoring the interplay of perspectives in the novella's structure, the narrative shifts to Karlinsky and Marina before allowing Globov to answer his son's question. The intervening segment of the text opens with Karlinsky's words to Marina: "It all depends, dear Marina Pavlovna, on your point of view" (284).

17. The sentence beginning "Planets and stars . . ." does not appear in the cited edition (in the *Sobranie sochinenii*); it seems to have been dropped by mistake. It is present in the version of *The Trial Begins* printed in *Fantasticheskii mir Abrama Tertz*, 232–33.

18. Tolstoi, "Smert' Ivana Il'ycha," 10:180.

19. I take the expression "killed into art" from Gilbert and Gubar, *Madwoman in the Attic*, 17. In equating Marina with a museum exhibit, Karlin-

sky echoes Marina's own attempts throughout the text to turn her body into a work of art, to stop time and freeze her image on the glass of the mirror. The evidence of her body's aging exposes the inherent difference between body and representation: while the human body decays, the body of the sign remains fixed. I would like to thank Richard Borden for having pointed to the link between the text born out of an abortion and Marina, "killed into art." Representation is a form of death, which can, however, give birth to the new body of the text.

20. Oedipus's name means both "swollen foot" and "I know the foot." It is therefore the key to the duality of his identity, because it identifies him as both the child Laius and Jocasta left to die and the ruler of Thebes by virtue of having solved the riddle of the Sphinx. Recognition of his true identity, embedded in the name, entails a recognition of the duality of the self, a realization that he is both son and husband to his mother and both father and brother to his children. Globov's situation resonates with Sophocles's dramatization of the Oedipus myth in the disintegration of his roles as father and husband in relation to his public persona, a rift he attempts to negate by rejecting his family and subordinating himself completely to the Master. Also like Oedipus, Globov sets out to investigate a murder only to discover in the end that he himself is a murderer. For an excellent discussion of naming, self, and reversal in Sophocles's *Oedipus Tyrannus*, see Knox, *Word and Action*, 87–111.

21. Globov pokes his finger into the brain, which does not register any physical reaction to his prodding. Rabinovich's full comment is: "It doesn't hear. It just thinks and thinks, invents ideas. Perhaps it has in his hometown a girl it loves. But it has no legs to go to a rendezvous. How far could you go on its convolutions?" (309–10). This grotesque image of the brain severed from the body plays out the implications of Karlinsky's explication of original sin. Rabinovich's apparently inappropriate response—"It doesn't hear"—to Globov's touching of the brain in fact links the possibility of physical contact with the ability to participate in dialogue. The brain is deprived of both, and the basis of its knowledge is therefore called into doubt, knowledge including, of course, the series of goals that it has generated and that Rabinovich will exhibit to Globov. This image of the brain in *The Trial Begins* may look ahead to Sinyavsky's discussion of Lenin's "hyperbolic cranium" in *Soviet Civilization* (see Sinyavsky, *Soviet Civilization*, 55).

22. I am grateful to Olga Meerson for having pointed out that these lines are from the *Internationale*.

23. In January 1953 a group of doctors, most of them Jewish, were arrested for supposedly conspiring to do away with high-ranking Soviet officials by medical means. The arrests in connection with the "Doctors' Plot" probably were intended to serve as a prelude to a new wave of purges, which was only averted by Stalin's death on March 5, 1953.

24. An enormous crowd gathered to view Stalin's body lying in state in the Hall of Columns in central Moscow. The authorities were unable to manage the situation, and hundreds, perhaps thousands, were crushed to death in the compressed mass of people.

25. It is a measure of the extent to which Sinyavsky fathomed the basic

workings of his society that the charges brought against the narrator—"for slander, pornography, and the divulging of state secrets" (309)—are almost exactly the accusations that were leveled against Sinyavsky himself in the Soviet press and courtroom.

26. This proposition is played out figuratively in the novella in the scene in which Karlinsky stays home from the celebration of the November 7 holiday to listen to the radio. Switching back and forth through Western radio stations, he is overwhelmed by the diversity of voices:

> Yury was an antenna. But he wanted to be a transmitter. To radiate powerful signals of any wave-length. "Attention! Attention! Karlinsky is at the microphone. Listen only to me alone!"
>
> The stations competed with each other in wailing, each about its own interests. They surrounded him like women hawking at the market. . . .
>
> And what could he propose to the world in his own name? One more potpourri of Freud and Hawaiian guitar? Who am I and where am I, original and unique, if the time has come for everyone to speak at once? (288)

When Karlinsky begins to listen to Radio Free Europe, however, the rival voice is literally drowned out by the Soviet authorities: "The angry thunder of a barrage became audible. Our silencers were joining battle" (289). When the foreign radio station is replaced by the sound of marches, Karlinsky turns the radio off. The desire to assert the "I" and the suppression of the "I" both end in a failure of dialogue.

Chapter 3. The Writer as Criminal

1. Ginzburg, *Belaya kniga*, 306.

2. The first Russian-language publication of Tertz writings under this title included five of the six stories generally grouped together under the heading "fantastic stories," as well as *The Trial Begins*. Like *The Trial Begins* and *What Is Socialist Realism*, it was issued by the house that published the journal *Kultura* in the series *Kultura* Library (see Terts, *Fantasticheskie povesti*). "Pkhents" was placed together with the other stories under the heading "fantastic stories" only in a later edition entitled *Fantasticheskii mir Abrama Tertsa*. Margaret Dalton maintains that "the title of the collection clearly points to E. T. A. Hoffmann ("Fantasiestuecke in Callots Manier," 1814–15)" (Dalton, *Andrei Siniavskii and Julii Daniel'*, 49). Andrew Field also traces the title to Hoffmann (Field, "Abram Tertz's Ordeal by Mirror," in Terts, *Mysli vrasplokh*, 10).

Aside from Dalton and Field, a number of other critics have written about the fantastic stories within the context of Tertz's writings. See, e.g., Lourie, *Letters to the Future*, 124–54; Aucouturier, "Writer and Text in the Works of Abram Terc"; Deming Brown, "Art of Andrei Sinyavsky"; Edward J. Brown, "Exodus into *Samizdat* and *Tamizdat*: Sinyavsky," in idem, *Russian Literature since the Revolution*, 238–50; Filippov, "Priroda i tyur'ma"; Mikhailov, *Abram Terts ili begstvo iz retorty;* and Woronzoff, "Writer as Artist and Critic."

However, only Andrew Durkin, in what remains one of the finest studies of Tertz's writings, has examined the stories as a unified whole: "The *Fantastic Tales* are not merely a random collection—they are interrelated by similarities in narrative situation and structure, by their concern with certain basic devices, and by their thematic affinities, in particular each protagonist's search for a way out of an existential impasse. In an intricate system of echoes, each story responds to and develops, in a new way, devices and themes suggested by one or more of its companions; the *Fantastic Tales* represent a set of variations on a limited number of motifs. In this sense the stories are recursive and centripetal, each one enhancing and illuminating our understanding of the others" (Durkin, "Narrator, Metaphor, and Theme," 133).

3. For articles specifically on "Pkhents," see Kolonosky, "Inherent and Ulterior Design"; and Peterson, "Writer as Alien". I have found a number of points made by Kolonosky in his suggestive article particularly helpful in developing my own argument.

4. Early critics had difficulty placing "Pkhents" chronologically in relation to Tertz's other fantastic stories, because it was published only after Sinyavsky's trial. According to Sinyavsky, he had shown it to Sergei Khmelnitsky, who later appeared as a witness against him at the trial and who served as the prototype for the character called alternately S. and Sergei in *Goodnight*. Sinyavsky delayed publication of the story because he feared that Khmelnitsky would give away his identity if the story appeared under the Tertz pseudonym in the West. "Pkhents" is accurately dated 1957 in the two-volume edition of Abram Tertz's writings published in Russia in 1992. It is worth noting that even the season of the year in which the alien arrives on earth seems to correspond to Sinyavsky's birthday. Sinyavsky was born in October, and it appears to be autumn when the spaceship crashes: "Besides, I felt a growing cold in the atmosphere" (Terts, *Sobranie sochinenii*, 1:244.) Page numbers from this edition will henceforth be given in parentheses in the text.

5. Sinyavsky is in fact one-quarter Polish.

6. Kolonosky points to the significance of naming in the story: "To examine the semantic field of names in 'Pxenc' is to discover the first clues to an underlying discourse about difference involving the alien, the author, and Soviet society" (Kolonosky, "Inherent and Ulterior Design," 331).

7. For a history of the evolution of the legend, including a provocative discussion of its sexual implications, see Kuryluk, *Veronica and Her Cloth*.

8. Quotes are from Simmons, *Malevich's Black Square*, 233. For an excellent discussion of the theoretical background of Malevich's conception of the Suprematist quadrilateral, see the chapter, "The Icon Unmasked: 1915," in ibid., 224–53.

9. For example, Kolonosky points out: "The alias of the alien, Andrej Kazimirovič Sušinskij, is a rather bold counterpoint of the name of the author, Andrej Donatovič Sinjavskij, who, like the alien, has also adopted another name" (Kolonosky, "Inherent and Ulterior Design,'" 331). Lourie remarks that "the word 'pkhentz,' which the hero remembers from his native tongue, sounds suspiciously like 'Tertz'" (Lourie, *Letters to the Future*,

154), and Olga Matich observes: "Tertz's alienation was much more extreme, as expressed in the image of the extraterrestrial outsider in the short story 'Pkhents,' whose title is reminiscent of the sound combination 'Tertz'" (Matich, "Russian Literature in Emigration," 17).

10. Kolonsky and Field make this assumption (Kolonosky, "Inherent and Ulterior Design,'" 332; Field, "Abram Tertz's Ordeal by Mirror," 34).

11. *Rezhut* here also has the connotation of slitting someone's throat.

12. Leopold Sergeevich, as a double who physically "mirrors" the narrator, suggests a subtle subversion of realism. While the narrator's body becomes a figure of the fantastic text, of that which has no referent in reality, Leopold Sergeevich, who has the ability to mimic human beings, to play the "classic role of the humpback" (240) and who turns out to be none other than what he appears to be, suggests an image of the realist text. We should also note that Veronica, spurned by the narrator, marries an actor from the Stanislavsky Theater.

13. I would like to thank Shawn Vietor for having pointed out that the image of the preserved corpse past which viewers file may be read as a parodic allusion to Lenin's mummified body preserved in a mausoleum on Red Square. Benjamin Cramer also suggested that the image recalls Peter the Great's collection of human organs, rarities, and monsters in the Kunstkammer in Petersburg. When I relayed these observations to Sinyavsky in May 1994, he pointed out that, as he writes in *Soviet Civilization*, Lenin's brain was preserved in alcohol (see the brain in Globov's dream in *The Trial Begins*).

14. I am grateful to Richard Borden for having suggested this observation to me.

15. The narrator also laments that one of his eyes was damaged in 1934. Kolonosky and Peterson have recognized this as a reference to the first Congress of Soviet Writers at which Socialist Realism was proclaimed the official method of Soviet literature (Kolonosky, "Inherent and Ulterior Design," 337; Peterson, "Writer as Alien," 49).

16. Aucouturier sees the title and conclusion of "Pkhents" as examples of what he terms "'Tercian' *zaum*," which, he argues, is the extreme manifestation of "the notion of 'the text as an object'" and gives "the effect of 'transmental language,' devoid of external reference" (Aucouturier, "Writer and Text," 6). Although he does not discuss the concept of the image "not made by hands" in relation to "Pkhents," Aucouturier does pose it as the impossible ideal to which "the poetics of the text as material object, independent of any external reference [3]" manifested in Tertz's works aspires. Durkin's reading of the ending complements Aucouturier's by implicitly seeing in it an image of the "death of the author": "While 'Pxenc' admits of interpretation as an allegory of the plight of the modern intellectual or as yet another reworking of the Platonic myth of the soul trapped in an inferior world dimly recalling its former existence, these readings may perhaps be best seen as corollaries to the basic 'linguistic' failure of the narrator, who finds language, as a conventional system devised by human culture, ultimately meaningless, useless, and uncontrollable, and who must seek tran-

scendence even at the price of annihilation" (Durkin, "Narrator, Metaphor, and Theme," 135).

17. See Kolonosky's reading of the alien as "a Christ-figure" ("Inherent and Ulterior Design,'" 333–34).

18. Lourie writes of "Pkhents" that "the story is really a portrait of man after the Fall, the Expulsion" (*Letters to the Future*, 151). Boris Filippov suggests a Neo-Platonic reading of the story: "The Platonic teaching about the soul-psyche, which flew into our corporeal world and is imprisoned in the prison of the flesh, is vividly incarnated in this small story" (Filippov, "Priroda i tyur'ma," 19).

19. The first mention of the diary comes when the narrator "penetrates" her room to borrow the ink. The episode both plays on the parallel with Christ, in the absence of physical contact, and simultaneously marks a "failure" in relation to the postulation of an equation between body and material inscribed in the legend of the veil.

20. Terts, "V tsirke," in his *Sobranie sochinenii*, 1:115. Page numbers from this edition will henceforth be given in parentheses in the text. For a complementary reading of this story in relation to Tertz's emigre criticism, see Nepomnyashchy, "Sinyavsky/Tertz." Tertz writes in *A Voice from the Chorus*, apparently playing with the name of this story and the image it embodies: "Generally speaking, almost all that remains from the fairy tale is now to be found in the circus. Sorcerer—magician—thief: the evolution of an image. With the circus I began. It's necessary to end with the circus as well." (Terts, "Golos iz khora," in his *Sobranie sochinenii* 1:577.) Despite the centrality of the imagery initiated in this story to Tertz's *oeuvre*, "At the Circus" has received relatively little attention from critics and has been discussed only in surveys.

21. Here Sinyavsky plays with the fact that the name Judas has become a synonym for traitor in Russian, as it has in English. Kostya does not think of Judas by name, but uses his name—uncapitalized in the expression *iuda predatel'*—metaphorically.

22. Aucouturier, "Writer and Text," 3, 8.

Chapter 4. Confrontations with God

1. Richard Lourie terms "You and I" "a mixed success" (*Letters to the Future*, 132), while Deming Brown finds it "hopelessly chaotic and abstruse" ("Art of Andrei Sinyavsky," 334). Margaret Dalton maintains that the story resists set interpretation altogether, that it "seems to be more of a grotesque and macabre exercise on a theme by Gogol' or Dostoevskii" and lacks a "key" (*Andrei Siniavskii and Julii Daniel'*, 71).

2. Henrikh Ivanovich Graube is in the tradition of such russified Germans as Pushkin's Hermann in "The Queen of Spades," while Lida recalls the recurring image of the virtuous prostitute. Andrew Field, who considers "You and I" one of Tertz's "two best" fantastic tales, views it as an "examination of paranoia and internal sexual conflict" ("Abram Tertz's Ordeal by Mirror," 11). Lourie considers the story not entirely successful, "in part be-

cause it deals with both paranoia and schizophrenia" (*Letters to the Future,* 136). There is a tantalizing echo of Lourie's remark in *In the Shadow of Gogol,* where Tertz suggests that Gogol was simultaneously paranoid and schizophrenic.

3. For a complementary reading of the story from this point of view, see Nepomnyashchy, "Andrei Sinyavsky's 'You and I.'" Mihajlo Mihajlov preceded me in identifying the narrator of "You and I" as God (*Begstvo iz retorty,* 18). Andrew Durkin, while he does not explicitly read the narrator as God, recognizes the significance of the epigraph: "The epigraph, the only one in the *Fantastic Tales,* also suggests the psychological illusory, or metaphorical nature of the duel between the doubles; from Genesis, it concerns Jacob who, though alone, wrestled with an angel until dawn. Without the transcendence of self possible through love, the ego is trapped in endless and sterile contemplation of and struggle with its mirror image, unable to resolve the contradiction of its own impotence and powerlessness" ("Narrator, Metaphor, and Theme," 141). Dalton, also pointing to the importance of the epigraph, asks: "But is this 'I' God in the literal sense? Tertz's vision, at least as far as it is possible to judge from his fiction up to that point, is hardly religious in a conventional orthodox sense. It appears rather that what Tertz wanted to express was a philosophical idea (distorted by his phantasmagoric devices), namely, the relativity of existence (Nikolai Vasilevich), which is conditioned by the presence of consciousness ('I')" (*Andrei Siniavskii and Julii Daniel',* 75–76). Edith Clowes, who views the relationship between the "I" and the "you" in the story as "a struggle between an omniscient author/ narrator, 'I', and his protagonist," argues: "Terts does begin his story with a quotation from Genesis 32:24 which refers to Jacob's nocturnal struggle with an unseen force, God. At dawn God calls a truce and appoints Jacob to lead the nation of Israel. This reference to God can only be seen as ironic: there is no such heroic outcome in *Ty i ia*" (Clowes, "Kafka and Russian Experimental Fiction," 153, 154).

4. Terts, "Ty i ya," in his *Sobranie sochinenii,* 1:128. Page numbers from this edition will henceforth be given in parentheses in the text.

5. Edith Clowes comments on this passage: "Early in the story Terts uses an extended pun with the word '*utka*' or 'duck' to give a witty clue that his whole narrative construct is a fraud perpetrated by an irresponsible author on his characters. A 'duck' in Russian is the same as a 'red herring' in English. Ducks are served at Graube's gala anniversary dinner, implying that the hosts' '*pustiat utku*' or are throwing out a red herring" (Clowes, "Kafka and Russian Experimental Fiction," 155). I agree that the "duck" is indeed a "red herring," but one that distracts the "you" from the true source of surveillance.

6. Alexander Woronzoff uses these passages as an illustration of his contention that, "From 'V cirke' to *Progulki s Puškinym,* Sinjavskij's method depends on the initial splitting, subsequent fragmentation, and final dissolution of narrative voice" (Woronzoff, "Writer as Artist and Critic," 139). "By the time Sinjavskij comes to write 'Ty i ja,'" Woronzoff maintains, "the narrator's panoramic perception of events is totally fragmented" (ibid, 142).

7. I am grateful to Sylvie Richards for having pointed out that Jacob is

himself a thief who has stolen his birthright from his brother Esau through deception and who, in struggling with God at Pēn-ī-ēl, seeks and in the end receives legitimacy as the keeper of the covenant.

8. The "third person" here refers not only to Lida's role in the triangle she forms with the "you" and the "I," but also to the grammatical third person, to which the narrator resorts in the fifth section for the first time. Just as the shift to the grammatical third person marks a final collapse of the aborted dialogue between the "you" and the "I," so Lida, rather than ameliorating the situation, spurs on the course of events.

9. Mihajlov suggests that "it is no accident that the name of the story is identical with Martin Buber's fundamental philosophical work, *I and Thou*" (*Begstvo iz retorty*, 18). Sinyavsky has maintained that he did not read *I and Thou* until after he had written "You and I." His vision nonetheless seems to dovetail with that of Buber.

10. Buber, *I and Thou*, 112. Page numbers from this edition will henceforth be given in parentheses in the text.

11. In this context, Lida's name suggests a conflation of Liza, a stock name for the type of the "fallen woman" (Karamzin's "Poor Liza," Dostoevsky's *Notes from the Underground*) and Leda. In Greek mythology Leda was seduced by Zeus in the guise of a swan and as a result of this union gave birth to Helen of Troy.

12. "KNYAZ' KHRISTOS," an epithet Dostoevsky recorded in the manuscript variants of *The Idiot* (Dostoevskii, "Idiot. Rukopisnye redaktsii," in his *Polnoe sobranie sochinenii*, 9:246, 249). See also Miller, "Notions of Narrative," 169.

13. Dostoevskii, *Polnoe sobranie sochinenii*, 8:338–39. Page numbers from this edition will henceforth be given in parentheses in the text. Julia Kristeva discusses the Holbein painting as a challenge to the limits of meaning and representation in the chapter "Holbein's Dead Christ" in idem, *Black Sun*, 107–38. I am grateful to Deborah Martinsen for having brought this book to my attention.

14. Terts, "Grafomany," in his *Sobranie sochinenii*, 1:154. Page numbers from this edition will henceforth be given in parentheses in the text.

15. As critics have pointed out, Tertz endows his characters with suggestive names in "Graphomaniacs" as well. *Straustin* derives from the Russian word for "ostrich" (*straus*), which alludes to the character's propensity to hide from a true vision of himself. Galkin's name comes from the word for "jackdaw" (*galka*). These bird names suggest a humorous allusion to Gogol, whose surname also means "golden-eye," a species of bird (see Durkin, "Narrator, Metaphor, and Theme," 138; Lourie, *Letters to the Future*, 144).

16. At the time of the story's writing Tverskoi Boulevard in Moscow was called Pushkin Boulevard. In a conversation with me in May 1994, Sinyavsky maintained that the idea behind this sentence is that literature is "drying up." It is worth noting in this context that the most famous monument to Pushkin, A. M. Opekushin's statue of the poet, stands on Pushkin Square, which is located at the intersection of Tverskaya (formerly Gorky) Street and Tverskoi Boulevard.

17. We should note here that, while Straustin plans to end *In Search of Joy* with this phrase, he begins "Graphomaniacs" with it.

18. Dalton argues: "Straustin tries to be a realist, even a socialist realist. This is evidenced by his themes (the Revolution and Civil War, both of which are personally unknown to him), by his optimistic titles ('In Search of Happiness,' 'The Sun Rises over the Steppe,' 'Man'), by his dislike of 'modern' poetry (such as Galkin's), and his attentiveness to realistic details (e.g. when he scrutinizes Galkin at the beginning of the story). . . . Yet despite his attempts to follow the official demands, he does not succeed—perhaps because an art form artificially forced upon a writer becomes nothing but a dead weight around his neck, and can never come to life" (*Andrei Siniavskii and Julii Daniel'*, 59.)

19. Aucouturier points to the importance of the concept of "self-elimination" articulated here by Galkin to Tertz's concept of creation and, looking ahead to the later Tertz writings, links it with role playing: "To imitate the speech of someone else, to 'play' it as one would a role, is the easiest way of 'self-elimination'" ("Writer and Text," 5). Dalton points out, adopting Tertz's terminology from *What Is Socialist Realism*, that it is "purposeless": "The question of greatness and fame is secondary to this involuntary, irrational, purposeless urge, in Galkin's opinion" (*Andrei Siniavskii and Julii Daniel'*, 62). It is worth noting that Straustin ends up by committing precisely the "crime" of which he accuses others: he "steals" Galkin's words in incorporating them into his own text. I am grateful to Mallika Ramdas for having suggested this aspect of the image of the writer as criminal, a thief of the words of others, in a discussion of *A Voice from the Chorus*.

20. Durkin reads this scene in terms of the metaphor of the author as God, claiming that "Straustin's flight into literature and metaphor reaches a crisis in which he metaphorically converts the world into a text, but himself into a mere instrument in the hands of its Author" ("Narrator, Metaphor, and Theme," 138). He further connects this insight to Tertz's portrayal of Gogol in *In the Shadow of Gogol* and maintains that "Straustin seems to be refusing to play the game and his revolt is directed against either Sinjavskij or God, depending on one's viewpoint" (143). Dalton, while not recognizing the "Author" here as God, does, like Mihajlov, discern an incursion of the supernatural: "Straustin's graphomanic urge acquires also some strange, supernatural overtones, suggestive of powers beyond his control, as seen during his walk home" (*Andrei Siniavskii and Julii Daniel'*, 64; see also Mikhailov, *Begstvo iz retorty*, 16).

21. Jonah's submission to God is temporary, however. When God sends him to Nineveh, he is angered by what he believes to be God's unwarranted mercy toward the sinners of the city and again rebels.

Chapter 5. The Fantastic as Metaphor

1. "Icy Weather" and *Lyubimov* are rendered in the standard English translations of the texts respectively "The Icicle" and *The Makepeace Experiment*. (See Abram Tertz, "The Icicle," in *Fantastic Stories*, translated by

Max Hayward and Ronald Hingley [New York: Pantheon, 1963]; and Abram Tertz, *The Makepeace Experiment*, translated by Manya Harari [New York: Pantheon, 1965]. Both of these translations have recently been reprinted by Northwestern University Press.) Since these translations of the titles mask and misrepresent their significance to the two texts, I have chosen to use more accurate English titles.

2. See Dalton, *Andrei Siniavskii and Julii Daniel'*, 65; Deming Brown, "Art of Andrei Sinyavsky," 335; and Lourie, *Letters to the Future*, 139. F. D. Reeve inexplicably suggests that, " 'The Tenants' is a dialogue between the self and an imaginary—or perhaps real—male friend, culminating in a suggested homosexual experience" (Reeve, "Listen for the Pistol Shot," 746).

3. Terts, "Kvartiranty," in his *Sobranie sochinenii*, 1:154. Page numbers from this edition will henceforth be given in parentheses in the text. The expression *napit'sya do chertikov* echoes an earlier phrase in "Tenants"; the narrator reports in this way the judgment passed on the writer by Shestopalov (initially introduced by the narrator as his former boss and the person who "decides apartment questions" [144]): "We won't particularly concern ourselves with the writer. Considering that he's an alcoholic and will soon be fancying he sees real devils [*emy nastoyashchie cherti skoro nachnut mereshchit'sya*]" (150). Both Dalton and Durkin point out that the name of one of the tenants, Anchutker, is derived from the word "anchutka," a dialect term for devil, which, Durkin observes, occurs in the expression "dopit'sya do anchutkov" (Durkin, "Narrator, Metaphor, and Theme," 143; Dalton, *Andrei Siniavskii and Julii Daniel'*, 179). In conversation in May 1994 Sinyavsky confirmed this derivation of Anchutker's name, but said he did not know the expression "dopit'sya do anchutkov." He added that he had affixed the ending "er" to make the name sound "Jewish."

4. The phrase "wordless creature" is in fact applied to another character, Ninochka, who was, the narrator maintains, transformed into a rat before the story began. The same fate apparently awaits the writer at the story's end.

5. Durkin, "Narrator, Metaphor, and Theme," 136.

6. The Russian text reads "*Za razglashenie ikhnikh sekretov*," echoing the official Soviet juridical formula, *za razglashenie gosudarstvennykh tain* ("for divulging state secrets").

7. Terts "Gololeditsa," in his *Sobranie sochinenii*, 1:180. Page numbers from this edition will henceforth be given in parentheses in the text.

8. The Russian here is *uchastie*, which also means "participation." Like the narrator of "Tenants," the narrator of "Icy Weather" is, in a sense, inviting his reader to participate in the process of narration.

9. Dalton, for instance, claims that the narrator's adduction of "proofs for his theory in various deviations from the norm, among the physically deformed, and the mad . . . raise[s] the question of the narrator's own sanity" (*Andrei Siniavskii and Julii Daniel'*, 84, 85).

10. I am grateful to Deborah Martinsen for having pointed out that this image suggests pregnancy.

11. This passage is echoed in statements on "character" in *A Voice from*

the Chorus, which will be discussed below, as well as in Sinyavsky's article "Dostoevskii i katorga."

12. Deming Brown and Margaret Dalton have commented on the ice imagery in the story. Brown maintains: "In the story 'The Icicle' an icicle hanging menacingly above a Moscow sidewalk becomes the symbol of inescapable fate, whose power transcends even that of the hero's clairvoyance and, as an ironic reminder of the ultimate freezing of the planet, of the absurdity of the 'march of history'" ("Art of Andrei Sinyavsky," 342). Dalton suggests that "the title of the tale is Tertz's answer to Erenberg's *Thaw*" and that "the symbol of the icicle and ice-covered ground that runs through the tale . . . refers not only to the time period of the plot, delineated by the narrator's first vision (the ice-covered ravine) and his last one (again, a glacial landscape); it seems also to suggest a certain cyclic repetition of historical periods: ice at the beginning of time, ice again in the future, rather than continuous progress of humanity, a 'golden age' of Communism. Perhaps there is also some significance in the fact that Natasha is killed by an icicle (a fact which could, perhaps, have been avoided, had colonel Tarasov not been so fearful of overstepping 'Soviet legality' in arresting her, as the narrator had requested" (*Andrei Siniavskii and Julii Daniel'*, 92, 91). Dalton's suggestion that it is precisely Tarasov's insistence on sticking to the letter of the law that brings on Natasha's demise, which is metaphorically equivalent to his own transformation into an icicle, is particularly interesting. It also calls to mind the association of classicism, "frozen" form, with ice in *What Is Socialist Realism* and *The Trial Begins.*

13. During his questioning at the trial, Sinyavsky defended *Lyubimov* against critics who would reduce it to political allegory: "*Lyubimov* is my last work. I gave this backwater my beloved traits of the wondrous and the fantastic. Specters walk through the town, people are transformed. This is invention. There is in much there the motif of seeming, invisibility. It is the unreal town of my soul. It is a lyrical, and not a political, work. And it is not political satire, as those who have compared my *Lyubimov* with Shchedrin's *Glupov* think. I am against such comparisons; one should at least know how to read the title. Shchedrin's *Glupov* comes from the word 'stupid' [*glupyi*], while my *Lyubimov* comes from the word 'beloved'—I love, to love [*lyubimyi, lyublyu, lyubit'*]" (Ginzburg, *Belaya kniga*, 229). Sinyavsky was clearly trying to distance *Lyubimov* from Saltykov-Shchedrin's *History of a Town,* a text subordinated to the ends of political satire. This should not, however, discredit the insights of those critics who have postulated textual echoes of the earlier work in *Lyubimov.* (See especially Dalton, *Andrei Siniavskii and Julii Daniel'*, 99, 108.)

14. The "two men in civilian clothes," Vitya and Tolya, reappear in *Lyubimov* endowed with the names of the official Soviet writers Vitaly Kochetov and Anatoly Sofronov. (Sinyavsky had published a disparaging review of Sofronov's writing in *Novyi mir,* and Kochetov seems to have taken revenge on the reference to him in an article after the trial attacking Sinyavsky [*Belaya kniga,* 373–75].) In a letter he writes to Tolya in *Lyubimov,* Vitya traces the fantastic premise of *Lyubimov* back to *The Trial Begins:* "'Do you remember, Tolya, how we strolled through quiet Moscow and, discussing

books we had read, exchanged news about the technology of security? What did we, rookie spooks, understand? I think that it was nothing but a beautiful dream. However, Tolya, we, like children, dreamed of an apparatus for servicing the brain, which would photograph the thoughts in a person's head. Now I can give you the glad tidings that such an apparatus exists, and even more technological in relation to our utopia" (Terts, "Lyubimov," *Sobranie sochinenii,* 1:85). (Page numbers from this edition will henceforth be given in parentheses in the text.) Despite the continuities between the earlier and later works, Lourie goes a bit far in suggesting that "there are so many similarities [between *Lyubimov* and *The Trial Begins*] that, in fact, the former can be seen as something of a rewrite of the latter" (Lourie, *Letters to the Future,* 169).

15. Aucouturier observes: "When the story ends, and the dissidence of Ljubimov has been suppressed, the city of Ljubimov no longer exists, has never existed. All that is left is *Ljubimov* the book, for which Savely Kuz'mič carries full responsibility. The book has become his own subject matter. There is no reality of reference but the text itself" (Aucouturier, "Writer and Text," 3). (This represents a slightly modified restatement of an argument he makes in Aucouturier, *"Lioubimov,"* 275.)

16. Here Tertz seems to be playing on the Russian expression for "scapegoat" (*kozel otpushcheniya*), which ironizes Lenya's insistence on the Russian etymology of her name. The name Serafima suggests an allusion to Pushkin's "The Prophet," in which a seraphim acts as the intermediary between God and the man summoned to be His prophet. Thus, like the Master in *The Trial Begins*, Serafima is marked as usurping a divine prerogative in assigning her task. Here Lenya is explicitly prompted to pursue his goal, at least initially, by desire, thus suggesting that the roots of teleology lie in eros. In conversation in May 1994, Sinyavsky also suggested that Serafima's name is a play on the expression "Ty ne serafima, ty khiroshima" ("You're not an angel, you're Hiroshima").

17. The concluding words of Tishchenko's speech and the description of the crowd's reaction, "The people were silent" (*Narod bezmolvstvoval,* 22), echo the concluding line (in which the False Dmitry is named tsar) and the final stage direction ("the people are silent" [*Narod bezmolvstvuet*]) of Pushkin's *Boris Godunov,* suggesting that Lenya, like his historical predecessor, should be viewed as an impostor.

18. See, Dalton, *Andrei Siniavskii and Julii Daniel',* 111; Filippov, "Priroda i tyur'ma," 17; Lourie, *Letters to the Future,* 168.

19. Three of the four gospels make mention of two criminals—identified as "thieves" in the King James Edition of the Bible (*razboiniki* in the Russian)—crucified to the right and the left of Christ at Golgotha. Matthew 27:44 and Mark 15:32 merely state that these other victims "reviled" Jesus. Luke 23:39–43, however, differentiates the two: "And one of the malefactors which were hanged railed on him, saying, If thou be Christ, save thyself and us. But the other answering rebuked him, saying, Dost not thou fear God, seeing thou art in the same condemnation? And we indeed justly; for we receive the due reward of our deeds: but this man hath done nothing amiss. And he said unto Jesus, Lord, remember me when thou comest into

thy kingdom. And Jesus said unto him. Verily I say unto thee. To day shalt thou be with me in paradise."

20. Deming Brown has termed it "in part, a novel about novel-writing, a novel that talks to itself" ("Art of Andrei Sinyavsky," 339).

21. For various readings of the interaction of narrative voices in *Lyubimov*, see Aucouturier, "Lioubimov," 275–76; idem, "Writer and Text," 4–5; Deming Brown, "Art of Andrei Sinyavsky," 339; Edward Brown, *Russian Literature since the Revolution*, 242–43; Dalton, *Andrei Siniavskii and Julii Daniel'*, 124–28; Woronzoff, "Writer as Artist and Critic," 142–43; Rufus W. Mathewson, Jr., *Positive Hero in Russian Literature*, 346–47.

22. The text reads: "I became a passionate reader when I became head of the town reading room. At first—from nothing to do, then—I became keen. Then I tried myself, with verses. I saw that it was turning out, even in rhyme. But it still seemed as if I was missing something, but what—I myself didn't know. Then I remembered the professor who came to Lyubimov in 1926. Oh, I thought, if only something [*istoriya*] were to happen in our town—like a fire or a judicial investigation [*sudebnoe sledstvie*]—I would immediately immortalize it on paper for future posterity" (17). Here there is clearly a play on the dual meaning of *istoriya* as both "story" and "history." Savely's reference to a "judicial investigation" as an appropriate plot moreover forms part of the counterpoint of legality and illegality that runs as a leitmotif throughout the text.

23. The Russian here, *samopishushchee pero*, literally means "self-writing pen," thus underscoring the idea of the writing process's being out of the author's control.

24. Vladimir Alexandrov's fine article comparing typographical devices as a means of representing the transcendent in *Lyubimov* and in Bely's *Petersburg* contains an extended discussion of the function of the footnotes in the Tertz novel in relation to other intrusive voices in the text (Alexandrov, "Typographical Intrusion"). Alexandrov points out that footnotes are "often the domain of the otherworldly in the novel" (178) and that "both Lyonya and the narrator are subject to the same transcendent forces" (177).

25. [N. Bokov], "Andrei Sinyavsky on Dissidence," 92.

26. Erica Haber points out that the "seemingly accidental mention of a pterodactyl represents the first sign of interference from the second narrator" and observes: "The pterodactyl that Savelij Kuzmič claimed did not exist in the town when Samson Samsonovič boldly slipped the word into the text in the prologue, suddenly appears at the end of chapter three. Not just a word in the text, this time it appears as a living creature. In this instance, Sinjavskij-Terc foregrounds the shift in signification between the verbal construct 'pterodactyl' and the flying reptile itself—the very naming of which is enough to make it a reality in the text" (Haber, "Dueling Narrators," 4, 8). I would like to express my gratitude to Erica Haber for having given me a copy of this paper.

27. Sinyavsky, *Soviet Civilization*, 88.

Chapter 6. "It Is Forbidden to Write Like That"

1. *"Opavshie list'ya" V. V. Rozanova* is based on a series of lectures Sinyavsky delivered at the Sorbonne in 1974–75. It is an "academic" work and is therefore attributed to Sinyavsky, rather than Tertz. For the influence of Rozanov on Tertz, see Edward Brown, *Russian Literature since the Revolution*, 247; Dalton, *Andrei Siniavskii and Julii Daniel'*, 129; Field, "Abram Tertz's Ordeal by Mirror," 33; Lourie, *Letters to the Future*, 97–116 passim; Gul', "Abram Terts: *Mysli vrasplokh*," 276; and Holmgren, *First-person Liberties*, 143–45.

2. Sinyavsky, *"Opavshie list'ya,"* 187. Page numbers from this edition will henceforth be given in parentheses in the text.

3. Marcus Levitt uses the locution "dead Rozanovian 'fallen leaves'" to distinguish Tertz's experiment in form in *A Voice from the Chorus* from Rozanov's writing (Levitt, "Siniavskii's Alternative Autobiography," 50).

4. Quotes are from Terts, *Mysli vrasplokh*, in his *Sobranie sochinenii*, 1:313, 338. Henceforth page numbers from this edition will be given in parentheses in the text. Lourie suggests that the opening and closing passages of *Thoughts Unawares* echo the opening of Rozanov's *Fallen Leaves* (Lourie, *Letters to the Future*, 104).

5. Woronzoff argues: "Sinjavskij's initial, creative impulse is located in his answer to the many voices he discovers in himself: 'Zhivesh' durak durakom, no inogda v golovu lezut prevoskhodnye mysli.' The author's divided voice becomes more and more fragmented until it can be compared to disconnected tracks in the snow. . . . In the end, fragmentation leads to a distrust of text, dissolution of narrative voice, and silence: Mysli konchayutsya i bol'she ne prikhodyat, kak tol'ko nachinaesh' ikh sobirat' i obdumyvat' . . . .' Thus, it is the last thought that completes the first, and all thoughts found in *Mysli vrasplokh* are the product of Sinjavskij's subjective, divided voice" (Woronzoff, "Writer as Artist and Critic," 140).

6. Field observes that the "random thoughts" presented in *Thoughts Unawares* "are, of course, far from random in thought or organization. . . . The first and last thoughts, most obviously, constitute a very 'literary' beginning and end" (Field, "Abram Tertz's Ordeal by Mirror," 31, 32).

7. The portrayal of sex and the body in Tertz's early works, especially *Thoughts Unawares*, has drawn a fair amount of attention from critics. Both Dalton and Lourie distinguish Tertz's portrayal of sex from Rozanov's. Dalton finds "a strong rejection of the flesh" in *Thoughts Unawares* and claims that "Tertz feels disgust for the body." She writes of "Tertz's negative feelings evoked by sex" (*Andrei Siniavskii and Julii Daniel'*, 129, 130). Lourie writes, "It is not that Sinyavsky is so much repelled by sex as that he is both strongly repelled and attracted by it. In fact, there is a sort of secondary repulsion for him—repulsion at being so attracted" (*Letters to the Future*, 107). Deming Brown observes, "Sinyavsky is not an erotic writer. Sterility and impotence, and the ugly, perverse, and spiritually destructive features of sex are so heavily emphasized that sex as an aspect of love is almost thoroughly excluded" (Brown, "Art of Andrei Sinyavsky," 349). Field

maintains that "Tertz-Sinyavsky seems to have a fierce aversion to the sex act" and even speculates that "it is a matter for serious debate as to whether Tertz-Sinyavsky's portrayal of women is an 'exorcism' of sex in general, or whether, on a lower plane, it is specifically an exploration of the latent homosexuality in all men" (Field, "Abram Tertz's Ordeal by Mirror," 17, 19).

While there is certainly a distinct difference between Tertz's treatment of sex in his early works and his later writings, I try here to suggest how *Thoughts Unawares* contains a hint of Tertz's later treatment of the subject as a metaphor for art. It is worth noting, in this context, that the postulation of the centrality of love to creation and the concomitant discovery of the ideal reader in the beloved woman, first introduced in "Icy Weather," does constitute one of the most significant features of Tertz's evolution.

8. This Ukrainian proverb lampoons non sequiturs. We might say in English, "The moon is shining; what's Jack Robinson got to do with it?"

9. At Sinyavsky's trial the judge was particularly incensed by these statements on the thievery and drunkenness of the Russian people: "Why did you hunt up this libel? This is our people, the Russian people, who make sacrifices, who made sacrifices in a terrible war, suffered, forged the steel of victory, lost twenty million people, but endured and created a great culture. These are 'thieves' and 'drunks'? Do not forget that you are being tried by a court of the Russian Federation!" (Ginzburg, *Belaya kniga*, 227).

10. Holmgren, *First-Person Liberties*, 152.

11. A number of critics have recognized a continuity between *Thoughts Unawares* and *A Voice from the Chorus* e.g., Ivask, "'Golos iz khora' Sinyavskogo," 101; Hayward, "Sinyavsky's *A Voice from the Chorus*," 276; Kolonosky, "Andrei Siniavskii: Chorus and Critic," 352; Muchnic, "Light from Above," 8; Tikos, "On Abram Tertz's *A Voice from the Choir*," 169. Beth Holmgren points specifically to the evolution of the kenotic model of self: "In his *Mysli vrasplokh* (1966), another journal of fragments completed before his arrest, Terts reveals that spiritual purity can be attained only by renouncing the material world and obliterating the personality, an ideal he finds already achieved in the self-effacing 'nobody' of Christ. This model is restated in *Golos iz khora* as both general article of belief and specific prerequisite for the artist" (Holmgren, "Transfiguring of Context," 968–69.) She elsewhere observes, however: "We find that *Golos*, while appropriating and elaborating the formal structure of *Mysli*, differs from its predecessor in its preponderant focus on art" (Holmgren, *First-Person Liberties*, 157–58.)

For discussions of *A Voice from the Chorus* (including substantive book reviews and surveys), see also Aucouturier, "Writer and Text," 3, 8; Clarence Brown, "*A Voice from the Chorus* by Abram Tertz (Andrei Sinyavsky)"; Gifford, "Andrey Sinyavsky: The Voice and the Chorus"; Golomshtok, "Posleslovie"; Kott, "A Voice from the Chorus"; Levitt, "Siniavskii's Alternative Autobiography"; Ruth Mathewson, "Sinyavsky's Mission"; Meerson, "Progulka s Tertsem"; Nussbaum, "Literary Selves"; Scammell, "Speculations of a Captive Monk," 626–27; Woronzoff, "Writer as Artist and Critic," 140–41. My analysis is particularly indebted to Marcus Levitt's excellent analysis of *A Voice from the Chorus*.

12. As Max Hayward points out in his introduction to the English trans-

lation (reprinted in idem, *Writers in Russia, 1917–1978*, 281), the title of *A Voice from the Chorus* is drawn from Aleksandr Blok's lyric poem of the same name. The poem presents an unremittingly gloomy vision of the "cold and darkness of coming days," exhorting the addressee: "Be satisfied with your life, quieter than water, lower than grass," for the imminent future will bring "the final age, most terrible of all" [Blok, "Golos iz khora," *Sobranie sochinenii* 3:62–63). While Blok's apocalypic vision would seem to find little resonance in *A Voice from the Chorus*, the image of the poet as prophet is, as I shall argue, central to Tertz's text. It is, moreover, tempting to suggest that Sinyavsky may have had at the back of his mind in choosing the title Blok's words (with which Sinyavsky is familiar) on the occasion of reading the poem at the Union of Poets on 29 September 1920:

> The session ended by their taking turns reading poems. Blok read no more than five or six poems. Everyone fell silent under the spell of his voice. And when no one expected him to continue, Aleksandr Aleksandrovich began the last: *A Voice from the Chorus*. His face, hitherto calm, was distorted by a tormented crease near his mouth; his voice rang hollowly, as if cracked. He hunched forward a little in his armchair, heavy lids fell over his eyes, half closing them. He pronounced the last lines almost in a whisper, with agonizing strain, as if forcing himself.
>
> And a kind of depressing feeling gripped us all. No one wanted to recite more. But Blok was the first to smile and said in his normal voice:
>
> "Very unpleasant lines. I don't know why I wrote them. It would have been better to leave these words unspoken. But I had to say them. One must overcome what is difficult. And afterward there will be a clear day. . . . And you know, let's read something from Pushkin. Nikolai Stepanovich, now it's your turn." Gumilyov was not at all surprised by this suggestion and after a moment's pause began:
>
> > Skirmish behind the hills;
> > Their camp and ours look:
> > On the hill in front of the Cossacks
> > The red cap waves.
>
> Pushkin's bright name discharged the general tension. [Mochulsky, *Aleksandr Blok*, 422.]

Sinyavsky was, of course, writing *Strolls with Pushkin* at the same time as *A Voice from the Chorus* (although he thought up the conception and title of the latter only later). Both works in a sense "overcome what is difficult."

13. [Nepomnyashchy], "Interview with Andrei Sinyavsky," 12. Original translation slightly altered.

14. Igor Golomshtok, in his afterword to the original Russian edition of *A Voice from the Chorus*, correlates the external history of Sinyavsky's incarceration in hard labor camps, in the system known under the umbrella term Dubrovlag, with the sections into which *A Voice from the Chorus* is divided:

> From March 1966 to January 1967 (i.e., for the duration of the first chapter-year of the book) Sinyavsky was in the small (several

hundred prisoners) camp with the peaceful name "Sosnovka [pine grove]", the basic contingent of which was made up of so-called "religious" offenders—chiefly old men with considerable, decades-long, terms of imprisonment, who were absolutely convinced of the truth of their faith and preferred the rigors of camp life to intercourse with the devil (i.e., from their point of view, with the Soviet authorities). Then he was transferred to the administrative center of this enormous country of prisoners—to Yavas (I—you! [*Ya—vas!*]—a name strangely appropriate to the place where the authorities punish offenders from the intelligentsia). Here a motley crowd of "war criminals," who were serving out their twenty-five year sentences, nationalists of every stripe, Moscow dissidents, and simply criminals created chairs and television boxes in a wood-working factory (chapters 2–4). In June 1969—a new displacement (the bosses did not like a prisoner to develop too many connections or become too familiar with the daily round in one place). Sinyavsky spent the last years of his imprisonment in a remote camp in the settlement of Barashevo in the vicinity of a "hospital zone" and a vast camp cemetery with nameless graves (chapters 4–6). ("Posleslovie," 332–33.)

Direct echoes of the "external history" of Sinyavsky's imprisonment can be discerned in the structure of *A Voice from the Chorus*, for instance, in the cluster of entries on religious believers (which, however, appears at the end of chapter 2, rather than in chapter 1), in that on thieves with which chapter 3 concludes, and in the passages concerning Sinyavsky's stay in the "hospital zone" toward the end of chapter 5. However, the passages from the letters of which *A Voice from the Chorus* is comprised are for the most part not arranged in any sort of strict chronological sequence.

15. I have chosen to use the term "author," rather than the more unwieldy "authorial persona" or the more marked "voice," throughout my discussion of *A Voice from the Chorus*. The paradox Tertz's later works pose by presenting Sinyavsky's autobiographical experiences in works signed by Tertz challenges conventional terminology just as it forces the reader to reexamine the relationship between flesh-and-blood author and text. In this context, several scholars have analyzed *A Voice from the Chorus* specifically as it relates to the writing of autobiography. Levitt has termed it an "anti-autobiography." "The ideal of *A Voice from the Chorus*," he concludes, "is an authorless text—the ultimate paradox, perhaps, of 'autobiographical' writing" (Levitt, "Siniavskii's Alternative Autobiography," 48, 53, 59). Holmgren observes that "through an intricate conflation of autobiographical reference and analytic method, the persona experiments with the connection between his concrete experience and its creative transformation; he gradually displaces his material context with the artistically transformed space of the text" (Holmgren, *First-Person Liberties*, 174–75.) Nussbaum views *A Voice from the Chorus* as only an "intermediate stage" in what he terms the "autobiographical triptych" including also *Little Tsores* and *Goodnight* (Nussbaum, "Literary Selves," 241, 239).

16. Golomshtok, for example, points to the hybrid nature of *A Voice from*

the Chorus: "It is difficult to define the genre of this work, in which the diary, confession, autobiography, literary essay, and philosophical treatise form, as it were, the facets—or strata—of its complex structure" ("Posleslovie," 332).

17. A number of critics have commented on Tertz's departure from the generally expected conventions of Russian writing about imprisonment. Holmgren has suggested how the sufferings of the writer's body traditionally are used to make claims on the reader: "The Soviet labor camp can function as an extreme synecdoche for a monitored and policed Soviet society. Rendered into text, it has been featured mainly in autobiographical narratives or works of realistic fiction, as if its harsh reality, by some collective moral consensus, is to be conveyed through a presumably objective record. Even in fiction its chroniclers often imply that they have been its real victims. Their time in camp serves them as a rite of initiation, a means of validating their hard-won spiritual and moral world view and commanding their readers' respect and (more urgently) belief" (Holmgren, "Transfiguring of Context," 967). Levitt has pointed to the centrality of an integral conception of self to such writings: "In Russia, perhaps due to autobiography's frequent function as a surrogate for the formal writing of history, and as carrier of political and ideological truth, traditional content-oriented autobiographical writing—with its concomitant implicit belief in the integrity of the self and the message it espouses—has predominated. Such is particularly true among prison memoirs" (Levitt, "Siniavskii's Alternative Autobiography," 48).

18. Terts, "Golos iz khora," in his *Sobranie sochinenii,* 1:551. Henceforth page numbers from this edition will be given in parentheses in the text.

19. Tokarev, *Mify narodov mira,* 2:438.

20. In looking at how the metaphors for art in *A Voice from the Chorus* correspond with the actual conditions of the work's creation, we should remember that the book's origin in Sinyavsky's letters to Rozanova obviously placed practical restraints on the text. Since all correspondence had to pass through censors, it was, of course, impracticable for the writer to complain about the physical rigors of his confinement or to make inflammatory political statements. In declaring the appropriateness of thinking about art while in prison, however, the writer transforms the limitations imposed on his writing into an affirmation of the proper concerns of art.

21. Terts, "Literaturnyi protsess v Rossii," 151 (emphasis in the original).

22. Avvakum's "hole" or "pit" refers to the "underground prison" in which Avvakum and others who challenged the reforms instituted in the Russian Orthodox Church by Patriarch Nikon in the seventeenth century were buried under the earth: "Then they covered us up with earth. There was a framework in the earth, and above the earth a second framework, and then again around the whole of it was a fence with four locks, and they set a watch to guard all the doors" (Avvakum, "Life of Archpriest Avvakum", 445, 446). Avvakum also wrote his "Life" while he was imprisoned. Sinyavsky devotes a chapter to this work in *Ivan the Fool,* expanding in a conventional scholarly format on observations made in *A Voice from the Chorus* (Sinyavskii, *Ivan-durak,* 297–318).

23. Golomshtok, "Posleslovie," 337. Gifford concurs with Golomshtok,

adding: "And in the second half of the book the Voice very largely takes over. But all it says now must be subtly different because of the earlier interchanges with the Chorus" (Gifford, "Andrey Sinyavsky," 36). Tikos sticks even more closely to Golomshtok's reading: "Even though the prison camp was a great school in which Siniavski discovered the 'real' Russian people (as Dostoevsky did) after a while he realizes that the dichotomy between the individual (especially the creative person) and the masses is just as real as it was for Pushkin or Dostoevsky. The Choir is always an enforced community for the individual singer, and even though he might be happy to join the Choir at times, he is always cramped by the restriction of community" (Tikos, "On Abram Tertz's *A Voice from the Choir*, 172). My reading, on the other hand, is closer to Levitt's: "The individual voice of the author is joined by the chorus. This is not, I would argue, to emphasize the author's alienation from the chorus; Golomshtok, in this regard, ultimately defines their relationship as inimical, and suggests that it mirrors the Pushkinian opposition of *poet* and *tolpa* [crowd]. Rather, the unidentified 'voices' become part of the author's own kaleidoscopic, multi-leveled alternative 'self' that transcends the boundaries of individual personality" (Levitt, "Siniavskii's Alternative Autobiography," 60).

24. Reinforcing the metaphorical connection between *A Voice from the Chorus* and *The Odyssey*, between the author and Odysseus, the fifth section ends with a passage (immediately following the one cited here in the text) in which the author's confinement is cast as a journey:

> With December we cut winter in half; it fell behind our back and lies without moving, while we, up to our knees in snow, drag ourselves along further—there toward May, toward June . . .
> Perhaps winter fears are also already behind us.
> All this savors of a journey [*otdaet puteshestviem*]. You estimate straits, obstructions on a map beforehand. January and February are compact. But March is expansible. March is always expansible. (639)

25. He was vindicated by telling a riddle. For the significance of riddles in *Voice from the Chorus*, see below.

26. Here we should note that in the course of this discussion Tertz rather wryly remarks: "In this sense Russia is the most congenial soil for the experience and fantasy of the artist, although his life-fate is at times terrible" (613). This remark recalls the persistent refrain throughout his works that life should *not* function like art.

27. Terts, "Otechestvo: Blatnaya pesnya . . . ," 81.

28. In *Soviet Civilization*, Sinyavsky, writing on what he terms the "criminalization" of Soviet society, observes: "The people were no longer people but masses, human dust. This dust naturally churned up criminals: people who had lost their social niche, their place in the sun, their land. Socialism brought about society's desocialization. Man, deprived of his roots and his ties, deprived of what gives life meaning, found himself naked; he became a rogue and a marauder whose only friends belonged to the same underworld based on an upside down morality, based on the 'thief's law'" (Sinyavsky, *Soviet Civilization*, 184).

Chapter 7. Decanonizing the Classics

1. One positive reviewer of V. V. *Rozanov's "Fallen Leaves"* poked fun at those who had been shocked by Tertz's Pushkin and Gogol books and remarked on the "dispassionate tone" of the Rozanov book. See E. Ternovskii, "V neyasnom i nereshennom mire Rozanova (O knige Sinyavskogo 'Opavshie list'ya' V. V. Rozanova)," *Russkaya mysl'*, no. 3429 (9 September 1982), 11.

2. [Nepomnyashchy], "Interview," 10–11.

3. As discussed in Chapter 1, a great deal has been written on *Strolls with Pushkin*. Much of it, however, has been primarily polemical in nature, with little analytical value. The most substantive statements on the work include: Batkin, "Sinyavskii, Pushkin—i my"; Genis and Vail, "Labardan!" Hayward, "Pushkin, Gogol, and the Devil"; Holmgren, *First-Person Liberties*, 176–97; Rubinshtein, "Abram Terts i Aleksandr Pushkin"; Sandler, "Sex, Death and Nation"; and Vozdvizhenskii, "Progulki s Shafarevichem i bez. . . ." The journal *Voprosy literatury* published an extensive discussion of the book and the controversy surrounding it followed by a response by Mariya Rozanova: Nepomnyashchii et al., "Obsuzhdenie knigi Abrama Tertsa 'Progulki s Pushkinym"; and Rozanova, "K istorii i geografii etoi knigi." See also Aucouturier, "Writer and Text," 6; Cohen and Fanger, "Abram Tertz," 168–69; Fanger, "Conflicting Imperatives," 118–19; and Woronzoff, "Writer as Artist and Critic," 143–44.

4. (Sinyavskii), "Progulki s Pushkinym," in *Sobranie sochinenii v dvukh tomakh*, 1:341. Page numbers to this edition will henceforth be given in parentheses in the text. Translations given here are taken from Tertz, *Strolls with Pushkin*, trans. C. Nepomnyashchy and S. Yastremski.

5. Reyfman, *Vasilii Trediakovsky*, 253.

6. Here Tertz is playing, as he does throughout *Strolls with Pushkin*, with one of the standard clichés of Pushkin criticism, initiated by Gogol in his 1834 article "Some Words about Pushkin" and elaborated and given its most famous expression in Dostoevsky's "Pushkin Speech" on the occasion of the unveiling of the Opekushin monument to Pushkin in Moscow in 1880. Both Gogol and Dostoevsky argued that Pushkin was the quintessential Russian precisely because of his universalism, his ability to transcend national boundaries and adopt foreign identities. Tertz subtly subverts this cliché of Pushkin criticism by taking it to its logical conclusion: if Pushkin can become anyone, then his very Russianness embraces the traditional other in Russian society, the Jew. By the same token, I would suggest that in reducing Pushkin the man to "zero," as I argue below, Tertz essentially inverts Apollon Grigorev's famous statement, "Pushkin is our all," into "Pushkin is our nothing."

7. Rozanova, "K istorii i geografii etoi knigi," 160.

8. In his "Little Tragedy" *Mozart and Salieri*, Pushkin has Salieri in his opening monologue describe how he has attained a high rank in the music world through hard work and devotion to art:

> Through persistent, strained constancy
> I finally reached in boundless art
> a lofty rank.

He ends his monologue by revealing his envy for Mozart, whom he considers unworthy of the gift of genius bestowed on him:

O, heavens!
Where is justice, when the sacred gift,
When immortal genius—is not granted as a reward
For fervent love, self-sacrifice,
Labor, diligence, prayers—
But illumines the head of a madman,
An idle reveler [*gulyaka*]? . . . O Mozart, Mozart!
(Pushkin, *Sobranie sochinenii,* 6:156, 157)

9. For an excellent discussion of the vampire metaphor, see Sandler, "Sex, Death and Nation," 302.

10. Tertz, "Chto takoe sotsialisticheskii realizm," 404.

11. [Nepomnyashchy.] "Interview," 13. Relatively little has been written on *In the Shadow of Gogol.* There was a flurry of controversy over the work among emigrants, but nothing of the magnitude of the response to *Strolls with Pushkin.* For an article that levels much the same accusations at the Gogol book as were leveled at *Strolls with Pushkin,* see Pletnev, "O zlom suemudrii knigi Abrama Tertsa." For a defense against such criticisms, see Pomerants, "Diaspora." The only relatively extended discussions of *In the Shadow of Gogol* are to be found in Genis and Vail, "Labardan!" 57–75; Hayward, "Pushkin, Gogol, and the Devil," 630–32; Holmgren, *First-Person Liberties,* 197–26; and Mann, "Nad bezdnoi Gogolya." Passing discussions of the work are included in Alexandrov, "Typographical Intrusion," 173–74; Fanger, "Conflicting Imperatives," 116–18; Sandler, "Sex, Death and Nation," 299–300; Woronzoff, "Writer as Artist and Critic," 143.

12. Tertz (Sinyavsky), "V teni Gogolya," *Sobranie sochinenii,* 2: 36. Henceforth page numbers from this edition will be given in parentheses in the text.

13. In 1847, five years before his actual death, Gogol published, under the title *Selected Passages from Correspondence with Friends,* excerpts from his private correspondence in which he aired his views, above all, on the means to personal salvation and the spiritual regeneration of Russia. Gogol writes in his preface to the work: "I would like at least with this to redeem the uselessness of everything I have published up until now, because in my letters, according to the admissions of those people to whom they were written, there is more that is necessary to the human being than in my works" (Gogol, "Vybrannye mesta iz pis'ma s druz'yami." In *Sobranie sochinenii,* 6:252). The tract, taken as an apologia for autocracy and the abuses of the hierarchical Russian social structure, was met with outrage by those in the Russian reading public who had valued Gogol's fictional works primarily as social and political satire. The most famous expression of the view that *Selected Passages* marked a sharp break with the earlier Gogol, a betrayal of the principles embodied in the writer's fiction, was Vissarion Belinsky's "Letter to Gogol" in which the critic accuses Gogol of, "under the cover of religion and defense of the whip" preaching "falsehood and immorality as

truth and virtue" (Belinskii, "Pis'mo k Gogolyu." In *Izbrannye sochinenii*, 889.)

14. In one of the several lyrical digressions in *Dead Souls*, the narrator claims the ability to look at life through "the laughter visible to the world and the tears that are invisible and unknown to it" (Gogol, "Mertvye dushi," *Sobranie sochinenii*, 5:157).

15. The title of the chapter, "The Dead Suffocate" (*mertvye dushat*), contains a play on the title of *Dead Souls* (*mertvye dushi*).

16. In *Ivan the Fool* Sinyavsky writes of the *skomorokhi* that, "They understood clownery, buffoonery, and conjuring themselves as a manifestation of a sort of sanctity" (*Ivan-durak*, 58). He then goes on to adduce as an example the same *bylina*, "Vavilo and the *skomorokhi*," that he cites at the end of *In the Shadow of Gogol*, concluding with a further meditation on *skomorokhi*: "Yes, they are saints. Only their sanctity is buffoonish. And as a result they defeat the evil Tsar Dog. But they emerge victorious not through any physical efforts or exhortations, but through their bewitching music. This, in my view, is the highest self-definition of the fairy tale and of art in general, of art as a whole, at all times. Art is sanctity" (59).

Chapter 8. Literature and Morality

1. Both *Little Tsores* and *Goodnight* were first published by the Sinyavskys' publishing house, "Syntax."

2. In a telephone conversation with me in July 1993, Sinyavsky used the word "parable" (*pritcha*) to describe *Little Tsores*. Vera Dunham writes that "Sinyavsky is a mysterious writer" and that *Little Tsores* is "tight, tricky, almost impenetrable" (Dunham, "Serenity," 110, 111.) On *Little Tsores*, also see Edward Brown, *Russian Literature since the Revolution*, 246–47; Numano, "Iz knigi 'Za odnu ostanovku do vechnost' 239; and Nussbaum, "Literary Selves," 238–59. Nussbaum, in particular, treats *Little Tsores* as a challenge to traditional autobiography, reaching the conclusions that "Kroshka's autobiographical act undermines itself. His text betrays and destabilizes his intention to construct a cohesive autobiography. . . . He suffocates in his metaphors, which become symbols without referents" (243) and "In *Kroshka Tsores* Sinyavsky's hero is ultimately silenced by his inability to appreciate the inadequacies of the traditional autobiography" (239).

3. While relatively little-known to American readers, "Little Zaches" is widely read among educated Russians, and the writer could therefore assume familiarity with it on the part of Russian readers of *Little Tsores*. Vera Dunham discusses the relationship between the two works in her article "Serenity," 112–14.

4. In *Lyubimov* Savely Proferansov offers the following meditation on the significance of the word *tsores:*

> Oh, I once had a Jewess in my life—I'll never forget that little Jewess. . . . She spoke Russian like a Russian—you couldn't tell the difference—and the only Jewish word she knew was *tsores*, which in their language means sorrow, unpleasantness, a kind of melancholy

rubbish stabbing the heart, and *tsores* comes from this rubbish of the heart. There was a grain of this *tsores* in her, a splinter that wasn't plucked out, but was plunged in, that splinter was buried in the very composition of her soul. . . . the dried-out desert looked out in sad numbness from under her black eyelashes, from under her camel eyelids, as if waiting for something and as if summoning you somewhere, so that all you could do was sit on the sand and weep inconsolably from historical memories. (32,33)

The narrator's mother also refers to her son in Russian as "my sorrow" on the opening page of the tale (Terts, "Kroshka Tsores," *Sobranie sochinenii*, 2:612). Page numbers from this edition will henceforth be given in parentheses in the text. The English rendering of this passage and of other citations from the first chapter of the work are taken from my translation of the first chapter of *Little Tsores* (Tertz, "From *Little Tsores*," 173–74).

5. It is notable in this context that Vasily's death is the only one of the five for which the narrator truly accepts guilt, which seems an acknowledgment that only in this instance was there a true war and a true enemy, not merely an imagined other designated as a scapegoat for society's ills.

6. The parallel with Khrushchev appears particularly compelling when we remember that Volodya is killed in a traffic accident when he rushes from his apartment to make an overture to Tsores/Sinyavsky, who, by that point in the narrative, has been clearly identified as a writer/scholar with dissonant tastes in literature. Volodya's death thus echoes Khrushchev's downfall in the wake of his relaxation of cultural policies in relation to the avant-garde wing of the intelligentsia.

7. A passage in the Tertz article "Otechestvo: Blatnaya pesnya" (The Fatherland: A thieves' song) resonates with the metaphor of Cain and Abel as it is deployed in *Little Tsores*. The writer here is speaking about the thief transfigured in song: "Before us, crowned, is a man torn away [*raz"edinennyi chelovek*]—torn away from his home, from society, from his past, from himself, and in this alienation—evil [*zloi*] (the people [*narod*], in principle, is always good [*dobryi*], as there is never a completely alienated people). This man is Cain (Abel is still the people): a monster, rebel, renegade. He becomes good [*dobrym*] in song" (Terts, "Otechestvo: Blatnaya pesnya," 95). This passage, read in connection with *Little Tsores*, suggests the connection between the writer as Jew and as thief, outcast, and scapegoat for the evil of the nation: Cain.

8. Terts, "Literaturnyi protsess," 185, 186.

9. In Soviet and post-Soviet Russia, Jews, even if thoroughly russified, were and are considered a nationality distinct from Russians.

10. Terts, "Literaturnyi protsess," 188.

11. During the uproar over *Strolls with Pushkin* in the Soviet Union, Sinyavsky was frequently attacked for having called Russia a "bitch" (*suka*, literally a female dog). Ironically, his reference to Russia in these terms appears not in *Strolls with Pushkin*, but in "The Literary Process in Russia" (Terts, "Literaturnyi protsess," 183). As Sinyavsky has remarked, if Russia is a bitch, then he is a son of a bitch.

12. I would like to express my gratitude to Marina Ledkovsky for having explained *grekh vo spasenie* to me.

13. It should, however, be noted that Sinyavsky's vision of the Fall, especially as it is laid out in *Little Tsores*, is distinctly Russian Orthodox, for, rather than viewing the individual human being as fallen, it assumes the essential goodness of the human soul trapped in a fallen world. Hence, the narrator's repeated lamentations on the subject of the source of evil not in intention, but in circumstance.

14. The writer suggests the same notion in *A Voice from the Chorus:* "A strange reply, from which it follows that evil is transformed into salvation [*zlo—vo spasenie*], purifies the soul. But not by means of repentance or punishment, as might be thought, but the crime itself is escape [*vykhod*]: 'I drove away my evil, and now I am at peace and feel no regret. Otherwise it would always have lain on my soul' " (570).

15. [Nepomnyashchy,] "Interview," 16.

16. As I have pointed out earlier, the author describes *Goodnight* on one occasion in the text as a novel and on another as a memoir. Critics have generally termed it an "autobiographical novel." Sinyavsky himself, however, considers this designation inaccurate, explaining in one interview that he prefers to consider it simply a novel:

> *A. S.* For the sake of simplicity sometimes when I am asked about *Goodnight!* I say that speaking in general terms it is an autobiographical novel, but I wouldn't want to subtitle it "an autobiographical novel." What I mean to say is that *Goodnight!* is simply a novel. It is autobiographical in that it is based on a real canvas, but it isn't, strictly speaking, an autobiographical novel. For example, I consider Gorky's *Childhood* an autobiographical novel, and Gorky's *My Apprenticeship* is an autobiographical novella.
> *C. N.* And how does an autobiographical novel differ from simple biography?
> *A. S.* There is a difference, because an autobiography is not a novel, and a novel is a work of literature. In the novel *Goodnight!* I don't simply describe my life. I didn't use a good deal of my life in it at all. For example, I didn't even mention my military service in it, it simply wasn't relevant. Only those episodes are included in the novel that have some connection with the fate of Abram Tertz. In general, the fate of the writer is my main theme, whether I am writing about myself or about Pushkin or Gogol.
> ([Nepomnyashchy,] "Interview," 10)

On *Goodnight,* see Bayley, *"Goodnight,"* 1, 26–27; Gachev, "Andrei Sinyavskii-Abram Terts," 235–66; Holmgren, *First-Person Liberties,* 227–313; Holmgren, "Transfiguring of Context," 965–77; Howe, "Do Not Go Gentle," 34, 36–37; Richard Lourie, "Introduction," in *Goodnight!,* vii–xiv; Maksudov, "Spokoinoi nochi," 93–96; Matich, *"Spokojnoj noči,"* 50–63; Nivat, ". . . Chtoby prevozmoch' otchayanie i odinochestvo," 10; Nussbaum, "Literary Selves," 238–59; and Tatarinov, "Andrei Sinyavskii i Abram Terts," 20–22.

17. The Russian here is "v skorlupu," echoing Tertz's identification of Pushkin the man as the "shell" of the Poet in *Strolls with Pushkin* and prefiguring the author's postulation of S. as an "empty shell" in the last chapter of *Goodnight*.

18. Terts, "Spokoinoi nochi," in his *Sobranie sochinenii*, 2:535. Page numbers from this edition will henceforth be given in parentheses in the text.

19. Sinyavsky has cited Céline's *Voyage au bout de la nuit* as one of his favorite works of French literature, although he does not believe that it has exercised any particular influence over his own work (see [Nepomnyashchy,] "Interview," 14).

20. The official date of Stalin's death was, of course, 5 March 1953. In his narrative, however, the author interlaces rumors that Stalin may have died several days earlier into his account of the public mourning for the dictator.

21. The writer's attribution of his novel-memoir, in which Sinyavsky figures as the major character, to Tertz poses the same terminological challenge as does *A Voice from the Chorus*. Here again, following the narrator's own self-designation (as illustrated in the preceding quotation from *Goodnight*), I have chosen to refer to the narrating subject as "the author" throughout.

22. In the English translation these passages are printed in boldface type.

23. Terts, "Otechestvo: Blatnaya pesnya," 88.

24. The Russian word here is *p'esa* (play). The author is presumably referring to the "fairy-play" "The Mirror," which will be discussed below.

25. This is clearly an ironic allusion to Stalin's designation of writers as "engineers of human souls."

26. The Russian here is "po dobrote nashikh bezopasnykh organov," a play on the name of the KGB—Komitet gosudarstvennoi bezopasnosti (the Committee for State Security)—and the fact that it was popularly referred to as the "organs."

27. Sinyavsky, *Soviet Civilization*, 203.

28. "Ochki" was originally published separately in *Sintaksis*, no. 5 (1979), 31–41.

29. The use of this adjective links the wall with the image of the cave in the fifth chapter of *Goodnight*.

30. The image of the tape recorder as a mouse gives rise to the one inserted red text in the second chapter of *Goodnight*, "A Treatise on Mice and on Our Inexplicable Fear of Mice." This curious piece begins as what seems to be a straightforward discussion of the author's and his wife's reactions to the appearance of mice in their house in France. Yet, as Beth Holmgren, points out: "Soon, however, despite his initial references to a real situation (his exile in France) and real persons (himself and his wife, Marija), Sinjavskij clearly indicates that he is permitting the artistic transformation of that reality. With each reference to his wife, he changes her name and sometimes her profession and nationality; he himself is called by another name; and the number of mice burgeons into the hundreds. The images of wife and mice, respectively, seem to metamorphose and escalate of their own accord" (Holmgren, *First-Person Liberties*, 256). Following Holmgren (257), I

would suggest that the image of the mouse draws a connection between the spying of the authorities (the mouse-like rustling of the tape recorder) and the author's "transformation of reality" in the "Treatise." I would contend, however, that the issue here, as throughout *Goodnight*, is the distinction the author draws between art and life. The artistic license taken in the "Treatise" figures the free play of the sign in the literary work: names become interchangeable and tropes self-generating. In this context, the "Treatise" also forms a contrast with the inserted texts on the False Dmitry in the fourth chapter of *Goodnight* (which will be discussed below). There the body becomes interchangeable, while the name remains the same. Reality claims the prerogative of the literary text, to bloody result.

31. Prefiguring the imagery of hunters vs. the hunted in the last chapter of *Goodnight*, the author's father is symbolically transformed from a hunter into a victim by the confiscation of his gun during the search of the family's apartment. They thus go into the woods the final time to "hunt" without a weapon.

32. The title of the chapter would seem to be drawn from Choderlos de Laclos' novel *Les liaisons dangereuses*, which, like the Tertz text, deals with words, deception, and sexual intrigue.

33. According to Sinyavsky, he was in fact reading this old and rare set of books—*Skazaniya inostrantsev o Smutnom vremeni, v pyati tomakh*—during the days that Stalin lay dying, and this reading clearly inspired the inserted texts on the Time of Troubles printed in red ink in the Russian text. The Time of Troubles (1605–1613) was a period of political confusion between the end of the ruling dynasty that traced its lineage back to Ryurik and the ascension of the Romanovs to power. It was initiated by the appearance of the pretender, the False Dmitry, who claimed to be the Tsarevich Dmitry, the murdered son of Ivan the Terrible.

34. Here the author plays on the dual meaning of the expression *zloba dnya*, which can mean either "news of the day" or "evil of the day."

35. In line with his vision of art as a sort of distorting mirror, discussed below, the author here plays with conventional Orthodox iconography. The three figures depicted as if from a single icon brought to life generally appear in a triptych of icons in the deisis of the iconostasis in a Russian Orthodox church, with Christ in the center, Mary on the viewer's right, and John on the left. The image of Christ in the deisis is not, however, the Pantocrator, nor is John depicted without his head in that context.

36. See Matich, "*Spokoinoj noči.*"

37. The "Octobrist star" here refers to the badges in the shape of a star depicting "baby Lenin" worn by Soviet children belonging to the children's group the Octobrists.

38. Khmelnitsky identified himself publicly, thereby helping to precipitate the scandal surrounding the events portrayed in the novel. Khmelnitsky published an article in the Israel-based, Russian-language journal *Dvadtsat' dva* disputing his portrayal in *Goodnight* and accusing Sinyavsky of having collaborated with the secret police. Both *Dvadtsat' dva* and *Vremya i my* subsequently printed responses by Sinyavsky and others challenging Khmelnitsky's statements. See Voronel', "Pravo byt' uslyshannym . . . ," 145–50;

Khmel'nitskii, "Iz chreva kitova," 151–80; Sinyavsky, *V redaktsiyu*, 221–23; "Izvinite za donos," 218–36; Bogoraz, "Dushevnye muki seksota," 210–14; Fanger, "A Change of Venue," 1321–22; I. Sh., "Pozitsiya izdatelya," 181–93.

39. According to Sinyavsky, this description of Hélène's soul is patterned after the model of the icon of the dormition of the Virgin.

40. This is an ironic reference to the nineteenth-century radical critic Nikolai Dobrolyubov's article by this title.

41. Significantly, the author prefaces his invocation of "enemy of the people" with a reference to the attacks on him for having called Russia a "bitch" in his Tertz article "The Literary Process in Russia." His ostracism by society is therefore implicitly linked with his pseudonymous writing.

42. Berdyaev, "Ethics of Creativity," 201. I am grateful to Richard Gustafson for having directed my attention to this passage.

43. The article was actually attributed, in both the Russian original and the English translation, to "Andrei Sinyavsky (Abram Tertz)." However, in the copy I was given by Sinyavsky the "Sinyavsky" was crossed out. It appears under Tertz in the Bibliography.

44. Sinyavsky (Tertz), " 'I' and 'They,' " 290. Page numbers to this edition will be given in the text.

Selected Bibliography

This bibliography is divided into the following sections: Works by Sinyavsky, Works by Tertz, Interviews with Sinyavsky, Works on Sinyavsky/Tertz, General References. Publication history includes the first publication in Russian, all republications in Russia, and English translations and editions in book form.

Works by Sinyavsky

"L'adieu à Iouli Daniel." *Le Monde*, 3 January 1989, 5.

"Akmeism." In *Kratkaya literaturnaya entsiklopediya*, 1:118–19. Moscow: Sovetskaya entsiklopediya, 1962.

"A. M. Gor'kii." In *Istoriya russkoi sovetskoi literatury*, 1:99–167. Moscow: Akademiya nauk, 1958.

"Andrei Siniavskii." In *The Red Pencil: Artists, Scholars, and Censors in the USSR*, edited by Marianna Tax Choldin and Maurice Friedburg, translated by Maurice Friedberg and Barbara Dash, 94–100. Boston: Unwin Hyman, 1989.

"André Siniavski." *Pourquoi écrivez-vous? 400 écrivains répondent*, 199. Paris: Libération, 1985.

"A. Sinyavskii—ital'yanskomu zhurnalu 'Ekspress.'" *Sintaksis*, no. 31 (1991), 190–91.

"Apofeoz knigi." *Cahiers du Monde russe et soviétique* 29, nos. 3–4 (1988): 293–301.

"Bez skidok (o sovremennom nauchno-fantasticheskom romane)." *Voprosy literatury*, no. 1 (1960), 45–59. English translation, "No Discount," in Sinyavsky, *For Freedom of Imagination*, 17–36.

"Chtenie v serdtsakh." *Sintaksis*, no. 17 (1987): 191–205. Reprinted in *Novyi mir*, no. 4 (1992): 204–10.

"Des langages différents." *Le Figaro*, 15 June 1977, 1–2.

"Dissidentstvo kak lichnyi opyt." *Sintaksis*, no. 15 (1986): 131–47. Reprinted in *Yunost'*, no. 5 (1989): 88–91. English translation by Maria-Regina Kecht,

"Dissent as a Personal Experience," *Yearbook of Comparative and General Literature*, no. 31 (1982): 21–29. Published in *Dissent* 31, no. 2 (Spring 1984): 152–61.

"Dostoevskii i katorga." *Sintaksis*, no. 9 (1981): 108–11.

"Eduard Bagritskii." In *Istoriya russkoi sovetskoi literatury*, 1:397–420. Moscow: Akademiya nauk, 1958.

"Emigré." *Encounter* 51, no. 3 (September 1978): 79–80.

"Encounters with the West." *Partisan Review* 50, no. 4 (1983): 517–25.

"Est' takie stikhi . . ." *Novyi mir*, no. 3 (1965): 244–48. English translation, "There Are Such Verses," in *For Freedom of Imagination*, 92–102.

For Freedom of Imagination. Translated by Laszlo Tikos and Murray Peppard. New York: Holt, Rinehart and Winston, 1971.

Introduction to *Kolyma*, by Varlam Chalamov. Translated by Catherine Fournier. 5–13. Paris: François Maspero, 1980.

"Isaac Babel." *Oeuvres et Opinions*, no. 8 (1964): 157–63. English translation in *Major Soviet Writers: Essays in Criticism*, edited by Edward J. Brown. New York: Oxford University Press, 1973.

Ivan-durak: Ocherk russkoi narodnoi very. Paris: Sintaksis, 1991.

"Izraztsy." *Sintaksis*, no. 18 (1987): 112–37.

"J'ai traversé un cimetière." Translated by Annie Apelboin. In *Culture et pouvoir communiste: l'autre face de "Paris-Moscou,"* 157–61. Paris: Recherches, 1979.

"Kafedra Galileya." *Literaturnaya gazeta*, no. 44 (28 October 1992): 6.

"Literatura perioda velikoi otechestvennoi voiny." *Istoriya russkoi sovetskoi literatury*, 3:5–53. Moscow: Akademiya nauk, 1961.

"Literaturnaya maska Alekseya Remizova." *Sintaksis*, no. 14 (1985): 98–114.

"M. A. Voloshin." *Kratkaya literaturnaya entsiklopediya*, 1:1021. Moscow: Sovetskaya entsiklopediya, 1962.

"Mify Mikhaila Zoshchenko." *Sintaksis*, no. 23 (1988): 82–103. Reprinted in *Voprosy literatury*, no. 2 (1989): 50–67.

"Nazyvaya imena (kommentarii)." *Sintaksis*, no. 2 (1978): 48–62. Reprinted in *Zhurnalist*, no. 10 (1991): 27–30.

"Ne verit'–znat'." *Sintaksis*, no. 34 (1994): 219–20.

"Ob estetike Mayakovskogo." *Vestnik Moskovskogo universiteta.* Seriya obshchestvennykh nauk, no. 1 (1950): 129–39.

"Odin den' s Pasternakom." *Sintaksis*, no. 6 (1980): 131–39. Reprinted in *Yunost'*, no. 2 (1990): 83–5.

"O khudozhestvennoi strukture romana 'Zhizn' Klima Samgina.'" In *Tvorchestvo M. Gor'kogo i voprosy sotsialisticheskogo realizma*, 132–74. Moscow: Akademiya nauk, 1958.

"O kritike." *Sintaksis*, no. 10 (1982): 146–55.

"O novom sbornike stikhov Anatoliya Sofronova." *Novyi mir*, no. 8 (1959): 248–

54. English translation, "On a Collection of Verses by Anatoly Sofronov," in Sinyavsky, *For Freedom of Imagination*.

"*Opavshie list'ya*" *V. V. Rozanova*. Paris: Sintaksis, 1982. Excerpts reprinted as "Preodolenie literatury: Zhanrovoe svoeobrazie 'Opavshikh list'ev' V. V. Rozanova." *Nashe nasledie*, no. 11 (1989): 84–94; "Iz lektsii o v. Rozanove," *Obshchestvennye* nauki, no. 2 (1990): 174–86; and "Rozanov," in *Ideology in Russian Literature*, ed. Richard Freeborn and Jane Grayson, 116–33 (London: Macmillan, 1990).

"O sebe." *Inostrannaya literatura*, no. 2 (1989): 241–43.

"Osnovnye printsipy estetiki V. V. Mayakovskogo." *Znamya*, no. 2 (1950): 151–57.

"Otkrytoe pis'mo A. Solzhenitsynu." *Sintaksis*, no. 31 (1991): 159–62.

"O V. Nekrasove." *Znamya*, no. 5 (May 1990): 49–50.

"Pamflet ili paskvil'?" *Novyi mir*, no. 12 (1964): 228–33. English translation, "Pamphlet or Lampoon?" in Sinyavsky, *For Freedom of Imagination*, 78–91.

"'Panorama s vynoskami' Mikhaila Kuzmina." *Sintaksis*, no. 20 (1987): 58–71.

"Poeticheskii sbornik B. Pasternaka." *Novyi mir*, no. 3 (1962): 261–63.

"Poeziya i proza Ol'gi Berggolts." *Novyi mir*, no. 5 (1960): 226–36. English translation, "The Poetry and Prose of Olga Berggolts," in Sinyavsky, *For Freedom of Imagination*, 37–62.

"Poeziya Pasternaka." *Stikhotvoreniya i poemy*, by B. Pasternak. Moscow-Leningrad: Sovetskii pisatel', 1965, 9–62. English translations: "Boris Pasternak," in *Pasternak: Modern Judgments*, edited by Donald Davie and Angela Livingstone. London: Macmillan, 1969; "Pasternak's Poetry," in *Pasternak: A Collection of Critical Essays*, edited by Victor Erlich, 68–109. Englewood Cliffs, N.J.: Prentice-Hall Inc., 1978; "The Poetry of Pasternak," in Sinyavsky, *For Freedom of Imagination*, 103–66; "The Poetry of Pasternak," in *Major Soviet Writers: Essays in Criticism*, ed. Edward J. Brown, 100–137 (New York: Oxford University Press, 1973).

"'Poidem so mnoi . . .'" *Novyi mir*, no. 1 (1964): 260–63. English translation, "Come Walk with Us," in Sinyavsky, *For Freedom of Imagination*, 63–71.

"Pokhvala emigratsii." *Sintaksis*, no. 24 (1988), 39–42. Reprinted in *Stalitsa* no. 40 (1992): 49–50.

"Prostranstvo prozy." *Sintaksis*, no. 21 (1988): 25–31. English translation, "The Space of Prose," in *The Louisiana Conference on Literature and Perestroika, 2–4. March 1988*, edited by Märta-Lisa Magnusson, translated by John Kendal, 73–80. Esbjerg, Denmark: South Jutland University Press, 1989.

"Qu'est-ce que 'Syntaxis'?" Translated by Annie Sabatier. In *Syntaxis: Réflexion sur le sort de la Russie et de la culture russe*, 9–12. Paris: Albin Michel, 1981.

"Raskovannyi golos (k 75-letiyu A. Akhmatovoi)." *Novyi mir*, no. 6 (1964): 174–76. English translation, "The Unfettered Voice," in Sinyavsky, *For Freedom of Imagination*, 72–77; "The Unshackled Voice: Anna Akhmatova," in *Major Soviet Writers: Essays in Criticism*, ed. Edward J. Brown, 54–57 (New York: Oxford University Press, 1973).

"Realizm fantastiki." *Literaturnaya gazeta*, no. 2 (5 January 1960), 3.

"Reka i pesnya." *Sintaksis*, no. 12 (1984): 121–38.

"Roman M. Gor'kogo Mat'—kak rannii obrazets sotsialisticheskogo realisma." *Cahiers du Monde russe et soviétique*, 29, no. 1 (1988), 33–40.

"Russkii natsionalizm." *Sintaksis*, no. 26 (1989): 91–110. Reprinted in part in "Iz stat'i 'Russkii natsionalizm.'" *Literaturnaya gazeta*, no. 14 (1 April 1992): 3.

"Russophobia." *Partisan Review* 57, no. 3 (1990): 339–44.

"S chem sravnivat'?" *Oktyabr'*, no. 9 (1961): 195.

"Sinyavskii o sebe." In *The Third Wave: Russian Literature in Emigration*, edited by Olga Matich with Michael Heim, 107–09. Ann Arbor, Mich.: Ardis, 1984.

"Sinyavsky on Art." *New York Times*, 18 November 1978, 21.

"Sny na pravoslavnuyu Paskhu." *Sintaksis*, no. 8 (1980): 7–14.

"Solzhenitsyn kak ustroitel' novogo edinomysliya." *Sintaksis*, no. 14 (1985): 16–32.

Soviet Civilization: A Cultural History. Translated by Joanne Turnbull with the assistance of Nikolai Formozov. New York: Little, Brown and Company–Arcade, 1990.

"Srez materiala." *Sintaksis*, no. 8 (1980): 180–86.

"Stalin—geroi i khudozhnik stalinskoi epokhi." *Sintaksis*, no. 19 (1987): 106–25.

"The State of Europe: Christmas Eve, 1989." Translated by Michael Glenny. *Granta* 30 (Winter 1990): 151–54.

"Stilisticheskie raznoglasiya." *Iskusstvo kino*, no. 7 (1989): 34–38.

"'Stoyala zima. Dul veter iz stepi . . .' O stikhotvoreniyakh Pasternaka na evangel'skie syuzhety i temy." *Vek Pasternaka: Dos'e: Prilozhenie k 'Literaturnoi gazete'* (February 1990): 22.

"Teatr Galicha." *Vremya i my*, no. 14 (February 1977): 142–50.

"'Temnaya noch' . . . .'" *Sintaksis*, no. 1 (1978): 11–22.

"Veseloe remeslo." Introduction to *Rodnaya rech'*, by Petr Vail' and Aleksandr Genis, 5–6. Tenafly, N.J.: Hermitage, 1990.

"V noch' posle bitvy." *Sintaksis*, no. 3 (1979): 41–66.

"V redaktsiyu zhurnala '22.'" *Dvadtsat' dva*, no. 49 (August–September 1986): 221–23.

"V zashchitu piramidy (Zametki o tvorchestve Evg. Evtushenko i ego poeme 'Bratskaya GES')." *Grani*, no. 63 (1967): 114–39. English translation, "In Defense of the Pyramid," in Sinyavsky, *For Freedom of Imagination*, 167–95.

"Vse eto uzhe bylo: Pochemu ya segodnya protiv El'tsina." *Nezavisimaya gazeta*, no. 195 (13 October 1993), 5. Reprinted as "Tak nachinalas' sovetskaya vlast'" in *Sintaksis*, no. 34 (1994): 197–99, and as "El'tsin? Pochemu?" in *Novoe russkoe slovo*, 1 November 1993, 4.

"Would I Move Back?" Translated by Catharine Theimer Nepomnyashchy. *Time*, 10 April 1989, 129–30, 132.

"Yazyk odinochestva." *Novosti* 1, no. 77 (28 December 1983): 5.

Sinyavskii, A., and A. Men'shutin. "Davaite govorit' professional'no." *Novyi mir,* no. 8 (1961): 248–52.

———. "'Den' russkoi poezii.'" *Novyi mir,* no. 2 (1959): 211–22.

———. *Poeziya pervykh let revolyutsii: 1917–1920.* Moscow: Nauka, 1964.

———. "Za poeticheskuyu aktivnost'" (zametki o poezii molodykh)." *Novyi mir,* no. 1 (1961): 224–41.

Sinyavsky, Andrei, and Günter Grass. "Letters." *Encounter* 43, no. 6 (December 1974), 94–95.

Sinyavskii, Andrei, and Igor' Golomshtok. *Pikasso.* Moscow: Znanie, 1960.

Sinyavskii, A., and M. Rozanova, "Prizhiznennyi nekrolog." Afterword to *Po obe storony okeana. Zapiski zevaki. Saperlipopet, ili Esli b da kaby, da vo rtu rosli griby,* by Viktor Nekrasov, 396–99. Moscow: Khudozhestvennaya literatura, 1991.

Sinyavskii, A., V. Maksimov, and P. Egides. "'Pod sen' nadezhnuyu zakona . . .'" *Nezavisimaya gazeta,* no. 198 (16 October 1993) 1. Reprinted under the same title in *Sintaksis,* no. 34 (1994), 200–202, and under the title "El'tsin—v otstavsku!" in *Novoe russkoe slovo,* 20 October 1993, 5.

Sinyavskii, A., and Yu. Daniel'. "Dialog." *Sintaksis,* no. 24 (1988), 168–73.

Works by Tertz

"Anekdot v anekdote." *Sintaksis,* no. 1 (1978): 77–95. English translation by Olga Matich, "The Joke Inside the Joke," *Partisan Review* 51, no. 3 (1984): 356–66.

Chto takoe sotsialisticheskii realizm. Paris: Sintaksis, 1988. Reprinted in *Dekorativnoe iskusstvo,* no. 5 (1989): 19–20, 29; *Literaturnoe obozrenie,* no. 8 (1989): 89–100; and *Teatr,* no. 5 (1989): 73–83. English translation by George Dennis, *On Socialist Realism,* translated by George Dennis, introduction by Czeslaw Milosz (New York: Pantheon, 1960). Reprinted in *The Trial Begins and On Socialist Realism* (New York: Vintage, 1965; and Berkeley: University of California Press, 1982).

Fantasticheskii mir Abrama Tertsa. Introduction by Boris Filippov. New York: Inter-language Literary Associates, 1967.

Fantasticheskie povesti. Paris: Instytut literacki, 1961. English translation by Max Hayward and Ronald Hingley, *Fantastic Stories* (New York: Pantheon, 1963). Reprinted; Evanston: Northwestern University Press, 1987.

Golos iz khora. Afterword by Igor' Golomshtok. London: Stenvalley Press, 1973. English translation by Kyril FitzLyon and Max Hayward, *A Voice from the Chorus,* with an introduction by Max Hayward (New York: Farrar, Straus, and Giroux, 1976). Reprinted; New Haven: Yale University Press, 1995.

"Gosti." *Sintaksis,* no. 15 (1986): 16–29.

"Iskusstvo i deistvitel'nost'." *Sintaksis,* no. 2 (1978): 111–19. English translation by Catharine Theimer Nepomnyashchy, "Art and Reality," *Formations* 6, no. 1 (Spring 1991): 1–5.

Kroshka Tsores. Paris: Sintaksis, 1980. English translation by Larry P. Joseph and Rachel May, *Little Jinx*, with a Foreword by Edward J. Brown (Evanston: Northwestern University Press, 1992). English translation of first chapter by Catharine Theimer Nepomnyashchy, "From *Little Tsores*," *Humanities in Society* 7, nos. 3–4 (1984): 173–74.

"Literaturnyi protsess v Rossii." *Kontinent*, no. 1 (1974): 143–90. Reprinted in *Daugava*, no. 5 (May 1990): 95–113. English translation by Michael Glenny, "The Literary Process in Russia," in *Kontinent*, 77–118 (Garden City, N.Y.: Anchor-Doubleday, 1976).

Lyubimov, Washington: B. Filipoff, 1964. Translated into English as *The Makepeace Experiment*, trans. and with an introduction by Manya Harari (New York: Pantheon, 1965). Reprinted by Northwestern University Press, Evanston, Ill., 1989.

"Lyudi i zveri (Po knige G. Vladimova 'Vernyi Ruslan. Istoriya karaul'noi sobaki')." *Kontinent*, no. 5 (1975): 367–404. Reprinted in *Voprosy literatury*, no. 1 (1990): 61–86. Abridged English translation by William E. Harkins, "Beasts and Men" [Review of Georgi Vladimov, *Faithful Ruslan: The Story of a Guard Dog*], *New York Review of Books* 26, nos. 21 and 22 (24 January 1980): 22–24.

Mysli vrasplokh. With an interpretative essay on the literary art of Abram Tertz by Andrew Field. New York: Rausen Publishers, 1966. Excerpts were reprinted as "Mysli vrasplokh. Otryvki iz knigi," *Ogonek*, no. 51 (1991): 14–16; and "Gospod' blagoslovil menya togda na etot smekh," *Ogonek*, no. 52 (1991): 29. English translation, "Thought Unaware," *New Leader* 48, no. 15 (19 July 1965): 16–26; and *Unguarded Thoughts*, translated by Manya Harari (London: Collins and Harvill Press, 1972).

"Otechestvo: Blatnaya pesnya . . ." *Sintaksis*, no. 4 (1979): 72–118. Reprinted in *Sel'skaya molodezh'*, no. 9 (1992): 57–60 and no. 10 (1992): 48–52.

"Pamyati pavshikh: Arkadii Belinkov." *Kontinent*, no. 2 (1975): 363–72. English translation, "In Memory of the Fallen: Arkady Belinkov," in *Kontinent 2* (Garden City, N.Y.: Anchor-Doubleday, 1977), 133–41.

"Posleslovie." *Sintaksis*, no. 7 (1980): 108–09.

Progulki s Pushkinym. London: Overseas Publications Interchange in association with Collins, 1975. Reprinted in Paris; Sintaksis, 1989. Reprinted in *Voprosy literatury*, no. 7 (1990): 155–75; no. 8 (1990): 81–111; and no. 9 (1990): 146–78; and in Saint Petersburg: Vsemirnoe slovo, 1993. Excerpts were printed as "Progulki s Pushkinym: Fragment," *Oktyabr'*, no. 4 (1989): 192–99; and as "Zolotoe sechenie: Iz knigi 'Progulki s Pushkinym.'" *Mir Pushkina. Dos'e. Prilozhenie k 'Literaturnoi gazete'* (June 1990): 22–23. English translation by Catharine Theimer Nepomnyashchy and Slava I. Yastremski, *Strolls with Pushkin*, introduction by Catharine Theimer Nepomnyashchy, notes by Slava I. Yastremski (New Haven: Yale University Press, 1993).

"Puteshestvie na Chernuyu rechku." *Sintaksis*, no. 34 (1994): 3–51.

Sobranie sochinenii v dvukh tomakh. Introduction by Vladimir Novikov. Moscow: SP Start, 1992.

Spokoinoi nochi: Roman. Paris: Sintaksis, 1984. A section of the book was originally published separatedly as "Ochki," *Sintaksis*, no. 5 (1979): 31–41. Excerpts were reprinted as "Spokoinoi nochi (fragmenty romana)," *Gorizont*, no. 9 (1989): 53–64. English translation by Richard Lourie, *Goodnight!* with an Introduction by Richard Lourie (New York: Penguin, 1989).

Sud idet. Introduction by Gustav Gerlin: Grudzinskii. *Kultura.* Russian issue (May 1960): 62–130. Published in English as *The Trial Begins.* Translated by Max Hayward. New York: Pantheon, 1960. Reprinted in *The Trial Begins and On Socialist Realism*, with an Introduction by Czeslaw Milosz (New York: Vintage, 1965; and Berkeley: University of California Press, 1982).

V teni Gogolya. London: Overseas Publications Interchange, in association with Collins, 1975. Reprinted by Sintaksis, Paris, 1981. A chapter was reprinted as "Dva povorota serebryanogo klyucha v 'Revizore,'" *Teatr*, no. 10 (1990): 126–46.

"'Ya' i 'oni': O krainikh formakh obshcheniya v usloviyakh odinochestva." *Vremya i my*, no. 13 (January 1977): 169–82. English translation, "'I' and 'They': An Essay on Extreme Forms of Communication under Conditions of Human Isolation," *Survey* 22, nos. 3–4 (Summer–Autumn 1976): 278–87.

"Zolotoi shnurok." *Sintaksis*, no. 18 (1987): 182–87.

Interviews with Sinyavsky

"André Siniavski." *L'autre Europe*, nos. 7–8 (November 1985): 112–13.

[Arc, Gabriela.] "Bez Dostojevskog se ne ziveti: Odlomak razgovora s Andrejom Sinjavskim." *Knjizevnost* 71, nos. 5–6 (May–June 1981): 1189–91.

[Beausang, Michael.] "Exile and Writer." *Mosaic* 8, no. 3 (1975): 15–20.

[Bershin, Efim.] "V Tupikakh svobody." *Literaturnaya gazeta*, no. 14 (1 April 1992): 3.

[Bokov, N.] "Andrei Sinyavsky on Dissidence." *Encounter* 52, no. 4 (April 1979): 91–94.

[Brezna, Irena.] "An Interview with Andrei Sinyavsky." Translated by Kevin Windle. *Australian Slavonic and East European Studies* 3, no. 2 (1989): 51–60.

[Carlisle, Olga.] "Solzhenitsyn and Russian Nationalism: An Interview with Andrei Sinyavsky." *New York Review of Books* 26, no. 18 (22 November 1979): 3–6.

[Daubenton, Annie.] "André Siniavski: Certains dissidents veulent remplacer la dictature communiste par une autre." Translated by Lucia Cathala. *Les Nouvelles littéraires*, no. 2779 (19–26 March 1981): 26.

[Davydova, N., and A. Tarkhanov.] "Kakim ne dolzhen byt' pamyatnik." *Dekorativnoe iskusstvo*, no. 5 (1989): 18.

[Ebanoidze, I.] "Ne bol'she chem pisatel': Interv'iu s Andreem Sinyavskim." *Literaturnoe obozrenie*, no. 10 (1992): 30–33.

[Epelboin, Annie.] "Siniavski: 'La prose: une second poésie.'" *La Quinzaine littéraire*, no. 345 (1–15 April 1981): 7–9.

[Glad, John.] "Antizapadnichestvo v sovremennykh usloviyakh—eto antikul'tura." *Vremya i my*, no. 88 (1986): 145–67.

[Karaulov, Andrei.] "Vsya zhizn'." *Teatral'naya zhizn'*, no. 14 (1989): 28–31.

[Laird, Sally.] "My Life as a Writer." *Index on Censorship* 15, no. 6 (June 1986): 7–10, 14.

[Lur'e, Samuil.] "Abrashka Terts, professor iz Sorbonny." *Literator*, no. 20 (1990): 4–5.

[Maksimov, Maksim.] "'Russkaya emigratsiya—eto kolossal'neishee kladbishche . . .'" *Smena*, no. 129 (5 June 1990): 2.

[Markish, David.] "Upasi bog ot shovinizma: Interv'yu s Andreem Sinyavskim." *Panorama*, no. 172 (25 July–1 August 1984): 23.

[Medvedev, Feliks.] "Besedy s Andreem Siniavskim i Mariei Rozanovoi o Pushkine, i ne tol'ko o nem." *Knizhnoe obozrenie*, no. 4 (26 January 1990): 8–9.

[Mendzheritskii, I. A.] "Vonnegut i Sinyavskii na fone . . . ukradennoi 'Anzheliki.'" *Knizhnoe obozrenie*, no. 31 (31 July 1992): 3.

[Mogutin, Yaroslav.] "Salman Rushdi russkoi literatury." *Stolitsa*, no. 40 (1992): 48–49.

[Nasaroff, Barbara.] "Andrei Siniavski." *Lire*, no. 161 (February 1989): 26–32, 44.

[Nekhoroshev, Grigorii.] "'Tam my schitaemsya krasnymi . . .'" *Knizhnoe obozrenie*, no. 2 (13 January 1989): 3.

[Nepomnyashchy, Catharine Theimer.] "An Interview with Andrei Sinyavsky." *Formations* 6, no. 1 (Spring 1991): 6–23.

[Novikov, Vl.] "Grenobl'skie grezy: Vstrechi s literaturovedami vo Frantsii." *Oktyabr'*, no. 12 (1990): 187–93.

[Platonova, Yelena.] "'Emigration Is a Horrible but Instructive Experience.'" *Moscow News*, no. 2 (15–22 January 1989): 16.

[Pomerantsev, K.] "Sinyavsky: Fiction and Reality." Translated by Michael Glenny. *Times Literary Supplement*, 23 May 1975, 560.

[Putrenko, T.] "'Pushkin—nash smeyushchiisya genii.'" *Literaturnaya gazeta*, no. 32 (8 August 1990): 7.

[Tsitrinyak, G.] "Progulki s professorom Sorbonny." *Nezavisimaya gazeta*, 14 January 1992, 7.

[Uvarova, N.] "Dlya ego pesen nuzhna rossiskaya pochva." *Teatr*, no. 10 (1990): 146–48.

[————.] "Pisatel'—tot zhe fokusnik." *Trud*, 27 February 1993, 7.

[Voina, Vladimir.] "Andrey Sinyavsky." *Bostonia* 64, no. 2 (March/April 1990): 34–36.

[Zhavoronkov, G.] "Mozhno li pokayatsya pod dulom pistoleta?" *Moskovskie novosti*, no. 48 (2 December 1990): 15.

[Zinkewych, Osyp.] "An Interview with Andrei Sinyavsky." *Smoloskyp* 1, no. 3 (Spring 1979): 12–13.

Works on Sinyavsky/Tertz

Abel, Lionel. "Art while Being Ruled: 'Abram Tertz,' Brecht, and Calderon." *Commentary* 39 (May 1960): 405–12.

Adams, Phoebe. "Fiction Here and Abroad." Review of *The Trial Begins*. *Atlantic*, October 1960, 123–24.

———. "Potpourri." Review of *The Makepeace Experiment*. *Atlantic*, September 1965, 151.

Adelman, George. Review of *Fantastic Stories*, by Abram Tertz. *Library Journal* 88, no. 9 (1 May 1963): 1905.

"L'Affaire Siniavski-Daniel." *Esprit*, no. 357 (February 1967): 227–310.

Alexandrov, Vladimir E. "Typographical Intrusion and The Transcendent in Bely's *Petersburg* and Sinyavsky's *Lyubimov*." *Slavonic and East European Review* 62, no. 2 (April 1984): 161–79.

Amurskii, Vitalii. "Igra v 'durachka.'" *Novoe russkoe slovo*, 9 March 1993, 11.

Anan'ev, Anatolii. "Kritika ili obvinenie?" *Literaturnaya Rossiya*, no. 35 (1 September 1989), 14–15.

———. "V sekretariat pravleniya SP SSSR v redaktsiyu 'Literaturnoi gazety.'" *Literaturnaya gazeta*, no. 37 (13 September 1989): 7.

Anan'ev, Anatolii, and Stanislav Lesnevskii. "'O slavyanofilakh, rusofobakh i lyubvi k Rossii . . .'" *Knizhnoe obozrenie*, no. 35 (1 September 1989): 3.

Anninskii, Lev. "A propos." *Soglasie*, nos. 8–9 (August–September 1992): 189–91.

Antonov, M. F., V. M. Klykov, I. R. Shafarevich. "Pis'mo v sekretariat pravleniya soyuza pisatelei RSFSR." *Literaturnaya Rossiya*, no. 31 (4 August 1989): 4.

Aucouturier, Michel. "Lioubimov." *Esprit*, no. 357 (February 1967): 271–76.

———. "Writer and Text in the Works of Abram Terc (An Ontology of Writing and A Poetics of Prose)." Translated by Alexandre Guérard. In *Fiction and Drama in Eastern and Southeastern Europe: Evolution and Experiment in the Postwar Period*, edited by Henrik Birnbaum and Thomas Eekman, 1–10. Columbus, Ohio: Slavica, 1980.

Azhgikhina, Nadezhda. "Samyi glavnyi dissident." Review of *Abram Terts (Andrei Sinyavskii), Sobranie sochinenii v dvukh tomakh]*. *Ogonek*, no. 9 (1993): 17.

———. "Vozvrashchenie Sinyavskogo i Danielya." Review of *Tsena metafory, ili Prestuplenie i nakazanie Sinyavskogo i Danielya*. *Oktyabr'*, no. 8 (August 1990): 203–05.

Bailey, George. "The Trial of Two Soviet Writers: A Special Report on the Failure of a Dogma." *Reporter* 34, no. 4 (24 February 1966): 34–38.

Bakhrakh, Aleksandr. "Vechnyi Rozanov." *Literaturnyi kur'er* (Fall 1985), 16–18.

Barrett, William. "Superfluous Man." Review of *On Socialist Realism*. *Atlantic* January 1962, 97–98.

Basinskii, Pavel. "Konets Tertsa, ili Andrei Sinyavskii vchera i segodnya." *Literaturnaya gazeta*, no. 4 (27 January 1993): 4.

Batkin, Leonid. "Sinyavskii, Pushkin—i my." *Oktyabr'*, no. 1 (January 1991): 164–93.

Bayley, John. "*Goodnight* by Abram Tertz (Andrei Sinyavsky)." *New York Times Book Review*, 17 December 1989, 1, 26–27.

"'Belaya kniga' o dele Sinyavskogo i Danielya." *Grani*, no. 63 (1967): 204–15.

Bergholz, Stefan. "On Reading Tertz." *Survey*, no. 41 (April 1962): 145–50.

Bloch-Michel, Jean. "Siniavski i Daniel." *Preuves*, no. 183 (1965): 76–78.

Blot, Jean. Review of *Goodnight*. *La Nouvelle revue française*, no. 384 (1 January 1985): 109–11.

Bogoraz, Larisa. "Dushevnye muki seksota: Otkrytoe pis'mo Aleksandru Voronelyu." *Vremya i my*, no. 93 (1986): 210–14.

Boroff, David. "Message from a New Dimension." Review of *Fantastic Stories*. *Saturday Review*, 13 April 1963, 28.

Bregel', Yurii. "Ob"yasnenie posle lagerya." *Vremya i my*, no. 91 (1986): 224–29.

Brown, Clarence. "*A Voice from the Chorus* by Abram Tertz (Andrei Sinyavsky)." *New Republic*, 25 September 1976, 41–43.

Brown, Deming. "The Art of Andrei Sinyavsky." In idem, *Soviet Russian Literature since Stalin*, 331–51. Cambridge: Cambridge University Press, 1978. Reprinted from *Slavic Review* 29, no. 4 (December 1970): 662–81. Also reprinted in *Major Soviet Writers: Essays in Criticism*, edited by Edward J. Brown, 367–87 (New York: Oxford University Press, 1973).

———. "Moscow: The Defense Does Not Rest." *Reporter* 35, no. 4 (22 September 1966): 43–45.

Brown, Edward J. *Russian Literature since the Revolution*. Rev. ed. Cambridge, Mass.: Harvard University Press, 1982.

Brumberg, Abraham. "In Quest of Justice." *Problems of Communism* 17, no. 4 (July–August 1968): 1–5.

———. "'Socialist Legality' On Trial." *Reporter* 34, no. 5 (10 March 1966): 34–36.

———. "Writers in Prison." *Problems of Communism* 15, no. 2 (March–April 1966): 65–78.

Bryden, Ronald. "Nineteen Sixty-Four." Review of *The Trial Begins*. *Spectator*, no. 6878 (29 April 1960), 633–34.

Burg, David. "Molodoe pokolenie sovetskikh pisatelei." *Mosty* 1 (1965): 211–29.

Carlisle, Olga. "A Voice from the Third Russian Emigration." *New York Times Book Review*, 30 October 1977, 15, 50–52.

Carrington, Ildikó de Papp. "Demons, Doubles, and Dinosaurs: *Life Before Man*, *The Origin of Consciousness*, and 'The Icicle.'" *Essays on Canadian Writing*, no. 33 (Fall 1986): 68–88.

Chapple, Richard L. "The Bible and the Zoo in Andrey Sinyavsky's *The Trial Begins*." *Orbis Litterarum: International Review of Literary Studies* 33 (1978): 349–58.

Clardy, J. V. "Andrei Sinyavsky's 'On Socialist Realism': An Analysis." *Cimarron Review*, no. 23 (1973): 29–32.

Clowes, Edith W. "Kafka and Russian Experimental Fiction in the Thaw, 1956–1965." *Modern Language Review* 89, no. 1 (January 1994): 149–65.

——. *Russian Experimental Fiction: Resisting Ideology after Utopia.* Princeton: Princeton University Press, 1993.

Cohen, Gordon, and Donald Fanger. "Abram Tertz: Dissidence, Diffidence, and Russian Literary Tradition." In *Soviet Society and Culture: Essays in Honor of Vera S. Dunham,* edited by Terry L. Thompson and Richard Sheldon, 162–77. Boulder and London: Westview Press, 1988.

Dalton, Margaret. *Andrei Siniavskii and Julii Daniel': Two Soviet "Heretical" Writers.* Würzburg: Jal-Verlag, 1973.

Davenport, Guy. "Two Straw Men and Gogol's Ghost." Review of *The Makepeace Experiment. National Review* 17, no. 34 (24 August 1965): 732, 734–35.

Devlin, Kevin. "Echoes of the Tertz Affair." *New Leader* 49, no. 7 (28 March 1966): 17–18.

Dolbier, Maurice. "'The Trial Begins' [Review of *The Trial Begins*]." *New York Herald Tribune,* 12 September 1960, 21.

Dovlatov, Sergei. "Andreyu Sinyavskomu—60 let." *Panorama,* no. 235 (11–18 October 1985): 18.

Dunham, Vera S. "Serenity: A Note on Sinyavsky's Style." In *The Third Wave: Russian Literature in Emigration,* edited by Olga Matich with Michael Heim, 110–17. Ann Arbor: Ardis, 1984.

Durkin, Andrew R. "Narrator, Metaphor, and Theme in Sinjavskij's *Fantastic Tales.*" *Slavic and East European Journal* 24, no. 2 (Summer 1980): 133–44.

[The Editors]. "In Quest of Justice." *Problems of Communism* 17, no. 5 (September–October 1968): 1.

Efimov, Igor'. "Vymysel demagoga." *Novoe russkoe slovo,* 22 February 1987, 3.

Emerson, Caryl. "Soviet Civilization: Its Discontents, Disasters, Residual Fascinations," *Hudson Review,* 44, no. 4 (Winter 1992): 574–84.

Eremin, Dm. "Perevertyshi." *Izvestiya,* no. 10 (13 January 1966): 6.

Eremina, L. S., ed. *Tsena metafory ili prestuplenie i nakazanie Sinyavskogo i Danielya.* Moscow: Kniga, 1989.

Etkind, Efim. "Der Doppelgänger: Über Andrej Sinjawskij und seinem Roman 'Gute Nacht.'" *Neue Rundschau* 97, no. 1 (1986): 84–90.

——. "Ispoved' shenapana." *Vremya i my,* no. 91 (1986): 230–36.

Fainsod, Merle. "From the Soviet Literary Underground." Review of *The Trial Begins. Herald Tribune Book Review,* 11 September 1960, 7.

Fanger, Donald. "A Change of Venue: Russian Journals of the Emigration." *Times Literary Supplement,* 21 November 1986, 1321–22.

——. "Conflicting Imperatives in the Model of the Russian Writer: The Case of Tertz/Sinyavsky." In *Literature and History: Theoretical Problems and Russian Case Studies,* edited by Gary Saul Morson, 111–24. Stanford: Stanford University Press, 1986.

————. "Homo Sovieticus: Utopia and Reality in the Russian Experience." Review of *Soviet Civilization. Times Literary Supplement*, 15 March 1991, 5–6.

Feifer, George. "Who's Been Spiking the Borscht? [Review of *The Makepeace Experiment*]." *Book Week* [*Washington Post*], 22 August 1965, 4, 15.

Feofanov, Yu. "Izoblichenie." *Izvestiya*, no. 36 (12 February 1966): 4.

————. "Logika padeniya." *Izvestiya*, no. 39 (16 February 1966): 4.

————. "Pora otvecat'." *Izvestiya*, no. 37 (13 February 1966): 5.

————. "Tut tsarit zakon." *Izvestiya*, no. 35 (11 February 1966): 4.

Field, Andrew. "Abram Tertz's Ordeal by Mirror." Abram Tertz, *Mysli vrasplokh*. New York: Rausen Publishers, 1966, 7–42. Incorporates "Abram Tertz's Ordeal by Mirror." *New Leader* 48, 15 (19 July 1965): 9–15, and "Prisoner in Fantasy," New Leader 49, no. 4 (14 February 1966): 17–18.

————. "The Arrest of Andrei Sinyavsky." *New Leader* 48, no. 22 (8 November 1965): 10–1.

Filippov, Boris. "Priroda i tyur'ma." In Tertz, *Fantasticheskii mir Abrama Tertsa*, 5–23. New York: Inter-language Literary Associates, 1967. Section on Tertz reprinted from "Priroda i Tyur'ma. (O tvorchestve Abrama Tertsa i Nikolaya Arzhaka)." *Grani*, no. 60 (1966): 75–93.

Foster, Ludmila A. Review of *Lyubimov* by Abram Terc. *Slavic and East European Journal* 10, no. 1 (1966): 106–07.

Frank, Joseph. "The Triumph of Abram Tertz." *New York Review of Books*, 27 June 1991, 35–43.

Frankel, Theodore. "Art, Politics, and the Soviet Writer." *Commentary* 41, no. 5 (May 1966): 52–59.

Frayn, Michael. "Lightning over Moscow." Review of *The Trial Begins. Guardian*, 29 April 1960, 11.

————. "Writers on Trial: Thoughts on the Sinyavsky-Daniel Case." *Encounter* 30, no. 1 (1968): 80–88.

Fremont-Smith, Eliot. "Serafima Was the Spur." Review of *The Makepeace Experiment. New York Times*, 9 July 1965, 27.

Frioux, Claude. "Siniavski, Daniel et la conscience publique." *Esprit*, no. 357 (February 1967): 227–34.

Gachev, Georgii. "Andrei Sinyavskii–Abram Terts i ego roman *Spokoinoi nochi* (Ispovest')." *Moskovskii vestnik*, no. 1 (1989): 235–66. English translation of excerpts from this article by Catharine Theimer Nepomnyashchy, "Andrei Siniavskii–Abram Tertz and His Novel *Goodnight!*" *Russian Studies in Literature* 28, no. 1 (Winter 1991–92): 25–44.

Genis, Aleksandr, and Petr Vail'. "Labardan! Andrei Sinyavskii kak Abram Terts." Chapter in *Sovremennaya russkaya proza*. Ann Arbor, Mich.: Hermitage, 1982, 57–75.

Gifford, Henry. "Andrey Sinyavsky: The Voice and the Chorus." *Encounter* 42, no. 2 (February 1974): 34–39.

Ginzburg, Aleksandr, ed. *Belaya kniga po delu A. Sinyavskogo i Yu. Danielya*. Frankfurt am Main: Posev, 1967.

Glenny, Michael. "Sinyavsky and Daniel on Trial." *Survey* 66 (1968): 145–47.

Golomshtok, Igor'. "Posleslovie." Abram Terts, *Golos iz khora*. London: Stenvalley Press, 1973, 329–39.

Gorbanevskaya, N. "Kto na chei kryuchok klyunul?" *Russkaya mysl'*, no. 3664 (13 March 1987): 4.

Gul', Roman. "Abram Terts: *Mysli vrasplokh.*" *Novyi zhurnal*, no. 84 (1966): 276–79.

———. "Progulki khama s Pushkinym," *Novyi zhurnal*, no. 124 (1976): 117–29. Partially reprinted in *Literaturnaya Rossiya*, no. 26 (30 June 1989): 18–19.

Gurvich, I. "Tol'ko li gipoteza?" *Novoe russkoe slovo*, 27 July 1993, 8.

Gusev, Vl. "Kraine Ser'ezno." *Literaturnaya Rossiya*, no. 38 (22 September 1989): 8.

———. "V poslednii raz." *Literaturnaya Rossiya*, no. 45 (11 November 1989): 2–3.

Gusev, Vladimir, and Andrei Turkov. "Nasmeshka gor'kaya . . ." *Literaturnaya gazeta*, 31 May 1989, 2.

Haber, Erika. "Dueling Narrators; or, *Ljubimov* as Metafiction." [Unpublished manuscript.]

Hayward, Max. "Awkward Voices in Russia." *London Times*, 1 February 1966, 11.

———. "The Case of Tertz-Sinyavski." *Dissent*, January–February 1966, 88–91.

———. "The Moscow Trial." *Partisan Review* 33, no. 2 (1966): 227–39.

———. "Pushkin, Gogol, and the Devil." In idem, *Writers in Russia*. Reprinted from *Times Literary Supplement*, 28 May 1976, 630–32.

———. "Sinyavsky's *A Voice from the Chorus.*" In idem, *Writers in Russia, 1917–1978*. Edited and with an introduction by Patricia Blake, 265–84. New York: Harcourt Brace Jovanovich Publishers–Harvest/HBJ Book, 1983. Reprinted from Introduction to Tertz, *A Voice from the Chorus*. Translated by Kyril Fitzlyon and Max Hayward, vii–xxiii. New York: Farrar, Straus and Giroux, 1976.

Hayward, Max, ed. and Trans. *On Trial: The Soviet State versus "Abram Tertz" and "Nikolai Arzhak."* 2d ed. New York: Harper and Row, 1967.

Hayward, Max, and Leopold Labedz. "Writers and the Police." *Encounter* 26, no. 1 (1966), 84–88.

Hingley, Ronald. "Arresting Episodes." Review of *Spokoynoy nochi. Times Literary Supplement*, 15 February 1985, 178.

Holmgren, Beth C. "First-Person Liberties: The persona in the work of Witold Gombrowicz and Abram Terc." Ph.D. diss., Harvard University, 1987.

———. "The Transfiguring of Context in the Work of Abram Terts." *Slavic Review* 50, no. 4 (Winter 1991): 965–77.

Howe, Irving. "Do Not Go Gentle." Review of *Goodnight!* by Abram Tertz (Andrei Sinyavsky). *New Republic*, 1 January 1990, 34, 36–37.

———. "Predicaments of Soviet Writing—I [Review of *Fantastic Stories*]." *New Republic*, 11 May 1963, 19–21.

Hugh-Jones, Stephen. "Worm's Eye View." Review of *The Makepeace Experiment*. *Encounter* 25, no. 1 (July 1965): 82–83.

Il'inskii, Oleg. "Neudachnye obobshchenya: Po povodu stat'i A. Tertsa." *Novyi zhurnal*, no. 118 (1975): 236–43.

Ivanova, Natal'ya. "Sindrom 'zheleznoi ruki.'" *Ogonek*, no. 37 (September 1989): 21–23.

Ivask, Yurii. "'Golos iz khora' Sinyavskogo: Zametki na polyakh." *Novyi zhurnal*, no. 116 (1974): 95–101.

———. "Rozanov v izobrazhenii Sinyavskogo." *Chast' rechi* 2/3 (1982): 308–13.

Ivsky, Oleg. Review of *The Makepeace Experiment*, by Abram Tertz. *Library Journal* 90, no. 13 (July 1965): 3074.

"Iz pochty *Oktybrya*." *Oktyabr'*, no. 9 (1989): 204–06.

Jameson, Donald. "What Yevgeny Knew." *New Republic* 196, no. 25 (22 June 1987): 39–41.

Kakutani, Michiko. "A Novel Illuminates a Shocking Soviet Reality." Review of *Goodnight! New York Times*, 13 December 1989, C29.

Kaniewicz, Georges. "Un anonyme." Review of *Fantastic Stories*. *Preuves*, no. 157 (March 1964): 86–88.

Kedrina, Z. "Nasledniki Smerdyakova." *Literaturnaya gazeta*, no. 10 (22 January 1966): 2, 4.

Khmel'nitskii, Sergei. "Iz chreva kitova." *Dvadtsat' dva*, no. 48 (June–July 1986): 151–80.

"Klevetniki-perevertyshi." *Izvestiya*, no. 4 (18 January 1966): 3.

Kochetov, V. "Skvernoe remeslo." *Oktyabr'*, no. 3 (March 1966): 211–18.

Kolonosky, Walter. "Andrei Siniavskii: The Chorus and The Critic." *Canadian-American Slavic Studies* 9, no. 3 (Fall 1975): 352–60.

———. "Andrej Sinjavskij as a Literary Critic." Ph.D. diss., University of Kansas, 1972.

———. "Inherent and Ulterior Design in Sinjavskij's 'Pxenc.'" *Slavic and East European Journal* 26, no. 3 (Fall 1982): 329–37.

Kott, Jan. "A Voice from the Chorus." *New York Times Book Review*, 27 June 1976, 1, 25–27.

Kozlovskii, Vladimir. "Vydalo li TsRU Sinyavskogo i Danielya?" *Novoe russkoe slovo*, 10 February 1987, 3–4.

Krymov, B. "Sud prodolzhaetsya." *Literaturnaya gazeta*, no. 19 (12 February 1966): 2.

Labedz, Leopold. "The Trial in Moscow." *Encounter* 26, no. 4 (April 1966): 82–91.

Laber, Jeri L. "The Trial Ends . . ." *New Republic*, 19 March 1966, 26–29.

Lask, Thomas. "Publishing: Sinyavsky." *New York Times*, 17 November 1978, C24.

Laurita, Mary. "The Transgression of Boundaries? Andrej Sinjavskij-Tertz's Cubist Approach to Narration." Unpublished manuscript.

Leatherbarrow, W. J. "The Sense of Purpose and Socialist Realism in Tertz's *The Trial Begins.*" *Forum for Modern Language Studies* 11, no. 3 (1975): 268–79.

Lebenson, Ol'ga. "Vizit posle donosa." *Vremya i my*, no. 91 (1986): 229–30.

Lehmann-Haupt, Christopher. Review of *A Voice From the Chorus*. *New York Times*, 2 July 1976, C25.

Leong, Albert. "The Literary Criticism of Abram Tertz." *Proceedings of the Pacific Northwest Conference on Foreign Languages* 28, i (1977): 118–20.

Levin, Martin. "A Reader's Report." Review of *The Makepeace Experiment*. *New York Times Book Review*, 11 July 1965, 40.

Levitt, Marcus C. "Siniavskii's Alternative Autobiography *A Voice from the Chorus.*" *Canadian Slavonic Papers* 33, no. 1 (March 1991): 46–61.

"Litso Klevetnikov." *Pravda*, no. 42 (11 February 1966): 6.

Lobanov, Mikhail, "Chelnochnye perestroishchiki," *Moskovskii literator*, no. 7 (10 February 1989): 4.

Lourie, Richard. *Letters to the Future: An Approach to Sinyavsky-Tertz*. Ithaca: Cornell University Press, 1975.

Maguire, Robert A. Review of *On Socialist Realism* and *The Trial Begins* by Abram Terc. *Russian Review* 21, no. 2 (1962): 193–95.

Maksudov, S. "Spokoinoi nochi. S dobrym utrom. Priglashenie k chteniyu." *Strana i mir*, no. 10 (1984): 93–96.

[Mal'gin, Andrei.] "Anatolii Anan'ev: Gost' 13 stranitsy." *Nedelya*, no. 34 (21–27 August 1989): 13.

Marchenko, Alla. "Opyt raznomysliya vnutri inakomysliya." *Literaturnoe obozrenie*, no. 8 (1989): 87–88.

[Martynenko, Ol'ga.] "Uvolen za ubezhdeniya." *Moskovskie novosti*, no. 2 (14 January 1990), 4.

Mann, Yu. "Nad bezdnoi Gogolya." Review of *V teni Gogolya*. *Literaturnoe obozrenie*, no. 1/2 (1993): 30–32.

Mathewson, Rufus W., Jr. *The Positive Hero in Russian Literature*. 2d ed. Stanford: Stanford University Press, 1975.

———. "Trapped in History: The Mind of Andrei Sinyavsky." Unpublished manuscript.

Mathewson, Ruth. "Sinyavsky's Mission." Review of *A Voice from the Chorus*. *New Leader*, 13 September 1976, 16–17.

Matich, Olga. "*Spokojnoj noči:* Andrej Sinjavskij's Rebirth as Abram Terc." *Slavic and East European Journal* 33, no. 1 (Spring 1989): 50–63.

———. "Russian Literature in Emigration: A Historical Perspective on the 1970s." In *The Third Wave: Russian Literature in Emigration*, edited by Olga Matich with Michael Heim, 15–20. Ann Arbor, Mich.: Ardis, 1984.

Mayne, Richard. "Technique [Review of *The Makepeace Experiment*]." *New Statesman* 69, no. 1779 (16 April 1965): 619–20.

McLean, Hugh. "Abram Tertz and His Translators." *Slavic and East European Journal* 8, no. 4 (1964): 434–40.

Meerson, Ol'ga. "Progulka s Tertsem." *Forum.* 3 (1983), 222–31.

Merkulov, Dmitrii. "Klevetnikam Rossii . . ." *Moskovskii literator,* nos. 30, 31 (15 September 1989): 4.

Mikhailov, Mikhailo. *Abram Terts ili begstvo iz retorty.* Frankfurt/Main: Possev-Verlag, 1969. English translation, "Flight from the Test Tube," in idem, *Russian Themes.* New York: Farrar, Straus and Giroux, 1968.

Morsberger, Grace Anne. "'The Icicle' as Allegory." *Odyssey* 4, no. 2 (August 1981): 15–18.

Muchnic, Helen. "It Happened in Lyubimov." Review of *The Makepeace Experiment. New York Review of Books,* 14 October 1965, 33–35.

——. "Light from Above." Review of *A Voice from the Chorus,* by Abram Tertz (Andrei Sinyavsky). *New York Review of Books* 23, no. 13 (5 August 1976), 5, 8.

Muggeridge, Malcolm. "Books." *Esquire,* March 1968, 26, 40.

Murav, Harriet. "The Case Against Andrei Siniavskii: The Letter and the Law." Unpublished manuscript.

Nepomnyashchii, Valentin, et al. "Obsuzhdenie knigi Abrama Tertsa 'Progulki s Pushkinym.' *Voprosy literatury,* no. 10 (October 1990): 77–153. English translation of excerpts by Catharine Theimer Nepomnyashchy, "A Discussion of Abram Tertz's Book *Strolls with Pushkin,*" *Russian Studies in Literature* 28, no. 1 (Winter 1991–92): 63–88.

Nepomnyashchy, Catharine Theimer. "Andrei Sinyavsky's 'Return' to the Soviet Union. *Formations* 6, no. 1 (Spring 1991): 24–44.

——. "Andrei Sinyavsky's 'You and I': A Modern Day Fantastic Tale." *Ulbandus Review* 2, no. 2 (1982): 209–30.

——. "Perestroika and the Soviet Creative Unions." In *New Perspectives on Russian and Soviet Artistic Culture: Selected Papers from the Fourth World Congress for Soviet and East European Studies, Harrogate, 1990,* edited by John O. Norman, 131–51. New York: St. Martin's Press, 1994.

——. "The Poetics of Motivation: Time, Narrative, and History in the Works of Solženitcyn, Sinjavskij, and Pasternak." Ph.D. diss., Columbia University, 1987.

——. "Sinyavsky/Tertz: The Evolution of the Writer in Exile." Special issue of *Humanities in Society* 7, nos. 3–4 (1984): 123–42.

Nepomnyashchy, Catharine Theimer, ed. "The Return of Abram Tertz: Siniavskii's Reception in Gorbachev's Russia." An issue of *Russian Studies in Literature* 28, no. 1 (Winter 1991–1992).

Nivat, Georges. "André Siniavski: l'écrivain est un assassin." *Magazine littéraire,* nos. 172–73 (May 1981): 92–3.

——. ". . . Chtoby prevozmoch' otchayanie i odinochestvo." Review of *Goodnight. Russkaya mysl',* no. 3546 (6 December 1984): 10.

——. "Le pistolet de Pouchkine." *Magazine littéraire,* no. 124 (May 1977): 60–63.

"Notes from Underground." *Time,* 29 October 1965, 37.

Novikov, Vladimir. "Sinyavskii i Terts." In Terts, *Sobranie sochinenii v dvukh tomakh* 1:3–12. Moscow: SP Start, 1992.

[Nudel'man, R.] "Dvadtsat' let spustya [Interview with Mark Azbel' and Nina and Aleksandr Voronel']." *Dvadtsat' dva*, no. 46 (January–March 1986): 132–77.

Numano, Mitsuësi. "Iz knigi 'Za odnu ostanovku do vechnosti.' Solzhenitsyn ili Sinyavskii!" *Inostrannaya literatura*, no. 2 (February 1990), 238–41.

Nussbaum, Andrew J. "Literary Selves: The Tertz-Sinyavsky Dialogue." In *Autobiographical Statements in Twentieth-Century Russian Literature*, edited by Jane Gary Harris. 238–59. Princeton: Princeton University Press, 1990.

Oberbeck, S. K. "Underground Letters." Review of *The Makepeace Experiment*. *Reporter* 33, no. 7 (21 October 1965): 58–59.

[Obozrevatel']. "Klevetniki v efire." *Izvestiya*, no. 88 (14 April 1966): 2.

Ohmann, Richard M. "Soviet and American Literature." Review of *On Socialist Realism*. *Commonweal* 75, no. 15 (5 January 1962): 391–92.

Orekhanova, G. "Posleslovie k replike." *Sovetskaya Rossiya*, 10 October 1989, 4.

"Otkrytoe pis'mo v redaktsiyu gazety 'Izvestiya.'" *Izvestiya*, no. 45 (23 February 1966): 3.

Perel'man, Viktor. "Kto obvinyaet Sinyavskogo." *Vremya i my*, no. 91 (1986): 218–22.

"Perestaralis'." *Literaturnaya gazeta*, no. 24 (24 February 1966): 4.

Peterson, Ronald E. "The Writer as Alien in Sinjavskij's 'Pxenc.'" *Wiener Slawistischer Almanach*, Band 12 (1983): 47–53.

Petrov, T. "Prigovor Klevetnikam." *Pravda*, no. 46 (15 February 1966): 4.

Pevear, Richard. "Sinyavsky in Two Worlds: Two Brothers Named Chénier." *Hudson Review* 25 (1972): 375–402.

Pipes, Richard. "The Soviet Jacobins." *New Leader* 49, no. 9 (25 April 1966): 9–11.

"Pis'ma na odnu temu." *Literaturnaya Rossiya*, no. 37 (15 September 1989): 16.

"Pis'ma na odnu temu." *Literaturnaya Rossiya*, no. 39 (29 September 1989): 20.

Pletnev, R. "O zlom suemudrii knigi Abrama Tertsa." Review of *V teni Gogolya*. *Novyi zhurnal*, no. 121 (1975): 72–80.

Pomerants, G. "Diaspora i Abrashka Terts." *Iskusstvo kino*, no. 2 (1990): 20–26.

Popova, Natal'ya. "Gal'skii petukh i rusofobiya." *Knizhnoe obozrenie*, no. 46 (17 November 1989): 16. English translation by Dobrochna Dyrcz-Freeman, "The Gallic Rooster and Russophobia," *Russian Studies in Literature* 28, no. 1 (Winter 1991–92): 56–62.

Porte, Joel. "The Laugh's on Us All." Review of *The Makepeace Experiment*. *Christian Science Monitor*, 5 August 1965, 7.

Radley, Philippe. "Reporting the Tertz Affair." *New Leader* 49, no. 1 (3 January 1966): 11–12.

Redaktsionnaya kollegiya. "K chitatelyam." *Oktyabr'*, no. 9 (1989): 207–08.

Redaktsiya "LR." "Provokatsiya." *Literaturnaya Rossiya*, no. 42 (20 October 1989), 2.

Reeve, F. D. "Listen for the Pistol Shot." Review of *Fantastic Stories*. *Kenyon Review* 25, no. 4 (Autumn 1963): 743–47.

Renshaw, John. "The Elusive 'Abram Tertz.'" *New York Times Magazine*, 31 October 1965, 52–53.

Roberts, Henry L. "Capitalize *P* in Purpose." Review of *On Socialist Realism. New York Times Book Review*, 26 November 1961, 10.

"Rossiiskie dokumenty po delu A. Sinyavskogo i Yu. Danielya." *Grani*, no. 62 (1966).

Rozanova, Mariya. "Abram da Mar'ya." *Nezavisimaya gazeta*, 12 January 1993, 5, and 13 January 1993, 5. Reprinted in *Sintaksis*, no. 34 (1994), 125–51.

——. "Fantasticheskii realizm." *Dekorativnoe iskusstvo* 3 (1967).

——. "K istorii i geografii etoi knigi." *Voprosy literatury*, no. 10 (October 1990), 154–61. Reprinted in Abram Terts, *Progulki s Pushkinym*, 147–59 (Saint Petersburg: Vsemirnoe slovo, 1993). English translation by Catharine Theimer Nepomnyashchy, "On the History and Geography of This Book," *Russian Studies in Literature* 28, no. 1 (Winter 1991–92): 89–98.

——. "Kto za kogo reshaet." *Moskovskie novosti*, no. 3 (28 January–2 February 1990): 6. English translation, "Who Decides for Whom?" *Moscow News*, no. 3 (28 January–2 February 1990): 3.

Rubinshtein, Natal'ya. "Abram Terts i Aleksandr Pushkin." *Vremya i my*, no. 9 (July 1976): 118–33.

Salisbury, Harrison E. "Russian Dissenters." Review of *Fantastic Stories. New York Times Book Review*, 5 May 1963, 35.

Sandler, Stephanie. "Sex, Death and Nation in the *Strolls with Pushkin* Controversy." *Slavic Review* 51, no. 2 (Summer 1992): 294–308.

Scammell, Michael. "Speculations of a Captive Monk." Review of *A Voice from the Chorus. Times Literary Supplement*, 20 May 1977, 626–27.

Schwartz, Harry. "Globov, Marina, and Seryozha of the Soviet New Class." Review of *The Trial Begins. New York Times Book Review*, 16 October 1960, 4.

——. "Man-Centered Theology." Review of *On Socialist Realism. Saturday Review*, 11 November 1961, 26.

Sekretariat pravleniya Soyuza pisatelei SSSR. "Otkrytoe pis'mo v redaktsiyu 'Literaturnoi gazety.'" *Literaturnaya gazeta*, no. 22 (19 February 1966): 1.

Sh., I. "Pozitsiya izdatelya. Po stranitsam zhurnalov '22' i 'Sintaksis.'" *Vremya i my*, no. 91 (1986): 181–93.

Shafarevich, I., "Fenomen emigratsii," *Literaturnaya Rossiya*, no. 36 (8 September 1989): 4–5. English translation by Dobrocha Dyrcz-Freeman, "The Emigration Phenomenon," *Russian Studies in Literature* 28, no. 1 (Winter 1991–92): 45–55.

——. "Rusofobiya." *Nash sovremennik*, no. 6 (1989): 167–92, and no. 11 (1989): 162–72. Reprinted from *Veche*, no. 32 (December 1988): 9–75, and no. 33 (March 1989), 5–54.

Sheppard, R. Z. "Notes from the Underground." Review of *Goodnight! Time*, 25 December 1989, 76.

"VI plenum pravleniya SP RSFSR." *Literaturnaya Rossiya*, no. 48 (1 December 1989): 2–13.

Shturman, Dora. "Spokoinoi nochi . . . ." *Novoe russkoe slovo*, 2 July 1993, 21.

Simmons, Ernest J. "The Trial Begins for Soviet Literature." *Massachusetts Review* 7, no. 4 (Autumn 1966): 714–24.

Simonov, Vladimir. "Vid iz okna." *Moskovskie novosti*, no. 8 (22 February 1987): 3.

Singer, Herman. "Fugitive from Socialist Realism." Review of *The Trial Begins*. *New Republic*, 5 December 1960, 19–20.

Sinyavskii i Daniel' na skam'e podsudimykh. New York: Inter-language Literary Associates, 1966.

"Socialist Surrealism." Review of *The Trial Begins*. *Time*, 3 October 1960, 84–85.

[Solov'eva, Yu.] "Monologi." [Interview with Mariya Rozanova]. *Sovetskii tsirk*, no. 22 (31 May 1990): 14, and no. 23 (7 June 1990): 14–15.

Solzhenitsyn, Aleksandr. ". . . Koleblet tvoi trenozhnik." *Vestnik russkogo khristianskogo dvizheniya*, no. 142 (1984): 133–52. Reprinted in *Novyi mir*, no. 5 (1991): 148–59.

———. "Otvetnoe slovo na prisuzhdenie literaturnoi nagrady amerikanskogo natsional'nogo kluba iskusstv, N'yu-Iork, 19 yanvarya 1993." *Novyi mir*, no. 4 (1993): 3–6. English translation, "The Relentless Cult of Novelty and How It Wrecked the Century," *New York Times Book Review*, 7 February 1993, 3, 17.

———. "Nashi plyuralisty." *Vestnik russkogo khristianskogo dvizheniya*, no. 139 (1983): 133–60. Reprinted in *Novyi mir*, no. 4 (1992): 211–25. English translation, "Our Pluralists," *Survey: A Journal of East and West Studies* 29, no. 2/125 (Summer 1985): 1.28.

Steinman, Maxine. Review of "Fantastic Stories" by Abram Tertz. *East Europe* 13, no. 10 (October 1964): 54–56.

Tatarinov, Aleksei. "Andrei Sinyavskii i Abram Terts." Review of *Spokoinoi nochi Strelets*, no. 11 (November 1985): 20–22.

"Témoignage pour Siniavski." *Le Monde*, 23 November 1965, 6.

Ternovskii, E. "V neyasnom i nereshennom mire Rozanova (O knige Sinyavskogo 'Opavshie list'ya' V. V. Rozanova)." *Russkaya mysl'*, no. 3429 (9 September 1982): 11.

Tikos, Laszlo M. "On Abram Tertz's *A Voice from the Choir*." *International Fiction Review* 2, no. 2 (July 1975): 168–73.

Tsyurupa, Aleksei. "Ne sotvori sebe kumira (Pochti vavilonskaya istoriya)." *Kamchatskii komsomolets*, 12 December 1989, 6.

Tvardovskii, A. "Po sluchayu yubileya." *Novyi mir*, no. 1 (January 1965): 3–18.

Updike, John. "The Lament of Abrashka Tertz." *New Leader* 49, no. 2 (1966): 3.

Viereck, Peter. "World Power Through Witchcraft." Review of *The Makepeace Experiment*. *Saturday Review*, 24 July 1965, 45–46.

Vinogradov, Igor'. "Osobyi put'? . . . ." *Moskovskie novosti*, no. 38 (17 September 1989): 16.

Volker, Levin. *Das Groteske in M. Bulgakov's Prosa. Mit einem Exkurs zu A. Sinjavsky.* Munich: Sagner, 1975.

Voronel', Aleksandr. "Pravo byt' uslyshannym. . . ." *Dvadtsat' dva,* no. 48 (June–July 1986): 145–51.

Vozdvizhenskii, Vyacheslav, "Progulki s Shafarevichem i bez . . . ." *Strana i mir,* no. 6 (1989): 166–71.

"V sekretariate moskovskoi pisatel'skoi organizatsii." *Literaturnaya gazeta,* no. 23 (22 February 1966): 4.

"Vse zaedino: stseny VI plenuma pravleniya Soyuza pisatelei RSFSR 13–14 noyabrya 1989 goda." *Ogonek,* no. 48 (November 1989): 6–8, 31.

West, Anthony. "Books: Inside the Wrong Skin." Review of *Fantastic Stories. New Yorker,* 21 September 1963, 181–88.

West, Paul. "New Novels." Review of *The Trial Begins. New Statesman* 59, no. 1520 (30 April 1960): 642–43.

Woronzoff, Alexander. "The Writer as Artist and Critic: The Case of Andrej Sinjavskij." *Russian Language Journal* 37, nos. 126–27 (1983): 139–45.

Yevtushenko, Evgeny. "Kontramarka na protsess." *Ogonek,* no. 19 (May 1989): 19. Abridged English translation, "A Pass to See the Trial," *Soviet Life,* February 1990, 58–59.

———. "A Poet's View of *Glasnost.*" *Time,* 9 February 1987, 32–33.

Zamoyska, Hélène. "Andrey Sinyavsky Arrives in Paris." *Encounter,* no. 41 (November 1973): 63–65.

———. "Pis'mo Elen Zamoyska (Pel'te) Andreyu Sinyavskomu." *Vremya i my,* no. 91 (1986): 222–23.

———. "Quelques souvenirs sur André Siniavski." *Esprit,* no. 357 (February 1967): 258–70.

———. "Siniavski et sa patrie." *Le Monde,* 17–18 April 1966, 1, 3.

General References

Avvakum. "The Life of Archpriest Avvakum by Himself." In *Medieval Russia's Epics, Chronicles, and Tales,* edited and translated by Serge A. Zenkovsky, rev. ed., 399–448. (New York: E. P. Dutton, 1974).

Barthes, Roland. *Image—Music—Text.* Translated by Stephen Heath. New York: Farrar, Straus and Giroux–Noonday Press, 1977.

———. *S/Z.* Translated by Richard Miller. New York: Hill and Wang–Noonday Press, 1974.

Belinskii, V. G. *Izbrannye sochineniya.* Moscow/Leningrad: Gosudarstvennoe izdatel'stvo khudozhestvennoi literatury, 1949.

Berdyaev, Nicholas. "The Ethics of Creativity." In *Russian Philosophy,* vol. 3, edited by James M. Edie, James P. Scanlan, and Mary-Barbara Zeldin, with the collaboration of George L. Kline, 198–203. Knoxville: University of Tennessee Press, 1968.

Blok, Aleksandr. *Sobranie sochinenii.* Moscow-Leningrad: Gosudarstvennoe iz-datel'stvo khudozhestvennoi literatury, 1960–63.

Booth, Wayne C. *A Rhetoric of Irony.* Chicago: University of Chicago Press, 1974.

Brooks, Jeffrey. "Readers and Reading at the End of the Tsarist Era." In *Literature and Society in Imperial Russia, 1800–1914,* edited by William Mills Todd III, 97–150. Stanford: Stanford University Press, 1978.

————. "Russian Nationalism and Russian Literature: The Canonization of the Classics." In *Nation and Ideology: Essays in Honor of Wayne S. Vucinich,* edited by Ivo Banac, John G. Ackerman, and Roman Szporluk, 315–34. New York: Columbia University Press, 1981.

————. *When Russia Learned to Read: Literacy and Popular Literature, 1861–1917.* Princeton: Princeton University Press, 1985.

Buber, Martin. *I and Thou.* Translated by Walter Kaufmann. New York: Charles Scribner's Sons, 1970.

Debreczeny, Paul. *"Zhitie Aleksandra Boldinskogo:* Pushkin's Elevation to Saint-hood in Soviet Culture." *South Atlantic Quarterly,* 90, no. 2 (Spring 1991): 269–92.

Derrida, Jacques. *Speech and Phenomena, and Other Essays on Husserl's Theory of Signs.* Translated by David B. Allison. Evanston: Northwestern University Press, 1973.

————. *Writing and Difference.* Translated by Alan Bass. Chicago: University of Chicago Press, 1978.

Dostoevskii, F. M. *Polnoe sobranie sochinenii v tridtsati tomakh.* Leningrad: Nauka, 1972–1988.

Eco, Umberto. *The Role of the Reader: Explorations in the Semiotics of Texts.* Bloomington: Indiana University Press, 1979.

Fitzpatrick, Sheila. "The Problem of Class Identity in NEP Society." In *Russia in the Era of NEP,* edited by Sheila Fitzpatrick, Alexander Rabinowitch, and Richard Stites, 12–33. Bloomington: Indiana University Press, 1991.

Foucault, Michel. *The Archaeology of Knowledge and the Discourse on Language.* Translated by A. M. Sheridan Smith. New York: Pantheon Books, 1972.

————. *Language, Counter-Memory, Practice: Selected Essays and Interviews.* Edited and with an introduction by Donald F. Bouchard. Translated by Donald F. Bouchard and Sherry Simon. Ithaca, N.Y.: Cornell University Press, 1977.

Gasparov, Boris, Robert P. Hughes, and Irina Paperno, eds. *Cultural Mytholo-gies of Russian Modernism: From the Golden Age to the Silver Age.* Berkeley: University of California Press, 1992.

Gilbert, Sandra M., and Susan Gubar. *The Madwoman in the Attic: The Woman Writer and the Nineteenth-Century Literary Imagination.* New Haven: Yale University Press, 1979.

Gogol', N. V. *Sobranie sochinenii v semi tomakh.* Moscow: Khudozhestvennaya literatura, 1966–67.

Johnson, Barbara. *The Critical Difference: Essays in the Contemporary Rhetoric of Reading.* Baltimore: Johns Hopkins University Press, 1980.

————. *A World of Difference.* Baltimore: Johns Hopkins University Press, 1987.

Bernard Knox. *Word and Action: Essays on the Ancient Theater.* Baltimore: Johns Hopkins University Press, 1986.

Kristeva, Julia. *Black Sun: Depression and Melancholia.* Translated by Leon S. Roudiez. New York: Columbia University Press, 1989.

Kuryluk, Ewa. *Veronica and Her Cloth: History, Symbolism, and Structure of a "True" Image.* Cambridge: Basil Blackwell, 1991.

Levitt, Marcus C. *Russian Literary Politics and the Pushkin Celebration of 1880.* Ithaca, N.Y.: Cornell University Press, 1989.

Lotman, Ju. M., and B. A. Uspenskii, "The Role of Dual Models in the Dynamics of Russian Culture (Up to the End of the Eighteenth Century)." In *The Semiotics of Russian Culture*, edited by Ann Shukman, translated by N. F. D. Owen. Ann Arbor: University of Michigan Press, 1984.

Mandel'shtam, O. E. "Chetvertaya proza." In his *Sobranie sochinenii v chetyrekh tomakh*, edited by G. P. Struve and B. A. Filippov, 2:177–92. Moscow: Terra, 1991.

Miller, Robin Feuer. "Notions of Narrative in the Notebooks for *The Idiot.*" *Ulbandus Review*, 2, no. 1 (Fall 1979): 160–74.

Mochulsky, Konstantin. *Aleksandr Blok.* Translated by Doris V. Johnson. Detroit: Wayne State University Press, 1983.

Parthé, Kathleen F. *Russian Village Prose: The Radiant Past.* Princeton: Princeton University Press, 1992.

Pushkin, A. S. *Sobranie sochinenii.* Moscow: Khudozhestvennaya literatura, 1967–70.

Reyfman, Irina. *Vasilii Trediakovsky: The Fool of the "New" Russian Literature.* Stanford: Stanford University Press, 1990.

Rozanov, Vasilii. *Izbrannoe.* Neimanis: [Munich,] 1970.

Simmons, W. Sherwin. *Kasimir Malevich's "Black Square" and the Genesis of Suprematism, 1907–1915.* New York: Garland, 1981.

Terras, Victor. "Some Observations on Puškin's Image in Russian Literature." *Russian Literature* 14 (1983): 299–315.

Tokarev, S. A., ed. *Mify narodov mira.* 2 vols. Moscow: Sovetskaya entsiklopediya, 1987–1988.

Tolstoi, L. N. "Smert' Ivana Il'ycha." In idem, *Sobranie sochinenii v dvenadtsati tomakh*, 10:133–86. Moscow: Khudozhestvennaya literatura, 1980.

Index